SHAKESPEARE
Select Bibliographical Guides

SHAKESPEARE

Select Bibliographical Guides

Edited by STANLEY WELLS

OXFORD UNIVERSITY PRESS
1973

Oxford University Press, Ely House, London W.1

GLASGOW NEW YORK TORONTO MELBOURNE WELLINGTON
CAPE TOWN IBADAN NAIROBI DAR ES SALAAM LUSAKA ADDIS ABABA
DELHI BOMBAY CALCUTTA MADRAS KARACHI LAHORE DACCA
KUALA LUMPUR SINGAPORE HONG KONG TOKYO

CASEBOUND ISBN 0 19 871026 7
PAPERBACK ISBN 0 19 871032 1

PRINTED IN GREAT BRITAIN
BY RICHARD CLAY (THE CHAUCER PRESS), LTD
BUNGAY SUFFOLK

CONTENTS

INTRODUCTION

This volume is planned as a selective guide to the best in Shakespeare scholarship and criticism. It recognizes that needs vary: that, for example, one reader may wish for nothing more elaborate than a well-printed text of a play, whereas another may seek a heavily annotated edition. Contributors have been free to organize their material in their own ways, though they have been asked to represent the main points of view on the plays with which they are concerned. They have been encouraged to recommend the good rather than castigate the bad. Though they do not offer histories of criticism, they recommend writings of earlier ages which still have something to offer. The most discussed plays have chapters to themselves; the rest are grouped with others of their kind. Chapters on important background subjects—textual scholarship and theatre history—are included. The first chapter offers guidance on writings of a still more general kind; its sections on Bibliographies and Periodicals should help readers to keep up with new writings as well as to find ones not mentioned elsewhere in this volume.

The References section to each chapter lists the writings there recommended. The lists are sub-divided in the same ways as the chapters, and are arranged in alphabetical order. Editions of books later than the first are cited when they are substantially revised. Many of the books are available in paperback reprints, listed in the catalogues *Paperbacks in Print* (U.K.) and *Paperbound Books in Print* (U.S.); and anthologies of criticism and scholarship often include chapters of books, and articles, listed here.

S.W.W.

ABBREVIATIONS

The following abbreviations are used in the References:

JEGP	*Journal of English and Germanic Philology*
MLR	*Modern Language Review*
N & Q	*Notes and Queries*
PMLA	*Publications of the Modern Language Association of America*
RES	*Review of English Studies*
SEL	*Studies in English Literature, 1500–1900*

The revised Arden edition of Shakespeare, which began publication under the general editorship of Una Ellis-Fermor in 1951 and is continuing under Harold Jenkins and H. F. Brooks, is here referred to as the new Arden edition.

1. The Study of Shakespeare

STANLEY WELLS

THE purpose of this volume is to help readers to find their way among the immense amount of scholarly and critical writings about Shakespeare's plays and poems. It is not intended as a comprehensive bibliography; on the contrary, contributors have been asked to be selective, and to provide critical guides to reading in the area each has been allotted. The bulk of the volume is made up of chapters on separate works or groups of works. Other chapters are devoted to studies of Shakespeare's text and of his plays in relation to the theatre both of his own time and of later ages. Authors of chapters on the plays touch on these topics where they are specially relevant, but it seemed desirable also to offer sustained independent treatments of them, since each has its own necessary background. This opening chapter attempts to provide guidance to other, more general, aspects of the study of Shakespeare: to reference books, background studies, and books concerned less with individual plays than with his over-all achievement.

BIBLIOGRAPHIES

Four volumes attempt to provide comprehensive bibliographies up to 1958. The first is the least reliable and the most idiosyncratic: it is William Jaggard's *Shakespeare Bibliography*, published in 1911. More reliable and more systematic is Ebisch and Schücking's continuation, published twenty years later, with a Supplement in 1936. Their work is continued in Gordon Ross Smith's *A Classified Shakespeare Bibliography, 1936–1958*, a massive volume with an over-complicated classification system that makes it difficult to use. These are primarily research tools, supplemented and carried forward by sections in the *Annual Bibliography of English Language and Literature*, *Shakespeare Jahrbuch*, and the summer numbers of *Shakespeare Quarterly*. The particular value of the last two is that they appear fairly soon after the publication of the works they list.

More useful to the student and general reader are deliberately selective bibliographies. Ronald Berman's *A Reader's Guide to Shakespeare's Plays*, though inelegantly produced, offers intelligent selection and helpful commentary. Selective lists are provided in *The Cambridge Bibliography of English Literature* and my *Shakespeare: A Reading Guide*. Detailed critical surveys of each year's publications appear in *The Year's Work in English Studies* and in *Shakespeare Survey*, where they are divided into three sections, one on the Life, Times, and Stage, another on Critical Studies, and a third on Textual Studies.

PERIODICALS

The oldest of the four main periodicals devoted to Shakespeare is the annual *Shakespeare Jahrbuch*, which was founded in 1864. Since 1965, two versions have appeared, from East and West Germany. Some of the articles are in English. *Shakespeare Survey* has appeared annually since 1948. Each volume has a main theme, and also includes critical surveys of scholarship, criticism, and performances. Some of the volumes include valuable retrospective surveys of writings related to the volume's main topic. The American *Shakespeare Quarterly* began in 1950. Each year it includes an annotated bibliography of the year's publications, and a collection of reviews of theatre productions, in America and elsewhere. The American *Shakespeare Studies*, first published in 1965, is an annual collection of essays and book reviews.

THE LIFE

The most systematic and scholarly study of Shakespeare's life and theatrical career is provided by E. K. Chambers in his monumental two-volume work, which includes studies of the facts and problems associated with each play, reprints and transcripts of all the records known at the time Chambers was writing, and of allusions to Shakespeare up to 1640, and other relevant material reliably presented. There is a useful abbreviation of Chambers's work by Charles Williams, giving as much as the general reader is likely to require. Another volume with a mainly documentary basis, though on a much smaller scale than Chambers's complete work, is G. E. Bentley's *Shakespeare: A Biographical Handbook*, which includes some interpretation of the evidence.

There have, of course, been many attempts to tell the story of Shakespeare's life and to set it in a historical context. Some have gone well beyond the boundaries of fantasy, but among more sober studies that can be recommended are the closely argued section on the life in Peter Alexander's *Shakespeare*, and Peter Quennell's more leisurely and discursive biography. F. E. Halliday has an attractive pictorial biography. There is a mass of information, especially about the Warwickshire background, in E. I. Fripp's *Shakespeare: Man and Artist*, which is on as large a scale as Chambers's two volumes, but presents its material in a narrative framework. Oddly enough, the best book on Shakespeare's life is in fact a study of other people's attempts to recount it, S. Schoenbaum's *Shakespeare's Lives*, a most authoritative and entertainingly written work which recounts the stages in the development of biographical studies of Shakespeare. Its excellent index makes it a valuable work of reference. Schoenbaum includes an account of attempts to prove that Shakespeare was someone else, a topic also studied in H. N. Gibson's *The Shakespeare Claimants*. Readers looking for an account of Shakespeare's life combined with a study of his achievement are probably best served by Alexander's book, or by M. M. Reese's *Shakespeare: His World and His Work*.

REFERENCE BOOKS

There are two particularly valuable handbooks, arranged in alphabetical order of entries, which provide information about a wide range of topics likely to be of interest to the student of Shakespeare and his times. The handier and less expensive is F. E. Halliday's *A Shakespeare Companion, 1564–1964*. Bulkier and more expensive, but also very good, is *A Shakespeare Encyclopaedia*, which includes more material relating to the criticism of the plays. *A New Companion to Shakespeare Studies* has eighteen chapters on various aspects of Shakespearian interest, some on the background, some on the writings, and others on stage history and criticism.

Bartlett's is still the standard concordance for the non-specialist who simply wants to track down particular words and passages in the plays and poems, though Marvin Spevack's computerized volumes, compiled on more scientific principles, are more ultimately reliable. Assistance with Shakespeare's language is probably best obtained from good, annotated editions, but two basic books are Onions's *A Shakespeare Glossary*, which is in effect a Shakespearian version of the *Oxford English Dictionary*, and E. A. Abbott's *A Shakespearian Grammar*, still valuable after over a century. More specialized assistance on an aspect of Shakespeare's vocabulary neglected in some reference books is provided by Eric Partridge's *Shakespeare's Bawdy*.

EDITIONS

Guidance on editions of individual plays is provided in the following chapters. Readers who need a collected edition in one volume are variously served. In England the tradition has been to print collected editions with no annotation, though sometimes with introductory material and collective glossaries. In America the most popular collected editions include explanatory notes printed on the page. The most generally approved text available in England in a single volume is that of Peter Alexander, which can also be had in a four-volume set. C. J. Sisson's edition has helpful introductions and appendices, and includes *Sir Thomas More*. The American Pelican editions have been revised and collected into a single volume available in both America and the United Kingdom; notes are printed on the page, and American spelling is used. The Signet editions have been published collectively, though without the selected critical commentaries, in New York. In America, other popular editions are Hardin Craig's and Irving Ribner's revision of G. L. Kittredge's.

SHAKESPEARE'S REPUTATION AND INFLUENCE

Raw material for the study of Shakespeare's reputation during the seventeenth century is provided in *The Shakespeare Allusion-Book*, a work which is in need of revision. A partial study of Shakespeare's reputation during the same period is G. E. Bentley's *Shakespeare and Jonson: Their Reputations in the Seventeenth Century Compared*, which should be read along with David Frost's article 'Shakespeare in the Seventeenth Century', which attempts a refutation of both Bentley's methods and his conclusions, of which the most striking is that Jonson's reputation stood higher than Shakespeare's during the period investigated.

Perhaps the most important single event in the development of Shakespeare's posthumous reputation was the jubilee organized in 1769 by David Garrick. The best account of this remarkable occasion is given by Johanne M. Stochholm, though Martha W. England's study represents a more serious attempt to assess its sociological significance. D. Nichol Smith's scholarly and concise study o eighteenth-century interest in Shakespeare is still worth reading. There is no equivalent for the nineteenth century, but F. E. Halliday and Louis Marder have each written readable general accounts of Shakespeare's reputation. Oswald LeWinter's anthology *Shakespeare in Europe* reprints some of the most important Continental writings from Voltaire to Jean-Louis Barrault.

There is no really good, full account of the history of the critical examination of Shakespeare's writings, but Arthur M. Eastman gives a thoughtful survey of the work of the major critics, and Patrick Murray has written about twentieth-century criticism. Shakespeare's influence on the visual arts, manifested especially through illustrations to editions, designs for the theatre, and paintings with Shakespearian subjects, is studied in W. Moelwyn Merchant's *Shakespeare and the Artist*, a book which makes interesting critical use of its material.

SOURCES AND INFLUENCES

The principal studies of the sources of individual plays are referred to in the appropriate chapters. The more important narrative and dramatic sources are well served by, especially, Geoffrey Bullough's volumes. There is no good, full study of Shakespeare's reading in general, but there are good essays on the topic by Frank Kermode, and by G. K. Hunter in *A New Companion to Shakespeare Studies*. Some writings exercised a pervasive influence on Shakespeare's work; the influence of others was more local. Notes to the more fully annotated editions often provide the best source of information about the latter. Among more generally influential books, the Bible is the subject of a scholarly but rather drily academic study by Richmond Noble, more valuable as a collection of allusions than as criticism. There is no comprehensive study of the important influence of Ovid. J. A. K. Thomson has a general study of *Shakespeare and the Classics*, which is of only limited value, being concerned mainly to assess Shakespeare's classical scholarship. E. C. Pettet's *Shakespeare and the Romance Tradition*, too, cannot be whole-heartedly recommended, since it takes a very partial view of romance, though it can be supplemented by Carol Gesner's more thorough study of a branch of the topic, *Shakespeare and the Greek Romance*. The matter of the relationship between the young Shakespeare and his contemporaries is often bedevilled by problems of chronology, but G. K. Hunter has an acute section on the relationship between Lyly and Shakespeare in his book on Lyly, and F. P. Wilson's *Marlowe and the Early Shakespeare* is both learned and readable. The relationship with Lyly and with Mundy is studied in articles in *Shakespeare Survey 14*, by Marco Mincoff and I. A. Shapiro respectively, and there is a useful essay by Norman Sanders on Greene and Shakespeare. A subtle and fascinating study concerned mostly with non-literary influences is E. A. Armstrong's *Shakespeare's Imagination*.

HISTORICAL, SOCIAL, AND PHILOSOPHICAL BACKGROUND

Readers sometimes feel the need for information on Shakespeare in relation to the society in which he lived. The two-volume work, *Shakespeare's England*, published in commemoration of the three-hundredth anniversary of his death, is still valuable. It is made up of thirty sections by many different contributors, and is full of information about Elizabethan society and culture. It is supplemented and brought up to date by *Shakespeare Survey 17*, which commemorates the four-hundredth anniversary of the birth, and by some of the chapters in *A New Companion to Shakespeare Studies*. J. Dover Wilson's *Life in Shakespeare's England* is a documentary anthology, partial in scope but enduring in popularity.

Special aspects of Shakespeare's environment are studied in a number of individual works. K. M. Briggs has two books concerned with fairies, witchcraft, and magic. D. H. Madden's *The Diary of Master William Silence: A Study of Shakespeare and Elizabethan Sport* is an imaginatively conceived book which has the status of an independent work of art while also being founded on sound scholarship. It is acknowledged as a special influence on T. R. Henn's *The Living Image*, which is particularly concerned with the imagery derived from field sports. One of Henn's topics is studied at greater length in Paul A. Jorgensen's *Shakespeare's Military World*.

Probably the most accessible of the books concerned with the intellectual environment of Shakespeare and his audience is E. M. W. Tillyard's *The Elizabethan World Picture*. It can be, and has been, criticized for presenting an excessively simplified and schematic picture, but remains a valuable introduction to an important topic. More detailed studies of the same subject are Hardin Craig's *The Enchanted Glass* and J. B. Bamborough's *The Little World of Man*. Shakespeare's religious background is a matter of perennial controversy. Roland Mushat Frye's *Shakespeare and Christian Doctrine* may be found useful for its learning even by those who cannot accept its basically secular position.

SHAKESPEARE AND MUSIC

Music plays a large part in Shakespeare's plays, which in turn have influenced and inspired much music. A standard study is Edward W. Naylor's *Shakespeare and Music*, first published in 1896 and revised in 1931. Richmond Noble's *Shakespeare's Use of Song* is rather badly dated by advances in both musical and textual scholarship, and by changes in critical attitudes. The most detailed work on the subject is Peter J. Seng's *The Vocal Songs in the Plays of Shakespeare: A Critical History*. Each song is printed, with information in a New Variorum style about texts, music, and critical commentary. F. W. Sternfeld's *Music in Shakespearean Tragedy* is a thorough, scholarly, and original study which extends beyond the limits suggested by its title. It includes transcriptions of early music, and an authoritative 'Retrospect of Schoiarship on Shakespeare and Music'. *Shakespeare in Music*, edited by Phyllis Hartnoll, includes a useful essay by John Stevens on 'Shakespeare and the Music of the Elizabethan Stage' and also Winton Dean's invaluable 'Shakespeare and Opera', which is virtually a monograph in its own right. There are also good chapters on 'Song and Part-Song Settings of Shakespeare's Lyrics, 1660–1960', and on 'Shakespeare in the Concert Hall'.

REFERENCES

BIBLIOGRAPHIES

Annual Bibliography of English Language and Literature (Modern Humanities Research Association, London, from 1920).

Bateson, F. W. (ed.), *The Cambridge Bibliography of English Literature*, vol. i (Cambridge, 1940); vol. v (Supplement), ed. George Watson (Cambridge, 1957).

Berman, Ronald, *A Reader's Guide to Shakespeare's Plays: A Discursive Bibliography* (Chicago, Ill., 1965).

Ebisch, W., and Schücking, L. L., *A Shakespeare Bibliography* (Oxford, 1931); *Supplement for the Years 1930–35* (Oxford, 1937).

Jaggard, William, *Shakespeare Bibliography* (Stratford-upon-Avon, 1911).

Smith, Gordon Ross, *A Classified Bibliography, 1936–1958* (University Park, Pa., 1963).

The Year's Work in English Studies (The English Association, London, from 1921).

Wells, Stanley, *Shakespeare: A Reading Guide* (London, 1969; 2nd edn., 1970).

PERIODICALS

Jahrbuch der Deutschen Shakespeare-Gesellschaft (1865–1964). (Two separate publications thereafter: *Jahrbuch 1965*, etc., published by the Deutsche Shakespeare-Gesellschaft West, Heidelberg, and *Shakespeare Jahrbuch* 100/101 (1964–5), etc., published by the Shakespeare-Gesellschaft East, Weimar.)

Shakespeare Quarterly, ed. James G. McManaway (to Spring, 1972) and R. J. Schoeck (from Summer, 1972) (Washington, D.C., from 1950).

Shakespeare Studies, ed. J. Leeds Barroll (Cincinnati, Ohio, from 1965).

Shakespeare Survey, ed. Allardyce Nicoll (to 1965) and Kenneth Muir (1966–) (Cambridge, from 1948).

THE LIFE

Alexander, Peter, *Shakespeare* (London, 1964).

Bentley, G. E., *Shakespeare: A Biographical Handbook* (New Haven, Conn., 1961).

Chambers, E. K., *William Shakespeare: A Study of Facts and Problems*, 2 vols. (Oxford, 1930).

——, abridged by Charles Williams, *A Short Life of Shakespeare with the Sources* (Oxford, 1933).

Fripp, E. I., *Shakespeare, Man and Artist*, 2 vols. (London, 1938).

Gibson, H. N., *The Shakespeare Claimants* (London, 1962).

Halliday, F. E., *Shakespeare: A Pictorial Biography* (London, 1953).

Quennell, Peter, *Shakespeare* (London, 1963; Penguin Shakespeare Library, Harmondsworth, 1969).

Reese, M. M., *Shakespeare: His World and His Work* (London, 1953).

Schoenbaum, S., *Shakespeare's Lives* (Oxford, 1970).

REFERENCE BOOKS

Abbott, E. A., *A Shakespearian Grammar* (London, 1869).

Bartlett, John, *A New and Complete Concordance or Verbal Index to Words, Phrases, and Passages in the Dramatic Works of Shakespeare with a Supplementary Concordance to the Poems* (London, 1894).

Campbell, O. J., and Quinn, E. G. (eds.), *The Reader's Encyclopedia of Shakespeare* (also published as *A Shakespeare Encyclopedia*) (New York, 1966).

Halliday, F. E., *A Shakespeare Companion 1550–1950* (London, 1952; 2nd edn., *A Shakespeare Companion 1564–1964*, Harmondsworth, 1964).

Muir, Kenneth, and Schoenbaum, S. (eds.), *A New Companion to Shakespeare Studies* (Cambridge, 1971).

Onions, C. T., *A Shakespeare Glossary* (Oxford, 1911).

Partridge, Eric, *Shakespeare's Bawdy* (London, 1947; 2nd edn., 1968).

Spevack, Marvin, *A Complete and Systematic Concordance to the Works of Shakespeare*, 6 vols. (Hildesheim, 1968–70).

EDITIONS

Alexander, Peter (ed.), *William Shakespeare: The Complete Works* (London, 1951).

Barnet, Sylvan (ed.), *The Complete Signet Classic Shakespeare* (New York, 1972).

Craig, Hardin (ed.), *The Complete Works of Shakespeare* (Chicago, Ill., 1951).

Harbage, A. (ed.), *William Shakespeare: The Complete Works* (Baltimore, Md., and London, 1969).

Kittredge, G. L. (rev. I. Ribner), *The Complete Works of Shakespeare* (Boston, Mass., 1970).

Sisson, C. J. (ed.), *William Shakespeare: The Complete Works* (London, 1954).

SHAKESPEARE'S REPUTATION AND INFLUENCE

Bentley, G. E., *Shakespeare and Jonson: Their Reputations in the Seventeenth Century Compared*, 2 vols. (Chicago, Ill., 1945).

Eastman, Arthur M., *A Short History of Shakespearean Criticism* (New York, 1968).

England, Martha W., *Garrick's Jubilee* (Columbus, Ohio, 1964).

Frost, David, 'Shakespeare in the Seventeenth Century', *Shakespeare Quarterly* 16 (1965).

Halliday, F. E., *The Cult of Shakespeare* (London, 1957).

LeWinter, Oswald, *Shakespeare in Europe* (Cleveland, Ohio, 1963; Penguin Shakespeare Library, Harmondsworth, 1970).

Marder, Louis, *His Exits and His Entrances* (London, 1964).

Merchant, W. Moelwyn, *Shakespeare and the Artist* (London, 1959).

Munro, J., revised by E. K. Chambers, *The Shakespeare Allusion-Book*, 2 vols. (London, 1932).

Murray, Patrick, *The Shakespearean Scene: Some Twentieth-Century Perspectives* (London, 1969).

Smith, D. Nichol, *Shakespeare in the Eighteenth Century* (Oxford, 1928).

Stochholm, Johanne M., *Garrick's Folly: The Stratford Jubilee of 1769 at Stratford and Drury Lane* (London, 1964).

SOURCES AND INFLUENCES

Armstrong, E. A., *Shakespeare's Imagination: A Study of the Psychology of Association and Inspiration* (London, 1946).

Bullough, Geoffrey, *Narrative and Dramatic Sources of Shakespeare*, 8 vols. (London, 1957—).

Gesner, Carol, *Shakespeare and the Greek Romance* (Lexington, Ky., 1970).

Hunter, G. K., 'Shakespeare's Reading', in *A New Companion to Shakespeare Studies*, ed. K. Muir and S. Schoenbaum (Cambridge, 1971).

——, *John Lyly: The Humanist as Courtier* (London, 1962).

Kermode, J. F., 'On Shakespeare's Learning', *Bulletin of the John Rylands Library, Manchester*, 48 (1965).

Mincoff, Marco, 'Shakespeare and Lyly', *Shakespeare Survey 14* (1961).

Noble, Richmond, *Shakespeare's Biblical Knowledge and Use of the Book of Common Prayer* (London, 1935).

Pettet, E. C., *Shakespeare and the Romance Tradition* (London, 1949).

Sanders, Norman, 'The Comedy of Greene and Shakespeare', in *Early Shakespeare* (Stratford-upon-Avon Studies 3, ed. J. R. Brown and B. Harris, London, 1961).

Shapiro, I. A., 'Shakespeare and Mundy', *Shakespeare Survey 14* (1961).

Thomson, J. A. K., *Shakespeare and the Classics* (London, 1952).

Wilson, F. P., *Marlowe and the Early Shakespeare* (Oxford, 1953).

HISTORICAL, SOCIAL, AND PHILOSOPHICAL BACKGROUND

Bamborough, J. B., *The Little World of Man* (London, 1952).

Briggs, K. M., *The Anatomy of Puck: An Examination of Fairy Beliefs among Shakespeare's Contemporaries and Successors* (London, 1959).

——, *Pale Hecate's Team: An Examination of the Beliefs on Witchcraft and Magic among Shakespeare's Contemporaries and His Immediate Successors* (London, 1962).

Craig, Hardin, *The Enchanted Glass: The Elizabethan Mind in Literature* (New York, 1936).

Frye, Roland Mushat, *Shakespeare and Christian Doctrine* (Princeton, N.J., 1963).

Henn, T. R., *The Living Image* (London, 1972).

Jorgensen, Paul A., *Shakespeare's Military World* (Berkeley, Calif., 1956).

Lee, Sidney, and Onions, C. T. (eds.), *Shakespeare's England: An Account of the Life and Manners of his Age*, 2 vols. (Oxford, 1916).

Madden, D. H., *The Diary of Master William Silence: A Study of Shakespeare and Elizabethan Sport* (London, 1897; 2nd edn., 1907).

Tillyard, E. M. W., *The Elizabethan World Picture* (London, 1943).

Wilson, J. Dover, *Life in Shakespeare's England* (London, 1911; Penguin Shakespeare Library, Harmondsworth, 1968).

SHAKESPEARE AND MUSIC

Hartnoll, Phyllis (ed.), *Shakespeare in Music* (London, 1964).

Naylor, Edward W., *Shakespeare and Music* (London, 1896; 2nd edn., London, 1931).

Noble, Richmond, *Shakespeare's Use of Song* (Oxford, 1923).

Seng, Peter J., *The Vocal Songs in the Plays of Shakespeare: A Critical History* (Cambridge, Mass., 1967).

Sternfeld, F. W., *Music in Shakespearean Tragedy* (London, 1963).

2. Shakespeare's Text

NORMAN SANDERS

IT is ironical that Shakespeare, the most highly esteemed writer of the modern world, should have been served quite so badly by the printing process as he was. And although one might wish to believe that things would have been different if he had, in the words of his first editors, 'himself... lived to have set forth, and overseen his own writings', there is no real evidence that his death alone prevented our possessing an accurate, authoritative text of his plays. It would appear that in England plays were not considered as 'literature' at all until Ben Jonson produced his Folio of plays in 1616; and Shakespeare apparently made no effort to have his works published in good versions, although the existence of well-printed and perhaps personally supervised editions of his two narrative poems suggests that he knew how to go about the task had he so wished.

As it is, our knowledge of what Shakespeare wrote for the stage rests on a variety of publications which were set up from manuscripts of many different kinds and origins, and of which the standards of accuracy and printing range from the appallingly bad to the relatively good. The study of Shakespeare's text during the past two hundred and fifty years is the record of men's attempts, first, to correct the inaccuracies for which the Elizabethan printing process was responsible; second, to determine by examination of the early printed texts what kind of manuscripts lay behind them; and third, to arrive at a formula for editing that will record as near as we can get to what Shakespeare actually wrote, and that will incorporate the evidence on which this final form is based.

THE EARLY EDITIONS

During Shakespeare's lifetime thirteen of his plays were published singly in reasonably accurate texts usually called 'good quartos': *Titus Andronicus* (1594), *Richard II* (1597), *Richard III* (1597), *1 Henry IV* (1598), *Love's Labour's Lost* (1598), *Romeo and Juliet* (1599), *2 Henry IV* (1600), *The Merchant of Venice* (1600), *A Midsummer Night's Dream* (1600), *Much Ado About Nothing* (1600), *Hamlet* (1604–5), *King Lear* (1608), *Troilus and Cressida* (1609); and *Othello* was published in the same format, six years after his death, in 1622. In addition, the following plays were published in quarto form, and are usually called 'bad quartos' because they show various degrees of textual corruption when compared with other extant texts of the same plays: *2 Henry VI* (1594), which bears the title *The First Part of the Contention betwixt the Two Famous Houses of York and Lancaster*; *3 Henry VI* (1595 octavo), which is called *The True Tragedy of Richard Duke of York*; *Romeo and Juliet* (1597); *Henry V* (1600); *Hamlet* (1603); *The Merry Wives of Windsor* (1602). Quartos of two other plays which clearly have connection with Shakespeare's plays on the same subject were also published in corrupt form: *The Taming of A Shrew* (1594) and *The Troublesome Reign of King John* (1591). Facsimiles of the quarto texts were issued under the supervision of F. J. Furnivall in 1880–91 and are currently being published in collotype facsimile for the Shakespeare Association by Charlton Hinman, who succeeded W. W. Greg, the first editor.

All the plays that appeared first in some quarto form were also included in the First Folio edition of the collected works, edited by two of Shakespeare's fellow actors, John Heminges and Henry Condell, and published in 1623. In this volume an additional sixteen plays were printed for the first time: *The Tempest, The Two Gentlemen of Verona, Measure for Measure, The Comedy of Errors, As You Like It, All's Well That Ends Well, Twelfth Night, The Winter's Tale, 1 Henry VI, Henry VIII, Coriolanus, Timon of Athens, Julius Caesar, Macbeth, Antony and Cleopatra*, and *Cymbeline*. Of the facsimiles of the Folio most frequently referred to in Shakespeare studies, Sidney Lee's of 1902 and 1910 is the most accurate reproduction of mainly a single copy; but this has been superseded by Charlton Hinman's *Norton Facsimile*, which is based upon a complete collation of the eighty copies in the Folger Shakespeare Library, and is made up from the clearest and most correct pages available in the various copies. The facsimile produced by H. Kökeritz and C. T. Prouty in 1954 is usually considered too unreliable for scholarly use.

The 1623 volume was reprinted as the 'Second Folio' of 1632; as the 'Third Folio' of 1663, of which the issue of 1664 contains *Pericles* and six plays sometimes attributed to Shakespeare; and as the 'Fourth Folio' of 1685. The text of *Pericles* included in the Third Folio was reprinted from a quarto version of the play which appeared in 1609, facsimiles of which were published by Sidney Lee in 1905 and by W. W. Greg in 1940. Of the 'apocryphal' plays that appeared in the Third Folio only *Pericles* is generally accepted as being mainly by Shakespeare. The six others, along with seven other printed plays which have been attributed to Shakespeare, were edited by C. F. Tucker Brooke in *The Shakespeare Apocrypha*. They, along with the manuscript play *Sir Thomas More*, are discussed in Chapter 17 of this book. Facsimile editions of the non-dramatic works (*Venus and Adonis* (1593), *The Rape of Lucrece* (1594), *The Passionate Pilgrim* (1599), *The Phoenix and the Turtle* (1601), and the *Sonnets* (1609)) are listed in the References to Chapter 4.

THE EIGHTEENTH AND NINETEENTH CENTURIES

As, during the late seventeenth and early eighteenth centuries, Shakespeare's works came to be considered 'classics', the texts of his plays began to receive a great deal of scholarly attention. Of the editions that appeared during the eighteenth century the most important textually are those of Nicholas Rowe (1709), Thomas Hanmer (1744), William Warburton (1747), Samuel Johnson (1765), Edward Capell (1768), George Steevens (1778), and Edmond Malone (1790). All these editions (as well as many of those in the nineteenth century) have been reissued in the reprint series 'Major 18th and 19th Century Editions of the Works of Shakespeare'.

In almost every category of editorial change (correction of printing errors, emended readings, relineation, repunctuation, reassignment of speeches, correction and supplying of stage directions, act and scene divisions, the identification of locales, etc.) these editors supplied the vast bulk of the basic materials and possibilities, and contributed most to the texts as we now view them.

While it is dangerous to make large generalizations about so varied a body of editorial work, it is probably true to say: (1) that the work of these early editors was carried out in relative ignorance of the theatrical and printing conditions that prevailed in Shakespeare's day; (2) that the emendations they made were governed by the literary, grammatical, and linguistic standards of their time and by the stylistic and theatrical tastes of the individual editors; (3) that, while the 'good' and 'bad' quartos received a great deal of attention and use, scholarly opinion had not really crystallized into any settled view of their varying claims to authority. However, it should be noted that, for example, Dr. Johnson perceived the dependence of the Second, Third, and Fourth Folios on the First and denied them any independent textual value; and Capell sorted out with some accuracy the various claims of the 'good' and 'bad' quartos. The ways in which some of the eighteenth-century editors, Capell in particular, anticipated some of the twentieth-century methods can be sampled in the studies of S. K. Sen, R. B. McKerrow, and Alice Walker.

During the nineteenth century many other editions appeared, some from the hands of distinguished scholars like Charles Knight (1838–43), J. Payne Collier (1842–4), J. O. Halliwell-Phillipps (1853–65), and Alexander Dyce (1857), which added something of permanent value to the body of textual work already done. But the editorial methods employed and the principles governing emendation were not greatly different from those of their eighteenth-century pre-decessors. However, again there were some scholars who pursued studies on more scientifically analytical and less eclectic lines than their contemporaries. For example, Tycho Mommsen made a close scrutiny of the Folio and Quarto texts of *Romeo and Juliet* and *Hamlet*; W. Sidney Walker classified the errors found in Shake-speare's texts; T. Kenny argued the case for memorially reconstructed texts; and P. A. Daniel made a useful analysis of the 'bad quarto' of *The Merry Wives of Windsor* and did still-useful work on the relation-ship between the Folio text of *Richard III* and the various quartos from which it may have been set up.

The culmination of this century and a half of textual study was the Cambridge Shakespeare, edited by W. G. Clark and W. A. Wright, which appeared in its final revision in 1891–3. This edition was not only the basis for the famous one-volume 'Globe' edition, to which many standard works of reference like J. Bartlett's *Concordance* are keyed, but also led to the starting of the *New Variorum Shakespeare* which is still in progress.

THE NEW BIBLIOGRAPHY

The new approach to Shakespeare's text which was developed during the first part of the present century has been traced by F. P. Wilson in his model essay in the history of scholarship *Shake-speare and the New Bibliography*, and by J. Dover Wilson in a series of essays in *Shakespeare Survey*.

The nature of this new approach to the problems was defined by R. B. McKerrow in his review (quoted in Wilson's essay) of K. Deighton's *The Old Dramatists: Conjectural Readings* (1896), a book which is a glaring example of the kind of ingenious tinkering with textual possibilities that had become popular during the nineteenth century:

Until some curious inquirer makes a thorough investigation into all the technical details of Elizabethan printing, and from this and a comparison of handwritings arrives at some definite statement of the relative probability of various misreadings and misprintings, emendation must remain in much the same state as medicine was before dissection was practised.

These were the lines the 'New Bibliographers' followed. First, the work of ascertaining exactly what published materials were available for study began with the finding lists published by W. W. Greg in *The Library* at the turn of the century and led to the publication of the *Short-Title Catalogue*, edited by Pollard and Redgrave, and ultimately to Greg's *A Bibliography of English Printed Drama to the Restoration*. Second, the intricacies of the Elizabethan publishing system were explored. Edward Arber had published his transcript of the Registers of the Stationers' Company in 1875–7, and his work was supplemented by that of Greg, E. Boswell, and W. A. Jackson on the records of the Company's Court of Assistants. This material was studied with a view to establishing such things as the business relationships that could exist between printer, publisher, and bookseller; the methods by which plays could get into print; the interpretation of book entries in the Company's registers; the nature of the licensing process by the civil and ecclesiastical authorities; the Company's procedure for establishing a printer's ownership of a copy; and the nature of 'piracy' (illegal printing of plays against the wishes of the author and/or the Company, or in violation of the claims of another printer). Studies which clarified such matters appeared in various periodicals, particularly *The Library*, during the early years of this century, but many of the conclusions arrived at and the problems raised are discussed in such books as W. W. Greg's *Companion to Arber*, *Some Aspects and Problems of London Publishing between 1500 and 1650*, and *The Shakespeare First Folio*; A. W. Pollard's *Shakespeare Folios and Quartos* and *Shakespeare's Fight With the Pirates*; E. M. Albright's *Dramatic Publication in England*; J. Q. Adams's *Dramatic Records*; and Leo Kirschbaum's *Shakespeare and the Stationers*.

The most important area of research was the determining from the extant texts of the exact nature of the Elizabethan printing process. The still-standard description of the Elizabethan printing house and its methods is R. B. McKerrow's *An Introduction to Bibliography for Literary Students*, which was an expansion of his earlier 'Notes on Bibliographical Evidence'. The analytical techniques developed from the kind of knowledge McKerrow covers were applied first to the quartos, and many early successes were scored. Among the most notable of these were W. W. Greg's, W. J. Neidig's, and A. W. Pollard's demonstration that a collection of nine quartos variously dated were actually printed by Thomas Pavier in 1619; Greg's study of the variants of *King Lear*; and Fredson Bowers's analysis of the proof correction in the same play. Perhaps the best demonstration, between 1900 and 1950, of the application of such techniques on a large scale is E. E. Willoughby's *The Printing of the First Folio of Shakespeare* which, although many of its conclusions have been changed and vastly expanded by Charlton Hinman's later work, still offers a fine display of the methods and results of the New Bibliography.

All the bibliographers working at this time were aware that the object of their researches was to penetrate the printed surface of the plays so as to be able to postulate with accuracy the kind of manuscript the printer used. One aid to this end was the study of all extant dramatic manuscripts. W. W. Greg had made a beginning with the inclusion of several 'plots' (scene analyses prepared for theatre use) and a player's part in his *Henslowe Papers*; and the Malone Society and other publishers put out accurate transcriptions of the plays in manuscript between 1910 and 1929, the most important of which was Greg's edition of *Sir Thomas More*. The study of Elizabethan handwriting, of which these editions were a product, also led to a series of facsimiles illustrating the literary hands of the period in *English Literary Autographs 1500–1650*, to the discussions of dramatic manuscripts in E. K. Chambers's *The Elizabethan Stage* and *William Shakespeare*, to Greg's complete survey of the extant remains in his *Dramatic Documents from the Elizabethan Playhouses*, and to two notable studies of individual plays which well illustrate the conclusions arrived at by such research: Greg's analysis of two stage abridgements (of Robert Greene's *Orlando Furioso* and George Peele's *Battle of Alcazar*), and R. C. Bald's work on Thomas Middleton's *A Game at Chess*.

It was work of this kind used in conjunction with the analysis of the printed texts that enabled scholars to identify the various classes of manuscript which could lie behind any printed version: 'foul papers'—the author's first or early draft; fair copy—the author's final version which was submitted to the theatre company; the prompt book—the manuscript prepared for theatre production which could be either a theatrical editing of the fair copy or a newly prepared version; scribal copies of any of these; and memorially constructed copy—the hypothetical source of the 'bad quartos'. One particular manuscript study was to have far-reaching results so far as Shakespeare was concerned. This was the discovery of the writing characteristics of Ralph Crane, a scrivener who copied for Shakespeare's company, the King's Men, manuscripts designed for publication in the First Folio.

With the knowledge gained from the playhouse manuscripts, Elizabethan printing and publishing methods, and the probable day-to-day workings of the theatre company (derived principally from the study of *Henslowe's Diary*), scholars proceeded to determine the nature of the printer's copy used for the various printed versions of the plays. The best summary of the state of knowledge up to 1955 is to be found in W. W. Greg's *The Shakespeare First Folio*. The texts of *The Tempest*, *The Two Gentlemen of Verona*, *The Merry Wives of Windsor*, *Measure for Measure*, and *The Winter's Tale* seem to have been printed from manuscripts specially prepared for the First Folio by Ralph Crane. Theatre copy of some sort is thought to lie behind the Folio texts of *Julius Caesar*, *As You Like It*, *Twelfth Night*, *Macbeth*, *Cymbeline*, *Hamlet*, *Othello*, *Richard III*, and *King Lear*. Authorial manuscript was apparently used for *The Comedy of Errors*, *Titus Andronicus*, *The Taming of the Shrew*, *Love's Labour's Lost*, *Richard II*, *A Midsummer Night's Dream*, *King John*, *The Merchant of Venice*, *1 Henry IV*, *2 Henry IV*, *Much Ado About Nothing*, *Henry V*, *All's Well That Ends Well*, *Timon of Athens*, *2 Henry VI*, *3 Henry VI*, *Troilus and Cressida*, *Antony and Cleopatra*, *Coriolanus*, *1 Henry VI*, and *Henry VIII*. However, in many cases the Folio texts appear to have been set up with varying degrees of conflation of a manuscript and a printed text where one existed. Many of the 'good quartos' seem to have been based on Shakespeare's own manuscript at one or two removes.

So far as the origins of the 'bad quartos' are concerned the problems are very much more complex. To account for their characteristic features a theory of 'memorial reconstruction' was developed. This posits that these texts are versions of what an actor or actors could recall from having played one or more roles (usually of a comparatively minor sort) in an authorized production of the play. W. W. Greg was the first to explore the implications of the theory in connection with the 'bad quarto' of *The Merry Wives of Windsor*, and other studies of individual plays followed. Among the most important of these are: Peter Alexander's and Madeleine Doran's work on *The Contention* and *The True Tragedy*; H. Hoppe's on *Romeo and Juliet*; H. T. Price's on *Henry V*; J. Dover Wilson's and B. A. P. van Dam's on *Hamlet*; W. W. Greg's and Fredson Bowers's on *King Lear*; and two important studies of the same play by G. I. Duthie, who examined and rejected the possibility that transcription by one of the shorthand systems available to Elizabethans may have been responsible for many of the features exhibited by the 'bad quartos'. Two historical studies which show how the textual problems of plays have been tackled are Madeleine Doran's *The Text of 'King Lear'* and D. L. Patrick's *The Textual History of 'Richard III'*.

One other important matter occupied the attention of the New Bibliographers. This was how to use the results of their labours in producing a definitive edition of the works. Much consideration was given to such topics as the principles which should govern textual emendation, by W. W. Greg and others; the selection of the proper copy-texts for modern editions, by Greg, R. B. McKerrow, and Fredson Bowers; the faith that can be placed on the punctuation of Elizabethan printers, by R. M. Alden, Hilary Jenkinson, Percy Simpson, and Peter Alexander; how far the printer followed the orthography of the manuscript and how far his own system, by J. Dover Wilson and A. W. Pollard; and the possibility that plays were frequently revised by the author, by Dover Wilson in his New Cambridge editions of the plays.

THE AGE OF BOWERS

In general, textual work since the 1950s has continued along the lines of the New Bibliography; but new methods and refinements of older ones have been used to test the conclusions of earlier scholars. The best way of appreciating the kind of work done is to read through the volumes of *Studies in Bibliography* between 1947 and the present, the issues of *The Library* for the same years, and the annual review articles in *Shakespeare Survey* written by James G. McManaway, James Walton, and Richard Proudfoot. Representative examples of the employment of the newer techniques can be sampled in work of Philip Williams, Alice Walker, Harold Jenkins, John Russell Brown, R. J. Turner, Cyrus Hoy, G. Walton Williams, and G. I. Duthie, among others.

Certain large achievements stand out. First, methods by which the texts may be made to yield the secrets of the printing process have become greatly sophisticated. The identification of the work of individual compositors is now possible by the tabulation and analysis of the errors a man is prone to, the preferences he has in the layout of type, the preferred spellings he has when there are no mechanical factors inhibiting his choice. The idea that compositors can be identified by variations in spelling had first been suggested by Thomas Satchell in 1929, but the method was much refined by Alice Walker and Charlton Hinman. Perhaps the most convenient discussion of the theory behind this technique is to be found in T. Howard-Hill's 'Spelling and the Bibliographer'. Second, analysis of the process of sheets through the press, the distribution of the manuscript between various compositors, the breaks in the printing process, and the practice of leaving certain unvarying parts of the type standing from page to page and forme to forme have enabled bibliographers to work out time schedules for the printing of individual works.

The outstanding example of the kind of results such new techniques can produce is Charlton Hinman's *The Printing and Proof-reading of the First Folio of Shakespeare*. Using a machine of his own invention, Hinman collated all eighty copies of the First Folio in the Folger Shakespeare Library. This enabled him to chart in great detail such things as the compositors' habits, the occurrences of 'distinctive types' (pieces of type characteristically-enough damaged to be individually identified and associated with a single printer's case), the kinds of errors made and the degree of fidelity with which different compositors followed their copy, the implications of the practice of 'casting off copy' (i.e. the system of dividing a manuscript between two compositors for simultaneous setting, thus causing the necessity for spreading out or compressing the printed text at the points of juncture), the system of proof correction, the use of cancelled leaves, corrected and uncorrected pages, the transfer of standing type from one part of the volume to another, and the employment of lines and rules to divide the text on the page. The conclusions based on such researches allowed Hinman to provide us with probably the fullest account of how the First Folio came into being that we shall ever have.

Other scholars have reinvestigated many of the problems first tackled by the New Bibliographers. For example, the whole outputs of printers who handled Shakespeare's texts have been examined; and the results of such studies can be seen in G. Walton Williams's edition of *Romeo and Juliet*, prepared after a close scrutiny of Thomas Creede's shop. Alice Walker suggested new methods of approach to the Folio texts of some plays and offered new conclusions about the relationship between quarto texts and the Folio versions of the same plays, and J. K. Walton has discussed the nature of the copy used for the printing of the First Folio whenever a good quarto already existed before the Folio was printed. The enormously complex problems of *Richard III* have been re-examined at book-length by J. K. Walton and Kristian Smidt. Ernst Honigmann has looked again at the possibility of the original instability of Shakespeare's text first dealt with by J. Dover Wilson in his controversial New Cambridge editions. The vexed question of the manuscript of the Sonnets has been extensively reviewed by J. Dover Wilson, W. G. Ingram and T. Redpath, and Brents Stirling; and J. M. Nosworthy has illuminatingly grouped for textual discussion those plays which were apparently written by Shakespeare to order for a special occasion.

One scholar, C. J. Sisson, in preparing a complete edition of the plays, applied systematically for the first time the accumulated knowledge of theatre manuscripts and Elizabethan handwriting to the palaeographical solution of the principal cruces; while another editor, Peter Alexander, brought to his textual work a complete knowledge of modern bibliographical researches. Of the other major editions, the New Cambridge Shakespeare and the new Arden Shakespeare have devoted most space to absorption and presentation of textual scholarship, although many of the popular paperback editions give some account of recent textual work.

Many specialist studies, of a not strictly textual nature, have a bearing on emendation, among which may be mentioned H. Kökeritz's *Shakespeare's Pronunciation*, Hilda M. Hulme's *Explorations in Shakespeare's Language*, Geoffrey Bullough's *Narrative and Dramatic Sources of Shakespeare*, Sister Miriam Joseph's *Shakespeare's Use of the Arts of Language*, A. C. Partridge's *Orthography in Shakespeare and Elizabethan Drama*, and the numerous imagery studies.

Since the death of W. W. Greg, one name has dominated the study of Shakespeare's text—that of Fredson Bowers. In almost every field of bibliography he has assumed Greg's mantle: he has codified the principles of descriptive bibliography (in *Principles of Bibliographical Description*); under his editorship *Studies in Bibliography* has published much of the most exciting work done during the past twenty years; he has contributed fundamental research to the difficult problems posed by the texts of *Hamlet, King Lear*, and *Richard III*; and he has been ready to define the theory and objectives of the whole subject in books like *The Bibliographical Way, Textual and Literary Criticism*, and *On Editing Shakespeare and Other Elizabethan Dramatists*. Perhaps of even greater importance, his old-spelling editions of Dekker and Beaumont and Fletcher may be seen as clearing the ground for the long-awaited old-spelling text of Shakespeare's works.

Yet, lest optimism for the future and smugness about our new skills grow too great, perhaps it should be noted that as recently as 1966 D. F. Mackenzie's history of the Cambridge University Press from 1696 to 1712, which is based on very full records including workmen's vouchers for composition, correction, and presswork, contains indications that some of the techniques developed by the 'School of Bowers' may need to be viewed less confidently than at present. In textual studies as in all else concerning Shakespeare, it would appear *Grammatici certant et adhuc sub iudice lis est*.

REFERENCES

THE EARLY EDITIONS

Brooke, C. F. Tucker (ed.), *The Shakespeare Apocrypha* (Oxford, 1908; corrected 1918).

Furnivall, F. J. and others (eds.), *Plays and Poems in Quarto*, 43 vols. (Shakespeare Association Facsimiles, London, 1880–91).

Greg, W. W. (ed.), *Pericles. The Quarto of 1609* (Shakespeare Association, London, 1940).

—— and Hinman, Charlton (eds.), *Shakespeare Quarto Facsimiles* (Shakespeare Association, London and Oxford, 1939–).

Hinman, Charlton (ed.), *The Norton Facsimile. The First Folio of Shakespeare* (New York, 1968).

Kökeritz, H., and Prouty, C. T. (eds.), *Mr. William Shakespeares Comedies, Histories, and Tragedies* (New Haven, Conn., 1954).

Lee, Sidney (ed.), *Shakespeare's Comedies, Histories, and Tragedies* (Oxford, 1902; London, 1910).

—— (ed.), *Shakespeare's Poems and 'Pericles'*, 5 vols. (Oxford, 1905).

THE EIGHTEENTH AND NINETEENTH CENTURIES

Clark, W. G. and Wright, W. A. (eds.), *The Cambridge Shakespeare*, 9 vols. (Cambridge, 1863–6; 2nd edn., 1867; 3rd edn., 1891–3).

Daniel, P. A., Introductions to facsimiles of the 1st, 3rd, and 6th Quartos of *Richard III* (London, 1886, 1888, 1889).

——, Introduction to facsimile of the 1st Quarto of *The Merry Wives of Windsor* (London, 1881).

Furness, H. H., and others (eds.), *A New Variorum Edition of Shakespeare* (Philadelphia, Pa., 1871–).

Kenny, Thomas, *The Life and Genius of Shakespeare* (London, 1864).

McKerrow, R. B., *The Treatment of Shakespeare's Text by his Earliest Editors, 1709–1768*, British Academy Lecture 1933.

Major 18th and 19th Century Editions of the Works of Shakespeare (AMS Press, New York).

Mommsen, Tycho, *Shakespeares Romeo und Julie* (Oldenburg, 1859).

——, 'Hamlet', *Neue Jahrbücher für Philologie und Paedagogik*, 72 (1885).

Sen, S. K., *Capell and Malone, and Modern Critical Bibliography* (Calcutta, 1960).

Walker, Alice, *Edward Capell and his Edition of Shakespeare*, British Academy Lecture 1962.

Walker, W. Sidney, *A Critical Examination of the Text of Shakespeare*, ed. W. N. Lettsom (London, 1860).

THE NEW BIBLIOGRAPHY

Adams, J. Q. (ed.), *Dramatic Records of Sir Henry Herbert* (New Haven, Conn., 1917).

Albright, Evelyn M., *Drama Publication in England 1580–1640* (New York, 1927).

Alden, R. M., 'The Punctuation of Shakespeare's Printers', *PMLA* 39 (1924).

Alexander, Peter, *Shakespeare's 'Henry VI' and 'Richard III'* (Cambridge, 1929).

——, *Shakespeare's Punctuation*, British Academy Lecture 1945.

Bald, R. C. (ed.), *Thomas Middleton's 'A Game at Chess'* (Cambridge, 1929).

Bowers, Fredson, 'An Examination of the Method of Proof Correction in *Lear*', *The Library* 2 (1947).

——, 'Current Theories of the Copy-Text', *Modern Philology*, 48 (1950).

Chambers, E. K., *The Elizabethan Stage*, 4 vols. (Oxford, 1923).

——, *William Shakespeare: A Study of Facts and Problems*, 2 vols. (Oxford, 1930).

Crane, Ralph. (The best summary of his scribal habits is to be found in W. W. Greg's *The Shakespeare First Folio* (Oxford, 1956).)

Dam, B. A. P. van, *The Text of Shakespeare's 'Hamlet'* (London, 1924).

Doran, Madeleine, *Henry VI* (Iowa City, Iowa, 1928).

——, *The Text of 'King Lear'* (Stanford, Calif., 1931).

Duthie, G. I., *Elizabethan Shorthand and the First Quarto of 'King Lear'* (Oxford, 1949).

——, *Shakespeare's 'King Lear'*, a Critical Edition (Oxford, 1949).

Greg, W. W., *Henslowe's Diary*, 2 vols. (London, 1904–8).

——, *Henslowe Papers* (London, 1907).

——, 'On Certain False Dates in Shakespearian Quartos', *The Library*, 9 (1908).

——, *Two Elizabethan Stage Abridgements* (Malone Society Reprints, Oxford, 1923).

——, and others, *English Literary Autographs 1500–1650* (London, 1925–32).

——, *Principles of Emendation in Shakespeare*, British Academy Lecture 1928.

——, *Dramatic Documents from the Elizabethan Playhouses*, 2 vols. (London, 1931).

——, *Variants in the First Quarto of 'King Lear'* (London, 1940).

——, 'The Rationale of the Copy-Text', *Studies in Bibliography*, 3 (1950).

——, *A Bibliography of English Printed Drama to the Restoration*, 4 vols. (London, 1951–62).

——, *Some Aspects and Problems of London Publishing between 1500 and 1650* (Oxford, 1956).

——, *The Shakespeare First Folio* (Oxford, 1956).

——, *A Companion to Arber* (London, 1967).

—— (ed.), *Shakespeare's 'Merry Wives of Windsor', 1602* (Oxford, 1910).

—— (ed.), *The Booke of Sir Thomas More* (Malone Society Reprints, Oxford, 1911).

—— and Boswell, E. (eds.), *Records of the Court of the Stationers' Company 1576–1602* (London, 1930).

Hoppe, H. R., *The Bad Quarto of 'Romeo and Juliet'*, *a Bibliographical and Textual Study* (Cornell, N.Y., 1948).

Jackson, W. A. (ed.), *Records of the Court of the Stationers' Company 1602–1640* (London, 1957).

Jenkinson, Hilary, 'Notes on the Study of English Punctuation of the Sixteenth Century', *RES* 2 (1926).

Kirschbaum, Leo, *Shakespeare and the Stationers* (Columbus, Ohio, 1955).

McKerrow, R. B., *An Introduction to Bibliography for Literary Students* (Oxford, 1927).

——, *Prolegomena for the Oxford Shakespeare* (Oxford, 1939).

Neidig, W. J., 'The Shakespeare Quartos', *Modern Philology*, 8 (1910–11).

Patrick, D. L., *The Textual History of 'Richard III'* (Stanford, Calif., 1936).

Pollard, A. W., and Redgrave, G. R. (eds.), *A Short-Title Catalogue of Books Printed in England, Scotland, and Ireland 1475–1640* (London, 1926).

——, 'Elizabethan Spelling as a Literary and Bibliographical Clue', *The Library*, 4 (1923).

——, *Shakespeare's Fight with the Pirates* (Cambridge, 1920, 1967).

——, *Shakespeare Folios and Quartos, 1594–1685* (London, 1909).

Price, H. T., *The Text of 'Henry V'* (Newcastle-under-Lyme, 1920).

Simpson, Percy, *Shakespearian Punctuation* (Oxford, 1911).

Willoughby, E. E., *The Printing of the First Folio of Shakespeare* (London, 1932).

Wilson, F. P., *Shakespeare and the New Bibliography* (rev. and ed. Helen Gardner, Oxford, 1970).

Wilson, J. Dover, *The Manuscript of Shakespeare's 'Hamlet', and the Problems of its Transmission*, 2 vols. (Cambridge, 1934).

——, 'The New Way with Shakespeare's Texts', *Shakespeare Survey 7* (1954), *8* (1955), *9* (1956), *11* (1958).

THE AGE OF BOWERS

Alexander, Peter, *William Shakespeare: The Complete Works* (London, 1951).

Bowers, Fredson, *On Editing Shakespeare and Other Elizabethan Dramatists* (Philadelphia, Pa., 1955).

——, *Principles of Bibliographical Description* (Princeton, N.J., 1949).

——, *Textual and Literary Criticism* (Cambridge, 1959).

——, *The Bibliographical Way* (Lawrence, Kans., 1959).

——, *The Dramatic Works in the Beaumont and Fletcher Canon*, 4 vols. (Cambridge, 1966–).

——, *The Dramatic Works of Thomas Dekker*, 4 vols. (Cambridge, 1953–61).

—— and Beaurline, L. (eds.), *Studies in Bibliography* (Charlottesville, Va., annually since 1947).

Bullough, Geoffrey, *Narrative and Dramatic Sources of Shakespeare*, 8 vols. (London, 1957–).

Ellis-Fermor, Una, Brooks, Harold F., and Jenkins, Harold (gen. eds.), The new Arden Shakespeare (London, 1951–).

Hinman, Charlton, *The Printing and Proofreading of the First Folio of Shakespeare*, 2 vols. (Oxford, 1963).

Honigmann, Ernst, *The Stability of Shakespeare's Text* (London, 1965).

Howard-Hill, T. H., 'Spelling and the Bibliographer', *The Library*, 18 (1963).

Hulme, Hilda M., *Explorations in Shakespeare's Language* (London, 1962).

Ingram, W. G., and Redpath, T. (eds.), *Shakespeare's Sonnets* (London, 1964).

Joseph, Sister Miriam, *Shakespeare's Use of the Arts of Language* (New York, 1947).

Kökeritz, H., *Shakespeare's Pronunciation* (New Haven, Conn., 1953).

Mackenzie, D. F., *The Cambridge University Press, 1696–1712*, 2 vols. (Cambridge, 1966).

Nicoll, Allardyce, and Muir, Kenneth (eds.), *Shakespeare Survey* (Cambridge, annually since 1948).

Nosworthy, J. M., *Shakespeare's Occasional Plays* (London, 1965).

Partridge, A. C., *Orthography in Shakespeare and Elizabethan Drama* (London, 1964).

Sisson, C. J., *New Readings in Shakespeare*, 2 vols. (Cambridge, 1956).

Smidt, Kristian (ed.), *The Tragedy of King Richard III* (Oslo; New York, 1969).

——, *Injurious Impostors and 'Richard III'* (Oslo, 1964).

Stirling, Brents, *The Shakespeare Sonnet Order: Poems and Groups* (Berkeley, Calif., 1968).

Walker, Alice, *Textual Problems in the First Folio* (Cambridge, 1953).

Walton, J. K., *The Copy for the Folio Text of 'Richard III'* (Auckland, N.Z., 1955).

——, *The Quarto Copy for the First Folio of Shakespeare* (Dublin, 1971).

Williams, G. Walton (ed.), *Romeo and Juliet* (Durham, N.C., 1964).

Wilson, J. Dover (ed.), *The Sonnets* (Cambridge, 1966).

——, Quiller-Couch, A. T., and others (eds.), The New Cambridge Shakespeare (Cambridge, 1921–).

3. Shakespeare in the Theatre

MICHAEL JAMIESON

SHAKESPEARE was a popular playwright in his own day, and at most subsequent periods in our theatre his main works have been regularly staged. A critical approach to Shakespeare based on a study of the plays as works to be performed on the stage is illuminating in itself, and it can also be an antidote to the kind of literary criticism which occasionally conveys insights and nuances which no actor or director could communicate to an audience. All students of Shakespeare should have a general notion of the stage conditions of Elizabethan times because this knowledge helps to explain the form the play takes on the printed page. It is desirable that readers of Shakespeare should be playgoers also, and have some understanding of how individual plays by Shakespeare work in the modern theatre. Familiarity with Shakespeare's fortunes on the stage between his day and our own is less important, but the stage history of a particular play or a group of plays sometimes sheds fresh light on the characters and their interplay or reminds us that a scene which makes dull reading has been found significant or memorable in a past performance. Theatrical and critical views do not, or need not, conflict. The stage interpretation during the 1950s of Shakespeare's plays on English history, for example, showed that there had been a feedback from the critical and scholarly work of the forties. Any chronological list of interpreters of Shakespeare that included such names as Johnson, Hazlitt, Bradley, and Wilson Knight should not omit Garrick, Kean, Phelps, Poel, or Gielgud.

SHAKESPEARE AND THE ELIZABETHAN STAGE

Biographers have been unable to establish the exact moment at which Shakespeare entered the theatre, but his arrival in London coincided with the first and greatest upsurge in our history of regular, commercial, metropolitan play production. In 1576, twelve years after Shakespeare's birth at Stratford, James Burbage erected at Shoreditch the first custom-built public playhouse in London, the Theatre, the timbers of which were used in 1599 as the basis for the Globe on Bankside. From early in his career Shakespeare was associated with Burbage's sons, Richard and Cuthbert, in speculative theatrical enterprises as an actor, as a company-sharer in the leading troupe of the age, and as a part-owner of the Globe and later of Blackfriars. Shakespeare's standing gave him more authority within his company than any mere playwright, and he must have written his plays with unique knowledge of the capabilities of his friend Richard Burbage and their fellow players and of the artistic effects possible at the Globe and at Blackfriars.

Two massive works of scholarship and reference, E. K. Chambers's four-volume *The Elizabethan Stage* and its accompanying two-volume *William Shakespeare: A Study of Facts and Problems*, together with G. E. Bentley's seven-volume continuation *The Jacobean and Caroline Stage*, show that there is no lack of facts about playhouse buildings, about the organization, personnel, and repertories of the various companies, about players and playwrights, about the legislation and control of playing, and about performances at Court, in inn-yards, in halls and colleges, and in the public and private playhouses of London. The general reader will find all he wants to know about these facts, and the inferences that can legitimately be made from them, in two helpful introductory accounts, Andrew Gurr's *The Shakespearean Stage, 1574–1642* and A. M. Nagler's briefer *Shakespeare's Stage*. Gurr aimed at providing a redaction of Chambers and Bentley, but he has given a lucid summary of the ascertainable facts and of modern scholarly opinion on the main topics: the companies, the players, the playhouses, the staging, and the audiences. Among older scholars, F. P. Wilson distilled within a single lecture given in 1955 his views on the Elizabethan theatre, and George Fulmer Reynolds in *On Shakespeare's Stage* (four lectures, posthumously published in 1967, which deserve a wider readership) engagingly discussed the problems of Elizabethan staging, a subject on which he was the leading and the most judicious scholar for over fifty years. G. E. Bentley's *The Seventeenth-Century Stage* reprints four contemporary accounts as prologue to eleven scholarly articles on the theatrical background, and his collection serves as an introduction for graduate students to the problems and methods of theatre research in the Shakespearian period.

THE PUBLIC PLAYHOUSES

Unlike most of his contemporaries, Shakespeare never wrote for the boy companies, and most of his plays were first acted by his fellow players at public playhouses, notably the Globe between 1599 and 1609. In some ways we know less about the playhouses of Renaissance England than we do about the ancient theatres of Greece or Rome, which survive in the Mediterranean today. The public playhouses were not necessarily all alike and the documentary evidence about them is scanty. A copy exists of a sketch which a Dutch tourist made of the Swan around 1596, and there are builders' contracts for the Fortune (1599) and the Hope (1613). Various panoramic views of London show the exteriors of buildings on Bankside. Little of this relates directly to the playhouse we are most interested in, the Globe. Many scholars have attempted to reconstruct that particular 'wooden O', but A. M. Nagler believes that the evidence permits no more than the description of a generic type of Shakespearian stage. Where evidence is scanty, the kind of reconstruction which each scholar proposes is governed (a) by his theories of the origins and evolution of the public playhouse, and (b) by his ideas about how the plays were staged. Deductions often have to be made not just from the stage-directions but from the dialogue and implied action, which allow wide areas of interpretation. John Cranford Adams in *The Globe Playhouse: its Design and Equipment* produced confident designs for Shakespeare's playhouse, and his work, with that of his colleague Irwin Smith, has formed the basis for several theatres built on American campuses for performances along Elizabethan lines. Yet Adams's design no longer commands assent from scholars. He believed (a) that the public playhouse evolved from earlier improvised playing-places in inn-yards— so that his galleried Globe recalls in its architectural detailing Elizabethan domestic buildings, not to say 'Tudor Tea-shoppes'— and (b) that the Elizabethans staged plays with close attention to where each scene was set and that well-differentiated areas were used for particular kinds of locality. Adams's reconstruction gave great prominence to two areas, the *inner* and *upper* stages—the first term never used in Elizabethan texts and the second hardly ever. In *The Globe Restored*, first published in 1953, C. Walter Hodges suggested that the public playhouse evolved from strolling players setting up their trestle-stages with tiring-houses behind, inside the galleried bear- and bull-baiting houses which already existed on Bankside (a theory which one phrase in the Fortune contract seems to support). Hodges presented the visual evidence from contemporary English and Continental sources in a handsome book, and, being himself a brilliant draughtsman, he was able to convey the spirit of his reconstruction in a series of drawings and sketches. Influenced by George R. Kernodle's *From Art to Theatre*, Hodges adopted for the tiring-house façade a baroque style, recalling not Tudor domestic architecture but the elaborately carved Renaissance screens which adorn the halls of English palaces, country houses, colleges, and inns of court (themselves often playing-places). That the playhouse façade was not 'the bare machine for playing imagined by twentieth-century scholars' was argued by Kernodle in the 1959 issue of *Shakespeare Survey*—a volume which was principally concerned with past and current views of the Elizabethan theatre. Kernodle saw the playhouse as 'a complex symbol, combined out of several age-old medieval symbols'.

The publication in 1940 of G. F. Reynolds's influential *The Staging of Elizabethan Plays at the Red Bull Theater, 1605–25* led to rigorous and discriminating re-examination of the stage directions and dialogue of the plays in the various repertories. Scholars have agreed that disproportionate emphasis was put on inner and upper stages, and suggest that in most plays most of the action took place on the great rectangular stage and that Elizabethan requirements for acting space at the rear and 'above' or 'aloft' were less frequent than J. C. Adams had claimed. Alfred Harbage found in 1955 that of eighty-six plays (seventeen by Shakespeare) staged in public playhouses between 1576 and 1608, forty-eight required no use of a gallery, thirty-nine no use of an enclosed space at the rear, and twenty-five no use of either. Subsequently the more detailed re-searches by Richard Hosley, in a series of searching articles addressed to the specialist, and by T. J. King, in an authoritative book, have endorsed Harbage's findings that (*a*) when characters appear 'aloft' it is usually only for a brief scene in which one character overlooks others below, so that the gallery above the stage could normally be used by paying spectators as 'the Lords' Room', or after 1609 (when the customs of the private playhouses like Blackfriars extended to the Globe) by the musicians, or by both; and (*b*) that in those plays which require a curtained 'discovery-place' for tableau scenes the effect may have been contrived by curtaining the doors or by using a booth or 'tent'. No evidence exists for an inner stage, and hypoth-eses about playhouse architecture constantly involve speculations about techniques of production.

Two books on the Globe Theatre aroused controversy around the time of their first appearance. Leslie Hotson's provocative *Shake-speare's Wooden O* postulated that the audience sat all round the players, that the tiring-house was below and not behind the stage, and that the actors made their entrances from 'houses'. Dr. Hotson's argument was based on his own views of the way plays were pre-sented at Court. His hypothetical Globe, with its appalling sightlines, has not been accepted by scholars of the theatre. Frances A. Yates in *Theatre of The World* put forward a new theory of the evolution of the playhouse, suggesting that James Burbage in building the Theatre and later the Globe made use of Vitruvius' theories about ancient architecture as propagated in England by John Dee. She also maintained that an illustration, engraved in Germany for Robert Fludd's *Ars Memoriae* (1623), depicts the Globe (others have since suggested it shows Blackfriars or was imagined). Again scholars have not been convinced by the major argument, but the book fascinatingly explores that territory where magic, science, and Renaissance knowledge of Antiquity overlap. Miss Yates's insight into the Globe as a moral emblem reinforces Kernodle's comments about the symbolism of that 'wide and universal theatre'.

THE PRIVATE PLAYHOUSES

In 1575, the year before Burbage built the Theatre, Sebastian Westcott opened an indoor playhouse for Paul's Boys, and in 1576 Richard Farrant moved the boys from the Chapel Royal at Windsor into a similar theatre at Blackfriars. These were the so-called 'private' playhouses, where companies of well-trained boys, under their choir-master, acted Lilliputian entertainments, usually satirical or pastoral. Shakespeare alluded in *Hamlet* to their success. In 1596 the Burbages purchased and reconstructed Blackfriars, but did not succeed in opening it as an adult playhouse until about 1610. From then until 1642 the King's Men played by candle-light at the second Blackfriars in the winter and in the bigger, open-air Globe (rebuilt after the fire of 1613) in the summer. W. A. Armstrong's pamphlet, *The Elizabethan Private Theatres*, summarizes the main facts and problems. H. N. Hillebrand's superbly researched *The Child Actors: A Chapter in Elizabethan Stage History* evokes in detail the milieu of the 'little eyases'. The history and physical dimensions of the first and second Blackfriars are dealt with in Irwin Smith's bulky book, while Richard Hosley, with his customary incisiveness, has proposed a reconstruction of the second Blackfriars in a short article. G. E. Bentley, in an important paper, 'Shakespeare and the Blackfriars Theatre', speculated that the acquisition of the smaller theatre had implications for Shakespeare and suggested that in *Pericles*, *Cymbeline*, *The Winter's Tale*, and *The Tempest*, Shakespeare was making increasingly successful experiments in a new form of entertainment, influenced by Beaumont and Fletcher, and specifically designed both for the new stage conditions at Blackfriars and for a more courtly, aristocratic audience.

THE AUDIENCE

The size and social composition of the audiences at the public and private playhouses have stimulated research. An early attempt at this kind of theatrical sociology was Louis B. Wright's chapter in *Middle Class Culture in Elizabethan England*, and W. A. Armstrong has scrutinized evidence about private theatre audiences in the years 1575–1642 in an article. The most comprehensive coverage is Alfred Harbage's *Shakespeare's Audience*, which established that the Globe could hold about 2,400 people, from all ranks of society, whereas a private theatre would seat a more select audience of perhaps 700. Harbage explored the implications for practising playwrights of the two kinds of audience in his subsequent book *Shakespeare and the Rival Traditions* where he demonstrated that a split developed between the 'Theatre of the Nation' and the 'Theatre of the Coterie' with a gradual loss of vitality in private theatre plays. Though valid in essence, his arguments—like Bentley's—have been faulted on points of detail. The evidence does not establish that the King's Men themselves discriminated between Globe plays and Blackfriars ones. Shakespeare's perennial appeal may stem from the fact that he addressed a wide audience, but the decline of late Jacobean and Caroline drama cannot be attributed solely to certain fashionable writers' disdain of the old public.

THE STAGING

Much of the documentary evidence about Elizabethan staging (or what we would nowadays call production) occurs in property-lists which survive among the papers of Philip Henslowe, the chief rival to James Burbage, and further inferences can be made from the plays themselves, particularly their stage-directions. The Elizabethans seem to have combined realism of presentation with extreme stylization, even in the same play. Henslowe's lists show that large free-standing properties existed, and possibly painted back-cloths— e.g. 'rock', 'cage', 'tomb', 'Hell Mouth', 'the City of Rome'. Stage-directions are often ambiguous, but expressions like '*A bed thrust forth, on it Frank in a slumber*' seem to indicate that large properties were carried on to the stage. Since the publication in 1933 of J. Isaacs's pamphlet *Production and Stage Management at the Blackfriars Theatre* it has been assumed that techniques were more elaborate at Blackfriars than at the Globe, and that performances were similar in their visual and musical splendours to the Court masque. T. J. King in his exhaustive *Shakespearean Staging, 1599–1642* concluded that the staging requirements of public and private theatre plays show no significant differences, and he divided plays into four categories according to their basic requirements. His analysis of 276 plays establishes that eighty-seven require only a floor space in front of an unlocalized façade with two entrances through which properties can be brought on or thrust out; forty-five plays need in addition an acting place above the stage; 102 require a covered space where actors can hide, or where properties, or actors, or both, can be discovered; and forty-five plays require a trap-door thus necessitating a platform stage. King's book is a research aid, to be consulted rather than read. It is the only place where a student can find quickly *all* known contemporary performances of particular Elizabethan plays, and it is the first book to summarize the bibliographers' findings on each play. Where playhouse manuscripts or prompt-books exist, or where the printed text is demonstrably based on playhouse copy, the stage-directions reflect production methods. King shows that most plays could have been staged simply in a hall or in a playhouse. Henslowe's inventories also include details about the wardrobe. Using this and other evidence, Hal H. Smith in an informative article, 'Some Principles of Elizabethan Stage Costume', has demonstrated that Elizabethan costumes were often elaborate and that more use was made of historical costume, especially in plays about Classical Antiquity such as *Troilus and Cressida*, than earlier scholars have suggested. Music was a feature of private theatre entertainment and, from 1609, of public playhouse performances also. Hosley thinks that the gallery above the stage at the public theatres housed both spectators and musicians, as well as, on occasions, actors 'aloft'. Music in Shakespeare's tragedies has been studied by F. W. Sternfeld, and John H. Long has devoted two volumes to Shakespeare's use of music in the great comedies and in the last plays. A technical account of Shakespeare's use of sound-effects has been given by Frances Shirley.

THE PLAYERS AND THE PLAYING

Muriel Bradbrook's *The Rise of the Common Player* is the most illuminating commentary on the Elizabethan actors and on the high place their leaders won for themselves in society in their metamorphosis from strollers to servants of the king. The clowns Richard Tarlton and Will Kempe early achieved national celebrity, to be succeeded in popular esteem by the tragedians Edward Alleyn (Henslowe's leading player), and his rival, Richard Burbage. The biographical facts about the players (more revealing about their litigation than their prowess on the boards) are in Chambers and Bentley, and in Nungezer's useful *Dictionary of Actors*. It was to the company rather than to the owners of the playhouse that the players owed allegiance, though control of both often overlapped. No company in English stage history has survived as long as the Lord Chamberlain's/King's Men nor has any other group created a comparable repertory of plays. T. W. Baldwin in *The Organisation and Personnel of the Shakespearean Company* set forth all that can be recovered about the running of this troupe, even attempting the impossible by attributing each part in Shakespeare to a particular player. A challenging article by William A. Ringler, Jr., 'The Number of Actors in Shakespeare's Early Plays', raises questions about company organization and ultimately about the quality of the acting, for Ringler proved that, with doubling, as few as sixteen players could act all the parts in the eighteen plays Shakespeare wrote before his company moved to the Globe in 1599.

Acting is ephemeral, and Elizabethan playing eluded detailed description in its own day, so that its spirit and technique cannot be recaptured now. Some scholars argue that Elizabethan acting must have been extremely formal and rhetorical, others that it was realistic and convincing. Such terms are always relative and often ambiguous. The puzzle might be solved if we could only know what sort of gesture Burbage made when as Hamlet he said to the players, 'Nor do not saw the air *too much* with your hand *thus . . .*', and how consistent Burbage's own playing was with Hamlet's advice. Alan Downer's 'Prolegomenon to a Study of Elizabethan Acting' is a serious introduction to the problems of discussing the acting of the past. Bertram Joseph, between editions of his book *Elizabethan Acting* in 1951 and 1964, modified his view that acting was formal, and that its techniques were analogous to those of rhetoric and oratory as taught in grammar-schools. Joseph's comparison of theatrical gesture with the system of manual motions evolved for the deaf and dumb by John Bulwer in 1644 provoked discussion. Alfred Harbage had argued for formal acting in *PMLA* in 1939, a view he later modified. Marvin Rosenberg, answering the question 'Elizabethan Actors: Men or Marionettes?', put the case for Shakespeare's actors projecting human personalities. Andrew Gurr's views on actors are contained in articles upon which he drew in *The Shakespearean Stage*. He believes that Alleyn 'strutted and roared' but that Burbage did not, and he has discerned an ascending order of achievement in the Elizabethan words *playing* (the work of common strollers), *acting* (originally used only for the decorous 'action' of the orator), and *personation* (the art of individual characterization). The Elizabethans did not have a sophisticated language for analysing stage-playing. No doubt there were good and bad actors then as in other ages; and the robust playing to the holiday apprentices at the Red Bull was probably less admired by the judicious than the personated passion of Burbage as Lear or Macbeth. The fact that great moments in Elizabethan drama often show men in almost pathological states of rage or grief has led some scholars to seek clues about the acting of such scenes in Elizabethan writings on melancholy or madness. R. A. Foakes's excellent article 'The Player's Passion' explored the connections between Elizabethan psychology and acting, suggesting that Burton's description of a jealous man might indicate how Othello was originally played. Foakes pointed out that the order which the Elizabethan theorists imposed on experience might suggest stylized acting at times. Certainly stage-directions like '*Isabella falls in love*' in a minor play of the period reflect stock reactions; and there seem to have been conventional ways of portraying malcontents, of presenting ghosts and visions, and of conveying invisibility. The fact in the adult companies that youths played the women's parts might confirm that all playing was formalized. Michael Jamieson, after reviewing the evidence about the boy actors and their training in an article 'Shakespeare's Celibate Stage', concluded that some boys must have acted uncommonly well to have held the stage in roles like Rosalind or Cleopatra. Conventions are unquestioningly accepted in their own day. The realistic representation of fights, torture, mutilation, grief, rage, and hysteria may well have co-existed within a single play with conventionalized presentation and stylized acting (especially in dumb-shows, the subject of an entire book by Dieter Mehl). John Russell Brown's view that acting was changing in Shakespeare's age, that formalism was 'fast dying out', and that a new naturalism was 'a kindling spirit' in Shakespeare's theatre, is convincing. The development of Shakespeare's blank verse, for instance, seems to reflect an evolution in acting also.

What, then, is the significance and use of studying the background of Shakespeare's dramatic workshop when so many details about buildings, about techniques of play-presentation, and about acting style are irrecoverably lost? The Elizabethan players were, above all, adaptable and ready, the moment the plague-figures in London soared, to go off playing their repertory on provincial fit-up stages in halls and inn-yards. Thus what happened at a commissioned, subsidized performance by the players at Court need not reflect the

practice of the same men on Bankside. Isaacs may be right in saying
that Blackfriars staging was sumptuous, but King's lists show that
most Blackfriars plays could be simply staged. Baldwin's ingenious
cast-lists assume a good-sized company, but Ringler's statistics show
that sixteen players could act *all* the parts in any one of Shakespeare's
pre-Globe plays. King and Ringler may have pared things down, as
the players themselves had to do on tour. A general study like
Bernard Beckerman's *Shakespeare at the Globe, 1599–1609* shows how a
study of the material background can lead on to an illuminating
account of Shakespeare's dramaturgy. Some consideration of the
original stage conditions checks the over-ingenuities of interpretative
literary criticism and helps the director and the actors to find analogous methods of presenting Shakespeare's plays in modern playhouses. Tyrone Guthrie's theatre at Stratford, Ontario, for example,
is an attempt to recapture in modern terms the Shakespearian
actor-audience relationship. A remark of Walter Hodges deserves
pondering: 'The ancient tradition which nourished the Elizabethan
playhouses died when the last of them was pulled down; since when
it may almost be said that no play of Shakespeare's has been acted,
except in adaptation.'

SHAKESPEARE IN THE THEATRE, 1660–1970

If the evidence about Elizabethan, Jacobean, and Caroline performances of Shakespeare has tantalizing lacunae, the sheer bulk of information about presentations of the plays between the Restoration
and our own day is overwhelming. The facts are contained in old-
fashioned volumes of theatrical history, in magisterial works of
reference like *The London Stage*, in eye-witness accounts of great
performances, in modern scholarly discussions of the stage history of
separate plays or groups of plays, in the biographies of players like
Edmund Kean or William Charles Macready or of a scholar-crank
like William Poel, in books on the leading theatrical companies, and
in prompt-books, play-bills, press-cuttings, and ephemera preserved
in the theatrical collections of Britain and the United States.

The history of Shakespearian staging is itself inextricably linked
with changes in general and literary taste, and with innovations in
playhouse design, acting technique, and stage practice. The student
of Shakespeare who asks himself 'What did Dryden really do to
Antony and Cleopatra in *All for Love*?', or 'Why was Hazlitt so thrilled
by Mrs. Siddons and Edmund Kean in their Shakespearian roles?',
or 'Was Bernard Shaw fair in his incessant attacks in the *Saturday
Review* on Sir Henry Irving as an actor-producer of Shakespeare?',

gets involved in matters which take him beyond stage history (itself a branch of antiquarianism) to general questions about the culture of a period and specific questions about the theatrical and critical interpretation of Shakespeare at particular moments. These questions, in turn, may stimulate a student's own reading of the plays, since the way characters and scenes have been presented in the theatre often sheds light on their significance, and suggests possibilities of interpretation which might not occur in the study—a topic explored by John Russell Brown in a paper 'Theatre Research and the Criticism of Shakespeare and his Contemporaries'. His own book, *Shakespeare's Plays in Performance*, grounded on knowledge of the plays' fortunes on the stage in the past and in our own day, seeks to find in the text the 'stage reality that lies there waiting to be awakened'.

There have been, broadly speaking, three movements in the stage history of Shakespeare—the first dominated by the adapters, the second by the great players of the eighteenth- and nineteenth-century stage, and the third by that international figure of the twentieth-century theatre, the director. Two and a half centuries of Shakespearian staging have been surveyed by George C. D. Odell in *Shakespeare—from Betterton to Irving*, an old-fashioned theatrical chronicle which has been amplified and corrected but never replaced by later scholarship. Arthur Colby Sprague has given, in effect, a selective history of this same subject in *Shakespearean Players and Performances*, each chapter of which re-creates a significant stage interpretation—Betterton's Hamlet, Garrick's King Lear, Booth's Iago, etc. Sprague's earlier book, *Shakespeare and the Actors*, recovered from semi-oblivion the illustrative stage business which accumulated in successive performances, an aspect of theatrical custom which has always fascinated traditionalists like Sir John Gielgud and Sir Donald Wolfit. Writing for the playgoer, Norman Marshall has given a pleasant account of changes in Shakespearian staging in three chapters of *The Producer and the Play* which stress the final emergence of the director as the artist responsible for the over-all interpretation in the theatre of a Shakespeare script.

Other writers in the present volume discuss the critical usefulness of the stage histories of particular plays and groups of plays. The standard editions vary in the amount of such information they include. The New Cambridge Shakespeare carries full stage histories by Harold Child and, later, by C. B. Young, but those in the earlier volumes stop short in the twenties. The stage histories in O. J.

Campbell's *Shakespeare Encyclopaedia* are reliable and unusually full. Examples of books that go into stage history in more minute detail are A. C. Sprague's *Shakespeare's Histories: Plays for the Stage*, which chronicles the rediscovery of these plays in the theatre, Joseph G. Price's *The Unfortunate Comedy*, which deals with the seldom-staged *All's Well That Ends Well*, Dennis Bartholomeusz's *Macbeth and the Players*, and Marvin Rosenberg's *The Masks of Othello*. *Hamlet* has understandably preoccupied stage historians and at least two books have been devoted to individual actors in that play—Charles H. Shattuck's on Edwin Booth, who played Hamlet across the United States between 1853 and 1891, and Rosamund Gilder's on John Gielgud. An invaluable research tool for those interested in the stage history of Shakespeare is Shattuck's *The Shakespeare Prompt-books*, a catalogue of the surviving theatre copies which indicate the ways in which various actors and directors have handled, or mis-handled, Shakespeare's texts.

By consulting the eleven volumes of *The London Stage* (1960–5) a student can now find out what was happening at the principal London theatres almost day by day between 1660 and 1800. Scenes from Shakespeare had been performed clandestinely during the Commonwealth, as Leslie Hotson showed in *The Commonwealth and Restoration Stage*, but between 1660 and 1700 Shakespeare came second to Beaumont and Fletcher among the old dramatists, and his plays were either adapted as spectacular operas, as readers of Pepys will remember, or were regularized to comply with neoclassic taste. This movement has been described, and the main adaptations sum-marized, by Hazelton Spencer in *Shakespeare Improved*, to which Christopher Spencer has provided a convenient adjunct by editing *Five Restoration Adaptations of Shakespeare*. Nahum Tate's *King Lear* (1681), with its excision of the Fool, its romance between Cordelia and Edgar, and its restoration of King Lear to the throne, formed the basis of all acting texts, Shakespeare's play not being completely restored until Macready's revival in 1834. Colley Cibber's alteration of *Richard III* (1700) long remained the actor-manager's Saturday night stand-by, some of its melodramatic lines being retained in Laurence Olivier's film of 1956.

Betterton's acting created a vogue for some of Shakespeare's plays around 1700, but it was not until the 1730s that Shakespeare achieved pre-eminence among older dramatists and that a number of his plays became part of the staple fare of playgoers who judged a player's excellence by his powers in Shakespearian roles. In the period 1747–76, when David Garrick made Drury Lane the premier theatre in Europe, both for acting and stage presentation, about 20 per cent of his repertory was Shakespearian, albeit in adaptation. The annals of London performances are contained in C. B. Hogan's *Shakespeare in The Theatre, 1701–1800*, which is in some ways superseded by *The London Stage* (on which Hogan collaborated), where Shakespearian performances are listed in the illuminating context of general theatrical activities. In their prefaces the five editors, including Hogan, discuss the Shakespearian element in the London repertories, and one of them, A. H. Scouten, has analysed the significance of Shakespeare's growing stage fame in an article 'The Increase in Popularity of Shakespeare's Plays in the Eighteenth Century: A *Caveat* for Interpreters of Stage History'.

Eye-witness accounts of Burbage, Betterton, and even Garrick are disappointing to students of Shakespeare. The age that saw Mrs. Siddons in maturity and Edmund Kean at the height of his romantic powers was also the time of the great dramatic critics and theatrical reporters. To read Hazlitt or Leigh Hunt on Mrs. Siddons as Lady Macbeth or Constance and on Kean as Shylock or Richard III is to be reminded that the prime interpreter was the individual player and that critical attention also focused on Shakespeare's character portrayal. The nineteenth-century actor–producers, particularly Charles Kean and Henry Irving, lavished upon the plays a wealth of period costumes and scenery, archaeologically accurate, and such cumbersome staging necessitated ruthless cutting of the text. In the 1890s, when Shaw was attacking Irving for such extravagance, the scholarly, eccentric William Poel mounted a series of unfashionable, experimental presentations of Shakespearian and Elizabethan plays in which he tried to recapture the original conventions. Poel's theories (discussed in Robert Speaight's biography) were championed by Shaw in the *Saturday Review* and influenced Harley Granville-Barker, whose own productions of Shakespeare in the West End in 1912–14 proved seminal in their respect for their text, the pace of the verse-speaking, and the brilliant modern sets and costumes. Barker became frustrated at the absence of a subsidized National Theatre in England and turned to writing the series *Prefaces to Shakespeare* (1927–47). His elucidation of several of the plays showed the insight of a director, and led to greater understanding by academics of Shakespeare as a man of the theatre as well as influencing a new generation of producers at such specialized theatres as the Old Vic in London and the Shakespeare Memorial Theatre at Stratford. Changes in Shakespearian production in the years between

the wars are dealt with in such books as *Old Vic Saga* by Harcourt
Williams, himself a director there, and *The Stratford Festival* by T. C.
Kemp and J. C. Trewin. Trewin's own *Shakespeare on the English
Stage, 1900–1964*, is a comprehensive survey, and in collaboration
with A. C. Sprague he has examined attitudes to such matters as
cutting the text, stage business, verse-speaking, character portrayal,
and stage design in *Shakespeare's Plays Today: Some Customs and Conventions of the Stage*. More idiosyncratic impressions of Shakespearian
acting and production between the wars are contained in two
gatherings of theatre notices—*Brief Chronicles* by James Agate and
The Shakespearean Scene by Herbert Farjeon. The records of such
organizations as the Royal Shakespeare Company, the National
Theatre, and the Festival Theatre at Stratford, Ontario, often contained in glossy commemorative books and pamphlets, shed light on
innovating approaches to Shakespeare in the theatre in the 1950s
and 1960s. The British annual *Shakespeare Survey* has from its inception in 1948 carried review articles by scholars like Richard David,
John Russell Brown, and Gareth Lloyd Evans on key productions
of the plays, while the American *Shakespeare Quarterly* devotes its
autumn number to evaluative reports on the Shakespeare seasons
at the three Stratfords (Warwickshire, Ontario, and Connecticut)
and at such Elizabethan summer playhouses as those at San Diego
and Ashland, Oregon.

Roger Manvell's *Shakespeare on Film*, an informative record, reminds us that a vast, international audience now encounters
Shakespeare for the first time in the cinema. Olivier's *Henry V*,
Kurosawa's *Macbeth*, and Kosintsev's *King Lear* are masterpieces of
world cinema. Adapted into Japanese or translated into Russian,
Shakespeare's plays still 'work' upon audiences as they did in the
days of Burbage, Kean, and Booth. The study of his plays in performance keeps readers and students in touch with a living
Shakespeare.

REFERENCES

SHAKESPEARE AND THE ELIZABETHAN STAGE

Reference Books and General Accounts

Bentley, G. E., *The Jacobean and Caroline Stage*, 7 vols. (Oxford, 1941–68).
—— (ed.), *The Seventeenth Century Stage: A Collection of Critical Essays* (Chicago, Ill., 1968).
Chambers, E. K., *The Elizabethan Stage*, 4 vols. (Oxford, 1923); *William Shakespeare: A Study of Facts and Problems*, 2 vols. (Oxford, 1930); index to both works by Beatrice White (Oxford, 1934).
Foakes, R. A., and Rickert, R. T. (eds.), *Henslowe's Diary* (Cambridge, 1961).
Greg, W. W. (ed.), *Dramatic Documents from the Elizabethan Playhouses*, 2 vols. (Oxford, 1931).
Gurr, Andrew, *The Shakespearean Stage, 1574–1642* (Cambridge, 1970).
Nagler, A. M., *Shakespeare's Stage* (New Haven, Conn., 1958).
Reynolds, George Fulmer, *On Shakespeare's Stage*, ed. R. K. Knaub (Boulder, Colo., 1967).
Wilson, F. P., 'The Elizabethan Stage', *Neophilologus*, 39 (1955); repr. in his *Shakespearian and Other Studies*, ed. Helen Gardner (Oxford, 1969).

THE PUBLIC PLAYHOUSES

Adams, John Cranford, *The Globe Playhouse: its Design and Equipment* (Cambridge, Mass., 1942; 2nd edn., London, 1961).
Harbage, Alfred, *Theatre for Shakespeare* (Toronto, 1955).
Hodges, C. Walter, *The Globe Restored: A Study of the Elizabethan Theatre* (London, 1953; 2nd edn., London, 1968).
Hosley, Richard, 'The Origins of the Shakespearian Playhouse', *Shakespeare Quarterly*, 15 (1964).
——, 'The Discovery-space in Shakespeare's Globe', *Shakespeare Survey 12* (Cambridge, 1959); repr. in *The Seventeenth Century Stage*, ed. G. E. Bentley (Chicago, Ill., 1968).
——, 'The Gallery over the Stage in the Public Playhouse of Shakespeare's Time', *Shakespeare Quarterly*, 14 (1963).
——, 'Shakespeare's Use of a Gallery over the Stage', *Shakespeare Survey 10* (Cambridge, 1957).
——, 'The Staging of Desdemona's Bed', *Shakespeare Quarterly*, 14 (1963).
——, 'The Use of the Upper Stage in *Romeo and Juliet*', *Shakespeare Quarterly*, 5 (1954).
——, 'Was There a Music-room in Shakespeare's Globe?', *Shakespeare Survey 13* (Cambridge, 1960).
Hotson, Leslie, *Shakespeare's Wooden O* (London, 1959).
Kernodle, George R., 'The Open Stage: Elizabethan or Existentialist?', *Shakespeare Survey 12* (1959).
——, *From Art to Theatre: Form and Convention in the Renaissance* (Chicago, Ill., 1944).

King, T. J., *Shakespearean Staging, 1599–1642* (Cambridge, Mass., 1971).

Reynolds, George Fulmer, *The Staging of Elizabethan Plays at the Red Bull Theater, 1605–25* (New York, 1940).

Smith, Irwin, *Shakespeare's Globe Playhouse: A Modern Reconstruction* (New York, 1956).

Yates, Frances A., *Theatre of the World* (London, 1969).

THE PRIVATE PLAYHOUSES

Armstrong, William A., *The Elizabethan Private Theatres: Facts and Problems* (The Society for Theatre Research, London, 1958).

Bentley, G. E., 'Shakespeare and the Blackfriars Theatre', *Shakespeare Survey 1* (Cambridge, 1948; repr. in his *Shakespeare and His Theatre*, Lincoln, Nebr., 1964).

Hillebrand, Harold Newcomb, *The Child Actors: A Chapter in Elizabethan Stage History* (University of Illinois Studies in Language and Literature, Urbana, Ill., 1926).

Hosley, Richard, 'A Reconstruction of the Second Blackfriars', *The Elizabethan Theatre*, 1, ed. David Galloway (Toronto, 1969).

Smith, Irwin, *Shakespeare's Blackfriars Playhouse: Its History and Its Design* (New York, 1964).

THE AUDIENCE

Armstrong, William A., 'The Audience of the Elizabethan Private Theatres', *RES*, N.S. 10 (1959); repr. in *The Seventeenth Century Stage*, ed. G. E. Bentley (Chicago, Ill., 1968).

Harbage, Alfred, *Shakespeare's Audience* (New York, 1941).

——, *Shakespeare and the Rival Traditions* (New York, 1952).

Wright, Louis B., *Middle Class Culture in Elizabethan England* (San Marino, Calif., 1935; 2nd edn., London, 1964).

THE STAGING

Isaacs, J., *Production and Stage Management at the Blackfriars Theatre* (Shakespeare Association, London, 1933).

Long, John H., *Shakespeare's Use of Music: The Comedies* and *The Last Plays*, 2 vols. (Gainesville, Fla., 1955 and 1961).

Shirley, Frances Ann, *Shakespeare's Use of Off-Stage Sounds* (Lincoln, Nebr., 1963).

Smith, Hal H., 'Some Principles of Elizabethan Stage Costume', *Journal of the Warburg and Courtauld Institutes*, 25 (1962).

Sternfeld, F. W., *Music in Shakespearean Tragedy* (London, 1963).

THE PLAYERS AND THE PLAYING

Baldwin, Thomas Whitfield, *The Organisation and Personnel of the Shakespearean Company* (Princeton, N.J., 1927; repr. New York, 1961).

Beckerman, Bernard, *Shakespeare at the Globe, 1599–1609* (New York, 1962).

Bradbrook, M. C., *The Rise of the Common Player: A Study of Actor and Society in Shakespeare's England* (London, 1962).

Downer, Alan S., 'Prolegomenon to a Study of Elizabethan Acting', *Maske und Kothurn*, 10 (1965).

Foakes, R. A., 'The Player's Passion: Some Notes on Elizabethan Psychology and Acting', *Essays and Studies*, N.S. 7 (1954).

Gurr, Andrew, 'Elizabethan Action', *Studies in Philology*, 63 (1966).

——, 'Who Strutted and Bellowed?', *Shakespeare Survey 16* (1963).

Harbage, Alfred, 'Elizabethan Acting', *PMLA*, 54 (1939); repr. in his *Theatre for Shakespeare* (Toronto, 1955).

Jamieson, Michael, 'Shakespeare's Celibate Stage', in *Papers Mainly Shakespearian*, ed. G. I. Duthie (Edinburgh and London, 1964); repr. in *The Seventeenth Century Stage*, ed. G. E. Bentley (Chicago, Ill., 1968).

Joseph, Bertram, *Elizabethan Acting* (London, 1951; 2nd edn., 1964).

Mehl, Dieter, *The Elizabethan Dumb Show: The History of a Dramatic Convention* (London, 1965).

Nungezer, Edwin, *A Dictionary of Actors and of Other Personages Associated with the Public Presentation of Plays in England before 1642* (New Haven, Conn., 1929).

Ringler, W. A., Jr., 'The Number of Actors in Shakespeare's Early Plays', in *The Seventeenth Century Stage*, ed. G. E. Bentley (Chicago, Ill., 1968).

Rosenberg, Marvin, 'Elizabethan Actors: Men or Marionettes?', *PMLA*, 69 (1954); repr. in *The Seventeenth Century Stage*, ed. G. E. Bentley (Chicago, Ill., 1968).

SHAKESPEARE IN THE THEATRE, 1660–1970
WORKS OF SCHOLARSHIP AND REFERENCE

Avery, Emmett L., Hogan, Charles Beecher, and others (eds.), *The London Stage: A Calendar of Plays, Entertainments and Afterpieces, 1660–1800*, 11 vols. (Carbondale, Ill., 1960–5).

Campbell, Oscar James, and Quinn, Edward G. (eds.), *A Shakespeare Encyclopaedia* (London, 1966).

Hogan, Charles Beecher, *Shakespeare in the Theatre: A Record of Performances in London, 1701–1800*, 2 vols. (Oxford, 1952–7).

Shattuck, Charles II., *The Shakespeare Promptbooks: A Descriptive Catalogue* (Urbana, Ill., 1965).

STAGE HISTORY

(a) *General*

Brown, John Russell, *Shakespeare's Plays in Performance*, with 'Theatre Research and the Criticism of Shakespeare and His Contemporaries' as appendix (London, 1966; Penguin Shakespeare Library, Harmondsworth, 1969).

Marshall, Norman, *The Producer and the Play* (London, 1957).

Odell, George C. D., *Shakespeare—from Betterton to Irving*, 2 vols. (London, 1920; repr. New York, 1963).

Sprague, Arthur Colby, *Shakespeare and the Actors: The Stage Business in His Plays, 1660–1905* (Cambridge, Mass., 1944; repr. New York, 1963).

——, *Shakespearian Players and Performances* (London, 1954).

——, *The Stage Business in Shakespeare's Plays: A Postscript* (The Society for Theatre Research, London, 1953).

(b) *Special Studies*

Bartholomeusz, Dennis, *Macbeth and the Players* (Cambridge, 1969).

Gilder, Rosamund, *John Gielgud's Hamlet: A Record of Performance* with 'The Hamlet Tradition' by John Gielgud (London, 1937).

Price, Joseph G., *The Unfortunate Comedy: A Study of 'All's Well That Ends Well' and its Critics* (Liverpool, 1968).

Rosenberg, Marvin, *The Masks of Othello: The Search for the Identity of Othello, Iago and Desdemona by Three Centuries of Actors and Critics* (Berkeley, Calif., 1961).

Shattuck, Charles H., *The Hamlet of Edwin Booth* (Urbana, Ill., 1969).

Sprague, Arthur Colby, *Shakespeare's Histories: Plays for the Stage* (London, 1964).

(c) *Shakespeare in the Restoration and Eighteenth Century*

Hotson, Leslie, *The Commonwealth and Restoration Stage* (Cambridge, Mass., 1928).

Scouten, Arthur H., 'The Increase in Popularity of Shakespeare's Plays in the Eighteenth Century: A *Caveat* for Interpreters of Stage History', *Shakespeare Quarterly*, 7 (1956).

Spencer, Christopher (ed.), *Five Restoration Adaptations of Shakespeare* (Urbana, Ill., 1965).

Spencer, Hazelton, *Shakespeare Improved* (Cambridge, Mass., 1927).

(d) *Theatrical Criticism, Nineteenth and Twentieth Centuries*

Agate, James, *Brief Chronicles: A Survey of Plays by Shakespeare and the Elizabethans in Actual Performance, 1923–42* (London, 1943).

Farjeon, Herbert, *The Shakespearean Scene: Dramatic Criticisms, 1913–44* (London, 1949).

Houtchens, Lawrence and Carolyn (eds.), *Leigh Hunt's Dramatic Criticism, 1808–1831* (New York, 1949).

Howe, P. P. (ed.), *The Complete Works of William Hazlitt*, vol. xviii, *Art and Dramatic Criticism* (London, 1933).

Shaw, G. Bernard, *Our Theatre in the Nineties*, 3 vols. (London, 1932); ed. Edwin Wilson, *Shaw on Shakespeare* (New York, 1961; Penguin Shakespeare Library, Harmondsworth, 1969).

(e) *Shakespeare in the Twentieth Century*

Kemp, T. C., and Trewin, J. C., *The Stratford Festival* (Birmingham, 1953).

Speaight, Robert, *William Poel and the Elizabethan Revival* (London, 1954).

Sprague, Arthur Colby, and Trewin, J. C., *Shakespeare's Plays Today: Some Customs and Conventions of the Stage* (London, 1970).

Trewin, J. C., *Shakespeare on the English Stage, 1900–1964* (London, 1964).

Williams, Harcourt, *Old Vic Saga* (London, 1949).

SHAKESPEARE IN THE CINEMA

Manvell, Roger, *Shakespeare on Film* (London, 1971).

4. The Sonnets and Other Poems

J. M. NOSWORTHY

The Sonnets

TEXTS

The Scolar Press facsimile of the original edition, printed by George Eld for Thomas Thorpe in 1609, provides an interesting and inexpensive initiation since, whatever the doubts and difficulties, it enables the reader to form his own unprejudiced estimate of the 'problems' which the Sonnets present. For more detailed study Pooler's original Arden edition, though eventually to be replaced, remains a useful one, and that of Ingram and Redpath provides a very full apparatus. Dover Wilson's valedictory contribution to the New Cambridge series reflects his characteristic humanity and enthusiasm but is uneven and sometimes misleading, except, perhaps, to readers able to accept his arbitrary postulate that the Sonnets constitute the greatest love-poem ever written. Unfortunately the onset of blindness prevented Wilson from attempting the kind of independent bibliographical analysis that distinguished the New Cambridge edition as a whole. Hence the determination of the habits of Eld's two compositors and their respective stints, together with a consideration of what light, if any, these throw on the character of the manuscript that came rather mysteriously into Thorpe's hands, remains a desideratum. All that need here be said of Rollins's New Variorum edition is that it is one of the greatest achievements in the whole field of Shakespearian scholarship and therefore indispensable for enthusiasts, whose needs, incidentally, are well provided for at the opposite end of the scale by Levi Fox's companionable pocket-sized edition.

CRITICISM AND COMMENTARY

Thorpe's collection comprises 154 sonnets, dedicated to a certain 'Mr. W.H.', problematic in both their order and their dating. Numbers 1 to 17 are addressed to a fair youth, evidently of high rank, imploring him to marry and beget children; numbers 18 to 126 concern Shakespeare's seemingly intense affection towards the youth and relate to a period of estrangement and to the youth's acceptance of the tributes of a rival poet; numbers 127 to 154 (defined by Mackail as 'a miscellaneous and disorderly appendix') relate mainly to the so-called 'dark lady' who readily gratified the sexual appetites of Shakespeare, the youth, and others.

These, with the reservation that there may have been more than one youth, are the basic elements of 'the Sonnet-story' upon which conjecture has waxed fat. The general character of Shakespeare's writings over the period 1592 to 1596 affords adequate stylistic evidence that many of the sonnets were written during those years, and this is endorsed by Francis Meres's praise of the dramatist's 'sugred Sonnets among his private friends' in *Palladis Tamia* (1598), but others, more mature in thought and style, seem to be of later date. The problem is handled fully and thoughtfully in Schaar's monograph, but the results are inconclusive. Attempts to reorder the sonnets have proved equally fruitless. That of Brents Stirling has an appearance of objectivity and, as far as the final group is concerned, is accepted as conclusive in Wilson's commentary, but the bibliographical evidence is vulnerable and the order proposed is scarcely more coherent than the received one. E. K. Chambers's essay on 'The Order of the Sonnets' has a twofold value—as a model of systematic demolition (of the once-fashionable arrangement proposed by Sir Denys Bray), and as a persuasive affirmation that, at least for Sonnets 1–126, Thorpe's original order may well be substantially correct.

Since Chambers was, perhaps, the least credulous of all Shakespearians, his case for identifying the fair youth with William Herbert, Third Earl of Pembroke, merits consideration. It is accepted and effectively supplemented in Wilson's introduction but remains, at best, an attractive possibility. Chambers, in his *William Shakespeare*, provides a balanced survey of the various theories propounded prior to 1930, and those who aspire to a comprehensive knowledge of this fascinating but unfruitful field of inquiry will find their needs admirably provided for by Rollins's vast, and often hilarious, commentary (1944). Subsequent endeavours have introduced new candidates, such as Hotson's Mr. William Hatliffe, or resurrected old ones, such as the Earl of Southampton, but these do not signify. Gurr has argued that Sonnet 145 puns on the name 'Hathaway' and was written about 1582. Since the poem is an anomalous one, written in tetrameter, and conveys the impression of prentice work, his ingenious, though somewhat naïvely presented, case merits attention, especially as it involves someone to whom Shakespeare probably did address the occasional sonnet. It may yet emerge that Anne Hathaway appears in Thorpe's collection more frequently than has been hitherto supposed.

Shakespeare's Sonnets are part of a vogue precipitated by the publication of Sidney's *Astrophil and Stella* in 1591—a vogue which, in both its pride and poverty, can be best studied in Sidney Lee's exhaustive collection, *Elizabethan Sonnets*. Here Shakespeare's contribution can be seen in the right perspective; and the offerings of Sidney and Spenser, together with the best of Drayton and Drummond, establish that he did not stand alone. He stood, nevertheless, somewhat apart in that his treatment of stock themes reflects the attitudes and techniques of a practised dramatist. The differences resulting from a quasi-dramatic, as opposed to a purely lyrical, approach are subtly demonstrated in an important essay by G. K. Hunter.

Lee's prefaces, together with subsequent papers, are valuable for their examination of the debts owed by English sonneteers to Italian and French models and for their demonstration of Shakespeare's specific debts to Ovid, whom Lee regards as a major source, and to the Platonic ideas current in the Italian renaissance. These inquiries are lengthily extended by T. W. Baldwin, whose preoccupation with the 'genetics' of the Sonnets serves, perhaps, to explain why he regards them primarily, and quite unacceptably, as mere technical exercises. His capacity for conjecture and dubiously relevant inquiry, and his uncritical acceptance of Southampton as the fair youth, do not inspire confidence. A more sensitive and unencumbered approach is that of J. W. Lever, who scrutinizes the Italian and French influences operative in the sonnets of various Elizabethans, clarifies the distinction between the Petrarchan and anti-Petrarch modes, and explores fully the debts incurred by Shakespeare to Ovid and Horace. It may be objected that his efforts to amend the order of the 1609 quarto are no more convincing than those of other commentators and that he underestimates Shakespeare's dependence on Neoplatonic thought, but this does little to diminish the importance of his book. The notion that Petrarchanism reached Shakespeare through Samuel Daniel's *Delia* sonnets is a long-standing one which Claes Schaar's careful analysis and comparison have shown to be unlikely. Sonnets 153-4 are anomalous and belong to a curious tradition which is fully examined by James Hutton in a model essay which annihilates most of the nonsense that has been written about them.

The main themes of the Sonnets—friendship and love, mutability and immortality, procreation and death—have been variously handled. Hubler's attempt to extract 'the sense of Shakespeare's sonnets' is efficient but joyless. Leishman presents the themes as Love, Beauty, and Time and considers the variations which Shakespeare wove around them, comparing him, in this respect, both with predecessors—Pindar, Horace, and Michelangelo—and with successors—Donne and Herbert. The link between Shakespeare and Donne, along with other of the so-called metaphysicals, is also touched on by Cruttwell. Time and mutability are among the Shakespearian themes dealt with by L. C. Knights in a general study which admits a sensitive appraisal of their function in the sonnets. Wilson Knight's typically mystical and ritualistic meditations on Shakespeare's handling of time, death, and eternity seek to establish a close linkage between the Sonnets and *The Phoenix and the Turtle*, thereby creating a relationship which Shakespeare clearly did not intend. Even so, Knight's perceptions, when disentangled from his symbolism, are often original and valid. The theme of love and friendship has all too often led commentators into fruitless speculation about Shakespeare's supposed (but highly unlikely) homosexuality. For an understanding of the Elizabethan convention, Shakespeare is, perhaps, himself the best guide since the themes and tensions presented subjectively in the Sonnets are objectively treated in *The Two Gentlemen of Verona*. Clifford Leech offers some brief but helpful comments in his introduction to the new Arden edition of the play.

Winifred Nowottny's examination of 'form' ('that in virtue of which the parts are related one to another') covers Sonnets 1–6 but will, presumably, be usefully extended in her projected new Arden edition. Shakespeare's use of alliteration and assonance is discussed by U. K. Goldsmith, and the Sonnets are considered *inter alia*, in M. M. Mahood's study of the dramatist's word-play. Stephen Booth's essay moves from formal analysis into the field of interpretation—a field in which Landry and Philip Edwards have also made interesting contributions. Shakespeare's sexual innuendoes, an important element somewhat primly handled by most commentators, are frankly revealed in Partridge's handbook.

Sonnet sequences, whether by Shakespeare or anyone else, do not readily lend themselves to comprehensive aesthetic judgements. Barbara Herrnstein's *Discussions of Shakespeare's Sonnets* offers a useful collection of extracts from past and present critics, and Rollins's account (in his New Variorum edition) of the vogue of the Sonnets affords a valuable basis for the formation of critical estimates. Twentieth-century enthusiasm, not wholly divorced from 'bardolatry,' contrasts oddly with the tepid, sometimes hostile, attitudes of the great Romantic poets and critics, and, though we may justly contemn canons of taste that set Shakespeare so far below the Revd. William Lisle Bowles, such a comment as Keats's, that the Sonnets 'seem to be full of fine things said unintentionally—in the intensity of working out conceits', together with his objection that a Shakespearian sonnet 'appears too elegiac—and the couplet at the end of it has seldom a pleasing effect', must give us pause. Though many of the Sonnets (Nos. 30, 60, 64, 98, 116, and 146 may be cited as random samples) transcend these reservations, there is elsewhere altogether too much of the working out of conceits. A reading of the sonnets of later poets can help towards an orientation. Milton's 'Methought I saw my late espoused saint' and Wordsworth's 'Surprised by joy—impatient as the wind' are charged with emotional profundities frequently matched in the plays of Shakespeare's maturity but not, I think, in even the finest of his sonnets.

The Poems

TEXTS

Venus and Adonis and *The Rape of Lucrece* were both dedicated to the Earl of Southampton, and Shakespeare entrusted them to his fellow Stratfordian, Richard Field, who had established himself as one of London's leading printers. The quartos were evidently set from either the author's fair copy or a careful transcript, and, since both texts are remarkably clean and straightforward, the Scolar Press facsimiles again afford an attractive initiation. There is to be a Scolar facsimile of Robert Chester's *Love's Martyr* to which Shakespeare contributed *The Phoenix and the Turtle*. Rollins's New Variorum edition, little if at all inferior to that of the *Sonnets*, provides a full conspectus of all that was known or thought about these poems down to the time of its publication (1938). F. T. Prince's new Arden edition is solid though unremarkable, but prints the main sources, which are lacking in J. C. Maxwell's New Cambridge presentation. Maxwell, however, supplies a better text and a more business-like apparatus. The New Penguin decision to assign the narrative poems to separate volumes is more than vindicated by J. W. Lever's *The Rape of Lucrece*. Again, the sources are not included, but the relevant material for both poems, together with brief but judicious discussion, is provided in Geoffrey Bullough's *Narrative and Dramatic Sources of Shakespeare*.

Venus and Adonis and *Lucrece* serve as the starting-point for Coleridge's profound inquiry into 'the specific symptoms of poetic power' exhibited by Shakespeare (*Biographia Literaria*, Chapter XV) and also for his lecture on Shakespeare as a poet generally. Despite a rather prim moral attitude and the acceptance of a now discredited chronology, Coleridge's recognition of the intrinsic merits of these poems far surpasses that of most subsequent critics. The linkage which he establishes between the emergent genius of the poems and the fulfilment of the plays has effectively stimulated more recent commentators, notably A. C. Hamilton, M. C. Bradbrook, and Kenneth Muir, whose reflections on the seriousness of *Venus and Adonis* and the quality of *Lucrece* serve as a corrective to the 'comic' approach of Rufus Putney's 'Venus Agonistes'. Putney's essay is by no means implausible but those who, like J. W. Lever, observe distinct parallels between this poem and *Antony and Cleopatra* have every reason to doubt its basic validity.

Lever's own introduction to *The Rape of Lucrece* offers a valuable comparison with the earlier poem and a scholarly presentation of received facts and opinions. It enables the modern reader both to see and to share those things in the poem that appealed to Shakespeare's contemporaries and, in all its judgements, reveals the workings of a distinguished critical intelligence. It can be profitably read in conjunction with John Buxton's sensitive appraisal of *Venus and Adonis*.

Particular aspects of the two poems have often been discussed to little purpose, but H. T. Price's essay on the imagery of *Venus and Adonis* and D. C. Allen's study of the Lucrece legend merit attention. P. W. Miller's article on the Elizabethan minor epic is concerned mainly with Marlowe's *Hero and Leander*, which it associates with the erotic epyllion developed by Ovid from Greek models, but since it examines the standard ingredients of the genre—the theme of sexual love, the use of digression and set speech, and the insistence on brevity—it has obvious relevance to the study of Shakespeare's narrative poems.

The Phoenix and the Turtle is Shakespeare's sole contribution to a set of poetical essays, by Jonson, Marston, Chapman and others, appended to Robert Chester's *Love's Martyr*, a versified hotchpotch concerned basically with the activities, mainly amorous, of Chester's patron, Sir John Salusbury of Lleweni in Denbighshire. It is a ready inference that the purpose of these additions was to secure the publication of the unpublishable. If so, Shakespeare's poem is almost certainly a *tour de force* within a context that eludes definition and not, as G. Wilson Knight and others have supposed, the outcome of prolonged meditation upon Neoplatonism and the mystical symbolism of the Phoenix. Carleton Brown's scholarly edition of the poems of Salusbury and Chester offers a number of suggestive clues, several of which have been put to good use in William Empson's essay. Roger Lancelyn Green provides a short and useful account of the Phoenix myth, and this is also handled by Alvarez and Ellrodt, both of whom credit Shakespeare with philosophical powers which he is unlikely, on this occasion, to have invoked.

Discussion of *A Lover's Complaint* has concerned itself, almost exclusively, with authorship. Mackail's case against Shakespeare has won considerable support, but Kenneth Muir's arguments for authenticity are at least equally convincing. The poem was first printed in the Sonnets quarto of 1609 and ascribed to Shakespeare. There seem to be no grounds for suspecting either error or deception. This strangely haunting poem has, I think, been undervalued. It is delicately conceived and skilfully organized and displays, in some measure, a psychological adeptness similar to that which Coleridge discerned in the narrative poems. W. S. Walker's proposed source— the description of Pamphilus in Book II of Sidney's *Arcadia*—has been generally ignored but is cited, with approval, by Rollins, and certainly merits consideration.

Several general works contain material of importance. The central theme of *Shakespeare Survey 15* is 'Poems and Music in Shakespeare's World'. There are numerous useful entries relating to Shakespeare's use of classical themes in J. W. Velz's critical guide. *A New Companion to Shakespeare Studies* (1971) offers valuable estimates of the poems, and these should be read in conjunction with the corresponding section—George Rylands's 'Shakespeare the Poet'—in the original *Companion* (1934). Rylands responds to his material with an intelligence and sensitivity that few other critics can hope to match.

REFERENCES

The Sonnets

TEXTS

Fox, L. (ed.), *The Sonnets of William Shakespeare* (London, 1958).
Ingram, W. G., and Redpath, T. (eds.), *Shakespeare's Sonnets* (London, 1964).
Pooler, C. K. (ed.), *The Sonnets* (Arden Shakespeare, London, 1931).
Rollins, H. E. (ed.), *The Sonnets* (New Variorum Shakespeare, Philadelphia, Pa., 1944).

Shakespeare, William, *Shake-speares Sonnets* (1609; Scolar Press, Menston, 1968).

Wilson, J. Dover (ed.), *The Sonnets* (New Cambridge Shakespeare, Cambridge, 1966; 2nd edn. augmented and revised, 1967).

CRITICISM AND COMMENTARY

Baldwin, T. W., *On the Literary Genetics of Shakspere's Poems and Sonnets* (Urbana, Ill., 1950).

Booth, Stephen, *An Essay on Shakespeare's Sonnets* (New Haven, Conn., 1969).

Chambers, E. K., *William Shakespeare: A Study of Facts and Problems*, 2 vols. (Oxford, 1930).

——, 'The Order of the Sonnets', in *Shakespearean Gleanings* (Oxford, 1944).

——, 'The "Youth" of the Sonnets', in *Shakespearean Gleanings* (Oxford, 1944).

Cruttwell, P., *The Shakespearean Moment* (London, 1953).

Edwards, P. W., *Shakespeare and the Confines of Art* (London, 1968).

Goldsmith, U. K., 'Words out of a Hat', *JEGP*, 49 (1950).

Gurr, A., 'Shakespeare's First Poem: Sonnet 145', *Essays in Criticism*, 21 (1971).

Herrnstein, Barbara, *Discussions of Shakespeare's Sonnets* (Boston, Mass., 1964).

Hotson, J. L., *Mr. W. H.* (London, 1964).

Hubler, E., *The Sense of Shakespeare's Sonnets* (Princeton, N.J., 1952).

Hunter, G. K., 'The Dramatic Technique of Shakespeare's Sonnets', *Essays in Criticism*, 3 (1953).

Hutton, J., 'Analogues of Shakespeare's Sonnets CLIII–CLIV', *Modern Philology*, 38 (1941).

Knight, G. Wilson, *The Mutual Flame* (London, 1955).

Knights, L. C., *Some Shakespearian Themes* (London, 1959).

Landry, H., *Interpretations in Shakespeare's Sonnets* (Berkeley, Calif., 1963).

Lee, Sidney, *Elizabethan Sonnets*, 2 vols. (London, 1904).

——, *Shakespeare and the Italian Renaissance*, British Academy Lecture 1915.

——, 'Ovid and Shakespeare's Sonnets', in *Elizabethan and Other Essays* (London, 1929).

Leech, Clifford (ed.), *The Two Gentlemen of Verona* (new Arden Shakespeare, London, 1969).

Leishman, J. B., *Themes and Variations in Shakespeare's Sonnets* (London, 1961).

Lever, J. W., *The Elizabethan Love Sonnet* (London, 1956).

Mahood, M. M., *Shakespeare's Word-Play* (London, 1957).

Nowottny, W. M. T., 'Formal Elements in Shakespeare's Sonnets', *Essays in Criticism* 2 (1952).

Partridge, Eric, *Shakespeare's Bawdy* (London, 1947; 2nd edn., 1968).

Schaar, C., *An Elizabethan Sonnet Problem* (Lund, 1960).

——, *Elizabethan Sonnet Themes and the Dating of Shakespeare's 'Sonnets'* (Lund, 1962).

Stirling, Brents, *The Shakespeare Sonnet Order* (Berkeley, Calif., 1968).

The Poems

EDITIONS

Chester, R., *Loves Martyr* (*The Anuals of great Brittaine*) (London, 1611; Scolar Press, Menston, forthcoming).

Lever, J. W. (ed.), *The Rape of Lucrece* (New Penguin Shakespeare, Harmondsworth, 1971).

Maxwell, J. C. (ed.), *The Poems* (New Cambridge Shakespeare, Cambridge, 1966).

Prince, F. T. (ed.), *The Poems* (new Arden Shakespeare, London, 1960).

Rollins, H. E. (ed.), *The Poems* (New Variorum Shakespeare, Philadelphia, Pa., 1938).

Shakespeare, William, *Venus and Adonis* (London, 1593; Scolar Press, Menston, 1969).

——, *The Rape of Lucrece* (London, 1594; Scolar Press, Menston, 1968).

CRITICISM AND COMMENTARY

Allen, Don Cameron, 'Some Observations on *The Rape of Lucrece*', *Shakespeare Survey 15* (1962); repr. in his *Image and Meaning* (Baltimore, Md., 2nd edn., 1968).

Alvarez, A., 'The Phoenix and the Turtle', in *Interpretations*, ed. John Wain (London, 1955).

Bradbrook, M. C., *Shakespeare and Elizabethan Poetry* (London, 1951).

Brown, C. (ed.), *Poems by Sir John Salusbury and Robert Chester* (London, 1914).

Bullough, G., *Narrative and Dramatic Sources of Shakespeare*, vol. i (London, 1957).

Buxton, John, *Elizabethan Taste* (London, 1963).

Coleridge, S. T., *Coleridge on Shakespeare*, ed. T. Hawkes (New York, 1959; Penguin Shakespeare Library, Harmondsworth, 1969).

Ellrodt, R., 'An Anatomy of "The Phoenix and the Turtle" ', in *Shakespeare Survey 15* (1962).

Empson, W., 'The Phoenix and the Turtle', in *Essays in Criticism*, 16 (1966).

Granville-Barker, H., and Harrison, G. B. (eds.), *A Companion to Shakespeare Studies* (Cambridge, 1934).

Green, R. L., 'The Phoenix and the Tree', in *English*, 7 (1948).

Hamilton, A. C., *The Early Shakespeare* (San Marino, Calif., 1967).

Mackail, J. W., 'A Lover's Complaint', *Essays and Studies*, 3 (1912).

Miller, P. W., 'The Elizabethan Minor Epic', *Studies in Philology*, 55 (1958).

Muir, Kenneth, '*Venus and Adonis*: Comedy or Tragedy?', *Shakespearean Essays*, ed. A. Thaler and N. Sanders (Knoxville, Tenn., 1964).

——, ' "A Lover's Complaint": A Reconsideration', in *Shakespeare 1564–1964* (Providence, R. I., 1964).

——, and Schoenbaum, S. (eds.), *A New Companion to Shakespeare Studies* (Cambridge, 1971).

Price, H. T., 'The Function of Imagery in *Venus and Adonis*', *Papers of the Michigan Academy*, 31 (1945).

Putney, R., 'Venus Agonistes', in *University of Colorado Studies*, 4 (1953).

Velz, J. W., *Shakespeare and the Classical Tradition* (Minneapolis, Minn., 1968).

Walker, W. S., *A Critical Examination of the Text of Shakespeare* (London, 1860).

5. The Early Comedies

D. J. PALMER

Among several good modern-spelling editions of the plays in separate volumes, the new Arden Shakespeare provides the fullest critical apparatus on the text, date, sources, interpretation, and stage history. Neither *The Taming of the Shrew* nor *A Midsummer Night's Dream* has so far appeared in this series, but the student should consult both R. A. Foakes's admirable edition of *The Comedy of Errors* and Clifford Leech's *The Two Gentlemen of Verona*, the latter with its original approach to the play's notorious problems of interpretation. The usefulness of Richard David's edition of *Love's Labour's Lost* is diminished by its disproportionate emphasis upon conjectures about topical references.

In recent years the standard of inexpensive paperback editions of Shakespeare has improved considerably, and those mentioned here have all attracted the services of distinguished scholars. Choice between them must be determined by what is offered in addition to a reliable text. Each volume in the New Penguin Shakespeare contains a substantial and lucid introductory analysis of the play, with a summary of relevant works for further reading; the most valuable feature of this edition, however, is the ample commentary which, together with the textual apparatus, is printed at the back of the volume. The Signet Classic Shakespeare is less adequately annotated, but each volume in this series reprints three or four important critical essays and source material where appropriate, while the editorial introductions are sound and sometimes brilliant (particularly Harry Levin's introduction to *The Comedy of Errors*). The Pelican Shakespeare also contains some excellent editorial essays, notably by Paul A. Jorgensen on *The Comedy of Errors*, Richard Hosley on *The Taming of the Shrew*, and Alfred Harbage on *Love's Labour's Lost*; the commentaries, however, are too brief to be of much help for detailed study.

CRITICAL STUDIES AND COMMENTARY

Two factors have traditionally circumscribed the critical reputation of Shakespeare's early comedies: they are early, and they are comedies. Overshadowed by the later masterpieces, they have been patronized or defended as the uncertain prentice work of immaturity, until we have become more accustomed to make allowances for their supposed limitations than to recognize their subtlety, superb craftsmanship, and depth of vision. Moreover, they have suffered from what H. B. Charlton described, in the book with which the modern study of Shakespearian comedy begins, as 'the enormous lee-way into which the consideration of comedy has fallen in comparison with the progress which has been made in exploring the grounds of criticism in tragedy'. Developments in the criticism of the early comedies during the past twenty years have therefore been particularly concerned with overcoming this double barrier to a proper estimate of their value, by improving our knowledge of Shakespeare's cultural heritage, and by challenging what R. A. Foakes, in his introduction to *The Comedy of Errors*, refers to as 'a long tradition of regarding comedy in general as inferior to "serious" plays, and Shakespeare's comedies in particular, as entertainments, plays of escape into a careless world'. Researches into Shakespeare's early life and schooling, together with the evidence produced by textual scholars for accepting the integrity of the early plays as Shakespeare's own work, have exploded those hoary myths of the ill-educated dramatist who began his career by refurbishing other men's plays. Critics now have a more substantial foundation for regarding the early Shakespeare, in the words of A. C. Hamilton, 'as a sophisticated literary craftsman', and consequently are more predisposed to give the early plays their due as accomplished achievements without need of apology. But the special problem of interpreting the comedies is that posed for the critic by Foakes: 'let him, however, probe beneath the vocabulary commonly used to describe the comedies, gay, warm, enchanting, romantic, lively, and so forth, and he is at once liable to invite the scorn of the many who believe interpretation to be unnecessary, and provoke the hostility of those for whom the experience afforded by the comedies is a sort of inviolate glow, sacred and not to be profaned.' Through the insights and approaches summarized here, the reader may discover that by taking Shakespeare's early comedies seriously he improves both his enjoyment and his understanding of them.

Despite the progress of modern scholarship, in one fundamentally important respect our ignorance remains. There is not sufficient evidence to allow us to say exactly when the early comedies were written, or in what order. Most scholars would accept that the five plays were probably composed between 1590 and 1595, and that

The Comedy of Errors, The Taming of the Shrew, The Two Gentlemen of Verona, and *Love's Labour's Lost* preceded *A Midsummer Night's Dream.* This is the order now commonly accepted, but it is at best conventional and open to occasional dispute.

Where the objective criteria are more than usually inconclusive, critics considering the early comedies as a group have been free to arrange their own sequence according to their differing conceptions of the relationships between the five plays. This has sometimes proved a dangerous liberty to critics theorizing about Shakespeare's development, as for instance in Charlton's assumption that after *Love's Labour's Lost* and *The Two Gentlemen of Verona* Shakespeare underwent a 'recoil from romanticism' and produced *The Comedy of Errors* and *The Taming of the Shrew.* On the other hand Virgil Whitaker finds support for the conventional sequence listed above in 'a decreasing dependence upon the classics and a growing familiarity with contemporary literature' (though one wonders whether the Ovidian spirit of *A Midsummer Night's Dream* bears this out: we still await a proper study of Shakespeare's use of Ovid). Peter G. Phialas also accepts the conventional sequence of *The Comedy of Errors, The Taming of the Shrew,* and *The Two Gentlemen of Verona* on the grounds of 'the relative emphasis upon wooing and romantic love' between the three plays. B. O. Bonazza's highly schematic analysis of four kinds of plot-structure in the same sequence of plays, 'to follow the steps in his progress from tentative experimentation to full competence', is particularly vulnerable to the two principal objections to which all such reconstructions are open, namely the circular reasoning which assumes what it sets out to prove by approaching the plays in a certain order, and the supposition that Shakespeare's artistic growth necessarily followed the orderly progression of the critic's logic. Bonazza's argument is also considerably weakened by his omission of *The Taming of the Shrew.* Whatever grouping of these early comedies is adopted, it is more useful as a framework for comparison and mutual illumination than as a reliable indication of Shakespeare's development. There is general agreement, however, with Charlton's estimate of *A Midsummer Night's Dream* as 'Shakespeare's first masterpiece' and the crowning achievement of the early comedies.

The study of Shakespeare's work as a whole must, of course, take account of both the continuity and the development of his art, and most critics of the early comedies have observed in them the emergence of what were to become major characteristics of their successors. But beginning with Charlton, whose book is an 'attempt to

trace in Shakespeare's comedies the growth of his "comic idea"',
there has been a persistent tendency in dealing with the evolution of
Shakespearian comedy to relegate the first group of plays to the
status of preliminary and only partially successful drafts for the
incontestably superior plays that were to follow them, as though
Shakespeare at the start of his career was trying imperfectly to do
the same kind of thing he later did so well. Terms such as 'immature'
and 'experimental', so frequently applied to the early comedies,
have tended to obscure and undervalue their intrinsic qualities.

Of late, however, there are signs that criticism is turning from this
retrospective view of the early plays, in favour of an approach
through their antecedents in both learned and popular forms.
Thanks to T. W. Baldwin's indefatigable researches, we are now
aware that the Elizabethan school curriculum enabled Shakespeare
to begin his career already well versed in the principles of dramatic
composition, although we may not go all the way with Baldwin's
conviction that Shakespeare practised the regular five-act structure
as expounded by the Renaissance commentators on Terentian
comedy. Apart from his academic models, Shakespeare's debts to
contemporary dramatists in his early comedies include none greater
than that to the sophisticated court dramatist John Lyly, and the
relationship between them has been explored in detail by G. K.
Hunter, and more briefly outlined by Marco Mincoff. Geoffrey
Bullough's indispensable edition of the principal sources allows us to
judge for ourselves the remarkable adroitness with which from the
beginning of his career Shakespeare was adapting materials to his
own purposes. The image of the early Shakespeare which emerges
from these studies bears little resemblance to that of a novice working
with crude or elementary skills. Sophistication and complexity are
already the notable features of the early comedies, and A. C.
Hamilton summarizes what we can recognize if we are not prejudiced
by our admiration for the later achievements of Shakespearian
comedy, namely that 'the subtlety and comprehensiveness of Shakespeare's dramatic genius are present from the beginning of his life as
a writer.'

Charlton's antithesis between 'classical' and 'romantic' comedy,
which is the basis of his approach to the plays, was the first real
attempt to define the kind of comedy we call Shakespearian, to
understand its conventions, and to describe its characteristics. Following Charlton, E. C. Pettet has provided a fuller introduction to the
romance tradition underlying the comedies, and Nevill Coghill has
traced their non-classical character to medieval Christian ideas of

comedy. But the most original modern approaches to Shakespearian comedy are those of Northrop Frye and C. L. Barber. Both are concerned with a conception of comic form more highly developed than a rudimentary interest in plot and character. Frye regards the conventions of comedy as structural patterns related to an archetypal ritual celebration of the victory of summer over winter, life over death. He finds that Shakespeare's 'dramatic instinct' led him to shape his material into these conventional patterns, which organize human experience comprehensively and inclusively. Frye therefore tends to treat the plays as artefacts divorced from reality, contained within the structural patterns that give form and meaning to the dramatic actions. Barber's interpretation is related to Frye's in deriving comic structure from patterns of ritual celebration, but his approach is more specifically historical in its 'exploration of the way the social form of Elizabethan holidays contributed to the dramatic form of festive comedy'. He finds in the traditional pastimes and merry-making customs of Shakespeare's England a natural kinship to the 'saturnalian pattern' of the comedies, with their 'basic movement through release to clarification'. Alongside the academic and courtly models, therefore, the influence and meaning of many traditional kinds of games, pageants and revelry must be included in our awareness of the elements that compose Shakespearian comedy.

Modern criticism generally endorses Bertrand Evans's observation that in Shakespeare's early comedies 'technique itself occupies a proportionately large place in the total work'. If this is a genuine sign of the beginner, it also displays what H. F. Brooks points out as 'the command he shows, from the very outset of his career as a playwright, of the elements of dramatic construction'. For some critics, dexterity in plotting is a relatively humble mechanical skill; Charlton, for instance, saw Shakespeare in his 'classical' comedies as submitting himself to a discipline 'which, however uncongenial to the spirit, was a salutary apprenticeship to the mechanics of play-building'. One suspects that the spirit to which it is 'uncongenial' in this case is the critic's and not Shakespeare's; conceived as the prosaic carpentry of fitting a number of scenes together, structural technique is somewhat beneath the attention of the critic who wishes to dwell upon the higher beauties of poetic vision. Hence Charlton's evident distaste for the 'classical' kind of comedy represented in his view by *The Comedy of Errors* and *The Taming of the Shrew*, in which clever intrigue associates ingenious plotting with a low moral tone. But of course Shakespeare's virtuosity in the art of plotting is not confined to the so-called 'classical' plays; it is evident throughout his early comedies, and is nowhere more apparent than in *A Midsummer Night's Dream*. Moreover, it is far more than a matter of 'technical expertness in plotting', in the sense that Charlton uses that phrase. 'The supreme power manifest in Shakespeare's art of dramatic construction is the combinative power,' writes H. F. Brooks, referring to his skill in selecting 'great significant patterns' and in relating them analogously to each other. The study of Shakespeare's structural techniques in the early comedies is therefore not merely a matter of observing the ingenious complication and resolution of an intricate plot, but involves an understanding of the ways in which conventional motifs are employed, and of the relationship between different elements in the total design.

THE PLAYS

Emphasis upon the importance of structural design is particularly evident in modern interpretations of those two comedies which Charlton considered as Shakespeare's 'recoil from romanticism', *The Comedy of Errors* and *The Taming of the Shrew*. In the former, which may well have been Shakespeare's first comedy, and which is certainly his most classical in the sense that the main plot is derived from Plautus, Charlton noted that by doubling the set of twins in the source 'the plot becomes a sort of mathematical exhibition of the maximum number of erroneous combinations of four people in pairs'. Technical ingenuity of this kind was for Charlton of a very low order of artistic merit, and he regarded the play as a farce, in which 'the general temper of the life depicted' is 'crude, coarse, and brutal'. In treating the 'romantic' story of Aegeon and the love interest centred upon Luciana as 'alien' and 'incongruous' elements, Charlton was oblivious to the vital aspect of Shakespeare's structural method which concerns his skill in weaving disparate elements into a new whole. As Phialas notes, *The Comedy of Errors* 'shows his general predilection for combining multiple actions into mutually qualifying relationships'. Moreover, Madeleine Doran has made the point that 'it may have seemed to Renaissance dramatists that their romantic plots were less unclassical than we think of them', and therefore that 'Shakespeare, in having the parents as well as the children "lost" and discovered is only elaborating a familiar pattern'. This elaboration of the original Plautine plot, particularly when it is considered in connection with the play's extensive references to St. Paul's dealings with the Ephesians (explored by T. W. Baldwin), gives to the play a more substantial kind of interest than the term 'farce' suggests, and thus provides an instructive example of the relationship between structural design and meaning. 'His play deepens from farce,' writes Geoffrey Bullough, 'touching on the relations of husbands and wives, parents and children, in a moralizing way', and, while this last phrase seems to go too far in the opposite direction, we can surely endorse Foakes's view, expressed in the Introduction to his edition, that 'it does more than merely provoke laughter, or release us temporarily from inhibitions and custom into a world free as a child's affording delight and freshening us up. It also invites compassion, a measure of sympathy, and a deeper response to the disruption of social and family relationships which the action brings about'.

Charlton was too busy with what he called the 'rollickingly antiromantic' spirit of *The Taming of the Shrew* to notice the subtlety of a dramatic structure to which G. R. Hibbard pays tribute in his Introduction: 'It is no exaggeration to say that the first audience to witness a performance of the play . . . were seeing the most elaborately and skilfully designed comedy that had yet appeared on the English stage'. And apart from the other arguments concerning the relationship between Shakespeare's play and the anonymous *The Taming of a Shrew* (which many, but by no means all, scholars now regard as a corrupted version of Shakespeare's play), Richard Hosley makes a powerful point about the structural adroitness it displays: 'It is doubtful whether by 1594 any English dramatist other than Shakespeare was sufficiently skilled in plot-construction to write such a carefully and subtly integrated triple-action play.' At least, as C. C. Seronsy writes, 'agreement among Shakespearian editors and critics is well-nigh universal that in *The Taming of the Shrew* the three plot strands of shrew-taming, loving intrigue or "supposes", and induction are interwoven with great skill and that Shakespeare, as presumable author, has brought them into a unity far superior to that achieved by the anonymous contemporary play *The Taming of a Shrew*'. Here again it is Shakespeare's ability to bring different kinds of conventional material into significant relationship with each other which critics regard as the essence of his technique in this comedy. The induction was a familiar Elizabethan device for creating two levels of dramatic reality, but by making the trick played upon Christopher Sly turn upon what T. N. Greenfield terms 'an experiment in human nature' in which Sly 'is a part of a comic juxtaposition of two contrasting worlds . . . the unimaginative subject in a test of the power of the imagination', Shakespeare was creating an image of the relationship between the spectator and the play. 'Shakespeare's particular emphasis brings his Induction into an organic relationship with the main play', says Greenfield; 'the contrast between the literal world of Sly and the world of dramatic poetry is emphatic and meaningful'. Such a self-conscious reflection upon his own art anticipates Shakespeare's use in *A Midsummer Night's Dream* of that other Elizabethan convention of double illusion, the play-within-the-play, and indeed Sly has more than a little in common with Bottom. Seronsy, however, points out that the induction is even more closely related to the double plot of the main play in terms of the transformations of character that take place in each, a perception conveniently summarized by Hosley, who notes that 'taken together, the three actions constitute a complex of compared and contrasted poses and "supposes" '. The source of the plot of Bianca's wooing is the earlier Elizabethan comedy *Supposes*, Gascoigne's translation of a play by Ariosto, and Seronsy shows us how the idea of 'supposes' is the link between Sly's metamorphosis into a lord, the disguises and mistaken identities of the Bianca plot, and the method by which Petruchio supposes or assumes 'qualities in Katherina that no one else, possibly even the shrew herself, ever suspects', until she discovers them in herself. Thus, in Hibbard's words, 'whether at the elementary and obvious level of a transformation of the outward appearance, such as Lucentio and Tranio undergo, or at the deeper one of a psychological change like Katherina's, this idea runs all through the play'.

As with *The Comedy of Errors*, therefore, an analysis of the play's structural method has important implications for its interpretation. There is clearly more to it than Charlton suggests by treating it simply as a knockabout farce. 'Naturally,' wrote Charlton, 'a tale of taming makes both the tamer and the tamed more like dwellers in a menagerie than in the polite world.' But as we have seen, the shrew plot cannot be isolated from the total design, which directs our interest to a series of external and internal transformations. The coarseness and brutality of the traditional shrew-taming has been humanized, as Petruchio relies, not on physical force, but on a subtler psychological approach to convince Kate that she is not what she seems. The play is no less funny seen in this way, but it is considerably more interesting.

Of the five early comedies, *The Two Gentlemen of Verona* is the one unanimously declared a failure. Opinions differ only on the reasons for the disaster, and these have not been developed much further since Charlton's diagnosis that 'Shakespeare's first attempt to make romantic comedy had only succeeded so far that it had unexpectedly and inadvertently made romance comic'. Charlton's account of the disaster makes hilarious reading at Shakespeare's expense; there is just the possibility, however, as Clifford Leech and A. C. Hamilton believe, that the dissolution of romance into comedy was neither unexpected nor inadvertent, but that Shakespeare was in control and quite deliberately ridiculing the extravagances of the romantic code of behaviour upon which his plot is based. J. F. Danby, on the other hand, represents the school of interpretation which believes that a better understanding of the conventions will solve some at least of the difficulties in the play.

Certainly a great deal of the overt mockery comes from the two clowns, whose function reflects one of the more successful aspects of the play's dramatic structure. H. F. Brooks observes that 'Shakespeare, in the parts he has given to Speed and Launce, is developing his play by means of comic parallels that illustrate and extend his themes', and his essay is a perceptive analysis of the way in which the clowns (and the dog) are used to burlesque the situations of the main plot. We may not therefore agree with Charlton that 'both Launce and Speed come into the play for no reason whatever but to be unmistakably dolts', yet he does suggest an unfortunate consequence of this comic parallelism upon the romantic hero Valentine: 'one begins to feel that it will be extremely difficult to make a hero of a man who is proved to be duller of wit than the patent idiots of the piece'. Stanley Wells finds that the basic failure of the play 'arises from the fact that Shakespeare is still a tyro in dramatic craftsmanship', and more specifically that 'the organic deficiencies of the play are the result of Shakespeare's failure to devise a plot which will enable characters conceived within the conventions of romantic love to behave in a manner compatible with these conventions'. The structural method of juxtaposing different elements, which we have seen as a characteristic of the early comedies, here seems to have created the difficulties that these critics find with the play; for the composition of the play not only concerns the parallels between masters and servants, but also turns upon the conventional antithesis of the rival claims of love and friendship, and upon the 'balancing of character against character and situation against situation' described by Norman Sanders in his edition. As Bullough points out, the influence of Lyly is apparent 'in the dramatic use of the courtly and amorous code', and in the symmetries of character relationship. But G. K. Hunter observes that 'this Lylian kind of structure will, however, only work when the characters are as simple as Lyly's', and that Proteus is conceived too psychologically for the balance of conflicting ideals to be preserved in the notorious final scene. This assumes, of course, that we are not meant to laugh at that point. Inga-Stina Ewbank directs our attention to the rhetorical artifice of the play, and finds in it 'an awareness that conventionalized language, like conventionalized behaviour, may be false', but also a failure in the last scene to make the language adequate to the depth of feeling.

When Charlton referred to 'the insouciant romantic formlessness' of *Love's Labour's Lost*, he meant that 'it is deficient in plot and characterization. There is little story in it. Its situations do not present successive incidents in an ordered plot'. In fact none of the early comedies shows more clearly the principles of Shakespeare's structural technique, for, as M. C. Bradbrook says, 'the contrast of different characters in terms of their different idiom, played off or chiming in together, constitutes the "form" of the comedy'. And C. L. Barber points out that 'what is striking about *Love's Labour's Lost* is how *little* Shakespeare used exciting action, story, or conflict, how far he went in the direction of making the piece a set exhibition of pastimes and games . . . story interest is not the point: Shakespeare is presenting a series of wooing games, not a story'.

In the absence of a story in the play, several attempts have been made in the past to remedy the deficiency by discovering a story behind the play, in the form of covert allusions to court rivalries. Much ingenuity has been devoted to identifying the historical 'originals' of the *dramatis personae*, none more confidently than by Frances Yates, who declared more than thirty years ago that 'everyone is agreed that *Love's Labour's Lost* is the most topical of all Shakespeare's plays, that it bristles with allusions to contemporary events and living persons. . . . I think one may say that this theory is now more or less generally accepted. The studious young men in the play can be interpreted as representing either the Raleigh group, immersed in their studies, or the Essex–Southampton group who laugh at schemes of that kind'. A theory that permits two such quite contrary interpretations arouses suspicions about the validity of either, but for a refutation of the textual and historical basis of the theory, Strathmann's article should be consulted. As Hamilton observes, 'the characters most suspected of historical originals are the most conventional literary types'. Alfred Harbage, in his edition, roundly dismisses such theories: 'none of them carries conviction except to those under the hypnosis induced by the shimmering nature of the evidence. A few suggestive phrases in the play there certainly are, but neither the characters nor the episodes resemble in the least the persons and events they are supposed to shadow forth'.

The elaborate design of the play, as most modern critics describe it, rests upon the contrapuntal relationships of the various groups of characters—courtiers, academics, and rustics—and the sophistication and artifice of the design corresponds to the stylistic self-consciousness of the language; in Barber's words, 'the effect is that each social level and type is making sport with words in an appropriate way, just as the lords' infatuation with the ladies is paralleled by Costard's and then Armado's attentions to Jaquenetta'. Such a skilfully patterned structure might almost be enjoyed for its own sake, as Harley Granville-Barker suggests: 'We must think of it all in terms of music, of contrasts in tone and tune, rhythm and the breaking of rhythm. . . . All plays exist, plots and character schemes beside, as schemes of sound, as shifting pictures, in decoration of thought and phrase, and the less their dependence on plot or conflict of character the more must they depend on such means to beauty and charm. . . . We are, indeed, never very far from the formalities of song and dance.' And following Granville-Barker, Bobbyann Roesen (Anne Barton) finds that 'the quality of the whole is very much that of a musical composition, an inexorable movement forward, the appearance and reappearance in the fabric of the play of certain important themes, forcing the harmony into a series of coherent resolutions consistent with each other and with the drama as a whole'. But those 'certain important themes' concern the very idea of artifice for its own sake, divorced from reality: 'it is the most artificial of all Shakespeare's comedies', writes Miss Bradbrook, 'and comes nearer than any other to containing a manifesto against artifice'. The influence of Lyly upon the courtly mode of the comedy and its elaborate symmetries is patent, although G. K. Hunter notes an essential difference in *Love's Labour's Lost*, which is 'concerned, as Lyly's never are, with "placing" or judging wit and cultivation in terms which are outside these values themselves'. And in this critical awareness of the limits of artifice, itself an added dimension to the drama of self-conscious sophistication, Cyrus Hoy finds 'the basic pattern of Shakespearian comedy: a pattern which consists in a movement from the artificial to the natural, always with the objective of finding oneself'. Once again, therefore, structure and meaning are intimately related.

By common consent, *A Midsummer Night's Dream* is not only the most perfectly constructed of the early comedies, it is also the last of them and seems to occupy a special position in Shakespeare's development, as his first major triumph. Even Charlton was disposed to spare a few words of praise for its structural beauty, although not without the characteristically slighting reference to 'technical expertness in plotting'; 'the unity of the comic idea, not the joinery of episodes, is what makes the greatness of *A Midsummer Night's Dream*'. As we have seen, in more recent appraisals of the preceding comedies, this is a distinction without a difference as far as Shakespeare's methods of composition are concerned. David P. Young's comprehensive study of the play describes its construction in words that might well be applied to the aim, if not always the achievement, of Shakespeare's methods from the beginning of his career: 'the particular quality of his achievement in this case seems to have stemmed from his ability to bring a great variety of comic materials into a complete harmony, a synthesis or fusion by which he was able to make them his own'. 'Three contrasted worlds', writes Miss Bradbrook, —the lovers', the rustics', and the fairies'— have each their own idiom and their own codes, but in the woods of Athens . . . divided worlds meet and intermingle . . . *A Midsummer Night's Dream* combines in the most paradoxical way the natural and to Elizabethan eyes pastoral and humble beauty of the woodland and its fairies with the highly sophisticated pattern of the lovers' quarrel and the straight burlesque provided by the loves of Pyramus and Thisbe'. Even single elements of the play reflect Shakespeare's synthesizing and transforming power: the fairies, for instance, derive from a fusion of Ovidian mythology and English folklore. The background to Shakespeare's mutation of the dangerous fairies of rustic superstition into mischievous but benevolent 'spirits of another kind' has been studied by M. N. Latham and more recently by K. M. Briggs. 'They do illustrate the rich traditional meanings available in the materials Shakespeare was handling', as Barber says.

Of one of the play's most celebrated confrontations between contrasting worlds, described by Barber as 'the climax of the polyphonic interplay', David P. Young writes, 'as Bottom meets Titania, analogies begin to surround them: the popular stage joins hands with the world of court entertainment; folklore is introduced to myth; grossness chats with refinement; bestiality dwells with spirituality'. The play therefore proclaims through the analogies of its structure, as well as through the title and the incidents of its plot, the transforming power of the imagination, which most critics regard as its central preoccupation. 'The poet's confident assertion of the transforming power of the poetic imagination, in a play that is a testimony of that power,' says A. C. Hamilton, 'balances the dramatist's confidence in his craft that allows him the mockery of the poetic imagination in the Pyramus and Thisbe interlude.' Barber expands the point: 'the consciousness of the creative or poetic act itself, which pervades the main action, explains the subject matter of the burlesque accompaniment provided by the clowns . . . the clowns provide a broad burlesque of the mimetic impulse to become something by acting it, the impulse which in the main action is fulfilled by imagination and understood by humor'. And R. W. Dent emphasizes the importance of the last act of the play, with Theseus's speech as the prelude to the play-within-the-play: 'the heart of the comedy, its most pervasive unifying element, is the partially contrasting role of imagination in love and in art'. John Russell Brown also notes the structural analogy between the lovers' experiences and our own perception of the play, mirrored in burlesque fashion by the Pyramus and Thisbe interlude: 'Shakespeare was deeply concerned with the ways in which actors and audience accept the "truth" of dramatic illusion, and, as a poet, he saw in these relationships an image of man's recognition of imagined truths.'

Critics have therefore found in the highly-wrought dramatic structure Shakespeare's own reflections on his art; David Young, for instance, asks, 'may not this play, since it contains an inner play and discussions of drama, poetry, and the imagination, represent a very conscious effort on the part of the dramatist to advance the scope and level of his art and thus be a vital source for our understanding of Shakespeare's own ideas about the character and purpose of his art?' R. W. Dent calls it 'Shakespeare's closest approximation to a "Defense of Dramatic Poesy" in general'. So considered, A. C. Hamilton says, 'the play suggests Shakespeare's awareness of the rounding out of the first stage of his works'.

The emphasis of modern criticism upon the structural skill displayed by the early comedies has not been a limited interest in the mere technicalities of Shakespeare's art, but a recognition of his ability to combine conventional meanings. There are no better illustrations of this than the two comedies which, following Charlton, E. C. Pettet found to be 'the polar opposite of Shakespeare's romantic comedies'. Yet far from being antithetical to Shakespeare's characteristic preoccupations in comedy, *The Comedy of Errors* and *The Taming of the Shrew* have both been shown to exemplify in more than rudimentary form the abiding interests of Shakespearian comedy. The motif of mistaken identity which is the cause of so much hilarious confusion in *The Comedy of Errors* is one of the simplest of all comic devices, but Shakespeare exploits it to penetrate the more fundamental and disturbing questions of personal identity itself. The strange coincidence of identical twins presents the problem of identity most acutely, for, as Harry Levin observes, 'duplication, in particular, seems an affront to human dignity (one is almost tempted to call it a loss of face)—to be always mistaken for, to be indistinguishable from, somebody else'. Moreover, while the resultant errors in the play provide laughter for us, their victims speak of madness and hallucination, as Harold Brooks points out: 'mistakes of identity all but destroy relationship, and loss of relationship calls true identity in question; the chief persons suspect themselves or are suspected of insanity, or of being possessed, surrounded, or assailed by supernatural powers—madness or demoniac possession would be the eclipse of the true self, and sorcery might overwhelm it'. 'Real horror attaches to the notion of the *complete* identity of two human beings', says G. R. Elliott; 'all normal persons (and especially Shakespeare) set so much store by human individuality that they shrink from the thought of its being submerged. . . . And *The Comedy of Errors* has a note of real weirdness just when its mirth is keenest.' 'Yet,' Brooks adds, 'the hazard of metamorphosis and of the loss of present identity is also the way to fresh or restored relationship.'

Shakespeare did not introduce identical twins again until *Twelfth Night*, but all his comedies employ the device of mistaken identity, and the pattern of loss and recovery, which together form the action of *The Comedy of Errors*. The fact that Cyrus Hoy is writing with particular reference to *Love's Labour's Lost* when he describes the typical movement of Shakespearian comedy as having 'the objective of finding oneself' serves to corroborate the significance of *The Comedy of Errors*.

This profounder conception of identity has also been noticed in *The Taming of the Shrew* in terms of the unifying motif of 'supposes' analysed by Seronsy. Writing of Katherina's transformation of character, Bullough remarks that 'a mistake in identity is after all less deeply comic than one in assessing a person's nature. *The Taming of the Shrew* shows that Shakespeare was already moving from the outer world of appearances and situation to the inner world of character and ethical implication'. The theme of identity is here treated in relation to another characteristic preoccupation of Shakespearian comedy, which Hibbard describes as 'the notion of metamorphosis'. The transformation of Katherina, as Seronsy notes, is 'an interior one', revealing, in Hibbard's words, that 'Shakespeare is already very much interested, in this play, in the working of the imagination, which he was to explore further in *A Midsummer Night's Dream*'. Moreover, as Greenfield has shown, in its use of the induction

The Taming of the Shrew makes a typically Shakespearian association between the metamorphic power of the imagination and the art of theatrical illusion.

In the light of these recent interpretations, therefore, the radical distinctions drawn by Charlton between Shakespeare's 'classical' and 'romantic' comedies are seen to be misleading and inadequate. Levin's conclusion, that 'even within the venal and angular precincts of Latinate comedy, he can make us aware of unpathed waters, undreamed shores, and things in heaven and earth that philosophy has not fathomed', represents the emphasis of modern criticism upon Shakespeare's ability to transform convention, and upon the remarkable continuity of the comedies. The other comedies of the early group apply the same preoccupations with true and false identity, metamorphosis and illusion to the conventions of courtly behaviour, especially in love. Norman Sanders notes the interesting use of disguise in *The Two Gentlemen of Verona*, for instance, 'which makes Julia physically what Proteus is both nominally and morally: that is, a shape-changer, a metamorphosis'. Cyrus Hoy's summary of Shakespeare's comic 'objective', in the context of *Love's Labour's Lost*, 'to find oneself is to escape from artificiality into the natural, to leave off deceiving oneself by setting about to know oneself', is as relevant to *The Taming of the Shrew* as it is to *The Two Gentlemen of Verona*, which, as Phialas says, deals with 'the opposition between the conventions or poetics of love and the realistic or matter-of-fact concept of it'. Moreover, this 'escape from the artificial into the natural' as a process of psychological reorientation is often accompanied by a corresponding physical movement, from the court world to the pastoral. Northrop Frye sees this pattern adumbrated in *The Two Gentlemen of Verona*, where 'the action of the comedy begins in a world represented as a normal world, moves into the green world, goes into a metamorphosis there in which the comic resolution is achieved, and returns to the normal world', and in the forest where the characters assemble for the notorious dénouement of this play he finds 'the embryonic form of the fairy world of *A Midsummer Night's Dream*'. A similar preoccupation in *Love's Labour's Lost* is described by Bobbyann Roesen in terms of the movement from the world of enclosed artifice to the wider perspectives of reality. 'Through *Love's Labour's Lost*', she writes, 'the play has been a symbol of illusion, of delightful unreality, the masque of Muscovites, or the pageant of the Nine Worthies, and now it becomes apparent that there was a further level of illusion above that of the plays within the play. The world of that illusion has enchanted us; it has been possessed of a haunting beauty, the clear loveliness of the landscapes in the closing song. But Shakespeare insists that it cannot take the place of reality itself, and should not be made to'.

Not unexpectedly, these interrelated themes of identity, metamorphosis, and the role of imagination have been most extensively studied in *A Midsummer Night's Dream*, for of the early comedies it is the play that treats them most fully, and that develops furthest what J. L. Calderwood calls 'Shakespeare's continuing exploration of the nature, function, and value of art'. 'He does seem unusually and consistently aware', Calderwood writes 'of how the illusions foisted upon and generated by characters within the play are related to the master illusion which is the play, and which is similarly foisted upon and generated by the audience.' The episode which has attracted much attention in this respect is Theseus's speech and Hippolyta's reply at the beginning of the last act, after the lovers' 'dream' and before the interlude of Pyramus and Thisbe, for Theseus specifically associates the lover's imagination with that of the poet, not to mention the lunatic. It is a focal point for two divergent approaches to the play, as Calderwood points out: 'criticism of *A Midsummer Night's Dream* has on the whole followed the contrasting leads of Theseus and Hippolyta in their responses to the lovers' story of the night.'

Critics in the camp of Theseus share his allegiance to the values of reason as opposed to those of imagination; moreover they tend to assume that Theseus is the spokesman of Shakespeare's point of view. Thus Charlton: 'Sanity, cool reason, common sense, is the pledge of Theseus against the undue ravages of fancy and of sentiment in human nature. . . . With Theseus, the philosophy of comedy is finding its voice, and his "cool reason" is its prevailing spirit.' Here certainly is Charlton's 'recoil from romanticism'. Marco Mincoff also regards Theseus as 'a choric figure expounding objective values', values which he says are reflected in 'the mature, rational, unswerving love of Theseus and Hippolyta', that serves 'as a frame to the whole play and a standard by which love is to be measured'. In a learned but sometimes overburdened interpretation of the play's courtly symbolism, Paul A. Olson manages to side with Theseus's rationalism without slighting the value of poetic imagination, by suggesting that 'Theseus makes some implicit distinctions between the poet and his mad colleagues. It is only lovers and madmen who are said to exhibit fantasies which descend beyond the comprehension of reason. Implicitly, poets, however much they are possessed by a *furor poeticus*, may deal in imaginings apprehensible in more rational terms'. One wishes that Shakespeare (or Theseus) had not left such an important point merely 'implicit'.

'If we take our stand shoulder to shoulder with Theseus,' writes Barber, 'the play can be an agency for distinguishing what is merely "apprehensible" from what is "comprehended".' But, as he goes on to remind us, Theseus 'does not quite have the last word . . . his position is only one stage in a dialectic'. 'Hippolyta supplies the necessary corrective', writes Stanley Wells; 'she can conceive what the lovers have been through and her use of the word "transfigured" helps to suggest that the woodland scenes represent for them a genuine shaping experience.' R. W. Dent and David Young recognize that this 'dialectic' is a reflection of certain ambivalences within the Elizabethan conception of the imagination (their discussion of the relevant background should be supplemented by reference to Rossky's article). Dent suggests that 'being good Elizabethans, we may well remember that not all dreams are the product of divided, passion-stimulated, never-sleeping imagination. Some dreams are divine revelations of truth, however difficult to expound.' Young's point is that 'anyone who wished to undertake a defense of the imagination might easily have done so, drawing upon the inherent contradiction in contemporary theories between the feeling that imagination was deceitful and destructive, and the creative powers commonly granted it as part of the epistemological hierarchy'.

As for Theseus, Dent indicates the irony undermining his position: 'Himself a creation from "antique fable" unconsciously involved in "fairy toys", Theseus believes in neither. . . . A noble governor, quite willing to accept poetry for a wedding-night pastime and to acknowledge it as the well-intended offering of his faithful subjects, he at no time implies any respect for it. Shakespeare's entire play implies a contrary view, despite the humility of its epilogue.' J. L. Calderwood similarly believes that 'the modesty of Shakespeare's epilogue is transformed by humorous irony into something of this order: "If it makes you feel more 'reasonable', adopt Theseus's view and regard the play as an idle dream—at best a way of passing the time; but, like the lovers who also converted drama into dream, whether you realize it or not, you have experienced something here of enduring value and with a reality of its own".'

'A major kind of knowledge which *A Midsummer Night's Dream* makes available to its audience', says Calderwood, 'is the inner forms and impulses of the human mind itself—the tricks and shaping fantasies of strong imagination and the forces that direct it, but the range and limits of cool reason as well. The mind that comes to focus upon the play, and especially upon the drama of the forest, comes to focus upon itself. . . . The theatrical experience made possible by the play thus mirrors the fictional experience presented *in* the play.' It is above all in the significant ordering of this experience that we find the quality and value of the poetic imagination; in the words of David Young, 'the coherence and constancy are in the poet's art, and they spring from his consistent use of the metamorphic principle as a device not only for reflecting experience but for controlling it and expressing its unity.'

REFERENCES

TEXTS

Foakes, R. A. (ed.), *The Comedy of Errors* (new Arden Shakespeare, London, 1962).

Jorgensen, Paul A. (ed.), *The Comedy of Errors* (Pelican Shakespeare, Baltimore, Md., 1964).

Levin, Harry (ed.), *The Comedy of Errors* (Signet Shakespeare, New York, 1965).

Wells, Stanley (ed.), *The Comedy of Errors* (New Penguin Shakespeare, Harmondsworth, 1972).

Heilman, Robert (ed.), *The Taming of the Shrew* (Signet Shakespeare, New York, 1966).

Hibbard, G. R. (ed.), *The Taming of the Shrew* (New Penguin Shakespeare, Harmondsworth, 1968).

Hosley, Richard (ed.), *The Taming of the Shrew* (Pelican Shakespeare, Baltimore, Md., 1964).

Evans, Bertrand (ed.), *The Two Gentlemen of Verona* (Signet Shakespeare, London, 1964).

Jackson, Berners A. W. (ed.), *The Two Gentlemen of Verona* (Pelican Shakespeare, Baltimore, Md., 1964).

Leech, Clifford (ed.), *The Two Gentlemen of Verona* (new Arden Shakespeare, London, 1969).

Sanders, Norman (ed.), *The Two Gentlemen of Verona* (New Penguin Shakespeare, Harmondsworth, 1968).

Arthos, John (ed.), *Love's Labour's Lost* (Signet Shakespeare, New York, 1965).

David, Richard (ed.), *Love's Labour's Lost* (new Arden Shakespeare, London, 1951).

Harbage, Alfred (ed.), *Love's Labour's Lost* (Pelican Shakespeare, Baltimore, Md., 1963).

Clemen, Wolfgang (ed.), *A Midsummer Night's Dream* (Signet Shakespeare, London, 1963).

Doran, Madeleine (ed.), *A Midsummer Night's Dream* (Pelican Shakespeare, Baltimore, Md., 1959).

Wells, Stanley (ed.), *A Midsummer Night's Dream* (New Penguin Shakespeare, Harmondsworth, 1967).

CRITICAL STUDIES AND COMMENTARY

Baldwin, T. W., *Shakespeare's Five-Act Structure* (Urbana, Ill., 1947).

Barber, C. L., *Shakespeare's Festive Comedy* (Princeton, N.J., 1959).

Bonazza, B. O., *Shakespeare's Early Comedies* (The Hague, 1966).

Brooks, H. F., 'Themes and Structure in *The Comedy of Errors*', in *Early Shakespeare* (Stratford-upon-Avon Studies 3, ed. J. R. Brown and B. Harris, London, 1961).

Bullough, Geoffrey (ed.), *Narrative and Dramatic Sources of Shakespeare*, vol. 1 (London, 1957).

Charlton, H. B., *Shakespearian Comedy* (London, 1939).

Coghill, Nevill, 'The Basis of Shakespearian Comedy', *Essays and Studies* (1950); repr. in *Shakespeare Criticism 1935–1960*, ed. Anne Ridler (World's Classics, London, 1963).

Evans, Bertrand, *Shakespeare's Comedies* (Oxford, 1960).

Frye, Northrop, 'The Argument of Comedy', *English Institute Essays 1948* (New York, 1949); repr. in *Shakespeare: Modern Essays in Criticism*, ed. Leonard F. Dean (New York, 1957; 2nd edn., 1967).

Hamilton, A. C., *The Early Shakespeare* (San Marino, Calif., 1967).

Hunter, G. K., *John Lyly: The Humanist as Courtier* (London, 1962).

Mincoff, Marco, 'Shakespeare and Lyly', *Shakespeare Survey 14* (1961).

Pettet, E. C., *Shakespeare and the Romance Tradition* (London, 1949).

Phialas, Peter G., *Shakespeare's Romantic Comedies* (Chapel Hill, N.C., 1966).

Whitaker, Virgil K., *Shakespeare's Use of Learning* (San Marino, Calif., 1953).

THE PLAYS

Baldwin, T. W., *Shakespeare's Five-Act Structure* (Urbana, Ill., 1947).

Bradbrook, M. C., *Shakespeare and Elizabethan Poetry* (London, 1951).

Briggs, K. M., *The Anatomy of Puck* (London, 1959).

Brooks, H. F., 'Two Clowns in a Comedy (to say nothing of the Dog): Speed, Launce (and Crab) in *The Two Gentlemen of Verona*', *Essays and Studies* (1963).

Brown, J. R., *Shakespeare and his Comedies* (London, 1957; 2nd edn., 1962).

Bullough, Geoffrey (ed.), *Narrative and Dramatic Sources of Shakespeare*, vol. 1 (London, 1957).

Calderwood, J. L., '*A Midsummer Night's Dream*: The Illusion of Drama', *Modern Language Quarterly*, 26 (1965).

Charlton, H. B., *Shakespearian Comedy* (London, 1938).

Danby, J. F., 'Shakespeare Criticism and *The Two Gentlemen of Verona*', *Critical Quarterly*, 2 (1960).

Dent, R. W., 'Imagination in *A Midsummer Night's Dream*', *Shakespeare Quarterly*, 15 (1964).

Doran, Madeleine, *Endeavors of Art* (Madison, Wis., 1954).

Elliott, G. R., 'Weirdness in *The Comedy of Errors*', *University of Toronto Quarterly*, 60 (1939); repr. in *Shakespeare's Comedies: An Anthology of Modern Criticism*, ed. Laurence Lerner (Penguin Shakespeare Library, Harmondsworth, 1968).

Ewbank, Inga-Stina, ' "Were man but constant, he were perfect": Constancy and Consistency in *The Two Gentlemen of Verona*', in *Shakespearian Comedy* (Stratford-upon-Avon Studies 14, ed. M. Bradbury and D. J. Palmer, London, 1972).

Granville-Barker, Harley, *Prefaces to Shakespeare*, First Series (London, 1927).

Greenfield, T. N., 'The Transformation of Christopher Sly', *Philological Quarterly*, 33 (1954).

Hamilton, A. C., *The Early Shakespeare* (San Marino, Calif., 1967).

Hoy, Cyrus, '*Love's Labour's Lost* and the Nature of Comedy', *Shakespeare Quarterly*, 13 (1962).

Latham, M. W., *The Elizabethan Fairies* (New York, 1930).

Olson, Paul A., '*A Midsummer Night's Dream* and the Meaning of Court Marriage', *ELH*, 24 (1957).

Phialas, Peter G., *Shakespeare's Romantic Comedies* (Chapel Hill, N.C., 1966).

Roesen, Bobbyann, '*Love's Labour's Lost*', *Shakespeare Quarterly*, 4 (1953).

Rossky, W., 'Imagination in the English Renaissance: Psychology and Poetic', *Studies in the Renaissance*, 5 (1958).

Seronsy, C. C., ' "Supposes" as a Unifying Theme in the *Taming of the Shrew*', *Shakespeare Quarterly*, 14 (1963).

Strathmann, E. A., 'The Textual Evidence for "The School of Night"', *Modern Language Notes*, 56 (1941).

Wells, Stanley, 'The Failure of *The Two Gentlemen of Verona*', *Shakespeare Jahrbuch*, 94 (1963).

Yates, Frances A., *A Study of 'Love's Labour's Lost'* (Cambridge, 1936).

Young, David P., *Something of Great Constancy* (New Haven, Conn., 1966).

6. The Middle Comedies

GĀMINI SALGĀDO

Among relatively inexpensive and readily available editions, the new Arden is the most comprehensive (though the paperback version has an alarming tendency to fall apart). Only two of the five comedies, *The Merchant of Venice* and *The Merry Wives of Windsor*, have so far appeared. Each volume contains a carefully edited text with collations and explanatory notes and an introduction which deals with most relevant aspects of the play, including printing and stage history and literary sources. The edition of *The Merchant of Venice* has a particularly good critical introduction by John Russell Brown which traces, in terms of imagery and action, the metaphor of 'love's wealth' as it operates in the contrasting worlds of Venice and Belmont.

For the comedies not yet published in the new Arden series, the fullest available edition is the New Cambridge Shakespeare, which is in general more useful for its notes and stage history than for the strictly critical part of the introduction. (The stage-directions, however, and some of the notes, must be approached with judicious scepticism.) The reader who wants abundance rather than relevance may also care to consult the elephantine volumes of the New (now very old) Variorum, where there is some helpful criticism and much else; but caution is recommended, as the pursuit of triviality combined with single-mindedness and erudition often makes for compulsive reading.

The notes and collations printed below the text in the new Arden editions are so full that occasionally the reader's attention may be distracted from the thin trickle of text by the lush undergrowth of annotation. For sheer ease of reading, my own preference is for the Laurel Shakespeare under the general editorship of Francis Fergusson. The text pages are set in the largest and clearest type face of any popular edition and are completely uncluttered. There are no notes, but each volume contains a glossary that is at best adequate, at worst emaciated. The general editor contributes an introduction to each play and a workman-like account of Shakespeare and his theatre. Each volume also contains a 'modern commentary' usually by someone who has been professionally concerned in a production of the play; of the five comedies here discussed, the most interesting commentary is that by the American composer Vergil Thomson on 'Music for *Much Ado About Nothing*'. The Laurel Shakespeare is less an edition to study from than a text for pleasurable and continuous reading when one is already reasonably familiar with the play (though, again, the binding is far from durable). The text is that of C. J. Sisson.

An edition with a text page which is almost as easy to read but with much fuller glossarial and other notes (in a 'commentary' at the end of each volume) and a somewhat more comprehensive guide to further reading is the New Penguin Shakespeare. All the comedies except *The Merry Wives of Windsor* have already appeared, with freshly edited texts. The most stimulating critical introduction is that by M. M. Mahood to *Twelfth Night*, which discusses with freshness and clarity the themes of enjoyment, generosity, time, and patience in the play. Professor Mahood's comments on the uses and abuses of time are interestingly elaborated by Frederick Turner in a chapter entitled 'Season and Mask in *Twelfth Night*' in his book *Shakespeare and the Nature of Time*, which also has a chapter on 'subjective', 'objective', and 'natural' time in *As You Like It*. The New Penguin *Twelfth Night* also contains musical settings dating from Shakespeare's own time for the songs in the play. The (American) Pelican Shakespeare, under the general editorship of Alfred Harbage, is more modest in scope as regards the introductions and notes. In England it is generally available only as a one-volume edition of the complete works.

Another useful edition originating in America is the Signet Shakespeare, of which the general editor is Sylvan Barnet, who contributes a survey of Shakespeare's life and times to each volume. The introductions by individual editors are scant by comparison with those in the New Penguin Shakespeare, and some readers (myself included) find the practice of putting notes at the foot of the page and keying them to the line by a minuscule bubble disproportionately distracting. The strength of this series lies in the generous extracts from critical commentary reprinted in each volume and the fullness of the suggestions for further reading.

All these editions have texts with modernized spelling. Apart from facsimile reprints, the only old-spelling texts of these plays which are generally available are *Twelfth Night* in the Fountainwell Drama Texts and *Twelfth Night* and *As You Like It* in the Shakespeare

Workshop series; all these reproduce an edited version of the First
Folio text. Separate facsimiles include *As You Like It* and *Twelfth
Night* (Folio, edited by J. Dover Wilson), and *The Merchant of Venice*
(Hayes Quarto), *Much Ado About Nothing*, and *The Merry Wives of
Windsor* in the Shakespeare Quarto Facsimiles series edited by Sir
W. W. Greg and Charlton Hinman.

CRITICISM AND COMMENTARY
General

If the common reader (or at any rate, critic) has conspicuously
failed to concur with Dr. Johnson in his preference for Shakespeare's
comedies over the tragedies, Johnson's assertion that the comedies
were produced without art effectively side-tracked critical discussion
of them until almost our own day. Too often the comedies have been
presented as the artless outpourings of a Shakespeare carelessly
warbling his native wood-notes wild. This kind of approach, while
possibly therapeutic for the critic, is not usually very helpful to the
reader or playgoer, since there is little one can say about wild
warblings beyond drawing attention to them. Attempting to imitate
them in critical prose has been a temptation too little resisted;
critical discourse, generally speaking, is not profitably converted
into hey nonny nonny.

Johnson's comments on the comedies, like all his criticism of
Shakespeare, have a capacity to stimulate lines of inquiry which his
Augustanism could not easily accommodate. His remarks have a
fertile brevity (e.g. 'Falstaff could not love but by ceasing to be
Falstaff'). But between his time and ours there is little criticism of
the comedies which is of more than historical interest, apart from
Shaw's sprightly iconoclasm. The reader who dips into *Shaw on Shakespeare* may be surprised to find that as often as not the icon Shaw is
trying to topple is not Shakespeare so much as nineteenth-century
vulgarization of him; his views on *Much Ado About Nothing* are,
however, an exception to this general rule: 'The main pretension in
Much Ado is that Benedick and Beatrice are exquisitely witty and
amusing persons. They are, of course, nothing of the sort. . . . It took
the Bard a long time to grow out of the provincial conceit that made
him so fond of exhibiting his accomplishments as a master of gallant
badinage.'

One of the earliest books to make a sustained study of the comedies,
Charlton's *Shakespearean Comedy*, still retains its value because of the
elegance and unobtrusive learning with which the author traces the
two traditions of the 'romantic' and the 'classical' comedy back to

their respective sources and forward to their unique blending in Shakespeare's plays. But it should be added that Charlton, like most of those who have accepted and developed his approach, is more successful in tracking down origins than in elucidating their synthesis in Shakespeare. This' is true, for instance, of E. C. Pettet's *Shakespeare and the Romance Tradition*, a straightforward and comprehensive account of its subject.

All too often, criticism of the plays which takes Shakespeare's sources, actual or hypothetical, as its point of departure tends to content itself with merely pointing out the changes which Shakespeare made, without much attempt to show how and why these changes are important for our understanding and enjoyment of the plays. A partial exception is C. T. Prouty's exhaustive study of *The Sources of 'Much Ado About Nothing'*, which tries, by a careful examination of no fewer than eighteen analogues, to relate the many changes Shakespeare made to a consistent comic vision. For the reader who wants to make up his own mind about the relationship between Shakespeare and his sources, the second volume of Geoffrey Bullough's *Narrative and Dramatic Sources of Shakespeare* is invaluable. This reprints all relevant source texts with critical introductions which often contain useful hints. Somewhat similar in scope but with a more determinedly critical emphasis is Kenneth Muir's *Shakespeare's Sources*. As already indicated, both the Arden and the New Cambridge editions contain extensive discussions of sources and analogues.

Among studies which are mainly critical, rather than expository or historical (the division is of course a matter of emphasis), three are of special importance. Bertrand Evans's *Shakespeare's Comedies* sees their distinctive achievement in the artful handling of different degrees of awareness of the developing action as between different characters and between characters and audience. Working his way through this book, the reader may occasionally feel that the notion of 'discrepant awareness' is serving as blinkers rather than spectacles; an original and suggestive insight sometimes degenerates into a mechanically applied scheme, as in the chapter on *As You Like It*, where the author himself implies that discrepant awareness is not of major importance. But elsewhere, in the discussion of *Twelfth Night* for instance, and particularly of *Much Ado About Nothing*, the method triumphantly justifies itself in a richer understanding of Shakespeare's comic technique.

C. L. Barber's *Shakespeare's Festive Comedy* almost deserves Laurence Lerner's commendation of it as the best book ever written on the subject. Its subtitle, 'A Study of Dramatic Form in Relation to Social Custom', may perhaps sound restrictive, but the restriction, if it is one, enables the author to bring the comedies sharply into focus. The first three chapters of the book fill out, by extensive reference to non-dramatic sources, the shape of Elizabethan communal festivities and their relation to comic form. Nashe's *Summer's Last Will and Testament* is then discussed as an example of 'festive comedy' not yet fashioned into drama. The rest of the book is devoted to a series of chapters on individual comedies, including three of our five plays—*The Merchant of Venice, As You Like It,* and *Twelfth Night.* The last perhaps gains most from the context in which Barber sets it, though all three are very good indeed. If my summary implies that the author is guilty of the fashionable reductivism of dramatic literature into something else (anthropology, sociology, psycho-analysis, or whatever) a glance at any of these essays will show that the implication is entirely unjustified. In Barber's own words, 'To get at the form and meaning of the play . . . is my first and last interest'. It is an interest he pursues with sensitivity, wit, and scholarship throughout the book. Though the individual essays on the comedies can profitably be read on their own, the opening chapter in which the author sets out his view of the Saturnalian pattern of 'clarification through release' should be read first.

In endorsing Professor Lerner's praise of *Shakespeare's Festive Comedy*, I used the qualifying word 'almost' with a particular exception in mind. The only critic who surpasses Barber in the range and brilliance of his writings on Shakespearian comedy is Northrop Frye. Frye has the great virtue of taking comedy seriously as a valid mode of responding to experience and therefore does not need to indulge in either apologetic whimsy or irrelevant erudition. In 'The Argument of Comedy' he gives a concise and convincing account of the pattern of Terentian and Plautine New Comedy, pointing out that it moves towards a 'new social integration' which is both 'a kind of moral norm' and 'the pattern of a free society'. But the moral norm is 'not morality but deliverance from moral bondage'. He then suggests that Shakespeare sensed when he looked at Plautus and Terence that the 'argument of comedy' would yield a profounder pattern than that articulated by the Roman dramatists. What this pattern is (the 'green world' and its changing relationship to the 'normal' world) is sketched briefly in 'The Argument of Comedy' and more elaborately in *A Natural Perspective*, which also contains a pithy analysis of the characteristics of Shakespearian and Jonsonian comedy. If Frye's concern with structures occasionally leads him to take a greater interest in what Shakespeare's comedies have in common than in the distinctive flavour of each, this is of a piece with his effort to arrive at a coherent notion of Shakespearian comedy; and in any case *A Natural Perspective* contains enough isolated and often unelaborated insights into individual comedies to furnish half a dozen particular critical studies.

(In the sections on individual plays which follow, I shall make no further reference to the critical studies mentioned above.)

'Much Ado About Nothing'

While it has always been popular on the stage, *Much Ado About Nothing* has been a source of embarrassment to many critics. They have no difficulty (*pace* Bernard Shaw) in doing justice to the witty pair Benedick and Beatrice and the engaging idiocy of Dogberry and his fellows, but are uncomfortable in the presence of a self-regarding romantic hero and an insipid heroine (though Hazlitt did not find her so). A good deal of criticism has therefore taken a stance for or against Claudio, often ignoring or evading the question of the relationship of Claudio (and our attitude to him) to the play's more general concerns. Among distinguished counsel for the prosecution are E. K. Chambers in *Shakespeare: A Survey* ('Claudio stands revealed as the worm that he is'), John Palmer in *Comic Characters of Shakespeare*, and James Smith. Smith's *Scrutiny* essay makes a resolute if finally unconvincing attempt to relate Claudio to what the critic sees as the shallow, arrogant, and philistine society of Messina. Also in *Scrutiny* is a careful and sympathetic essay by T. W. Craik which sees Claudio's behaviour as understandable in terms of the conventions of his society.

The beginnings of the kind of criticism which attempts to account for Claudio's behaviour in terms of convention can be traced to E. E. Stoll's *Shakespeare Studies*, though Stoll is not always aware that the last word has not been said when one has shown that behaviour is 'conventional'. A more sophisticated handling of this line of argument is to be found in M. C. Bradbrook's *Shakespeare and Elizabethan Poetry*, where it is also argued that Claudio's self-deception is rooted in his complete ignorance of Hero. Also worth reading for its defence of Claudio by a careful distinction between the element of belief in slander and the act of repudiation is Kerby Neill's 'More Ado About Claudio: An Acquittal for the Slandered Groom'.

Mark Van Doren's *Shakespeare* deals well with the comic idiom of Benedick and Beatrice and the relation of this couple to the conventional hero and heroine. The two pairs and the attitudes which

they embody are even more closely and sensitively looked at by D. L.
Stevenson in *The Love-Game Comedy*. Brief but stimulating comments
on the play as a whole are offered by G. K. Hunter in *Shakespeare:
The Late Comedies* and Francis Fergusson in *The Human Image in
Dramatic Literature*.

'Of all the angles of approach to Shakespearean Comedy', wrote
George Gordon, 'the master angle is, and must be, the angle of
femininity.' His little book is worth looking at, if only for Lewis
Carroll's letter on *Much Ado About Nothing* to Ellen Terry, which
includes a delicious parody of what Beatrice might have answered in
church, and for Gordon's remark (improving on Hazlitt) that
Dogberry represents 'a profound and awful revelation of the official
mind'. But for a development of Gordon's viewpoint which is
consistently intelligent and stays close to the spirit as well as the
letter of the play I recommend Barbara Everett's essay. She shows
how the action confirms the victory of a woman's world, and,
more importantly, just what this victory implies in terms of human
values.

The most comprehensive critical account of *Much Ado About
Nothing* I know is by J. R. Mulryne. This unpretentious, stimulating,
and clear-headed study is especially good on the way in which the
comedy achieves its full impact in the three-dimensionality of
theatrical performance. The only essay which seems to me better
than Mulryne's is that by A. P. Rossiter. This is equally penetrating
on the uses of deception in the play, the function of Dogberry's
linguistic mishaps in the total action, the particular flavour of
Beatrice and Benedick's wit, and the comic vision towards which the
whole play moves. The final paragraph of Rossiter's essay is, to my
mind, the clearest and most acute statement of the *distinctive* quality
of *Much Ado About Nothing*.

'*The Merchant of Venice*'

The fact that some of the best critical writing on Shakespearian
comedy has been on *The Merchant of Venice* does not necessarily mean
that it is Shakespeare's best comedy. Indeed, in a sense it suggests
almost the contrary; for a good deal of critical interpretation has
been concerned with what has been regarded as the near-*tragic*
figure of Shylock. Not many critics have been as forthright as Heine
or John Palmer in asserting that in *The Merchant of Venice* Shakespeare,
though he set out to write a rabble-pleasing anti-Semitic comedy,
ended up, in spite of himself, with something very like a tragedy

(though Nicholas Rowe did, as early as the beginning of the eighteenth century). But some such assumption lies behind much criticism which takes a 'sympathetic' Shylock as its point of departure. It is no real answer to such criticism to argue, as Stoll and Bradbrook do, that the Elizabethans would not have felt sympathetic towards Shylock. First, because even if the existence of a fixed attitude towards Jews could be conclusively demonstrated, it does not follow that Shakespeare merely panders to that attitude. Secondly, even if he did, no ordinary playgoer or reader would be content merely to rest in a supposed Elizabethan response. Certainly we ought to try to develop a historical perspective, but only so that our own response may not be distorted through ignorance and misinterpretation. And generations of audiences and readers bear witness to sympathy as a crucially important thread in the mingled yarn of our feelings towards Shylock. Red wigs and waxen noses may have lessened our sympathy on occasion but it is difficult to believe that they have destroyed it completely.

The best Shylock criticism steps over the red herring of Shakespeare's anti-Semitism and tries to see the character not as a piece of isolated portrait painting but as rooted in the imaginative world of the play. Thus Palmer proceeds through a sensitive analysis of Shylock's language to a perception of the play's ironic structure: 'Christian and Jew mutually charging one another with an inhumanity which is common to both parties'. Harley Granville-Barker's essay also has some sensible remarks on Shylock's idiom together with this critic's characteristic feeling for the play in performance. Charles Mitchell in 'The Conscience of Venice: Shakespeare's Merchant' points out, plausibly and without over-insistence, some connections between the two outsiders in the play, Shylock and Antonio. The same approach provides the basis for a casually brilliant essay 'Brothers and Others' by W. H. Auden, in my view the best single piece on the play.

Almost as potent a source of imaginative criticism as the figure of Shylock has been the underlying structure of the plot, especially the casket scene and the trial scene. Freud's account of the relationship of the three-caskets theme to Lear's choice among his three daughters and of both to the idea of the recognition and overcoming of death in wish fulfilment is more fascinating than persuasive. Its strategy is represented, perhaps somewhat unfairly, by the following: 'If we had to do with a dream, it would at once occur to us that caskets are also women, symbols of the essential thing in woman, and therefore of woman herself, like boxes, large or small, baskets and so on.'

It is the breath-taking casualness of the 'and so on' and its implications for criticism which are worth pondering. Perhaps C. S. Lewis's 'Psychoanalysis and Literature' should be read along with Freud's essay. A sharper but shorter comment by Freud touching *The Merchant of Venice* is 'Portia's Verbal Slip'. A very different explanation of 'the hardest fact and soundest wisdom' lying beneath the fairy-tale surface of the three caskets is offered by Harold Goddard, who sees the three central elements of the plot—the casket motif, the court scene, and the incident of the ring—as miniature plays with Portia at the centre. Goddard's conclusion, that Shylock is the leaden casket with the spiritual gold within and Portia the golden casket, does not, in the context of his argument, seem to be merely a perverse up-ending of the conventional anti-Shylock view.

Some of the best comment on the trial scene is to be found in Nevill Coghill's 'The Basis of Shakespearean Comedy', where the play is seen as a conflict between the Old and the New Law and the necessary compromise between mercy and justice. Another brief view of the trial scene which is witty, learned, and sensitive to the play is Philip Brockbank's 'Shakespeare and the Fashion of these Times'. This reminds us, among other things, that scepticism is not enough.

Much of the finest recent criticism has been concerned, directly or indirectly, with the opposition of the worlds of Venice and Belmont. The best section of John Russell Brown's *Shakespeare and his Comedies* explores the metaphor of love's wealth as it operates in the two worlds. The opposition between love and usury is the theme of a short but packed essay by J. W. Lever, 'Shylock, Portia and the Values of Shakespearean Comedy'. The importance of the ideas of justice, redemption, and mercy in the play's action is well brought out by Frank Kermode in his section on the play in 'The Mature Comedies', while T. H. Fujimura argues, perhaps a little too neatly, that the three worlds of the play—the golden, the silver, and the leaden—are marked by the corresponding styles of the romantic, the realistic, and the ironic.

Carey Graham's 'Standards of Value in *The Merchant of Venice*' examines with care and understanding the distinct moral attitudes of the major characters and the conflicts arising from them.

The most sustained 'allegorical' interpretation of the play I know is Barbara Lewalski's 'Biblical Allusions and Allegory in *The Merchant of Venice*', which argues, at times in a rather desperate fashion, that Shakespeare's play fits into the fourfold Dantean pattern of allegory. In '*The Merchant of Venice*: The Gentle Bond', Sigurd Burckhardt gives a very persuasive account of the dramatic action of *The Merchant of Venice*, starting from our ordinary response to Shylock and showing how 'the circle of the plot' is closed by our understanding of the true nature of a human bond: 'The ring is the bond transformed, the gentle bond'.

Finally, a short but valuable book-length study by A. D. Moody presents a sustained and often convincing view of the play as profoundly ironical, with the Christians chiefly notable for their conspicuous lack of Christian virtue.

'*The Merry Wives of Windsor*'

Readers with a taste for paradox will relish the fact that this section, the leanest of all, is devoted to the play dominated by the huge hill of flesh himself. Indeed, the relation between the two facts is not accidental. It is not that a great deal has not been written about *The Merry Wives of Windsor*. (A great deal has been written about every Shakespeare play.) Rather, a good deal of what has been written has been taken up with not very profitable speculations about whether the Falstaff of this play is Shakespeare's original or some reach-me-down substitute hastily run up to gratify the whim of a queen. The result has been that there is very little good criticism about the play as we have it or even about the character of the later Falstaff; too often he is being roundly rated for not being his namesake in earlier plays or staunchly defended as being just that. The following paragraph is devoted to criticism which in general avoids this mock battle; readers interested in the debate can study it best in A. C. Bradley's 'The Rejection of Falstaff' and Hardin Craig's *An Interpretation of Shakespeare*.

A sensible account of the play which does not claim too much for it but points out clearly its very solid virtues of pace and construction is that of Chambers in *Shakespeare: A Survey*. F. S. Boas in *Shakespeare and His Predecessors* also writes well on the play as a mirror of bourgeois life, though he does not quite avoid the 'can this be the Falstaff we know and love?' trap. This view of the play as a fully developed example of realistic citizen comedy is elaborated in E. J. Haller's 'The Realism of *The Merry Wives of Windsor*'. On a similar topic, S. Sewell's 'The Relation between *The Merry Wives of Windsor* and Jonson's *Every Man in his Humour*' is worth reading. Anne Righter has a few characteristically thought-provoking remarks on the uses of comic deceit in the three illusions to which Falstaff falls victim. I break my rule (of not citing works already mentioned in the general section) to point out that Evans is particularly good on

the uses of deceit in the play. Wilson Knight's comments on the
language of the play in *The Shakespearean Tempest* are fitfully illuminating. A good study of Slender which elaborates Hazlitt's view
of that worthy is J. J. Schell's 'Shakespeare's Gulls'. There is an
extended account of chronological, textual, and other problems
connected with the play in W. Green's *Shakespeare's 'Merry Wives of
Windsor'*.

'As You Like It'

'Of this play', wrote Dr. Johnson, 'the fable is wild and pleasing'.
Most of the fable Shakespeare took from Thomas Lodge's romance
Rosalynde, and what he did with it is best studied in Marco Mincoff's
article which pays intelligent attention not only to Shakespeare's
alterations of the prose work but to his omissions. The pastoral
tradition behind the play is exhaustively studied in W. W. Greg's
Pastoral Poetry and Pastoral Drama; a stimulating short account is to
be found in Hallett Smith's *Elizabethan Poetry*. Mary Lascelles's
'Shakespeare's Pastoral Comedy' proceeds by a scholarly and careful summary of the origins of literary pastoral, through Lodge's
Rosalynde, to an eloquent account of the values embodied in Shakespeare's pastoral world and its relation to the workaday one:
'pastoral romance is, and must always remain, *elsewhere* and *some
other time*'.

Until very recently, most criticism of the comedies has approached
them through studies of individual characters. In the case of *As You
Like It*, Jaques has attracted the most critical and scholarly attention,
with Touchstone a poorish second. A useful résumé of views on
Jaques is in O. J. Campbell's article. James Smith has some shrewd
comments on Jacques's melancholy in his essay, which however is
not confined to character study but stresses the more sombre aspects
of *As You Like It* and attempts to relate it to the problem plays. His
view of the play, though it seems to ignore too much of the ordinary
playgoer's response, is a salutary corrective to the romantic excesses
of the hey-nonny school. A. D. Nuttall's 'Two Unassimilable Men'
manages to extract several useful insights from the (at first) surprising juxtaposition of Jaques and Caliban.

Two helpful studies of Touchstone are those by John Palmer in
Comic Characters of Shakespeare and R. H. Goldsmith in *Wise Fools in
Shakespeare*. Palmer's account, although it takes Touchstone at
rather more than his face value, offers a view of his relation to the
rest of the play which is worth disagreeing with: 'It is as though

Shakespeare, setting out for Arden, where so many excellent poets have lost themselves . . . had determined in advance to take with him a guide who should keep him in the path of sanity. Touchstone puts all things and every person in the play, including himself, to the comic test'. Goldsmith's study, which is in part historical, has some stimulating remarks on the role of the fool in the different plays; Touchstone gains from being discussed alongside Feste and Lear's Fool. In *Shakespeare and the Popular Dramatic Tradition* S. L. Bethell explores the implications of Touchstone's double nature as both fool and wit. (Chapter Five of the same book deals well with the part played by the verse in the formal patterning of the play. Bethell points out that the very naturalness of Rosalind's prose makes the verse an essential element in the achieving of aesthetic distance.)

Three other studies which are not mainly concerned with *As You Like It* nevertheless shed a good deal of light on the play. In 'The Two Worlds of Shakespearean Comedy' Sherman Hawkins develops, in a richly suggestive way, Frye's notion of the 'green world' of comedy which he contrasts with the 'closed world' which 'is a metaphor, a symbol for the human heart'. He suggests that the two basic patterns of Shakespearian comedy are the 'siege', of which *Twelfth Night* is an instance, and the 'journey', exemplified by *As You Like It*. Nevill Coghill's 'The Basis of Shakespearean Comedy', as its sub-title, 'A Study in Mediaeval Affinities', indicates, traces the romantic comedy of Shakespeare to its roots in medieval theory. (The same roots, Coghill maintains, nourished the very different plant of Jonsonian satirical comedy.) Coghill does not discuss *As You Like It*, but his remarks on the 'golden world' and 'redintegratio amoris' illuminate the play. (He also has some interesting remarks on the problem posed by Shylock for the producer of *The Merchant of Venice*.)

William Empson's *Some Versions of Pastoral* is, like all his books, a brilliant performance in which the reader, and perhaps the author, is occasionally dazzled rather than enlightened. It contains two characteristically stimulating pages on the 'fain—feign' pun in *As You Like It*.

Two perceptive essays written from a somewhat specialized standpoint are those by John Shaw and Jay L. Halio. Halio's essay (in some ways anticipating Frederick Turner's) contrasts the timeless world of Arden with the court and rural characters and their preoccupation with time, and sees Rosalind as holding the balance between them. John Shaw traces the opposition of an essentially 'good' Nature and a perfidious Fortune in the action of *As You Like It*, a theme touched on by John Masefield in his book, *Shakespeare*.

Among general critical studies of the play the fullest is Michael Jamieson's careful scene-by-scene commentary which occasionally suffers from the self-imposed obligation to say something about every scene. Mark Van Doren's *Shakespeare* has an elegant, intelligent discussion of what attitude to the pastoral world the play wants us to take. Bernard Shaw's comments on nineteenth-century productions of *As You Like It* are among his most trenchant and are certainly worth looking at.

The two best-known separate essays on *As You Like It* are also the best. In one of them Harold Jenkins elucidates in convincing detail his general observation that 'Shakespeare then builds up his ideal world and lets his idealists scorn the real one. But into their midst he introduces people who mock their ideals and others who mock *them*. One must not say that Shakespeare never judges, but one judgement is always being modified by another. Opposite views may contradict one another, but of course they do not cancel out.' In the other essay Dame Helen Gardner deals not only with the many levels of comedy and the many worlds which meet in Arden, but also works out, or at least sets out, a view of comedy as free of time while tragedy is haunted by it: 'In Shakespeare's comedies time goes by fits and starts. It is not so much a movement as a space in which to work things out.' To try and work out why this is *not* true of *As You Like It* may be as fruitful an approach as any to the play, and to an understanding of Shakespearian comedy.

'Twelfth Night'

A very good introduction to this most elusive of Shakespeare's comedies is L. G. Salingar's 'The Design of *Twelfth Night*', which stresses the emotional coherence of the play and its working out of the themes of self-deception in love and the erratic but providential workings of fate. Salingar uses the sources of the play with fine tact to make strictly critical points.

Character-based criticism has centred mainly on Feste and Malvolio. A. C. Bradley's essay 'Feste the Jester' is worth reading for its sensitive and humane outlook even by those who find the Bradleian approach ('characters as real people') generally unacceptable. An equally sympathetic view which relates Feste more closely to the ethical concerns of the play is Alan Downer's 'Feste's Night'. A somewhat similar view of Feste is offered by R. H. Goldsmith in

Wise Fools in Shakespeare where the clown is viewed as the human norm of the play. Two perceptive and widely differing appraisals of Malvolio are those by Mark Van Doren and M. Seiden. The former compares Malvolio and Shylock in their relation as outsiders to the comic world of the play, while Seiden sees Malvolio's annihilation as the necessary price to be paid for the survival of the comic world.

One other approach through character, this time that of Viola, is worth mentioning. William B. Bache's 'Levels of Perception in *Twelfth Night*' is a persuasive account of Viola's redemptive role in the comic action.

A useful account of the background of revelry and misrule traditionally associated with *Twelfth Night* is to be found in Enid Welsford's *The Fool*. A good many critics have written on the tricky topic of the play's atmosphere or mood, but on the whole neither wisely nor well. Two exceptions are G. K. Hunter in *Shakespeare: The Late Comedies* and the brief but very pertinent comments by W. H. Auden in 'Music in Shakespeare', where he makes the point that 'Taken by themselves the songs in this play are among the most beautiful that Shakespeare wrote. . . . But in the contexts in which Shakespeare places them, they sound shocking.'

The structure of deception and disguise underlying the comedy and its relation to the major themes of the play is the subject of a very good essay, 'The Masks of *Twelfth Night*', by Joseph H. Summers. Frank Kermode has some good things to say about mistaken identity in 'The Mature Comedies', and the same topic is treated at length in Porter Williams's 'Mistakes in *Twelfth Night* and their Resolution', where the writer aims to show that mistakes in this play have a significance beyond their mere theatrical effectiveness. On the subject of the comedy as a text for performance, John Russell Brown's 'Directions for *Twelfth Night*' is excellent. He argues that in many modern productions some essential element of the play seems to have been missed and suggests that ambiguities of interpretation rise almost unbidden from the text.

Two important essays are by the American poet and critic John Hollander. The first, 'Musica Mundana and *Twelfth Night*', considers the metaphor of music as a key to the play's structure. The other and perhaps more central essay is entitled '*Twelfth Night* and the Morality of Indulgence'. It argues with close and intelligent attention to the language that the world of revelry, by providing an excess of certain undesirable activities, rids us of our desire for them. The thesis is subtler than my bald summary suggests and deserves close consideration even if ultimately we may reject it as not doing justice to our full sense of the play.

Two book-length studies, by Leslie Hotson and Clifford Leech, set the play in very different but equally stimulating contexts. Hotson's *The First Night of 'Twelfth Night'* sees the play as holding a mirror up to the queen and her court. (A very different view of the play's original setting is offered in J. W. Draper's *The 'Twelfth Night' of Shakespeare's Audience*, which in turn has been challenged, to my mind effectively, by N. A. Brittain in 'The *Twelfth Night* of Shakespeare and of Professor Draper'). Professor Leech's study of *Twelfth Night and Shakespearean Comedy* places the play in relation to Shakespeare's earlier and later work and sees its distinctive quality in the way in which it is lightly touched by a sense of real human time and its destructive potentialities. The cold wind of the dark comedies is here the merest breeze but even so it strikes an occasional chill.

REFERENCES

TEXTS

Fergusson, Francis (ed.), *As You Like It*, with Commentary by Esmé Church (Laurel Shakespeare, New York, 1959).

Furness, H. H. (ed.), *As You Like It* (New Variorum Shakespeare, Philadelphia, Pa., 1890).

Gilman, A. (ed.), *As You Like It* (Signet Shakespeare, New York, 1963).

Oliver, H. J. (ed.), *As You Like It* (New Penguin Shakespeare, Harmondsworth, 1968).

Quiller-Couch, A., and Dover Wilson, J. (eds.), *As You Like It* (New Cambridge Shakespeare, Cambridge, 1926).

Sargent, R. (ed.), *As You Like It* (Pelican Shakespeare, Baltimore, Md., 1959).

Wilson, J. Dover (ed.), *As You Like It* (facsimile of the First Folio text, Cambridge, 1928).

Wright, Martin (ed.), *As You Like It* (Shakespeare Workshop, London, 1968).

Brown, John Russell (ed.), *The Merchant of Venice* (new Arden Shakespeare, London, 1955).

Fergusson, Francis (ed.), *The Merchant of Venice*, with an introduction by Morris Carnovsky (Laurel Shakespeare, New York, 1959).

Furness, H. H. (ed.), *The Merchant of Venice* (New Variorum Shakespeare, Philadelphia, Pa., 1888).

Greg, W. W. (ed.), *The Merchant of Venice; Hayes Quarto 1600* (Shakespeare Quarto Facsimiles 2, Oxford, 1957).

Merchant, W. Moelwyn (ed.), *The Merchant of Venice* (New Penguin Shakespeare, Harmondsworth, 1967).

Myrick, Kenneth (ed.), *The Merchant of Venice* (Signet Shakespeare, New York, 1965).

Quiller-Couch, A., and Wilson, J. Dover (eds.), *The Merchant of Venice* (New Cambridge Shakespeare, Cambridge, 1926).

Stirling, Brents (ed.), *The Merchant of Venice* (Pelican Shakespeare, Baltimore, Md., 1959).

Bowers, F. T. (ed.), *The Merry Wives of Windsor* (Pelican Shakespeare, Baltimore, Md., 1963).

Fergusson, Francis (ed.), *The Merry Wives of Windsor*, with Commentary by Charles Shattuck (Laurel Shakespeare, New York, 1966).

Green, William (ed.), *The Merry Wives of Windsor* (Signet Shakespeare, New York, 1965).

Greg, W. W. (ed.), *The Merry Wives of Windsor: 1602* (Shakespeare Quarto Facsimiles 3, Oxford, 1957).

Oliver, H. J. (ed.), *The Merry Wives of Windsor* (new Arden Shakespeare, London, 1971).

Quiller-Couch, A., and Dover Wilson, J. (eds.), *The Merry Wives of Windsor* (New Cambridge Shakespeare, Cambridge, 1921).

Bennett, Josephine Waters (ed.), *Much Ado About Nothing* (Pelican Shakespeare, Baltimore, Md., 1958).

Fergusson, Francis (ed.), *Much Ado About Nothing*, with Commentary by Vergil Thomson (Laurel Shakespeare, New York, 1960).

Foakes, R. A. (ed.), *Much Ado About Nothing* (New Penguin Shakespeare, Harmondsworth, 1968).

Furness, H. H. (ed.), *Much Ado About Nothing* (New Variorum Shakespeare, Philadelphia, Pa., 1899).

Hinman, Charlton (ed.), *Much Ado About Nothing* (Shakespeare Quarto Facsimiles 15, Oxford, 1971).

Quiller-Couch, A., and Dover Wilson, J. (eds.), *Much Ado About Nothing* (New Cambridge Shakespeare, Cambridge, 1923).

Stevenson, David (ed.), *Much Ado About Nothing* (Signet Shakespeare, New York, 1964).

Baker, Herschel (ed.), *Twelfth Night* (Signet Shakespeare, New York, 1965).

Brimble, N. (ed.), *Twelfth Night* (Shakespeare Workshop, London, 1970).

Fergusson, Francis (ed.), *Twelfth Night*, with Commentary by E. Martin Browne (Laurel Shakespeare, New York, 1958).

Furness, H. H. (ed.), *Twelfth Night* (New Variorum Shakespeare, Philadelphia, Pa., 1901).

Mahood, M. M. (ed.), *Twelfth Night* (New Penguin Shakespeare, Harmondsworth, 1968).

Musgrove, S. (ed.), *Twelfth Night* (Fountainwell Drama Texts, Edinburgh, 1969).

Prouty, C. T. (ed.), *Twelfth Night* (Pelican Shakespeare, Baltimore, Md., 1958).

Quiller-Couch, A., and Dover Wilson, J. (eds.), *Twelfth Night* (New Cambridge Shakespeare, Cambridge, 1930).

Wilson, J. Dover (ed.), *Twelfth Night* (facsimile of the First Folio text, Cambridge, 1928).

CRITICISM AND COMMENTARY

General

Barber, C. L., *Shakespeare's Festive Comedy: A Study of Dramatic Form and its Relation to Social Custom* (Princeton, N.J., 1959).

Bullough, Geoffrey, *Narrative and Dramatic Sources of Shakespeare*, vol. ii (London, 1958).

Charlton, H. B., *Shakespearean Comedy* (London, 1938).

Evans, B., *Shakespeare's Comedies* (Oxford, 1960).

Frye, Northrop, 'The Argument of Comedy', in *English Institute Essays (1948)* (New York, 1949).

——, *A Natural Perspective: The Development of Shakespearean Comedy and Romance* (New York, 1965).

Johnson, Samuel, ed. W. K. Wimsatt, *Samuel Johnson on Shakespeare* (New York, 1960; published as *Dr. Johnson on Shakespeare*, Penguin Shakespeare Library, Harmondsworth, 1969).

Muir, Kenneth, *Shakespeare's Sources*, vol. i (London, 1957).

Pettet, E. C., *Shakespeare and the Romance Tradition* (London, 1949).

Prouty, C. T., *The Sources of 'Much Ado About Nothing'* (New Haven, Conn., 1950).

Shaw, G. B., ed. Edwin Wilson, *Shaw on Shakespeare* (New York, 1961; Penguin Shakespeare Library, Harmondsworth, 1969).

'*Much Ado About Nothing*'

Bradbrook, M. C., *Shakespeare and Elizabethan Poetry* (London, 1951).

Chambers, E. K., *Shakespeare: A Survey* (Oxford, 1925).

Craik, T. W., '*Much Ado About Nothing*', *Scrutiny*, 19 (1952–3).

Everett, Barbara, '*Much Ado About Nothing*', *Critical Quarterly*, 3 (1961).

Fergusson, Francis, *The Human Image in Dramatic Literature* (New York, 1957).

Gordon, George, *Shakespearian Comedy and Other Studies* (Oxford, 1944).

Hunter, G. K., *Shakespeare: The Late Comedies* (Writers and Their Work, No. 143, London, 1962).

Mulryne, J. R., *Much Ado About Nothing* (Studies in English Literature, No. 16, London, 1965).

Neill, K., 'More Ado About Claudio: An Acquittal for the Slandered Groom', *Shakespeare Quarterly*, 3 (1952).

Palmer, John, *Comic Characters of Shakespeare* (London, 1946).

Rossiter, A. P., *Angel With Horns* (London, 1961).

Smith, James, '*Much Ado About Nothing*', *Scrutiny*, 13 (1945–6).

Stevenson, D. L., *The Love-Game Comedy* (New York, 1946).

Stoll, E. E., *Shakespeare Studies, Historical and Comparative in Method* (New York, 1927).

Van Doren, Mark, *Shakespeare* (New York, 1953).

'*The Merchant of Venice*'

*Auden, W. H., 'Brothers and Others', in *The Dyer's Hand* (New York, 1948).

Bradbrook, M. C., *Shakespeare and Elizabethan Poetry* (London, 1951).

Brockbank, Philip, 'Shakespeare and the Fashion of These Times', *Shakespeare Survey 16* (1963).

*Brown, John Russell, *Shakespeare and His Comedies* (London, 1957; 2nd edn., 1962).

*Burckhardt, S., '*The Merchant of Venice*: The Gentle Bond', *ELH*, 29 (1962).

Coghill, Nevill, 'The Basis of Shakespearean Comedy', *Essays and Studies*, 1950 (revised and shortened version in *Shakespeare Criticism 1935–60*, ed. Anne Ridler, World's Classics, London, 1963).

*Freud, S., *Collected Papers*, vol. iv (London, 1925).

——, *Introductory Lectures on Psycho-analysis*, Standard Edition vol. xv (London 1915) (first published in *Psychopathology of Everyday Life*, London, 1914).

Fujimura, T. H., 'Mode and Structure in *The Merchant of Venice*', *PMLA*, 81 (1966).

*Goddard, H. C., *The Meaning of Shakespeare* (Chicago, Ill., 1951).

Graham, C., 'Standards of Value in *The Merchant of Venice*', *Shakespeare Quarterly*, 4 (1953).

*Granville-Barker, H., *Prefaces to Shakespeare*, Second Series (London, 1930).

*Heine, Heinrich, *Shakespeares Mädchen und Frauen*, trans. C. G. Leland (London, 1891).

Kermode, F., 'The Mature Comedies', *Early Shakespeare* (Stratford-upon-Avon Studies 3, ed. J. R. Brown and B. Harris, London, 1961).

Lever, J. W., 'Shylock, Portia and the Values of Shakespearean Comedy', *Shakespeare Quarterly*, 3 (1952).

Lewalski, B., 'Biblical Allusions and Allegory in *The Merchant of Venice*', *Shakespeare Quarterly*, 13 (1962).

Lewis, C. S., 'Psychoanalysis and Literature', in his *They Asked for a Paper* (London, 1962).

Mitchell, Charles, 'The Conscience of Venice: Shakespeare's Merchant', *JEGP*, 63 (1964).

Moody, A. D., *The Merchant of Venice* (Studies in English Literature No. 21, London, 1964).

*Palmer, John, *Comic Characters of Shakespeare* (London, 1946).

Stoll, E. E., *Shakespeare Studies, Historical and Comparative in Method* (New York, 1927).

* Starred items are included in the Casebook Series volume on *The Merchant of Venice*, ed. John Wilders (London, 1969).

'*The Merry Wives of Windsor*'

Boas, F. S., *Shakspere and His Predecessors* (London, 1896).

Bradley, A. C., 'The Rejection of Falstaff', *Oxford Lectures on Poetry* (London, 1909).

Chambers, E. K., *Shakespeare: A Survey* (Oxford, 1925)..

Craig, Hardin, *An Interpretation of Shakespeare* (New York, 1948).

Evans, B., *Shakespeare's Comedies* (Oxford, 1960).

Green, William, *Shakespeare's 'Merry Wives of Windsor'* (Princeton, N.J., 1962).

Haller, E. J., 'The Realism of *The Merry Wives of Windsor*', *West Virginia University Studies*, 3 (1937).

Knight, G. Wilson, *The Shakespearean Tempest* (London, 1932).

Righter, Anne, *Shakespeare and the Idea of the Play* (London, 1962).

Schell, J. J., 'Shakespeare's Gulls', *Shakespeare Association Bulletin*, 15 (1940).

Sewell, S., 'The Relation between *The Merry Wives of Windsor* and Jonson's *Every Man in his Humour*', *Shakespeare Association Bulletin*, 16 (1941).

'*As You Like It*'

Bethell, S. L., *Shakespeare and the Popular Dramatic Tradition* (London, 1944).

Campbell, O. J., 'Jaques', *Huntington Library Bulletin*, 8 (1935).

Coghill, Nevill, 'The Basis of Shakespearean Comedy', *Essays and Studies 1950* (revised and shortened version in *Shakespeare Criticism 1935–60*, ed. Anne Ridler, World's Classics, London, 1963).

Empson, William, *Some Versions of Pastoral* (London, 1935).

Gardner, Helen, '*As You Like It*', in *More Talking of Shakespeare*, ed. John Garrett (London, 1959).

Goldsmith, R. H., *Wise Fools in Shakespeare* (East Lansing, Mich., 1955).

Greg, W. W., *Pastoral Poetry and Pastoral Drama* (Stratford-upon-Avon, 1906).

Halio, J. L., 'No Clock in the Forest: Time in *As You Like It*', *SEL*, 2 (1962).

Hawkins, S., 'The Two Worlds of Shakespearean Comedy', *Shakespeare Studies*, 3 (1967).

Jamieson, Michael, *As You Like It* (Studies in English Literature No. 25, London, 1965).

Jenkins, Harold, '*As You Like It*', *Shakespeare Survey 8* (1955).

Lascelles, Mary, 'Shakespeare's Pastoral Comedy', in *More Talking of Shakespeare*, ed. John Garrett (London, 1959).

Masefield, John, *Shakespeare* (London, 1911).

Mincoff, Marco, 'What Shakespeare did to *Rosalynde*', *Shakespeare Jahrbuch* 96 (1960).

Nuttall, A. D., 'Two Unassimilable Men', *Shakespeare's Comedies* (Stratford-upon-Avon Studies 14, ed. M. Bradbury and D. J. Palmer, London, 1972).

Palmer, John, *Comic Characters of Shakespeare* (London, 1946).

Shaw, John, 'Fortune and Nature in *As You Like It*', *Shakespeare Quarterly*, 6 (1955).

Smith, Hallett, 'Pastoral Poetry: the Vitality and Versatility of a Convention', *Elizabethan Poetry* (Cambridge, Mass., 1952).

Smith, James, '*As You Like It*', *Scrutiny*, 9 (1940).

Turner, Frederick, *Shakespeare and the Nature of Time* (Oxford, 1971).

Van Doren, Mark, *Shakespeare* (New York, 1953).

'*Twelfth Night*'

Auden, W. H., 'Music in Shakespeare', in his *The Dyer's Hand* (New York, 1948).

Bache, William B., 'Levels of Perception in *Twelfth Night*', *Forum*, 5 (1964).

Bradley, A. C., 'Feste the Jester', in *A Book of Homage to Shakespeare*, ed. I. Gollancz (London, 1916); repr. in his *A Miscellany* (London, 1929).

Brittain, N. A., 'The *Twelfth Night* of Shakespeare and of Professor Draper', *Shakespeare Quarterly*, 7 (1956).

Brown, John Russell, 'Directions for *Twelfth Night*', *Shakespeare's Plays in Performance* (London, 1966; Penguin Shakespeare Library, Harmondsworth, 1969).

Downer, Alan, 'Feste's Night', *College English*, 13 (1952).

Draper, J. W., *The '*Twelfth Night*' of Shakespeare's Audience* (New York, 1950).

Goldsmith, R. H., *Wise Fools in Shakespeare* (East Lansing, Mich., 1955).

Hollander, John, 'Musica Mundana and *Twelfth Night*', *English Institute Essays, 1956* (New York, 1957).

——, '*Twelfth Night* and the Morality of Indulgence', *Sewanee Review*, 67 (1959).

Hotson, Leslie, *The First Night of '*Twelfth Night*'* (New York, 1954).

Hunter, G. K., *Shakespeare: The Late Comedies* (Writers and Their Work No. 143, London, 1962).

Kermode, Frank, 'The Mature Comedies', *Early Shakespeare* (Stratford-upon-Avon Studies 3, ed. J. R. Brown and B. Harris, London, 1961).

Leech, Clifford, '*Twelfth Night*' and Shakespearean Comedy (Toronto, 1965).

Salingar, L. G., 'The Design of *Twelfth Night*', *Shakespeare Quarterly*, 9 (1958).

Seiden, M., 'Malvolio Reconsidered', *University of Kansas City Review*, 28 (1961).

Summers, J. H., 'The Masks of *Twelfth Night*', *University of Kansas City Review*, 22 (1955).

Van Doren, Mark, *Shakespeare* (New York, 1953).

Welsford, Enid, *The Fool* (London, 1935).

Williams, Porter, 'Mistakes in *Twelfth Night* and their Resolution', *PMLA*, 76 (1961).

7. The Problem Comedies

Troilus and Cressida
All's Well that Ends Well
Measure for Measure

JOHN WILDERS

GENERAL STUDIES

Of all Shakespeare's plays, these three have probably provoked the most extreme critical controversy. They have sometimes baffled the critics—Dowden omitted all consideration of *Troilus and Cressida* from the first edition of his *Shakspere: His Mind and Art* because, as he admitted, he did not know how to deal with it—and they have been given extremely divergent and conflicting interpretations. Although their dates are uncertain it is generally agreed that they were written when Shakespeare was in his late thirties. *Troilus and Cressida* was probably composed in 1602 (a year later than *Hamlet*), *All's Well that Ends Well* in 1603, and *Measure for Measure* in 1604, the same year as *Othello*. One obvious feature of them is that they apparently do not fit into any of the conventional dramatic forms. As W. W. Lawrence said, they 'clearly do not fall into the category of tragedy, and yet are too serious and analytic to fit the commonly accepted conception of comedy'. Since all three were also written during a fairly short space of time they have usually been regarded as a separate and independent group. The critics have disagreed, however, about the characteristics which distinguish the group as a whole.

Dowden thought these plays were the product of a period in Shakespeare's life when he had 'ceased to be able to smile genially' and 'must be either ironical, or else take a deep, passionate and tragical view of life' which 'spoilt him, at that time, for a writer of comedy' (Preface to the Third Edition). Later critics also have assumed that these plays are primarily an expression of pessimism and despair and have discerned in them 'the note of disillusionment and cynicism', an outlook which is 'cheerless and often unwholesome' (Dover Wilson).

This romantic notion that the plays were the work of a desperate man was later forcefully attacked by C. J. Sisson in *The Mythical Sorrows of Shakespeare*, but already, a year before Dowden published the words quoted above, F. S. Boas was attempting to describe the plays in terms of subject-matter and effect rather than the mind which created them. 'All these dramas', he affirmed, 'introduce us into highly artificial societies whose civilisation is ripe unto rottenness. Amidst such media abnormal conditions of brain and of emotion are generated, and intricate cases of conscience demand a solution by unprecedented methods. . . . At the close our feeling is neither simple joy nor pain; we are excited, fascinated, perplexed, for the issues raised preclude a completely satisfactory outcome.' It was Boas who first applied to them the term 'problem plays'.

The first full-length study of them was published in 1931 by W. W. Lawrence, who disagreed with the autobiographical approach, asserting that there was 'no evidence that the problem comedies were composed . . . for the gratification of Shakespeare's aesthetic interests, or to give expression to his views on conduct or morality'. For him their essential characteristic was 'that a perplexing and distressing complication in human life is presented in a spirit of high seriousness' and 'that the theme is handled so as to arouse not merely interest or excitement, or pity or amusement, but to probe the complicated interrelations of character and action, in a situation admitting of different ethical interpretations'. Although subsequent critics have sometimes agreed with Lawrence's description, Schanzer has pointed out that his discussion of the plays individually is designed to show that such ethical ambiguities were not felt in Shakespeare's own time but have accrued as a consequence of changes in the moral assumptions of his audiences. Our judgement of the plays, Lawrence argued, is different from that made by Shakespeare's contemporaries: for the Elizabethans the problem comedies held no problems.

Lawrence claimed that the evidence for his case was historical. The sources used for all three plays were familiar to his audience and the poet was 'not free' to make 'sweeping changes in the meaning of traditional stories, in situations made familiar to people by centuries of oral narrative'. Since Shakespeare's sources contained no moral ambiguities, and the dramatist was not at liberty to alter their meaning, the plays themselves must therefore be 'direct and straightforward'.

Many of Lawrence's assumptions are open to question. We are

unable to reconstruct the precise effect on Shakespeare's contemporaries either of his plays or their sources. We may also doubt
whether he was seriously hampered by his sources, especially since
we know that he changed them substantially for all three plays. We
should, moreover, find it a hard task to 'discard as far as possible
the emotional and moral effect which the plays produce on us today':
if we could do so, says Rossiter, 'I fail to see what we are left talking
about.'

Rossiter agreed, however, that the plays were distinguished by
moral ambiguity. He summed up what were, for him, their main
qualities under five headings: (i) 'noble heroes' are deflated and
'with the deflations there runs concurrently the critical devaluation
of man at large'; (ii) 'Interpolated into the critical–analytical
patterns we find "ideal" figures' such as Ulysses in his speech on
degree and the Duke in *Measure for Measure* 'in his quasi-regal
moments'; (iii) 'these plays involve us in discoveries, always of a
bad reality beneath the fair appearances of things'; (iv) 'All the
Problem Plays are profoundly concerned with seeming and being';
(v) 'All the firm points of view or *points d'appui* fail one, or are felt to
be fallible. . . . Hence the "problem"-quality, and the ease with
which any critic who takes a firm line is cancelled out by another.'
This last point is very close to Lawrence's 'different ethical interpretations'.

Rossiter's five points were challenged by Schanzer who showed
that some of them were more relevant to plays outside the group
than to the three within it and that all of them could be applied to
other plays of Shakespeare. *Julius Caesar* and *Antony and Cleopatra* are
as ethically 'shifting' as any of the problem plays and both *Timon of
Athens* and *King Lear* come within the scope of Rossiter's other
definitions. The habit of grouping the three plays together had,
Schanzer believed, caused harm 'by fencing plays off from their
kindred, exaggerating the supposed similarities between those within
the pale and their supposed differences from those outside it', and
should therefore be abandoned.

It appears that discussion of the three 'problem comedies' as a
group has now ceased to be useful. Although the 'ethical ambiguity'
which Lawrence perceived in them can be found in all three plays,
it also appears in other works of Shakespeare's maturity. Recent
criticism of each play individually has made us see, on the one hand,
their connections with Shakespeare's development as a whole and,
on the other hand, their extraordinary distinctiveness and individuality.

Troilus and Cressida

TEXTS

The most useful texts for students are at present the New Cambridge edition, edited by Alice Walker, which has a helpful commentary but a somewhat biased introduction, and the Signet paperback edited by Daniel Seltzer. The Arden and New Penguin editions are still in preparation.

CRITICAL STUDIES AND COMMENTARY

Although the title-page of the First Quarto edition of *Troilus and Cressida* (1609) says that it was acted at the Globe theatre, the Epistle which prefaced the second issue (also 1609) implies that it had never been performed and was perhaps never designed for the public theatre. Peter Alexander has suggested that it was written for performance at the Inns of Court. For a long time it was one of Shakespeare's least popular plays in the theatre; although a wholesale adaptation by Dryden with the same title held the stage from 1679 to 1734, Shakespeare's original was not performed in England until 1907 when 'the main result' of the production, according to *The Times*, 'was the conviction that it was impossible to arrange for the stage.' Since then, however, there have been a number of successful productions. Some notable ones, such as Tyrone Guthrie's at the Old Vic in 1956, have been in modern dress; the Royal Shakespeare Company has offered distinguished productions in classical costume by Peter Hall and John Barton in collaboration (1960), and by John Barton alone (1968).

Strongly opposing views have been expressed about its characters, the quality of its achievement, the moral standpoint from which it was written, and its dramatic genre. The uncertainty about its genre began in the year it was first published. The First Quarto described it as a history, the Epistle to the Second Quarto called it a comedy, and in the First Folio (1623) it was inserted between the tragedies and histories. It has also been called a 'comical satire' and a 'heroic farce'.

Everyone seems to agree, however, that it is a highly argumentative, intellectual play. It is, according to Wilson Knight, 'more peculiarly analytic in language and dramatic meaning than any other work of Shakespeare'. S. L. Bethell agrees that it is 'a consciously philosophical play' and complains that 'the thought, only partially embodied in character and action, flows over into the dialogue which . . . is frequently developed almost independently of the situation to which it refers.'

Two of the longest and most crucial scenes consist of philosophical debates, the one in the Greek camp about the nature of social order, the other in the Trojan camp about the nature of value, and several critics have shown that these deliberations are conducted on the basis of two opposing sets of principles. Wilson Knight equates the Greeks with 'reason' or 'intellect' and the Trojans with 'emotion' or 'intuition'; R. A. Foakes more cautiously defines the Greek debate as 'political and concerned with the conduct of the war' and the Trojan as ethical and 'concerned with the motives and justice of the war'. What is clear is that the ideals propounded in both debates are abandoned in practice by the very characters who have expressed them. 'The Trojans, debating even now whether the war is worth fighting, can achieve nothing decisive with their chivalric code of war with honour. The Greeks, crippled by disaffection and insubordination, can achieve nothing even with the resources of rhetoric and contrivance which lie in Ulysses' (Philip Edwards). As L. C. Knights observes, 'none of the Greek generals in any significant sense embodies the order that is talked about . . . the impression we get from their counsels is one of "policy" rather than of "wisdom".' Ulysses's rhetoric is, moreover, the prelude to nothing more than a ruse to trick Achilles into action and, in order to achieve this result, Ulysses is prepared to turn 'his back on all the absolute values implicit in his "Degree" oration . . . telling Achilles . . . that "honour" is the dividend in a ceaseless business of self-advertisement' (Rossiter). Nor is Ulysses' 'policy' any more effective than his 'philosophy'. It merely makes the boorish Ajax more conceited. Achilles is certainly roused to action at the end of the play but his motive is not public duty but the private and unthinking impulse to revenge.

Many critics have noticed that, in the Trojan camp, Hector, though morally more attractive than Ulysses, is just as inconsistent. At first he proposes that they should accept Nestor's invitation to return Helen and end the war on the grounds that she is 'not worth what she doth cost the keeping'. Troilus, however, while admitting that Hector's argument is reasonable, declares that reason is itself inimical to the ideals of chivalry. His plea for the continued defence of Helen is on the grounds of 'manhood and honour'. Hector perceives that they are engaged in a clash of principles and decries Troilus' arguments as naïve and impulsive, yet agrees, nevertheless, that the war should go on. The wisdom of Hector's sudden change of heart is, moreover, further challenged when Helen's entrance in the third act 'makes it clear that the face that launched a thousand ships belongs to a woman of extreme silliness and affectation' (Muir). Hence 'the principal characters defy the sound political theories which they expound with so much eloquence' (Campbell) and their public orations, subsequently ignored, seem little more than 'rant and cant' (Patricia Thomson).

There has been disagreement about the soundness of Troilus' political principles. O. J. Campbell believes that he abandons common sense and allows himself to 'become the servant of his appetites', and Rossiter substantially agrees: his speeches are 'quite specious and self-deluding. . . . His argument is nonsense and meant to be taken as nonsense.' Wilson Knight holds an entirely opposite view. For him 'the Trojan party stands for human beauty and worth', their 'cause is worthy if only because they believe in it', and their 'idealism' is favourably contrasted with the 'stagnant, decadent, paralysed' cynicism of the Greeks.

Similar disagreement has arisen about Troilus' role as a lover and the quality of his feelings for Cressida, though opinions of Cressida herself are pretty well unanimous. She is, as Rossiter says, 'not simply a harlot', for her passion for Troilus is 'quite genuine' so far as it goes. Troilus' feelings for her, however, are seen by Wilson Knight as essentially 'pure, noble . . . hallowed by constancy', a 'mystic apprehension of romantic love', whereas Campbell regards him as 'an expert in sensuality', 'a sexual gourmet' towards whom we are induced to feel 'continuously critical and derisive'. Both critics have assumed extreme positions and the impression created by Troilus, as by the whole play, is not as simple as either has suggested. The impression he makes in the early scenes to some extent determines critical interpretations of the climactic moment when he discovers Cressida's infidelity. For some readers he rises to tragic proportions in an experience which is 'brutally and pitilessly effective' (Brian Morris); to others he displays a hysterical disregard of reason in which he has no 'tragic potentiality' (Campbell and Alice Walker). His final return to battle has similarly been considered as a chivalrous enterprise undertaken for 'the fine values of humanity, fighting against the demon powers of cynicism' (Knight), and as the futile refuge of a man 'crazy with disappointed passion' (Campbell).

Whatever their attitude towards Troilus, most critics agree that the unity of the love-story and the political action lies in the fact that both show the collapse of the ideals which inspired them. Ulysses' ideal of order and his political manœuvring are both defeated, Hector's rationalism is overruled, Troilus' aspirations as a lover are shattered, 'reason is shown as compromised by honour', and 'honour is seen to be unreasonably fixed on an unworthy object' (Morris). The effect of these parallel developments is to induce in us a kind of moral nihilism in which all ideals appear to be illusory, but about which the critics have again disagreed. Mrs. Nowottny believes that Troilus' idealism remains intact in spite of Cressida's infidelity: 'its existence is not thereby cancelled or negated'; it 'survives because it is created in the teeth of fact', an opinion close to Wilson Knight's. Her view does not sufficiently take account of the role of Pandarus, whose sexual pragmatism modifies our view of Troilus as our judgement of the Greeks is modified by the debasing invective of Thersites. Troilus' 'impassioned rhapsodizing', as Rossiter calls it, is made absurd 'by the presence—and the comments —of a buffoonish old Pandarus' whose view of the lovers is frankly and comically practical.

A further adjustment has to be made in our view of the play when we remember that the characters are frustrated not simply by personal blindness or stupidity but by sheer human fallibility and fickleness, which Shakespeare embodied in the pervasive image of Time, an element discussed in detail by Knights and Muir. Indeed the passion of Troilus for Cressida and Ulysses' vision of an ordered society may be seen as differing but equally futile attempts to wrest a durable ideal out of the relentless flux of time. Hence their defeat has elements of pathos as well as satire.

The uncertainty about the genre of the play is therefore not simply a disagreement about its structure or the irresolution of its ending. It arises from the effect on the reader of a highly complex and ambiguous work. Brian Morris believes that it is essentially a tragedy focusing on Troilus, who alone has 'the energy to initiate significant action' and 'alone possesses the capacity for experiencing the extremes of joy and suffering which is the mark of the poetic temperament'. Campbell, holding an equally extreme view, sees the play as a 'comical satire' in which Troilus 'did not deserve the dignity of a death on the field of battle'. Una Ellis-Fermor believed that the play was an expression of moral nihilism in which the 'passions, ideas, and achievements annihilate each other with no promise of compensation or solution', and where 'we fall more and more into agreement with Thersites, the showman who is ever at hand to point the futility, the progressive cancelling out to negation.' Kenneth Muir argues, more moderately, that although Shakespeare shows the ideals of these people to have been futile, he is not demolishing idealism itself: he merely implies that 'men are foolish to engage in war in support of unworthy causes; that they are deluded by passion to fix their affections on unworthy objects; that they sometimes act in defiance of their consciences and that, in the pursuit of self-interest, they jeopardize the welfare of the state. He was not saying that absolute values are illusions.' R. A. Foakes agrees that 'Shakespeare is not being cynical but merely showing the muddle in which most people move, approving the good but too often following the bad.' Muir and Foakes are among the most reliable critics' because they avoid any extreme critical point of view by taking into account as many of the play's shifting and subtle implications as possible. Its meaning can obviously not be reduced to any simple formula. It accords, as Lawrence concluded, 'with the facts of experience'.

All's Well that Ends Well

TEXTS

The Arden edition, edited by G. K. Hunter, and the New Penguin, edited by Barbara Everett, are the most suitable texts for students. Each has an excellent critical introduction and explanatory notes, the Arden more detailed and scholarly than the New Penguin. The New Cambridge edition, edited by Quiller-Couch and Dover Wilson has a poor introduction and the textual emendations, though sometimes brilliant, are occasionally eccentric. The Signet edition, edited by Sylvan Barnet, is also useful.

CRITICAL STUDIES AND COMMENTARY

All's Well that Ends Well was first published in the First Folio edition of Shakespeare's plays (1623), but no record exists of its performance before March 1741. It has never been popular in the theatre. Joseph G. Price, who gives a thorough account of its theatrical and critical history, remarks that it 'has been produced infrequently and the productions have received scant critical attention'. He also thinks that no 'really satisfying production of *All's Well* has yet been accomplished in a major theatre'. He was writing, however, before the Royal Shakespeare Company's production in 1968.

The literary critics have also, on the whole, reacted to the play with qualified approval, though none has been as hostile as Quiller-Couch, who declared it 'a nasty play . . . one of Shakespeare's worst'. The general view, eloquently challenged by Barbara Everett, is that it is a fascinating failure, though there has been more agreement about what Shakespeare was attempting than about the reasons why he failed. The themes of *All's Well that Ends Well* have been fully examined by G. K. Hunter in his edition. These are the contrast between youth and age, the 'moral frailty' of the young, and the moral stability of the old as exemplified in Bertram's dead father, the King, the Countess, and Lafew. Another contrast discussed by Hunter, and which Miss Bradbrook sees as the play's central concern, is that between the inherited rank of Bertram and the innate virtue of the more humbly born Helena, two different kinds of 'honour' which the King discusses formally in his *ex cathedra* speech (II.iii.117–44). Barbara Everett defines this theme slightly differently as the distinction between 'the way a man appears to his fellows, and the consonance (or lack of it) between the outward and the inward man'. Closely connected with this distinction, as Wilson Knight points out, is the question of feminine 'honour'—or virginity—and the honourable state of matrimony consummated by the loss of virginity, a paradox examined in the dialogue between Helena and Parolles in the first scene: 'the final use of her virginity is the purchase of honour not only for herself but also, as a ransom, for her husband' (Hunter). These contrasts are accompanied by the idea that human beings are never wholly good or bad but made, as the First Lord says, 'of a mingled yarn, good and ill together'. This idea, discussed by Tillyard and Rossiter, is implied in the moral ambiguity present in the characters themselves and the conflicting judgements which the critics have passed on them.

Bertram received a forceful condemnation from Dr. Johnson who denounced him as 'a man noble without generosity, and young without truth; who marries *Helen* as a coward, and leaves her as a profligate; when she is dead by his unkindness, sneaks home to a second marriage, is accused by a woman whom he has wronged, defends himself by falsehood, and is dismissed to happiness'. Coleridge, on the other hand, found himself 'unable to agree with the solemn abuse which the critics have poured on Bertram. . . . He was a young nobleman in feudal times, just bursting into manhood, with all the feelings of pride and birth and appetite for pleasure and liberty natural to a character so circumstanced. Of course he had never regarded Helena otherwise than as a dependant in the family . . . [He] had surely good reason to look upon the King's forcing him to marry as a very tyrannical act.' These two attitudes, the one denouncing Bertram as 'weak, cowardly, mean-spirited, false and ill-natured' (Rossiter), the other defending him as 'a high-bred brave and spirited lad' (Quiller-Couch), recur throughout the play's critical history. There is no doubt that Shakespeare made him more disagreeable than his counterpart in Boccaccio's *Decameron* but he also made his callousness understandable by emphasizing his youth.

Bertram is a 'young cub', an 'unseasoned courtier', an example of 'unbaked and doughy youth' who seeks honour in battle but is trapped into marriage. What Barbara Everett calls his 'well-bred loutishness' is 'fitted to his age and understanding'. Shaw, though unsubtle, is not far from the truth when he calls Bertram 'a perfectly ordinary young man, whose unimaginative prejudices and selfish conventionality make him cut a very fine mean figure in the atmosphere created by the nobler nature of his wife'. And it is not only Helena's superiority which puts Bertram in an unfavourable light. In adapting his source, Shakespeare also made the older characters, the King, the Countess, and Lafew, speak disparagingly of him.

Helena's character has also provoked critical disagreement. The plot requires that she should behave with a determination and deviousness largely uncongenial to modern taste. In John Masefield's tendentious summary, she 'practises a borrowed art, not for art's sake nor for charity, but, woman-fashion, for a selfish end. She put a man in a position of ignominy quite unbearable and then plot[ted] with other women to keep him in that position.' Clifford Leech, though more moderate and fairer to Shakespeare, also believes that her love is not presented altogether sympathetically and that 'ambition is the force that turns Helena from a passive love-sickness to active planning.' Yet Dowden saw her as an agent of providence whose mission was to heal the King's body and 'the spirit of the man she loves', a view amplified by Wilson Knight in one of the few exciting and original essays on this play. For him Helena has not only the simplicity, sincerity, integrity, and humility which Bertram lacks, she is the agent of a sacrificial and redeeming love which makes her 'a semi-divine person, or some new type of saint'. It is true that, in healing the King, Helena becomes the agent of a supernatural grace, but in the later part of the play her personality is scarcely strong enough to carry the power Knight attributes to her. Barbara Everett is nearer the mark when she draws attention to Helena's 'inwardness', her 'female self-containedness' which makes her attractive but hard to fathom.

Opinions of Parolles have been more unanimous. He is, as his name suggests, a man of 'words' rather than deeds (Bradbrook), whose words are 'not only boastful, but of the newest cut. . . . The latest slang, the latest fashionable clothes are Parolles' stock-in-trade' (Hunter). His role in the play is to serve as a foil to Bertram. Bertram's immaturity is revealed by his initial respect for Parolles; his final exposure is paralleled by the earlier unmasking of Parolles (Rossiter), and his growth in experience is marked by his rejection of Parolles. Yet, as Leech remarks, Parolles also grows in maturity at the end and 'acquires an awareness of his own nature that Bertram never reaches'. He is not therefore merely despicable, though the comparisons of him with Falstaff once made by Dr. Johnson and others now seem exaggerated.

The conflicting interpretations of the major characters have arisen largely as a result of the fullness and depth with which Shakespeare created them. Indeed Roger Warren may well be right in his conjecture that *All's Well that Ends Well* owes its life-like complexity and intensity of feeling to personal experience, the poet's love for a shallow, high-born man, recorded in the Sonnets. But though the apparent inconsistencies of the characters can be defended as true to life, there has been justifiable complaint that they are incompatible with the actions they are made to perform, that the life-like characters and fictional plot fail to cohere.

W. W. Lawrence tried to account for this lack of coherence. The 'different ethical interpretations' which he saw as characteristic of the problem comedies were, he argued, the result of an inconsistency between Boccaccio's opinion of the characters of this comedy and the judgements which Shakespeare imposed on them in the process of adaptation, and a further inconsistency between Shakespeare's moral assumptions and our own. The latter could be removed by historical scholarship, the former was ineradicable. Helena's story, he demonstrated, falls into two stages, the first 'the healing of the King', the second 'the fulfillment of the tasks', both derived ultimately from folklore (an element also discussed by Miss Everett), and both, in their original form, illustrating the devotion, skill, and assiduity of the heroine. The psychology in the folk-tales and Boccaccio's story was, however, rudimentary and raised no disturbing questions (such as the worthiness of the hero as the recipient of the heroine's love). But Shakespeare endowed the characters with the complex psychology of real life, and in making them credible raised uncomfortable doubts about the motives for Helena's pursuit of Bertram, the reasonableness of Bertram's rejection of Helena, and the genuineness of their reconciliation. 'Shakespeare . . . set before us real men and women, and then made them act in strangely irrational fashion.' Furthermore, says Lawrence, a modern audience, unfamiliar with folk-legend, tends to judge the behaviour of the characters by the standards of twentieth-century society. Hence we regard Bertram as 'a cad and a villain', Helena as a social climber, the bed-trick as either offensive or absurd, and the conclusion as casual or arbitrary. Lawrence's opinions have been challenged

directly by E. E. Stoll, who disregards the inconsistencies and so finds
no problems, and tacitly by Wilson Knight, who finds coherence in
the play's symbolic structure but is not much concerned about its
verisimilitude.

The most intractable problem is the genuineness of Bertram's
reconciliation with Helena, a point on which ultimate agreement is
unlikely. The brevity of the rhyming couplet in which he protests his
love (V.iii.309–10) and the conditional clause on which his pro-
testation depends make the play 'an open-ended work indeed' (Miss
Everett). Miss Bradbrook thinks the ending 'neither hypocritical
nor cynical' and Miss Everett, after reasonable cautiousness, feels
'a good deal of hope' for the couple's future. Yet Philip Edwards
asserts that 'Helena never saves Bertram. He is irredeemable:
Shakespeare could not save him'; and R. G. Hunter, a critic generally successful in reconciling the play's apparent contradictions,
admits that Bertram's regeneration is unconvincing, though he
believes that 'a Christian audience would not have needed convincing'.

The various difficulties discussed above have led many critics to
conclude that the play as a whole is insufficiently co-ordinated. 'We
lack the sense of fusion,' says Leech; 'The esemplastic power does
not seem to have been fully at work.' G. K. Hunter defines its prevailing effect as one of strain, 'of striving through intractable
material for effects which hardly justify the struggle' and which
appears in the tortuousness of the verse as well as in the larger
dramatic effects. Miss Everett, incidentally, believes the verse, though
difficult, to be one of the play's major achievements.

Paradoxically the very disunity of the play has been applauded as
evidence of Shakespeare's integrity. Certainly he rejected the easy
success which could have been achieved by a simple dramatization
of Boccaccio's story and chose to struggle with far more demanding
questions than Boccaccio was capable of asking. Philip Edwards is
impressed by the 'honesty' of a craftsman who 'tries to bring the
deep hopes of the soul into the images of art and finds them countered by even deeper doubts'.

Measure for Measure

TEXTS

The most useful edition is the Arden edited with an excellent introduction by J. W. Lever. Good scholarly notes can also be found in
the New Cambridge edition, though Quiller-Couch's introduction

leaves much to be desired. The Signet (edited by S. Nagarajan) and, more especially, the New Penguin (edited by J. M. Nosworthy) also contain sufficient material for all but the most advanced students.

CRITICAL STUDIES AND COMMENTARY

A play called 'Mesur for Mesur' by 'Shaxberd' is recorded as having been performed before James I at Whitehall on 26 December 1604 but allusions in the text, examined by Lever, suggest that it had been written and probably performed during the preceding summer. Like *All's Well that Ends Well* it was first printed in the 1623 Folio and, like the other two plays considered here, this 'great undefinable poem or unclassifiable play', as Swinburne called it, has been interpreted in widely differing ways. Schanzer is probably right in his claim that 'no other play by Shakespeare . . . has aroused such violent, eccentric and mutually opposed responses.' Its three leading characters have been variously extolled and reviled and the play has been seen, at one extreme, as an expression of Shakespeare's disgust with humanity and, at the other, as a Christian parable of the atonement. Whereas for Coleridge it was 'the most painful—say rather the only painful' work Shakespeare wrote, in which the comic scenes were 'disgusting' and the tragic scenes 'horrible', it has also been called 'a more Christian piece of thinking' than that of 'nine out of ten professional Renaissance theologians' (Miss Pope).

The most controversial character has been Isabella. Her refusal to sacrifice her virginity to redeem her brother's life has been judged as evidence either of her saintliness or of her rigid inhumanity. As early as 1817 Hazlitt confessed that he was 'not greatly enamoured of Isabella's chastity' and did not feel 'the same confidence in the virtue that is sublimely good at another's expense as if it had been put to some less disinterested trial'. Mrs. Charlotte Lennox, writing in 1753, went so far as to denounce Isabella as 'a mere vixen in her virtue' with 'the Manners of an affected Prude, outrageous in her seeming Virtue', an attack which prompted the Victorian critic Mrs. Jameson to retort that Isabella had 'a certain moral grandeur, a saintly grace, something of a vestal dignity. . . . She is like a stately and graceful cedar, towering on some alpine cliff, unbowed and unscathed amid the storm.' The divergency of opinion, though not the emotionalism, of both ladies has reappeared in the work of subsequent commentators: R. W. Chambers compared Isabella's single-minded virtue to that of a Christian martyr whereas Quiller-Couch saw 'something rancid in her chastity'. An accurate interpretation lies between—or, perhaps, encompasses—both extremes.

F. R. Leavis is right to insist that although, in her confrontation with Angelo, she 'must command a measure of sympathy in us', nevertheless we should not 'regard her with pure uncritical sympathy as representing an attitude endorsed by Shakespeare himself'. 'That she has admirable qualities is clear,' says R. G. Hunter, 'but she lacks the essential quality of charity', and this seems fair. As so often in the plays of this period, Shakespeare has created a character more complex than most critics have been willing to perceive. We may not be invited to approve of Isabella's moral rigidity even though we can sympathize with the youth, inexperience, and religious conviction which motivate it.

Although no one has so far attempted to exculpate Angelo there has been some argument about his motivation. The most naïve explanation is that of Mrs. Lennox, who was in no doubt that his 'Attempts on the Chastity of *Isabella*, his villainous breach of Promise, and Cruelty to *Claudio*, prove him to be a very bad Man, long practised in Wickedness.' It is not surprising that she finds his agonized expressions of guilt inconsistent with this view of his character. There is now, however, general agreement that Angelo's fault is 'self-deception, not cold and calculated wickedness. Like many another man, he has a lofty, fanciful opinion of himself, and his public acts belong to this imaginary person' (Raleigh). Wilson Knight agrees that 'Angelo, indeed, does not know himself: no one receives so great a shock as he himself when temptation overthrows his virtue.' An interesting footnote to his character is provided by R. G. Hunter (and noted some years earlier by D. J. McGinn): in attempting to impose the death penalty for adultery Angelo is applying a policy recommended by several strict puritan divines. 'In proposing the situation that obtains at the beginning of *Measure for Measure*, Shakespeare was asking his audience to imagine a legal and political possibility that was anything but far-fetched.'

Although there have been differences of opinion about the success of the Duke's characterization, practically all recent critics have agreed about his dramatic functions. These are to initiate the conflict by handing over the responsibility of government to Angelo in what Leavis calls 'a controlled experiment', to take charge of the situation when its consequences threaten to become dangerous, and to sit in judgement on his subjects when they have recognized their own inadequacies. W. W. Lawrence objected, however, that the Duke was no more than a structural device, 'a puppet manufactured to meet the exigencies of dramatic construction'. Wilson Knight, disagreeing, was the first person to point out that the relationship of the Duke to the other characters was comparable to that of God towards his creatures. His character, Knight believed, is 'that of the prophet of an enlightened ethic. . . . His sense of human responsibility is delightful throughout; he is like a kindly father, and all the rest are his children.' Others have been reluctant to judge him so favourably. Clifford Leech in particular has revealed his less attractive qualities and the contradictions in his character, regarding the Duke's behaviour in the middle scenes as far from godlike. 'It is difficult to believe', he writes, 'that [Shakespeare] looked with favour on a man who deceived a condemned criminal with a pretence of priestly power and who tricked Mariana into giving him his confidence.' Moreover the Duke's clemency in the last scene, which Knight regarded as a demonstration of the 'Gospel-ethic' of love and mercy, is to Leech inconsistent with his original exhortation that the law should be imposed with greater rigour. This last objection may be answered by Stevenson and R. G. Hunter who believe that the Duke actually revises his earlier opinion as a result of his own moral education in the play, discovering that clemency is the better policy. Yet Shakespeare nowhere allows the Duke overtly to express a change of heart.

We may be tempted to conclude that the various elements in the Duke's character are not components in a complex, human personality but contradictory elements which simply fail to cohere. Yet several scholars, including Miss Bradbrook, Miss Pope, and Schanzer, have shown that he displays a strong resemblance to an actual person, James I. The Duke's dislike of crowds and his fondness for subterfuge are known to have been characteristic of James, and the tempering of justice with mercy which the Duke applies in the last scene corresponds both with the King's principles, set out in his own treatise on 'the properties of government', the *Basilicon Doron*, and with his actual, often capricious practice. Josephine Waters Bennett, in a full-length study of the play, has no doubt that the Duke was a character 'whose acts and whose theories of government would be interesting to the new age and its new King because they were so carefully like the ones which the King had identified as his own'.

The chief complaint to be brought against the play as a whole has been that it lacks consistency of tone. Knights, Mincoff, and Edwards all protest that with the intervention of the Duke in Isabella and Angelo's affairs (III.i.151 onwards) a potential tragedy is clumsily turned into a comedy of intrigue and, our dramatic expectations having been aroused, 'we are thoroughly cheated' (Edwards). Their case is more convincing than that of Leavis and, more recently,

Herbert Weil, who affirm that the last two acts are 'a consummately right and satisfying fulfilment of the essential design'. There is little or no foundation for Josephine Waters Bennett's argument that the tone of *Measure for Measure* is comic throughout. In claiming that it is 'from beginning to end, pure comedy, based on an absurdity, like *The Mikado* full of topical allusions to a current best-seller', she shows a failure to appreciate a profoundly serious play.

Some interpreters have tried to rescue the play from the charges of inconsistency of tone and characterization by affirming a consistency in its moral scheme. Wilson Knight advises us first to 'have regard for the central theme, and only second look for exact verisimilitude to ordinary processes of behaviour' (advice of small use to an actor). For him 'the persons tend to illustrate certain human qualities. . . . Thus Isabella stands for sainted purity, Angelo for Pharasaical righteousness, the Duke for a psychologically sound and enlightened ethic.' This Christian symbolic interpretation, which Knight was the first critic to expound, was carried very much further by R. W. Battenhouse who described the play as 'a parable of the Atonement', containing 'a cycle of action which participates by analogy in the biblical cycle of sin, law, sentence, intervention, faith, suffering and reconciliation'. Of the presence of a moral, symbolic scheme there can be no doubt, but few critics would agree that it is as rigidly allegorical as Battenhouse believes. Miss Bradbrook puts forward a much more flexible scheme and affirms that its problems are ethical rather than religious, concerned with justice and mercy rather than sin and redemption. She is the more reliable guide to the play's themes.

Although *Measure for Measure* overtly raises many basic moral questions and some of its most tensely dramatic scenes show characters caught up in moral dilemmas, the play is nevertheless conceived in vividly human terms. The eighteenth-century critic Charles Gildon, though not the most perceptive of readers, nevertheless found the last act 'wonderful, and moving to such a Degree, that he must have very little Sense of Things, and Nature who finds himself Calm in the reading it'. It is this 'Sense of Things, and Nature' which is seriously underestimated by D. L. Stevenson who sees it as 'an intellectual comedy' which 'we follow with our minds, not with our emotions.' The right emphasis is given by Lever and by Josephine Waters Bennett when she insists that Shakespeare 'begins with human beings, and whatever ideal significance they may suggest on reflection, they remain human beings'. Indeed it is the very human complexity of *Measure for Measure* which has provoked such widely differing critical responses.

REFERENCES

GENERAL STUDIES

Boas, F. S., *Shakspere and his Predecessors* (London, 1896).
Dowden, Edward, *Shakspere: His Mind and Art* (London, 1875).
Lawrence, W. W., *Shakespeare's Problem Comedies* (New York, 1931; Penguin Shakespeare Library, Harmondsworth, 1969).
Rossiter, A. P., *Angel with Horns* (London, 1961).
Schanzer, Ernest, *The Problem Plays of Shakespeare* (London, 1963).
Sisson, C. J., *The Mythical Sorrows of Shakespeare*, British Academy Lecture, 1934.
Wilson, John Dover, *The Essential Shakespeare* (London, 1932).

Troilus and Cressida

TEXTS

Seltzer, Daniel (ed.), *Troilus and Cressida* (Signet Shakespeare, New York, 1963).
Walker, Alice (ed.), *Troilus and Cressida* (New Cambridge Shakespeare, Cambridge, 1957).

CRITICAL STUDIES AND COMMENTARY

Alexander, Peter, '*Troilus and Cressida*, 1609', *The Library*, 9 (1928).
Bethell, S. L., *Shakespeare and the Popular Dramatic Tradition* (London, 1944).
Campbell, O. J., *Shakespeare's Satire* (New York, 1943).
Edwards, Philip, *Shakespeare and the Confines of Art* (London, 1968).
Ellis-Fermor, Una, *The Frontiers of Drama* (London, 1945).
Foakes, R. A., '*Troilus and Cressida* Reconsidered', *University of Toronto Quarterly*, 32 (1962–3).
Knight, G. Wilson, *The Wheel of Fire* (London, 1949).
Knights, L. C., *Some Shakespearean Themes* (London, 1959).
Morris, Brian, 'The Tragic Structure of *Troilus and Cressida*', *Shakespeare Quarterly*, 10 (1959).
Muir, Kenneth, '*Troilus and Cressida*', *Shakespeare Survey 8* (1955).
Nowottny, Winifred, ' "Opinion" and "Value" in *Troilus and Cressida*', *Essays in Criticism*, 4 (1954).
Thomson, Patricia, 'Rant and Cant in *Troilus and Cressida*', *Essays and Studies*, 22 (1969).

All's Well that Ends Well

TEXTS

Barnet, Sylvan (ed.), *All's Well that Ends Well* (Signet Shakespeare, New York, 1965).
Everett, Barbara (ed.), *All's Well that Ends Well* (New Penguin Shakespeare, Harmondsworth, 1970).

Hunter, G. K. (ed.), *All's Well that Ends Well* (new Arden Shakespeare, London, 1959).

Quiller-Couch, A. T., and Wilson, John Dover (eds.), *All's Well that Ends Well* (New Cambridge Shakespeare, Cambridge, 1929).

CRITICAL STUDIES AND COMMENTARY

Bradbrook, M. C., *Shakespeare and Elizabethan Poetry* (London, 1951).

Coleridge, S. T., *Coleridge's Shakespeare Criticism*, ed. T. M. Raysor (2 vols., London, 1930; Everyman's Library, London, 1962); *Coleridge on Shakespeare*, ed. Terence Hawkes (Penguin Shakespeare Library, Harmondsworth, 1969).

Dowden, Edward, *Shakspere: His Mind and Art* (London, 1875).

Edwards, Philip, *Shakespeare and the Confines of Art* (London, 1968).

Hunter, Robert Grams, *Shakespeare and the Comedy of Forgiveness* (New York, 1965).

Johnson, Samuel, *Samuel Johnson on Shakespeare*, ed. W. K. Wimsatt (New York, 1960; repr. as *Dr. Johnson on Shakespeare*, Penguin Shakespeare Library, Harmondsworth, 1969).

Knight, G. Wilson, *The Sovereign Flower* (London, 1958).

Lawrence, W. W., *Shakespeare's Problem Comedies* (New York, 1931; Penguin Shakespeare Library, Harmondsworth, 1969).

Leech, Clifford, 'The Theme of Ambition in *All's Well*', *ELH*, 21 (1954).

Masefield, John, *William Shakespeare* (London, 1911).

Price, Joseph G., *The Unfortunate Comedy* (Toronto and Liverpool, 1968).

Rossiter, A. P., *Angel with Horns* (London, 1961).

Stoll, E. E., *From Shakespeare to Joyce* (New York, 1964).

Tillyard, E. M. W., *Shakespeare's Problem Plays* (London, 1950).

Warren, Roger, 'Why Does it End Well?', *Shakespeare Survey 22* (1969).

Measure for Measure

TEXTS

Lever, J. W. (ed.), *Measure for Measure* (new Arden Shakespeare, London, 1965).

Nagarajan, S. (ed.), *Measure for Measure* (Signet Shakespeare, New York, 1964).

Nosworthy, J. M. (ed.), *Measure for Measure* (New Penguin Shakespeare, Harmondsworth, 1969).

Quiller-Couch, A. T., and Wilson, John Dover (ed.), *Measure for Measure* (New Cambridge Shakespeare, Cambridge, 1922).

CRITICAL STUDIES AND COMMENTARY

Battenhouse, R. W., '*Measure for Measure* and Christian Doctrine of the Atonement', *PMLA*, 61 (1946).

Bennett, Josephine Waters, '*Measure for Measure*' as *Royal Entertainment* (New York, 1966).

Bradbrook, M. C., *Shakespeare and Elizabethan Poetry* (London, 1951).

Chambers, R. W., *Man's Unconquerable Mind* (London, 1939).

Coleridge, S. T., *Coleridge's Shakespeare Criticism*, ed. T. M. Raysor (2 vols., London, 1930; Everyman's Library, London, 1962); *Coleridge on Shakespeare*, ed. Terence Hawkes (Penguin Shakespeare Library, Harmondsworth, 1969).

Edwards, Philip, *Shakespeare and the Confines of Art* (London, 1968).

Gildon, Charles, 'Remarks on the Plays of Shakespeare', appended to Shakespeare, *Works*, ed. Rowe, 7 vols. (London, 1709–10).

Hazlitt, William, *Characters of Shakespeare's Plays* (London, 1817; World's Classics, London, 1917).

Hunter, Robert Grams, *Shakespeare and the Comedy of Forgiveness* (New York, 1965).

Jameson, Anna, *Characteristics of Women*, 2 vols. (London, 1832).

Knight, G. Wilson, *The Wheel of Fire* (London, 1949).

Knights, L. C., 'The Ambiguity of *Measure for Measure*', *Scrutiny*, 10 (1942).

Lawrence, W. W., *Shakespeare's Problem Comedies* (New York, 1931; Penguin Shakespeare Library, Harmondsworth, 1969).

Leavis, F. R., '*Measure for Measure*', in *The Common Pursuit* (London, 1952).

Leech, Clifford, 'The "Meaning" of *Measure for Measure*', *Shakespeare Survey 3* (1950).

Lennox, Charlotte, *Shakespear Illustrated*, 3 vols. (London, 1753).

McGinn, D. J., 'The Precise Angelo', in *J. Q. Adams Memorial Studies*, ed. J. G. McManaway and others (Washington, D.C., 1948).

Mincoff, Marco, '*Measure for Measure*: A Question of Approach', *Shakespeare Studies*, 2 (Cincinnati, Ohio, 1966).

Pope, E. M., 'The Renaissance Background of *Measure for Measure*', *Shakespeare Survey 2* (1949).

Raleigh, Walter, *Shakespeare* (London, 1907).

Schanzer, Ernest, *The Problem Plays of Shakespeare* (London, 1963).

Stevenson, David Lloyd, *The Achievement of Shakespeare's 'Measure for Measure'* (Ithaca, N.Y., 1967).

Weil, Herbert, 'Form and Contexts in *Measure for Measure*', *Critical Quarterly* 12 (1970).

8. The Late Comedies

PHILIP EDWARDS

TEXTS

For each of Shakespeare's four late comedies, or romances, there is only one early text. *Cymbeline, The Winter's Tale,* and *The Tempest* were first printed in the First Folio of 1623. The fourth, *Pericles,* exists only in an inferior text, probably pirated, of 1609 (twice reprinted in Shakespeare's lifetime). For different reasons, therefore, a reader need not have serious worries about the authenticity and purity of the texts provided in any particular edition he may be using: for three plays there are no major problems, for the fourth, there is no authoritative version.

The student of *Pericles* is strongly advised to look at a reproduction of the original 'bad' Quarto of 1609; a facsimile edited by Greg was published by the Shakespeare Association. After that, he may choose one of three good modern annotated editions. The New Cambridge edition was prepared by J. C. Maxwell in 1956; F. D. Hoeniger's edition for the new Arden series has the fullest introduction and notes; Ernest Schanzer's Signet edition compresses much into a small compass and is helpful in guidance to further reading.

Two very good modern editions of *Cymbeline* are the new Arden edition, edited with an important introductory essay by J. M. Nosworthy, and the New Cambridge edition, again edited by J. C. Maxwell.

J. H. P. Pafford's new Arden edition of *The Winter's Tale* gives the source, Greene's *Pandosto,* as an Appendix; the introduction and commentary are cautious but sound. Ernest Schanzer's edition for the New Penguin Shakespeare can be warmly recommended.

The New Cambridge edition of *The Tempest,* by Quiller-Couch and Dover Wilson, appeared in 1921 and, as the first in that notable but eccentric series, has considerable historical interest. A modern reader may find the punctuation fussy and the stage-directions sentimental. Frank Kermode's learned introductory essay to the new Arden edition has become a classic, and the whole edition is helpful. The New Penguin Shakespeare edition by Anne Righter (now Barton) is well annotated, and contains a very interesting introductory essay, particularly helpful on the opening and the close of the play.

THE ROMANCES AS A GROUP

Chronology

The romances seem to have been written between the end of 1607 and the beginning of 1612; probably they were the only plays which Shakespeare wrote during those years, and the last of them, *The Tempest*, was the last complete play that he composed. The special interest which this century has shown in these plays as a group simply could not exist until chronological study had established their kinship in time. A description of Malone's pioneer work (using the discoveries of Tyrwhitt and Steevens) to 'Ascertain the Order in which the Plays of Shakespeare Were Written', published in 1778, is given in S. Schoenbaum's *Shakespeare's Lives*. *Pericles* and *The Winter's Tale* Malone recognized as belonging together, but he first thought them to be very early works. *Cymbeline* he dated 1604, and *The Tempest* after 1609. He later moved *The Winter's Tale* to 1613, and in his unpublished papers he hit upon the accepted date of 1610–11. Coleridge was sceptical of the value of documentary evidence for dating and wished to rely on 'the internal evidences furnished by the writings themselves'. In his *Shakespearean Criticism*, collected by T. M. Raysor, it is possible to follow his attempts over the years to establish a poetic order. Once again the assumption (deriving from Dryden) that *Pericles* was very early is a hindrance. He knows that *The Winter's Tale* and *Cymbeline* are allied to *Pericles*, so he places them as the successors of that play. *The Tempest* was separate, belonging to Shakespeare's mid-career. In the chronological list published in *Literary Remains*, which probably reflects not only his own later judgement but Malone's later findings, *The Tempest*, *The Winter's Tale*, and *Cymbeline* appear as a final group—with *Pericles* still as an early work. Work by J. P. Collier on the text and authorship of *Pericles* in 1839 and 1857 enabled Dyce to perceive in 1866 that the Shakespearian parts of the play 'manifestly belong to his latest style of composition'. All was therefore ready for Dowden in his *Shakspere: A Critical Study of his Mind and Art* of 1875, moving forward from Furnivall's 'Trial Table of the Order of Shakspere's Plays' (which he prints), to initiate his powerful and influential conception of Shakespeare's final period, with its 'pathetic yet august serenity', including *Pericles* and ending with *The Tempest*. A cheapened version of this 'final period' appeared in Dowden's *Shakspere* of 1877, a contribution to J. R. Green's Literature Primers; but it is also this primer which confidently uses the term 'romances' for the last plays, and weds *Pericles* more firmly to its fellows: 'in some respects a slighter and earlier *Tempest*, in which Lord Cerimon is the Prospero'. Exactitude is impossible in dating Shakespeare's plays, especially *Cymbeline*; by and large, the dates given by E. K. Chambers in Chapter VIII of *William Shakespeare* (1930) still stand.

Histories of Criticism, Special Collections, and Studies

Many studies of the last plays narrate in some form the not un-exciting story of the 'discovery' of the romances, their growing magnetism for critics, and the rapid and radical changes in esteem and interpretation. There are succinct surveys of criticism in the introductions to the new Arden editions of *Cymbeline* (Nosworthy), *The Winter's Tale* (Pafford), and *The Tempest* (Kermode). An earlier survey of my own, more acidulous and even more selective than this present one, appeared in *Shakespeare Survey 11*. It deals with criticism from 1900 to 1957, and attempts to sort out the bewildering variety of assessment of the last plays by grouping criticism according to the fundamental assumptions about literature which the critics appeared to me to hold.

A good collection of previously written essays on the romances, many of which are discussed later in this survey, has been made by D. J. Palmer for the Penguin Shakespeare Library: *Shakespeare's Later Comedies*. The eleventh volume of *Shakespeare Survey* (1958) concentrated on the last plays. *Later Shakespeare* (edited by J. R. Brown and B. Harris) contains six specially written studies of differ-ent aspects of the last plays: like *Shakespeare's Later Comedies*, it con-tains recommendations of books for further reading. Frank Ker-mode's *Shakespeare: The Final Plays*, in the 'Writers and their Work' series, gives in fifty pages a very sound introduction to the romances as a whole and individually, and has a five-page reading-list.

There are not many books exclusively on the last plays. Tillyard's *Shakespeare's Last Plays* and Wilson Knight's *The Crown of Life* (1947) are the best-known, and are discussed in their place later, with Derek Traversi's *Shakespeare: The Last Phase*. There is also D. R. C. Marsh's *The Recurring Miracle*. Two books on Shakespearian comedy which pay special attention to the last plays are Northrop Frye's *A Natural Perspective* and R. G. Hunter's *Shakespeare and the Comedy of Forgiveness*.

Criticism and Commentary

It is often in the study of an individual play that a strikingly new approach to the romances as a whole is worked out, and, provided some overlapping and inconsistency is forgiven, the rough-and-ready division adopted here between general and particular criticism has many advantages, for, as with the tragedies and the histories, there are problems common to the whole genre, and there are problems peculiar to each play. Chronology has not been observed, yet I would have observed it if I could, because the *Zeitgeist* has every critic in thrall whether he knows it or wants it or not, and it is important to observe that criticism of the late plays falls in large bands of colour generation by generation. The spectrum is like this: the romantic search for the soul of Shakespeare, of which Dowden is the not-to-be-despised high priest, yields early in this century to the curt realism of Thorndike and Stoll; after the First World War there follows the first period of myth-and-ritual criticism, establishing the romances as fundamentally symbolic plays (though *The Tempest* had been read as an allegory for the previous hundred years). The period of the Second World War and its immediate aftermath may be seen as the main period of Christian interpretation, and it was followed by the Aristotelian structuralism (of many variants) which still prevails.

The main problem of the romances is the combination of form and time: they are (at least on the surface) so different from what Shakespeare wrote before; they are (at least on the surface) so much less imposing than what has gone before; they are so grotesquely incredible; they are so repetitive in their themes and incidents—that they really importune the critic with the question, 'what *was* Shakespeare trying to do at this time of his life with this kind of play?'

That the romances are, absolutely, feebler than their predecessors has been widely held, most famously by Lytton Strachey in his brilliant essay of 1904, 'Shakespeare's Final Period', which demolished the notion of the serenity of the last plays and offered instead a picture of Shakespeare, bored with people and bored with drama, writing carelessly fashioned plays in which flights of ethereal poetry are interrupted by violent moments of disgust. Dr. Johnson's comment on the 'unresisting imbecility' of *Cymbeline* was echoed 150 years later by Bernard Shaw. *Pericles* also has come in for some very hard knocks ever since, in its own day, Ben Jonson called it a 'mouldy tale'. Late Victorians like Dowden and Walter Raleigh felt that a carelessness and indifference about the quality of the plays was part and parcel of the very serenity of achieved wisdom which they thought the plays contained. But in 1955, in *The Growth and Structure of Elizabethan Comedy*, Muriel Bradbrook was able to talk of 'a general agreement' that the last plays provide us with 'perhaps the most characteristic and inimitable manifestation of Shakespeare's dramatic art'. One hears now and again voices saying that one or more of the plays is a failure (D. G. James and F. R. Leavis, for example) and occasional protests at overvaluation (from R. A. Foakes, for example, in his introduction to the new Arden *Henry VIII*), but it sometimes seems that we have reached the stage when Shakespeare's failings are seen as part of his conscious design. At any rate, castigation has certainly yielded to recognition. The most solid work on the romances in recent years has been in defining their kind. In considering these labours of definition, the reader must remember that the strange similarities and reciprocities of the romances may conceal from him and the critics basic differences in type in the four plays; the existence of these differences was well argued by F. R. Leavis in an essay of 1942, 'The Criticism of Shakespeare's Last Plays: A Caveat'.

That in shaping the romances Shakespeare was following the dramatic fashions or the theatrical needs of the day is an explanation that has been given in several different forms. A. H. Thorndike published *The Influence of Beaumont and Fletcher upon Shakespeare* in 1901; his thesis was that the popularity of the heroic romance created by Beaumont and Fletcher led Shakespeare to imitate them; the happy endings of Shakespeare's experiments in tragicomedy have no relation to his mood or his vision of life: they are the endings which plays of this sort have. F. H. Ristine's *English Tragicomedy* supports this unromantic view of the last comedies, but it must be noted that Ristine was a pupil of Thorndike's, and that the whole matter of the dependence of Shakespeare on the work of his younger comrades is founded on a suppositious dating of the plays involved. The view that, dating apart, the similarities between Shakespeare's romances and Beaumont and Fletcher's tragicomedies have been exaggerated is advanced by A. Harbage in *Shakespeare and the Rival Traditions*, who insists that Shakespeare's plays are different in kind from the decadent coterie drama of the private theatres. This matter is not easily dismissed, however, even if the direct influence of Beaumont and Fletcher's plays remains questionable. In his Preface on *Cymbeline* in 1930, Harley Granville-Barker laid great stress on the importance of Shakespeare's company beginning to use the indoor private theatre of Blackfriars as well as the less select open-air Globe in 1609. In the Blackfriars theatre, said Granville-Barker, modern drama was born, more subtle, less powerful; and its intimacy, lighting, and scenery may have been the direct cause of some of the idiosyncrasies of *Cymbeline*. In 1948, G. E. Bentley, in 'Shakespeare and the Blackfriars Theatre', greatly extended Granville-Barker's suggestion. He thought that the taking over of the Blackfriars lease by the King's Men must have led Shakespeare and his fellows to plan the kind of plays they wanted for their new theatre and more select audience, and that the writing of the romances, as well as the engagement of Beaumont and Fletcher as dramatists, is evidence of the concern to have the right kind of drama. Further consideration of the possible influence on Shakespeare of both new theatrical circumstances and new kinds of drama is given in two essays in *Later Shakespeare*; by Daniel Seltzer in 'The Staging of the Last Plays', and by Richard Proudfoot in 'Shakespeare and the New Dramatists'; some of the essays on *Cymbeline* mentioned later bear on this subject, particularly that of A. C. Kirsch, '*Cymbeline* and Coterie Dramaturgy', which entirely denies Harbage's view that the romances are not coterie drama—and J. Q. Adams's curious opinion expressed in his *Life of Shakespeare* that Shakespeare, though forced to meet fashion half-way, tried to preserve his own moral tone in a decadent kind of drama. Kirsch thinks that the late Shakespeare, with Beaumont and Fletcher, was infected with Marston's parody-compulsion, and that *Cymbeline* belongs to that tradition of self-conscious dramaturgy, mocking the conventions it uses, which the private theatres had evolved.

An original and appealing juxtaposing of the romances with their contemporaries is provided by Patrick Cruttwell in *The Shakespearean Moment*; he compares them with the spirit of Donne's 'Anniversaries'. He feels that the last plays should not be seen as an end, but as a new beginning, a bridge to a later development that Shakespeare (unlike Donne) did not live to achieve. Cruttwell argues that there are resemblances between Donne's treatment of Elizabeth Drury and Shakespeare's treatment of his last heroines; both writers go in for a certain 'extremeness' and show a certain indifference to the requirements of form and commonsense. He notes the tendency to deal in pure evil and pure good, and the irrational transference of the women from very flesh to goddesses.

In trying to relate these late comedies to their times, many writers have dealt with the revival of interest in dramatic romance and many more writers have dealt with the relation of Shakespeare's romances to romance as a whole in the sixteenth and seventeenth centuries including *Arcadia* and *The Faerie Queene*, or have been concerned to show that the plays are strictly within the general category of European romance, particularly in its pastoral forms. Carol Gesner's

Shakespeare and the Greek Romance is helpfully descriptive of the background that it studies, and makes a convincing case for the influence of the romances, especially on *Cymbeline*. E. C. Pettet's book, *Shakespeare and the Romance Tradition*, usefully traces the importance of romance and its conventions to Shakespeare throughout his writing career; a short study, Stanley Wells's 'Shakespeare and Romance', which gives a sketch of the history of romance, also treats Shakespeare's use of romance in his earlier as well as the late plays: there is a good section on *Twelfth Night*. Wells thinks that the seriousness and solemnity of romance—its didactic element—may have been over-emphasized; perhaps it was Shakespeare who made romance serious by turning it inside out. Three studies published in England in the early fifties show how helpful it is to see Shakespeare's romances against the dramatic and literary romance of the sixteenth century: J. F. Danby's *Poets on Fortune's Hill*, Frank Kermode's introduction to the new Arden *Tempest*, and James Nosworthy's introduction to the new Arden *Cymbeline*. I believe that these three critics made an important contribution to the study of Shakespeare's last plays, and I gave a fuller description of their work than is possible here in my 1957 survey mentioned above.

A succession of adventures, magic and marvels, journeyings and shipwrecks, riddles and quests, romantic love, the strange loss and stranger recovery of children, rural settings, extremes of characterization, happy endings—these are some of the things we find in romance. Auerbach in *Mimesis* despised the political and practical emptiness of all these adventures which are the reading-matter (whenever romance appears) of a secure upper class. But it is the very emptiness of purpose which makes romance so hospitable to profounder meanings; take away the practical importance of a journey and you may make it big with symbolic possibility. Uncontaminated with realism or respect for verisimilitude, romance is free to engage us at the level of our deeper dreams (which is why *Pericles*, the most clumsily written of all the thirty-seven plays, is one of the most moving when seen in the theatre). No one has written better on the essential significance of romance than Northrop Frye. In all his writings on comedy over the years, Shakespeare's romances have been at the centre of his thought, and *The Winter's Tale* has been at the centre of the romances. From the famous essay 'The Argument of Comedy' of 1948, through *Anatomy of Criticism* and 'Recognition in *The Winter's Tale*', to *A Natural Perspective* of 1965, he has pursued and developed his view of the deep structure of the romances with the same fertile intelligence. If there has been a lot of repetition, there is also the feeling that no one of these discussions can be read and understood entirely on its own. *A Natural Perspective* gives the fullest and best display of his views. Shakespearian comedy, moving steadily towards the achievement of the romances, takes us from 'reality' into illusion, from which we emerge into a recognition of an order of transcendent nature which we cannot know otherwise than by the symbols of art, symbols which derive from the great renewing power of the green world. The primitivism of Shakespeare's romances is especially fitting for an art which takes us, as myth took our ancestors, beyond tragedy into the participation, which all men desire, in a higher order of reality.

C. L. Barber, whose omission of the romances from his important study of Shakespeare's 'festive comedy' was a disappointment, has given us a tantalizingly brief but very suggestive reading of the code of the later comedies in ' "Thou that beget'st him that did thee beget" : Transformation in *Pericles* and *The Winter's Tale*'. He argues that whereas in the earlier comedies youth burst through to create a new society with its disruptive sexual energy, the later comedies show the transformation of love in the older generation, by means of which family ties are freed from the threat of sexual degradation. Incest is purged in *Pericles* and homosexuality in *The Winter's Tale*; the recovery of mother–wife–child at the end of each play is charged with a sacredness that suggests the discovery of a new meaning in life. The thesis is important enough for fuller and bolder treatment.

In 1921 Colin Still published a remarkable book, *Shakespeare's Mystery Play; A Study of 'The Tempest'*. He republished it in an enlarged form as *The Timeless Theme* in 1936. He claimed that the play had striking analogies with pagan mystery cults and rites of initiation, and Christian doctrine as well, and therefore joined with all these in being a symbolic representation of mankind's unchanging spiritual pilgrimage. The author of another book of the twenties thought it necessary to republish it when the times were more ripe to receive symbolic interpretations of Shakespeare's last plays. The book was *Myth and Miracle*, by G. Wilson Knight, republished in Knight's major study of the last plays, *The Crown of Life*. The last plays he saw as 'myths of immortality'; Shakespeare was trying to give voice to his 'more directly religious apprehension' which made the writing of 'a normal play' impossible. The earlier work remains a pioneer interpretation in an idiom which later became common currency; the later book is rather a remorseless juggernaut. Another early book of Wilson Knight's has much to say about the last plays: *The Shakespearian Tempest*; this gives his imaginative reaction to sea-imagery throughout Shakespeare; he saw tempest (discord) and music (harmony) as the poles of the plays, reconciled at last in the romances.

D. G. James's chapter on the last plays in his book *Scepticism and Poetry* is called 'The Failure of the Ballad Makers'; Shakespeare does not, he believes, achieve the proper symbolic language for his vision of the loss and recovery of spiritual possessions. James is specially interesting on the symbol of royalty.

Richard Wincor's essay 'Shakespeare's Festival Plays' may seem a little elementary now, but as an undergraduate prize essay at Harvard in 1942 it is a most surprising achievement. Wincor suggested that the last plays are related to the folk festival plays which survived until this century in Europe, and which probably had their origins in the most ancient religious rituals; he emphasized particularly the relevance of the Mock Death and Cure in folk plays.

Finally in this section we may mention Derek Traversi's *Shakespeare: The Last Phase*. This is a standard work for criticism of its kind. Traversi gives his own definition of symbolism and shows how Shakespeare creates plays to show an organic relation between breakdown and reconciliation. He is particularly good on *Pericles*. He seems to feel that *The Winter's Tale* is the crown of the romances—better than *The Tempest*. Traversi seems to me at times to confuse insight and moral education and I do not now want to labour the point which I made in my earlier survey that to treat the plays as symbolic utterances is by no means always to deepen and enrich them.

A not recondite answer to the importunate question is that Shakespeare wrote these romances because he needed a different form of drama in order to say something different. Quiller-Couch put the point as well as anyone in his *Shakespeare's Workmanship* of 1918. The Shakespeare who had done everything possible set out to do the impossible: to transfer into the brevity of a play the long-drawn-out process of repentance, forgiveness, reconciliation. In *Shakespeare's Last Plays*, E. M. W. Tillyard argued the thesis that essentially the romances are a working out of the third and last stage of the tragic cycle: prosperity, destruction, and regeneration. Although the work is too schematic, it has been properly influential in its claim that the last works are not a breakaway from Shakespeare's tragic world, but an extension of it. For both these critics the romances belong to a *late* period of Shakespeare's art and not just a new period. Ever since the romances have been discussed, interpretation has been entwined with imaginative biography. Shakespeare as Prospero is the icon, and 'Is it not thus that we should imagine him in the last years of his life?' (Strachey) is the motto. Dowden, as we have seen, heads the school of those who see Shakespeare reaching peace after passing through the fire of the tragedies; one might add to his school Walter Raleigh's *Shakespeare* and Morton Luce's introduction to the old Arden *Tempest*. Sir Edmund Chambers made the last major statement of this view in 1925 in *Shakespeare: A Survey*. As against Tillyard, he sees the move to the romances as a fundamental break, and supposes that Shakespeare had had a complete breakdown. Having been nursed back to health by his son-in-law, John Hall, he had something like a conversion; his mind was at peace with itself and in the last plays the world is the ordered and sunlit garden of God. John Dover Wilson in *The Essential Shakespeare* objected to the crudity of this; like Quiller-Couch, he sees the ageing Shakespeare as the past master of drama struggling to stretch the boundaries of art still further. Retirement to Stratford is certainly involved; Dover Wilson thinks Shakespeare was physically moving away from the theatres as he was moving away from plays to the non-dramatic poetry he would have written had he lived. He claims we can only understand Shakespeare's development in these last years if we compare the history of his peers, other great artists like Beethoven and Dostoevsky, who have moved into mysterious new regions of art in their later years. Comparisons with the 'last periods' of other writers and artists have often been fruitfully made: Kenneth Muir has a book devoted to the subject, *Last Periods of Shakespeare, Racine and Ibsen*; the introduction makes further helpful comparisons with the later work of Strindberg and Yeats.

We have already seen Lytton Strachey reacting violently, not against the biographical school, because he is a deep-dyed 'biographer', but against the notion of serenity. Many people now feel that the particular glory of the romances is their fragile chiaroscuro, where the dark is always threatening the light and the light is the more luminous for the surrounding dark. And many people have followed Strachey in attributing the unease and uncertainty that lurk in these last plays to the psyche of the writer. Two essays by Clifford Leech in *Shakespeare's Tragedies* investigate the 'puritanic tinge' of the last plays and the 'moral exhaustion' with which *The Tempest* ends. C. L. Barber's essay (mentioned earlier) hints rather than states that the psycho-sexual problems which he sees in *Pericles* and *The Winter's Tale* are primarily Shakespeare's. (See also Barbara Melchiori's essay, 'Still Harping on My Daughter', and Roy Fuller's poem mentioned below.)

An important fact about the romances is that they seem to have had a special attraction for other poets and writers. It is chiefly *The*

Tempest but not *The Tempest* only. In 'With a Guitar, to Jane', Shelley writes as Ariel to Miranda; Browning gives us the theological musings of 'Caliban upon Setebos'; Renan wrote a sequel (*Caliban*) to *The Tempest* in which Caliban represents the uncontrollable force of nineteenth-century democracy. 'Marina', T. S. Eliot's response to *Pericles*, is a most beautiful and poignant poem. W. H. Auden's 'The Sea and the Mirror', published in *For the Time Being*, is 'a commentary on Shakespeare's *The Tempest*'. Louis MacNeice has his 'Autolycus'. Roy Fuller has several poems which are essentially meditations on the last plays; the best is 'The Final Period', in which the old artist forces his rebellious mood into 'some utopia of forgiving'—

> Frozen in their betrothal kiss
> The innocent boy will never move
> To loose the codpiece, and his miss
> Stay spellbound in her father's love . . .

But perhaps the most important of these contributions is not a poem or a play or a novel, but a formal critical introduction, which Henry James wrote to *The Tempest* in 1907. Here the master, at sixty-four, expresses his bafflement that Shakespeare should have stopped writing at forty-six, when he was obviously at the height of his powers. He is led on to think of the total inscrutability of Shakespeare the man, and feels that he is never nearer to Shakespeare than when, having shown in *The Tempest* a quite new power and energy, freed from every compromise and sacrifice he has formerly had to make, and at last totally dedicated to his art—he commits the finally incomprehensible gesture of giving up writing.

ADDITIONAL STUDIES OF INDIVIDUAL PLAYS
'Pericles'
Questions of text and authorship precede all assessments of the value of *Pericles* or interpretations of any kind. My own study of the text in 'An Approach to the Problem of *Pericles*' suggested that the corruption was not only very extensive but was of more than one kind; I argued that it was possible that *Pericles* as performed could have been a coherent piece written by one author. Full discussions of the problems of text and authorship will be found in the introductions to the three editions recommended in the first section of this survey. A convenient reprint of the enigmatic *Painfull Adventures of Pericles Prince of Tyre* by George Wilkins, advancing itself as 'The true

History of the Play of *Pericles*', was edited by Kenneth Muir with an introduction in 1953; it almost certainly contains portions of the performed *Pericles* omitted from the corrupt Quarto. Volume vi of Bullough's *Narrative and Dramatic Sources* does well by *Pericles*, giving not only Wilkins but an interesting essay on the 'verse-fossils' in Wilkins, as well as the Pericles/Apollonius story as given in Gower and Twine. A. H. Smyth's *Shakespeare's 'Pericles' and Apollonius of Tyre* is a valuable study of the history of the widespread folk-tale which is the play's main source. G. A. Barker's 'Themes and Variations in *Pericles*' examines the changes in the traditional story which the play makes. There are very many studies of the authorship problem: Kenneth Muir's *Shakespeare as Collaborator* should be consulted.

A number of the general studies of the romances show how important *Pericles* is as the gateway to the other plays: the studies of Danby, Traversi, Wilson Knight, M. C. Bradbrook, and Kermode are recommended. John Arthos considers the important question of the adjustment of narrative and drama in '*Pericles, Prince of Tyre: A Study in the Dramatic Use of Romantic Narrative*'. Hoeniger's introduction to the new Arden edition makes an interesting connection with medieval saints' plays.

'*Cymbeline*'

Though they are of an entirely different kind, the problems of *Cymbeline* are as severe as those of *Pericles*. There is, unfortunately, no doubt that Shakespeare wrote it, although the vision of Jupiter was suspect until Wilson Knight gave it what still seems excessive praise. *Pericles* is just the play we want—but the text is all wrong; *Cymbeline* is all text and no play. Bernard Shaw's hilarious review of the famous Henry Irving–Ellen Terry production at the Lyceum in 1896 is well worth reading, as are his letters to Ellen Terry trying to help her in her perplexing role of Imogen; both are given by Edwin Wilson in *Shaw on Shakespeare*. As actress and theatre-critic confer, it becomes clear that the central impossibility is Imogen's awakening by the headless Cloten. Fifty years later Shaw did his best for Shakespeare by rewriting the last act for him: this Wilson also includes. Granville-Barker's 1930 preface to *Cymbeline*, which I have already mentioned, still makes a good introduction to the play. Granville-Barker gives us the keynote of modern criticism in suggesting that the 'mature and rather wearied' Shakespeare was going in for an ostentatious display of naïve showmanship. Nosworthy's very interesting introduction to the new Arden *Cymbeline* sees Shakespeare responding with enthusiasm to the structural challenge of tragicomic romance and yet reaching out to a transcendent world at the very end of the play. A. C. Kirsch's '*Cymbeline* and Coterie Dramaturgy' is an extension of this point of view. All the discontinuities, deceptions, and surprises in the play show Shakespeare mockingly exploring the tragicomic mode of the private theatres and still being able to deal seriously with loss, rebirth, and redemption.

J. P. Brockbank's 'History and Histrionics in *Cymbeline*' is an original and interesting, though tentative, examination of the sources to see if *they* can reveal what Shakespeare was up to in this puzzling play; his examples of what use was made by contemporaries of those early parts of Holinshed are most helpful. He notes, as Northrop Frye had done in 1948, the importance of Cymbeline's reign being contemporaneous with the birth of Christ. This fact is the centre of Emrys Jones's ingenious 'Stuart *Cymbeline*'. Wilson Knight had emphasized the importance of the interweaving of Rome and Britain in the play, and the final peace; Jones moves on from there to suggest an identification of Cymbeline and James I as peacemakers with Christ the Prince of Peace behind the play all the time. Jones also suggests that the prominence of Milford Haven is a tribute to the unification of Britain under James—worked hard for by the Tudors.

'*The Winter's Tale*'

Fitzroy Pyle's *The Winter's Tale: A Commentary on the Structure* is an observant and wise 'companion' to the play; it is perhaps at fault in believing that Shakespeare can do no wrong, but its discussions of Shakespeare's alterations of Greene's *Pandosto* are all good. Among its smaller attentions is the matter of whether Hermione should be seen to be pregnant in Act I, Scene ii. S. L. Bethell's *The Winter's Tale: A Study* is a thoroughgoing Christian interpretation. The use of romance to inculcate Christian theology is well established enough, and Bethell's thesis should not be rejected out of hand; he has in any case interesting things to say about the play as he proceeds.

Northrop Frye's contributions to the study of *The Winter's Tale* have been discussed earlier. Other 'mythic' interpretations of the fertility ritual are by F. C. Tinkler in *Scrutiny*, by F. D. Hoeniger, and by Paul Arnold.

Three features of *The Winter's Tale* which have evoked a great deal of debate are: the sudden onrush of Leontes's jealousy; the argument on art and nature between Perdita and Polixenes; and the statue scene in which Hermione is restored to Leontes. The first is a matter of psychological credibility and has been interestingly dealt with from a Freudian point of view by J. I. M. Stewart in *Character and Motive in Shakespeare*, followed by A. D. Nuttall in *William Shakespeare: 'The Winter's Tale'*, and by C. L. Barber in the study mentioned earlier. On the second, H. S. Wilson's 'Nature and Art in *The Winter's Tale*' succinctly describes the philosophic background. On the theatrical effectiveness of the last scene I am prepared to surrender my own scepticism in view of the very interesting comments of nineteenth-century theatre-goers—and Helen Faucit herself—collected by Kenneth Muir in *Shakespeare: 'The Winter's Tale': A Casebook*.

A valuable study of the language of *The Winter's Tale* is contained in M. M. Mahood's *Shakespeare's Wordplay*. In '*The Winter's Tale* and Jacobean Society' Charles Barber makes a lonely and brave attempt to relate the play to the processes of social change in seventeenth-century England.

'*The Tempest*'

A short account of the long history of allegorical interpretations of *The Tempest* is given in A. D. Nuttall's book, *Two Concepts of Allegory*. Nuttall makes *The Tempest* the centre of a philosophical discussion of allegory which is rapid and energetic in pursuit but somewhat tame in its conclusions. A standard allegorical interpretation of the early part of this century is Churton Collins's 'Poetry and Symbolism'. It was this kind of criticism which Elmer Edgar Stoll attacked in a famous essay in *PMLA* in 1932; he chiefly disliked the identification of Prospero saying good-bye to his art with Shakespeare and the 'now traditional expository style of "He too had" '. The positive side of his essay is his insistence that Ariel, Caliban, and the magician Prospero are not at all mysterious creatures who *have* to be interpreted but standard fictional beings of the Elizabethan era. Colin Still's historically important attempt to read *The Tempest* as a new rendering of mankind's perennial myth of initiation and redemption shows the river of allegorical interpretation finding a new channel as Stoll tries to block the old.

It is always interesting when two branches of criticism unite. In the general part of this survey, I spoke of the work done on the last plays and the nature of romance, especially in its pastoral form. Kermode's introduction to the new Arden edition (a good introduction to the play) examines in detail how the conventions of pastoral comedy enable Shakespeare to explore the distinctive roles and values of art, nature, and nurture. There has also been for a very long time a great interest in *The Tempest* as a play about the New

World and the problems of the colonists as they confronted its inhabitants. In 'Shakespeare's American Fable', the second chapter of his book *The Machine in the Garden*, Leo Marx marries the pastoral and the New World, and by placing *The Tempest* at the head of the great tradition of the American pastoral he gives an original focus to the play. From its beginning, he suggests, the pastoral is always conscious of the reality which threatens its ideal peace and simplicity. And from the beginning also, the Old World met the New with a combination of wonder at the realization of the Golden Age and terror of the ferocity of the natives and untamed elements. Marx sees Shakespeare satirizing the primitivism of Montaigne and Gonzalo, and he takes a rather rosy view of Prospero's taming of the wilderness and wild man by effort and science; but he sees Shakespeare also insisting that civilization needs baptism in the values of simple and instinctual life. So in its ambiguous treatment of the values of the wilderness, and its final optimism about man, refreshed by simplicity, taming the wild by science, *The Tempest* 'anticipates the moral geography of the American imagination'.

For most people these days, the really unforgettable speech in the play is likely to be Caliban's outcry against his master in Act I, Scene ii ending 'You taught me language, and my profit on't / Is, I know how to curse', rather than Prospero's speech in Act IV which includes 'We are such stuff / As dreams are made on.' A very much more sombre view than Marx's of the relations between Prospero and Caliban is given in O. Mannoni's fascinating *Prospero and Caliban: The Psychology of Colonisation*, originally published in France in 1950. The colonial, says Mannoni, goes into exile from his own people because he cannot adjust to them; he can only relate to others in a form of dual domination which every colony provides; he needs on the one hand will-less, sexless, devoted servants, and on the other a populace to be regarded as hostile, to be dominated by force, on to whom he projects, as infamies, all his suppressed longings. Mannoni is astonished to find Shakespeare creating in Prospero, Ariel, and Caliban a myth of the colonial situation before it properly existed. Prospero's harsh treatment of Caliban for having tried to violate his daughter seems to him the archetype of the colonial's irrational punishment of the native for sexual proclivities which exist in fact deep in the colonial's mind. Caliban's big speech talking of initial kindness then rejection seems to Mannoni also centrally true to the dependence-psychology of the native. The colonized longs to become the equal of the colonial and fears above all the rejection and abandonment which plunges him into inferiority.

Another study of the 'colonial aspect' of *The Tempest* which is interesting on Caliban is D. G. James's *The Dream of Prospero*; Shakespeare could have learned about the religion of the Indians and may have been influenced by what he learned in making Caliban primordial man living in a god-filled world. In '*The Tempest*: Conventions of Art and Empire', Philip Brockbank argues that the Bermuda pamphlets, like *The Tempest*, show a concern for order and discipline in the face of man's permanent tendency to brutishness and anarchy, and an abiding belief in the hand of providence behind mishap and disaster.

To conclude with some miscellaneous studies: W. C. Curry's *Shakespeare's Philosophical Patterns* is helpful on Prospero's magic; R. A. Brower's study of the play's metaphoric patterns in *The Fields of Light* well illustrates the extraordinary echoic nature of the play and the intricacy of its verbal interweaving; D. C. Allen's chapter on *The Tempest* in *Image and Meaning* compares the moral meaning of the journey to Prospero's island with those given to other island-journeys in world literature from Homer to Ariosto; Bernard Knox in '*The Tempest* and the Ancient Comic Tradition' claims that the play is 'the most rigidly traditional of all Shakespeare's comedies' except *The Comedy of Errors*, and shows its links with Plautus, Terence, and Menander.

REFERENCES

TEXTS

Greg, W. W. (ed.), *Pericles 1609* (Shakespeare Quarto Facsimiles 5, London 1940, Oxford, 1963.)

Hoeniger, F. D. (ed.), *Pericles* (new Arden Shakespeare, London, 1963).

Maxwell, J. C. (ed.), *Pericles, Prince of Tyre* (New Cambridge Shakespeare, Cambridge, 1956).

Schanzer, Ernest (ed.), *Pericles, Prince of Tyre* (Signet Shakespeare, New York, 1965).

Maxwell, J. C. (ed.), *Cymbeline* (New Cambridge Shakespeare, Cambridge, 1960).

Nosworthy, J. M. (ed.), *Cymbeline* (new Arden Shakespeare, London, 1955).

Pafford, J. H. P. (ed.), *The Winter's Tale* (new Arden Shakespeare, London, 1963).

Schanzer, Ernest (ed.), *The Winter's Tale* (New Penguin Shakespeare, Harmondsworth, 1969).

Righter (Barton), Anne (ed.), *The Tempest* (New Penguin Shakespeare, Harmondsworth, 1968).

Kermode, Frank (ed.), *The Tempest* (new Arden Shakespeare, London, 1954).

Quiller-Couch, A. T., and Wilson, John Dover (eds.), *The Tempest* (New Cambridge Shakespeare, Cambridge, 1921).

THE ROMANCES AS A GROUP

Chronology

Chambers, E. K., *William Shakespeare: A Study of Facts and Problems*, 2 vols. (Oxford, 1930).

Coleridge, S. T., *Shakespearean Criticism*, ed. T. M. Raysor, 2 vols. (Cambridge, Mass., 1930; Everyman's Library, London, 1960).

Collier, J. P., *Further Particulars Regarding Shakespeare and his Works* (London, 1839).

——, Introduction to *The Painfull Adventures of Pericles*, ed. T. Mommsen, (Oldenburg, 1857).

Dowden, Edward, *Shakspere: A Critical Study of his Mind and Art* (London, 1875).

——, *Shakspere* (Literature Primers, London, 1877).

Dyce, Alexander (ed.), *The Works of Shakespeare* (2nd edn., London, vol. viii, 1866).

Malone, Edmond, *Supplement to the Edition of Shakespeare's Plays Published in 1778 by Samuel Johnson and George Steevens* (London, 1780).

Schoenbaum, S., *Shakespeare's Lives* (Oxford, 1970).

Histories of Criticism, Special Collections, and Studies

Brown, J. R., and Harris, B. (eds.), *Later Shakespeare* (Stratford-upon-Avon Studies 8, London, 1966).

Edwards, Philip, 'Shakespeare's Romances: 1900–1957', *Shakespeare Survey 11* (1958).

Frye, Northrop, *A Natural Perspective: The Development of Shakespearean Comedy and Romance* (New York, 1965).

Hunter, R. G., *Shakespeare and the Comedy of Forgiveness* (New York, 1965).

Kermode, Frank, *Shakespeare: The Final Plays* (Writers and their Work, No. 155, London, 1963).

Knight, G. Wilson, *The Crown of Life: Essays in Interpretation of Shakespeare's Final Plays* (London, 1947).

Marsh, D. R. C., *The Recurring Miracle: A Study of 'Cymbeline' and the Last Plays* (Pietermaritzburg, 1962).

Palmer, D. J. (ed.), *Shakespeare's Later Comedies: An Anthology of Modern Criticism* (Penguin Shakespeare Library, Harmondsworth, 1971).

Tillyard, E. M. W., *Shakespeare's Last Plays* (London, 1938).

Traversi, Derek, *Shakespeare: The Last Phase* (London, 1954).

Criticism and Commentary

Adams, J. Q., *A Life of William Shakespeare* (London, 1923).

Auden, W. H., 'The Sea and the Mirror', in *For The Time Being* (London, 1945).

Barber, C. L., ' "Thou that beget'st him that did thee beget": Transformation in *Pericles* and *The Winter's Tale*', *Shakespeare Survey 22* (1969).

Bentley, G. E., 'Shakespeare and the Blackfriars Theatre', *Shakespeare Survey 1* (1948).

Bradbrook, M. C., *The Growth and Structure of Elizabethan Comedy* (London, 1955).

Browning, Robert, 'Caliban upon Setebos; or, Natural Theology in the Island', in *Dramatis Personae* (*Poetical Works*, London, 1889, vol. vi).

Chambers, E. K., *Shakespeare: A Survey* (London, 1925).

Cruttwell, Patrick, *The Shakspearean Moment and its Place in the Poetry of the Seventeenth Century* (London, 1954).

Danby, J. F., *Poets on Fortune's Hill: Studies in Sidney, Shakespeare, Beaumont and Fletcher* (London, 1952; later retitled *Elizabethan and Jacobean Poets*).

Dowden, Edward, *Shakspere: A Critical Study of his Mind and Art* (London, 1875).

Eliot, T. S., 'Marina', *Collected Poems 1909–1935* (London, 1936, etc.).

Foakes, R. A. (ed.), *King Henry VIII* (new Arden Shakespeare, London, 1957).

Frye, Northrop, *Anatomy of Criticism* (Princeton, N.J., 1957).

——, 'The Argument of Comedy', in *English Institute Essays 1948* (New York, 1949).

——, *A Natural Perspective: The Development of Shakespearean Comedy and Romance* (New York, 1965).

——, 'Recognition in *The Winter's Tale*', in *Essays on Shakespeare and Elizabethan Drama in Honor of Hardin Craig* (Columbia, Mo., 1962).

Fuller, Roy, *Collected Poems, 1936–61* (London, 1962).

Gesner, Carol, *Shakespeare and the Greek Romance: A Study of Origins* (Lexington, Ky., 1970).

Granville-Barker, Harley, '*Cymbeline*' (*Prefaces to Shakespeare*, Second Series, London, 1930).

Harbage, Alfred, *Shakespeare and the Rival Traditions* (New York, 1952).

James, D. G., *Scepticism and Poetry* (London, 1937).

James, Henry, Introduction to *The Tempest* (University Press Shakespeare, Renaissance Edition, 1907, vol. xvi); repr. in Shakespeare, *The Tempest: A Casebook*, ed. D. J. Palmer (London, 1968).

Johnson, Samuel, *Samuel Johnson on Shakespeare*, ed. W. K. Wimsatt (New York, 1960; repr. as *Dr. Johnson on Shakespeare*, Penguin Shakespeare Library, Harmondsworth, 1969).

Jonson, Ben, 'Come leave the loathèd stage', in *Works*, ed. Herford and Simpson, vol. vi (Oxford, 1938).

Kirsch, A. C., '*Cymbeline* and Coterie Dramaturgy', *ELH*, 34 (1967); repr. in *Shakespeare's Later Comedies*, ed. D. J. Palmer (Penguin Shakespeare Library, Harmondsworth, 1971).

Knight, G. Wilson, *Myth and Miracle* (London, 1929; included in *The Crown of Life*, London, 1947).

——, *The Shakespearian Tempest* (London, 1932).

Leavis, F. R., 'The Criticism of Shakespeare's Last Plays: A Caveat', *Scrutiny*, 10 (1942; repr. in *The Common Pursuit*, London, 1952).

Leech, Clifford, *Shakespeare's Tragedies and Other Studies in Seventeenth Century Drama* (London, 1950).

Luce, Morton, Introduction to *The Tempest* ([Old] Arden Shakespeare, London, 1902).

MacNeice, Louis, 'Autolycus', in *Collected Poems* (London, 1966).

Melchiori, Barbara, 'Still Harping on My Daughter', *English Miscellany* (Rome, 1960).

Muir, Kenneth, *Last Periods of Shakespeare, Racine and Ibsen* (Liverpool, 1961).

Nosworthy, J. M., Introduction to *Cymbeline* (new Arden Shakespeare, London, 1955).

Pettet, E. C., *Shakespeare and the Romance Tradition* (London, 1949).

Proudfoot, Richard, 'Shakespeare and the New Dramatists', in *Later Shakespeare* (Stratford-upon-Avon Studies 8, ed. J. R. Brown and B. Harris, London, 1966).

Quiller-Couch, Arthur, *Shakespeare's Workmanship* (London, 1918).

Raleigh, Walter, *Shakespeare* (London, 1907).

Renan, Ernest, *Caliban*, in *Drames Philosophiques*, 1888 (*Œuvres complètes*, Paris, 1949, vol. iii).

Ristine, F. H., *English Tragicomedy: Its Origin and History* (New York, 1910).

Seltzer, Daniel, 'The Staging of the Last Plays', in *Later Shakespeare* (Stratford-upon-Avon Studies 8, ed. J. R. Brown and B. Harris, London, 1966).

Shaw, George Bernard, *Shaw on Shakespeare*, ed. E. Wilson (New York, 1961; Penguin Shakespeare Library, Harmondsworth, 1969).

Shelley, P. B., 'With a Guitar, to Jane', *Complete Poetical Works*, ed. T. Hutchinson (London, 1905, etc.).

Still, Colin, *Shakespeare's Mystery Play; A Study of 'The Tempest'* (London, 1921; enlarged version published as *The Timeless Theme*, London, 1936).

Strachey, Lytton, 'Shakespeare's Final Period', *Independent Review*, 3 (1904; repr. in *Books and Characters*, London, 1922, and *Literary Essays*, London, 1948).

Thorndike, A. S., *The Influence of Beaumont and Fletcher upon Shakespeare* (Worcester, Mass., 1901).

Tillyard, E. M. W., *Shakespeare's Last Plays* (London, 1938).

Traversi, Derek, *Shakespeare: The Last Phase* (London, 1954).

Wells, Stanley, 'Shakespeare and Romance', in *Later Shakespeare* (Stratford-upon-Avon Studies 8, ed. J. R. Brown and B. Harris, London, 1966); repr. in *Shakespeare's Later Comedies*, ed. D. J. Palmer (Penguin Shakespeare Library, Harmondsworth, 1971).

Wilson, J. Dover, *The Essential Shakespeare: A Biographical Adventure* (Cambridge, 1932).

Wincor, Richard, 'Shakespeare's Festival Plays', *Shakespeare Quarterly*, 1 (1950).

ADDITIONAL STUDIES OF INDIVIDUAL PLAYS
'Pericles'

Arthos, John, *'Pericles, Prince of Tyre*: A Study in the Dramatic Use of Romantic Narrative', *Shakespeare Quarterly*, 4 (1953).

Barker, G. A., 'Themes and Variations in *Pericles', English Studies*, 44 (1963); repr. in *Shakespeare's Later Comedies* ed. D. J. Palmer (Penguin Shakespeare Library, Harmondsworth, 1971).

Bullough, Geoffrey, *Narrative and Dramatic Sources of Shakespeare*, vol. vi (London, 1966).

Edwards, Philip, 'An Approach to the Problem of *Pericles', Shakespeare Survey 5* (Cambridge, 1952).

Muir, Kenneth, *Shakespeare as Collaborator* (London, 1960).

——, ed., *The Painfull Adventures of Pericles Prince of Tyre*, by George Wilkins (Liverpool, 1953).

Smyth, A. H., *Shakespeare's 'Pericles' and Apollonius of Tyre* (Philadelphia, Pa., 1898).

'Cymbeline'

Brockbank, J. P., 'History and Histrionics in *Cymbeline', Shakespeare Survey 11* (1958).

Granville-Barker, Harley, *'Cymbeline'*, in *Prefaces to Shakespeare*, Second Series (London, 1930).

Jones, Emrys, 'Stuart *Cymbeline', Essays in Criticism* 11 (1961); repr. in *Shakespeare's Later Comedies*, ed. D. J. Palmer (Penguin Shakespeare Library, Harmondsworth, 1971).

Kirsch, A. C., *'Cymbeline* and Coterie Dramaturgy', *ELH*, 34 (1967); repr. in *Shakespeare's Later Comedies*, ed. D. J. Palmer (Penguin Shakespeare Library, Harmondsworth 1971).

Shaw, Bernard, *Shaw on Shakespeare*, ed. E. Wilson (New York, 1961; Penguin Shakespeare Library, Harmondsworth, 1969).

'The Winter's Tale'

Arnold, Paul, 'Ésoterisme du *Conte d'hiver', Mercure de France*, 318 (1953).

Barber, Charles, *'The Winter's Tale* and Jacobean Society', in *Shakespeare in a Changing World*, ed. A. Kettle (London, 1964).

Bethell, S. L., *The Winter's Tale: A Study* (London, 1947).

Hoeniger, F. D., 'The Meaning of *The Winter's Tale', University of Toronto Quarterly*, 20 (1950).

Mahood, M. M., *Shakespeare's Wordplay* (London, 1957).

Muir, Kenneth (ed.), *Shakespeare: 'The Winter's Tale': A Casebook* (London, 1968).

Nuttall, A. D., *William Shakespeare: The Winter's Tale* (Studies in English Literature 26, London, 1966).

Pyle, Fitzroy, *'The Winter's Tale': A Commentary on the Structure* (London, 1969).

Stewart, J. I. M., *Character and Motive in Shakespeare: Some Recent Appraisals Examined* (London, 1949).

Tinkler, F. C., '*The Winter's Tale*', *Scrutiny*, 5 (1937).

Wilson, H. S., 'Nature and Art in *The Winter's Tale*', *Shakespeare Association Bulletin*, 18 (1943).

'*The Tempest*'

Allen, D. C., *Image and Meaning: Metaphoric Traditions in Renaissance Poetry* (Baltimore, Md., 1960; 2nd edn., 1965).

Brockbank, J. P., '*The Tempest*: Conventions of Art and Empire', in *Later Shakespeare* (Stratford-upon-Avon Studies 8, ed. J. R. Brown and B. Harris, London, 1966).

Brower, R. A., *The Fields of Light: An Experiment in Critical Reading* (New York, 1951).

Churton Collins, J., 'Poetry and Symbolism: A Study of *The Tempest*', *Contemporary Review*, 93 (1908).

Curry, W. C., *Shakespeare's Philosophical Patterns* (Baton Rouge, La., 1937).

James, D. G., *The Dream of Prospero* (Oxford, 1967).

Knox, Bernard, '*The Tempest* and the Ancient Comic Tradition', in *English Stage Comedy* (English Institute Essays 1954, ed. W. K. Wimsatt, New York, 1955).

Mannoni, O., *Prospero and Caliban: The Psychology of Colonisation*, trans. P. Powesland (New York, 1956; originally published as *Psychologie de la colonisation*, Paris, 1960).

Marx, Leo, *The Machine in the Garden: Technology and the Pastoral Ideal in America* (New York, 1964).

Nuttall, A. D., *Two Concepts of Allegory: A Study of Shakespeare's 'The Tempest' and the Logic of Allegorical Expression* (London, 1967).

Still, Colin, *Shakespeare's Mystery Play: A Study of 'The Tempest'* (London, 1921; enlarged version published as *The Timeless Theme*, London, 1936).

Stoll, E. E., '*The Tempest*', *PMLA*, 47 (1932).

9. *Titus Andronicus* and *Romeo and Juliet*

G. R. HIBBARD

These two plays have certain things in common: they are the earliest of the plays included among the Tragedies in the First Folio of 1623; each had appeared in print before 1600; both seem to have been popular on the Elizabethan stage; neither receives more than a passing mention in A. C. Bradley's *Shakespearean Tragedy*. Nevertheless, they are so different in kind, and their fortunes both on the stage and in the study during the last three hundred years have been so diverse, that they ask for separate treatment.

Titus Andronicus

TEXTS

The two most important modern editions are those by J. Dover Wilson and J. C. Maxwell. Each has a comprehensive textual apparatus, a full and informative commentary, and a substantial introduction. Since these editors disagree over a number of fundamental issues, there is no readier way of recognizing some of the main problems the play raises than to consult both. A good plain text is to be found in Peter Alexander's edition of the *Complete Works*; and the edition by Gustav Cross is equipped with brief but useful explanatory footnotes. All editions prior to 1936 are unreliable, because they are not based on the First Quarto of the play which came out in 1594. This quarto survives in a unique copy discovered in Sweden in 1904 and now in the Folger Shakespeare Library. It was the publication of a facsimile of this quarto, edited by J. Q. Adams, in 1936, that first made the text generally available to editors.

CRITICISM AND COMMENTARY

Up to a little more than thirty years ago practically everything that was written about *Titus Andronicus* was devoted to a consideration of two interrelated problems which are not yet completely solved: its authenticity and its date. A judicious and accurate account of these matters is given by Maxwell in his edition, but something must be said here about the question of authenticity, because it has profoundly affected judgements on the play and been affected by them. Normally the evidence for Shakespeare's sole authorship—the fact that it was attributed to him by Francis Meres in his *Palladis Tamia* (1598), and its inclusion in the First Folio—would be accepted as decisive; but *Titus Andronicus* happens to be the one play of the First Folio about which doubts were voiced in the seventeenth century. In 1687 the Restoration playwright Edward Ravenscroft published an adaptation of it which held the stage down to 1725, and stated in his preface that he had 'been told by some anciently conversant with the Stage, that it was not his [Shakespeare's], but brought by a private Author to be Acted, and he only gave some Master-touches to one or two of the Principal Parts or Characters', adding, 'this I am apt to believe, because 'tis the most incorrect and indigested piece in all his Works; It seems rather a heap of Rubbish than a Structure.'

This story of the play's origin was eagerly seized on by editors and critics of the eighteenth and nineteenth centuries, since it relieved Shakespeare of the responsibility for a play which they too saw as 'a heap of Rubbish'. Dr. Johnson spoke for most when he wrote: 'All the editors and criticks agree with Mr. *Theobald* in supposing this play spurious. . . . That Shakespeare wrote any part . . . I see no reason for believing.' As more was discovered about Elizabethan drama generally, there developed in the late nineteenth and early twentieth centuries a kind of learned parlour game in which critics vied with one another in assigning wholes or parts of Shakespeare's plays, and especially *Titus Andronicus*, to Peele, Greene, Kyd, Marlowe and so forth on so-called stylistic grounds. The game went merrily on until 1924, when E. K. Chambers made a devastating attack on the methods being employed, following it up a year later by devoting a chapter in his *Shakespeare: A Survey* to the specific case of *Titus Andronicus*. The conclusion he came to was that until more verifiable evidence than had yet been adduced could be brought to bear on the problem there were no solid grounds for doubting Shakespeare's authorship.

This was the real turning-point in the critical history of the play. In 1943 Hereward T. Price, in his 'The Authorship of *Titus Andronicus*', boldly asserted that Shakespeare was the sole author, basing his case on literary considerations. Far from being 'a heap of Rubbish', the structure of the play is, he argues, characteristically Shakespearian in its use of contrasts between character and character and between scene and scene. The plot is superior to anything that Shakespeare's early contemporaries were capable of. There are marked parallels between this experiment in tragic form and such later masterpieces as *Othello* and *King Lear*. Moreover, there is already in it the typical Shakespearian preoccupation with the relationship between the individual and the state. The influence of this splendid pioneering essay on later critics has been enormous. The view that the tragedy is ambitiously and masterfully plotted has become something of a commonplace among them. But editors have proved harder to convince. Dover Wilson, in his edition, not only holds that Act I was largely the work of George Peele but also considers that Peele was responsible for the main plan of the whole. Shakespeare's part in it was that of revising and remoulding the last four acts, a task which he carried out, Dover Wilson thinks, in 1593. Maxwell, however, while seeing signs of Peele's hand in Act I, regards the rest of the play as Shakespeare's, and would like to date it around 1590. Some additional weight has been given to this dating by R. F. Hill in his article 'The Composition of *Titus Andronicus*', where, after comparing the style with that of the Three Parts of *Henry VI*, he decides that 'if *Titus* is entirely Shakespeare's, it must have been written before the *Henry VI* plays.'

Another seminal study, as fruitful in its effect on later studies as Price's, appeared in 1939. Up to that date it had been generally assumed that J. W. Cunliffe was right in ascribing to Seneca the major influence on *Titus Andronicus*. Howard Baker, in Chapter III of his *Induction to Tragedy*, made a frontal attack on Cunliffe's position, maintaining that the play is in the tradition of English narrative tragedy (e.g. *A Mirror for Magistrates*), that it owes much to *The Spanish Tragedy*, and that it is indebted, above all, not to Seneca but to Ovid's account of the myth of Tereus and Philomel in the *Metamorphoses*. This recognition of Ovid as the chief formative agent on the drama has led to new insights. The view that the central theme of the play is the idea of metamorphosis is put in a most persuasive manner by Eugene M. Waith in his article 'The Metamorphosis of Violence in *Titus Andronicus*', where he argues that Titus, presented at the beginning as a man of absolute integrity, is transformed by the cruelties inflicted on him into a monster, and that the effect Shakespeare was seeking to produce on his audience was that sense of 'admiration' (wonder) which Sir Philip Sidney thought proper to tragedy.

A third line of interpretation was opened up by E. M. W. Tillyard in his *Shakespeare's History Plays* (1944), though he had been partially anticipated by Price. Convinced that the play is the sole work of Shakespeare, written very early in his career, Tillyard brings out its political implications, evident in its concern with 'the wounds of civil war and their cure', thus linking it with the English history plays which are the main subject of his book. Corroboration that the play is indeed a 'history', but of a peculiarly Elizabethan kind, is provided by T. J. B. Spencer in an article that combines learning with wit.

Yet another issue of importance was raised by M. C. Bradbrook in her *Shakespeare and Elizabethan Poetry*, in which she drew attention to the way in which the characters tend to become 'emblematic', and to the startling contrast between the violence of the action and 'the formal quality of the writing, which is learned, rhetorical, full of conceits'. In consequence, she holds, what happens on the stage is carefully distanced from the spectator, so that the final effect is that of a pageant rather than a play. Peter Brook's production of the play, with Sir Laurence Olivier in the title role, at Stratford-upon-Avon in 1955 did not bear out this last contention; but the contrast Professor Bradbrook sees is indubitably there and is one of the play's most intriguing features. An interesting and debatable attempt to elucidate its significance is that of C. L. Calderwood. He advances the theory that Shakespeare, the poet of *Venus and Adonis* and *The Rape of Lucrece*, wrote *Titus Andronicus* as a protest against having to sacrifice his art as a poet to 'the rude demands of the theater'.

With the growing confidence that *Titus Andronicus* is wholly or substantially Shakespeare's, there has developed among critics a greater readiness to look at it for what it is and for what it offers, instead of judging it in the light of Shakespeare's later achievement or of any monolithic notion of what tragedy ought to be. Alan Sommers emphasizes its preoccupation with justice, which Titus flouts in the first act, thus leaving the way open to the reign of injustice, which transforms Rome, hitherto the embodiment of civilization, into 'a wilderness of tigers'. In rather similar fashion Irving Ribner takes the line, in Chapter II of his *Patterns in Shakespearian Tragedy*, that it depicts man giving way to an excess of passion and thus making himself a beast. More questionably, in a play that is studiedly pagan in atmosphere, he argues that the hero 'moves towards inevitable damnation'. Particularly helpful, both in their fulness and their flexibility, are the chapters given over to the play in two recent books. A. C. Hamilton sets it in the context of all Shakespeare's early works, including the two narrative poems, with which it has so much in common; and Nicholas Brooke deals with it as the first of the six plays that he handles in his *Shakespeare's Early Tragedies*.

But, while critics over the last thirty years have provided many reasons for taking *Titus Andronicus* seriously, they have not found a wholly satisfactory answer, though Hamilton goes some way towards doing so, to the strictures of a voice that cannot be ignored. Dover Wilson, in the Introduction to his edition, puts the case against the play with picturesque force, saying that it 'seems to jolt and bump along like some broken-down cart, laden with bleeding corpses from an Elizabethan scaffold, and driven by an executioner from Bedlam dressed in cap and bells'. His verdict is that much in *Titus Andronicus* is designed as a burlesque of the popular revenge play.

Yet even Dover Wilson cannot resist the appeal of Aaron the Moor, whom all the critics find fascinating in his evolution—the reverse of Titus's—from monster to human being. It is this figure that Eldred Jones concentrates on, with very illuminating results, in the relevant section of his *Othello's Countrymen: The African in English Renaissance Drama*.

Romeo and Juliet

TEXTS

Of the older editions, the most useful is the New Variorum by H. H. Furness, since it contains a compilation of earlier commentary and criticism that is not easily accessible elsewhere. The most austere of modern editions is that by George Walton Williams. Designed for the scholar rather than the general reader, it preserves the spelling and the punctuation of the copy-text, the Second Quarto of 1599. A valuable feature is the Staging Notes. The following editions, both in modernized spelling, have good introductions and commentaries: by J. Dover Wilson and G. I. Duthie; by T. J. B. Spencer. Richard Hosley's edition has a useful commentary but no introduction.

CRITICISM AND COMMENTARY

Unlike *Titus Andronicus*, which has been the least performed of all Shakespeare's plays since the closing of the theatres in 1642, *Romeo and Juliet* has been one of the most popular on the stage. Only *Hamlet* has been performed more often. It has also attracted the attention of many critics. The consequences are most intriguing, for criticism of this play, read *in extenso*, tells one quite as much, if not more, about critics and their preconceptions as it does about the play.

One of the main reasons for the wide range of opinions that *Romeo and Juliet* has given rise to lies in the fact that it is, as H. B. Charlton among many others well points out, a highly original work. At a time when tragedy was regarded as the preserve of the great—kings, emperors, military leaders—Shakespeare chose to write a tragedy about two young people of no particular standing. Moreover, he wrote a tragedy about a love relationship, not about the fate of a country; and, on top of this, he conducted the first two acts in a vein that is predominantly comic. It is not until Mercutio is killed, in III. i, that tragedy really takes over. Nevertheless, there has been no hesitation on the part of critics in accepting the play as a tragedy of some kind. Dr. Johnson, who preferred the comic parts to the tragic because he deplored the fact that Shakespeare's characters 'however distressed, *have a conceit left them in their misery, a miserable conceit*', still found 'the catastrophe irresistibly affecting, and the process of the action carried on with such probability, at least with such congruity to popular opinions, as tragedy requires'.

But, granted that *Romeo and Juliet* is a tragedy, what sort of tragedy is it, and how successful a tragedy is it? Here there is indeed 'God's plenty' of views. Charlton demands of tragedy that it should give a sense of inevitability, and contends that Shakespeare sought to achieve this effect by making the feud between the two families the immediate cause of the disaster that overtakes the lovers, and fate, of which the feud is the agent, the ultimate cause. Having attributed this intention to Shakespeare, he then blames him for not making the feud the implacable rivalry that it should be, and for resorting to the old pagan deities of fate and fortune, which have neither the reality nor the authority that is needed. Thus, instead of being fated, Romeo and Juliet are merely unlucky, victims of accident not of design. There is no inevitability. The play is therefore, he concludes, imperfect as a tragic work of art.

To some extent Charlton was going over old ground which, as Gordon Ross Smith amply demonstrates in his essay 'The Balance of Themes in *Romeo and Juliet*', had already been well trodden in the nineteenth century, and he was not alone in doing so. Granville-Barker expresses a similar opinion in his Preface to the play, a piece of critical writing that still deserves study, because of the way in which it keeps the demands of the stage very much in mind. Since Charlton's book appeared both D. A. Stauffer, who sees the lovers as 'the innocent victims of a general moral order that operates with an inhuman, mechanical severity', and G. I. Duthie (in his introduction to the New Cambridge edition), who thinks that the dominant idea is that of a malicious fate, have endorsed his findings, though this is by no means all that they do.

In opposition to the interpretation outlined above stands another group of critics which seeks to pull the play into the Aristotelian pattern of tragedy by laying the responsibility for the disaster on the lovers themselves. Their fault, it is argued, is their impulsiveness, their total surrender to passion, evident especially in Romeo. The play is a tragedy of character not of fate. John Masefield, for example, defines the subject of the play as 'the storm in the blood'. Virgil K. Whitaker, quoting the Friar—regarded by critics of this persuasion as a choric figure whose function it is to guide the reactions of the audience—on the subject of the relationship between 'grace and rude will', charges Romeo with giving way to violence of passion; and Franklin M. Dickey, in an exhaustive consideration of the play which is by no means confined to this point, requires no fewer than sixteen pages in which to add up all the evidence that can be brought against Romeo.

In the nineteenth century there was no middle ground between those who thought the lovers were at fault and those who looked on them as patterns of true love, deserving unqualified admiration and approval. Critics in the mid-twentieth century are in an easier position, since they can evoke the blessed idea of order. Like Touchstone's 'If', it is 'the only peacemaker'. For Duthie, as for Dickey, the true principal actors in the drama are not the lovers but the warring families. It is they who are responsible for the final disaster, which is both a punishment on them for their sins and the cause of their reconciliation with each other. A similar idea, put with more flexibility, informs H. S. Wilson's interpretation in his book *On the Design of Shakespearian Tragedy*. Starting from a consideration of the play's structure, he notes that the action is divided into three parts by the three entrances of the Prince, and he goes on to maintain that the Prince is there to bring out the meaning of the whole, 'to show a chain of seeming accidents issuing in a moral design adumbrated in the sonnet-prologue, implicit from the beginning'. The entire action is, in the last analysis, under the control of Divine Providence, moving in its inscrutable way to turn hatred into love. But, while Dickey thinks that the play 'celebrates the great vision of order by which the English Renaissance still lives', Wilson and Duthie both admit that the Prince's final entrance comes as something of an anticlimax after the emotional climax of the lovers' deaths. Thus the completion of the total design goes unheeded. Once again Shakespeare has failed to carry out the intention his critics credit him with.

A new approach to the play, much less dependent on any theory of what tragedy is or ought to be, was initiated by Caroline Spurgeon in her *Shakespeare's Imagery and What It Tells Us* (1935). Seizing on 'light', the radiance that the lovers find in each other, as the dominant image in the play, she suggests that the experience conveyed is that of brilliance quickly quenched by darkness. The brilliance is, of course, the vivid lightning flash of love, set against the dark night of hatred by which it is surrounded. That the image of light is, in fact, the most important of the play's images has not been accepted by all who have approached it along these lines. But the notion that it is about great fundamental oppositions, about polarities which exist in relation to one another, has won wide support. Molly Mahood singles out the idea of Death as Juliet's lover as the true *leitmotif* of the play, posing the basic problem of whether Death chooses the lovers or whether they choose it. In her reading *Romeo and Juliet* ends in a tragic equilibrium, the frustration of the lovers by fate and the feud being balanced by the fulfilment they find in a permanent and unchangeable union with each other. Tragedy is paradox in action. This notion is carried further by Marion B. Smith in the chapter on *Romeo and Juliet* in her *Dualities in Shakespeare*. As she sees it, the entire play deals with elemental oppositions—love and hate, life and death, day and night—which are the very conditions of human existence. A somewhat similar idea about the close connection between love and death is expressed by Norman Rabkin in the section on the play in his *Shakespeare and the Common Understanding*, while John Lawlor, also much interested in the wordplay, holds that the truth lying at the heart of the play is that 'Death has no final power over the lovers.'

Two studies of the style of the drama support the idea that it is concerned with basic oppositions. In his penetrating article 'Form and Formality in *Romeo and Juliet*' Harry Levin establishes the naturalness of the lovers' diction in contradistinction to the stylization and artificiality of speech which dominate the rest of the play, seeing it as an index of their mutuality, 'the one organic relation amid an overplus of stylized expressions and attitudes'. The rhetorical devices with which the play abounds are the subject of a short book by Robert O. Evans, which emphasizes its extensive use of the oxymoron.

The general move away from such problems as that of whether *Romeo and Juliet* is a tragedy of fate or a tragedy of character is confirmed by readings such as that of A. C. Hamilton, who describes it as 'an anatomy of love' and rejects the notion that the healing of the feud is the central theme. Philip Edwards, in his *Shakespeare and the Confines of Art*, maintains that it is human actions, not an outside power, that cause things to turn out as they do, and that the play sets two worlds in conflict with each other: the place of rancour and irrational hostility, and the place of love. Nicholas Brooke concludes his examination of its preoccupations with contrast and paradox by calling it 'a highly perceptive exploration of the love–death embrace of the sonneteering tradition'. T. J. B. Spencer's account of the play in the Introduction to his edition is tolerant of other views and wide-ranging. Ill luck has its part in what happens; so have the choices the lovers make; but the centre of interest is love in all its various manifestations. H. A. Mason, in the three chapters he gives to *Romeo and Juliet* in his *Shakespeare's Tragedies of Love*, holds that what Shakespeare was doing was to dramatize his source, Arthur Brooke's poem *Romeus and Juliet* (1562), making the most of each incident in it, but not attempting to impose any total significance on it. It is a tempting conclusion, but before accepting it we do well to remember that Coleridge found the tragedy to be a work of art created by 'a single energy' and informed throughout by a 'totality of interest'.

REFERENCES

Bradley, A. C., *Shakespearean Tragedy* (London, 1904).

Titus Andronicus

TEXTS

Adams, J. Q. (ed.), *Titus Andronicus, 1594* (New York, 1936).

Alexander, Peter (ed.), *William Shakespeare: The Complete Works* (London, 1951).

Cross, Gustav (ed.), *Titus Andronicus* (Pelican Shakespeare, Baltimore, Md., 1967).

Maxwell, J. C. (ed.), *Titus Andronicus* (new Arden Shakespeare, London, 1953).

Wilson, John Dover (ed.), *Titus Andronicus* (New Cambridge Shakespeare, Cambridge, 1948).

CRITICISM AND COMMENTARY

Baker, Howard, *Induction to Tragedy: A Study in a Development of Form in 'Gorboduc', 'The Spanish Tragedy', and 'Titus Andronicus'* (Baton Rouge, La., 1939).

Bradbrook, M. C., *Shakespeare and Elizabethan Poetry* (London, 1951).

Brooke, Nicholas, *Shakespeare's Early Tragedies* (London, 1968).

Calderwood, C. L., *Shakespeare's Metadrama* (Minneapolis, Minn., 1971).

Chambers, E. K., *The Disintegration of Shakespeare*, British Academy Lecture 1924.

——, *Shakespeare: A Survey* (London, 1925).

Cunliffe, J. W., *The Influence of Seneca on Elizabethan Tragedy* (London, 1893).

Hamilton, A. C., *The Early Shakespeare* (San Marino, Calif., 1967).

Hill, R. F., 'The Composition of *Titus Andronicus*', *Shakespeare Survey 10* (1957).

Johnson, Samuel, *see* Raleigh, W., and Wimsatt, W. K.

Jones, Eldred, *Othello's Countrymen: The African in English Renaissance Drama* (London, 1965).

Price, Hereward T., 'The Authorship of *Titus Andronicus*', *JEGP*, 42 (1943); partially reprinted in *Shakespeare: The Tragedies*, ed. Alfred Harbage (Englewood Cliffs, N.J., 1964).

Raleigh, W. (ed.), *Dr. Johnson on Shakespeare* (London, 1908).

Ravenscroft, Edward, *Titus Andronicus, or The Rape of Lavinia* (London, 1687).

Ribner, Irving, *Patterns in Shakespearian Tragedy* (London, 1960).

Sommers, Alan, ' "Wilderness of Tigers": Structure and Symbolism in *Titus Andronicus*', *Essays in Criticism*, 10 (1960).

Spencer, T. J. B., 'Shakespeare and the Elizabethan Romans', *Shakespeare Survey 10* (1957).

Tillyard, E. M. W., *Shakespeare's History Plays* (London, 1944).

Waith, Eugene M., 'The Metamorphosis of Violence in *Titus Andronicus*', *Shakespeare Survey 10* (1957).

Wimsatt, W. K. (ed.), *Samuel Johnson on Shakespeare* (New York, 1960; repr. as *Dr. Johnson on Shakespeare*, Penguin Shakespeare Library, Harmondsworth, 1969).

Romeo and Juliet

TEXTS

Furness, H. H. (ed.), *Romeo and Juliet* (New Variorum Shakespeare, Philadelphia, Pa., 1871).

Hosley, R. (ed.), *Romeo and Juliet* (Yale Shakespeare, New Haven, Conn., 1954).

Spencer, T. J. B. (ed.), *Romeo and Juliet* (New Penguin Shakespeare, Harmondsworth, 1967).

Williams, G. W. (ed.), *Romeo and Juliet: A Critical Edition* (Durham, N.C., 1964).

Wilson, John Dover, and Duthie, G. I. (eds.), *Romeo and Juliet* (New Cambridge Shakespeare, Cambridge, 1955).

CRITICISM AND COMMENTARY

Brooke, Nicholas, *Shakespeare's Early Tragedies* (London, 1968).

Charlton, H. B., *Shakespearian Tragedy* (Cambridge, 1948).

Dickey, Franklin M., *Not Wisely But Too Well: Shakespeare's Love Tragedies* (San Marino, Calif., 1966).

Edwards, P. W., *Shakespeare and the Confines of Art* (London, 1968).

Evans, Robert O., *The Osier Cage: Rhetorical Devices in 'Romeo and Juliet'* (Lexington, Ky., 1966).

Granville-Barker, Harley, *Prefaces to Shakespeare, Second Series* (London, 1930); the Preface to *Romeo and Juliet* is partially reprinted in *Twentieth Century Interpretations of 'Romeo and Juliet'*, ed. Douglas Cole (Englewood Cliffs, N.J., 1970).

Hamilton, A. C., *The Early Shakespeare* (San Marino, Calif., 1967).

Lawlor, John, *'Romeo and Juliet'*, in *Early Shakespeare* (Stratford-upon-Avon Studies 3, ed. J. R. Brown and B. Harris, London, 1961).

Levin, Harry, 'Form and Formality in *Romeo and Juliet'*, *Shakespeare Quarterly*, 11 (1960); repr. in *Modern Shakespearean Criticism*, ed. Alvin B. Kernan (New York, 1970), and in *Twentieth Century Interpretations of 'Romeo and Juliet'*, ed. Douglas Cole.

Mahood, M. M., *Shakespeare's Wordplay* (London, 1957).

Masefield, John, *William Shakespeare* (London, 1911).

Mason, H. A., *Shakespeare's Tragedies of Love* (London, 1970).

Rabkin, Norman, *Shakespeare and the Common Understanding* (New York and London, 1967).

Smith, Gordon Ross, 'The Balance of Themes in *Romeo and Juliet'*, in *Essays on Shakespeare*, ed. Gordon Ross Smith (London, Pa., 1965).

Smith, Marion B., *Dualities in Shakespeare* (Toronto, 1966).

Spurgeon, Caroline F. E., *Shakespeare's Imagery and What It Tells Us* (Cambridge, 1935). The section on *Romeo and Juliet*, originally given as a lecture in 1930, is reprinted in *Shakespeare: Modern Essays in Criticism*, ed. Leonard F. Dean (2nd edn., New York, 1967), and in *Twentieth Century Interpretations of 'Romeo and Juliet'*, ed. Douglas Cole (Englewood Cliffs, N.J., 1970).

Stauffer, D. A., *Shakespeare's World of Images* (New York, 1949); comments on *Romeo and Juliet* are reprinted in *Shakespeare: The Tragedies*, ed. Alfred Harbage (Englewood Cliffs, N.J., 1964).

Whitaker, Virgil K., *The Mirror up to Nature* (San Marino, Calif., 1965).

Wilson, H. S., *On the Design of Shakespearian Tragedy* (Toronto, 1957).

10. *Hamlet*

JOHN JUMP

Hamlet must be the most famous of all European plays. It has been performed again and again in country after country. It has been printed repeatedly and translated into many languages. It has been endlessly discussed. Scholars debate the intricate textual problems with which it confronts them; thoughtful readers and theatre-goers debate the psychological and ethical problems suggested by its characters, and especially by Hamlet himself. Ought it perhaps to be classified as a 'problem play'? E. M. W. Tillyard is not alone in thinking so. But vast numbers of less sophisticated readers and theatre-goers respond to it without concerning themselves consciously with its notorious problems. The sheer bulk of the studies devoted to *Hamlet* has necessitated a policy of ruthless selectivity in the present essay.

TEXTS AND TEXTUAL STUDIES

There are three early printed versions of *Hamlet*. That in the 'bad' Quarto of 1603 is roughly half the length of that in the 'good' Quarto of 1604. The 1604 version is 200 lines longer than that in the Folio of 1623, but omits 85 lines which are included in the later publication. Moreover, the three differ considerably in their wording and punctuation of the passages which occur in more than one of them. All other editions of the play necessarily derive from these versions.

Until the present century, most editors based their texts mainly upon what they found in the Folio. But in 1934 John Dover Wilson published a detailed examination of the versions of 1604 and 1623 which has encouraged subsequent editors to rely principally upon the 'good' Quarto. Arguing vigorously and persuasively, if at certain points a little over-confidently, he maintains that this was printed from Shakespeare's somewhat damaged autograph—his original manuscript, or 'foul papers'—but that the 1603 Quarto was consulted when his writing was illegible; and that the Folio text of *Hamlet* was printed from a transcript of the theatre's prompt-book. These views have been widely influential.

So have the conclusions arising from George Ian Duthie's searching analysis, published in 1941, of the 'bad' Quarto. He maintains that the printer of this used a manuscript containing a memorial reconstruction of the play made for a provincial performance by a touring company. The person responsible for this report was, he suggests, an actor, who had taken the part of Marcellus and perhaps another part or parts in the full play, and who was able, when his memory failed, to knock out rough blank verse of his own. The reporter's verse incorporates reminiscences of an earlier *Hamlet* than Shakespeare's.

In 1955, Sir Walter Greg gave his authoritative support to Duthie's general view of the nature of the 1603 version and to Dover Wilson's general view of that of the 1604 version. In the light of recent bibliographical and textual investigation, however, he disagreed with Dover Wilson so far as to trace the Folio text to a collation of the 'good' Quarto with either the prompt-book or a transcript of it.

Naturally, Dover Wilson relied mainly upon the 1604 Quarto in the edition of the play that he published in the same year as his study of the two principal early versions. The result is that his text differs significantly at many points from the texts of those editors who have relied mainly upon the Folio. Thus his punctuation of Hamlet's meditation beginning 'What a piece of work is a man' (ii.ii) divides it into quite different sense-units from those recognized by earlier editors and familiar to most readers. Again, instead of the Folio's 'too too solid Flesh' (i.ii), he follows the 1604 Quarto's 'too too sallied flesh', emending 'sallied' to 'sullied'. It is interesting that Fredson Bowers, writing in *Shakespeare Survey 9*, accepts this reading but argues that the emendation is unnecessary, since 'sallied' is not a misprint for 'sullied' but a legitimate though rare form of it. Dover Wilson's edition was preceded by the elaborate textual study already mentioned and was to be followed by the elaborate critical study to be mentioned later. Despite this diversion of material to other publications, it remains, thanks to its copious annotation, one of the most substantial volumes in the New Cambridge Shakespeare. Taken together, these three works of Dover Wilson's constitute the most considerable individual contribution to *Hamlet* studies of the past half-century.

Dover Wilson's edition is available as a paperback. A more modest paperback edition is that by Edward Hubler in the Signet Classic Shakespeare. Though Hubler bases his text upon that of the 1604 Quarto and follows Dover Wilson in printing 'sullied flesh', he restores the more familiar punctuation to Hamlet's meditation beginning 'What a piece of work is a man'. A distinctive feature of his volume, as of all the Signet Shakespeares, is its inclusion of generous extracts from the principal critics. The play is also available separately in a number of other paperback Shakespeares. Bernard Lott supplies it with copious annotation in the New Swan Shakespeare, and Willard Farnham's edition of it in the American Pelican Shakespeare has an introduction which is of particular interest. T. J. B. Spencer is editing it for the New Penguin Shakespeare.

Another edition now in preparation is that by Harold Jenkins in the new Arden Shakespeare. The New Clarendon *Hamlet*, designed above all for the use of students in schools and colleges, is fully and serviceably annotated and includes well-chosen extracts from the main critics. George Rylands is its editor. J. Q. Adams's American edition of the play, now more than forty years old, has an elaborate and original Bradleian commentary which has maintained a deservedly high reputation.

CRITICAL STUDIES AND COMMENTARY

The earlier critics are well represented in *Readings on the Character of Hamlet 1661–1947*, edited by C. C. H. Williamson. More accurate textually than Williamson's collection is *Shakespeare Criticism: A Selection*, edited by D. Nichol Smith in the World's Classics series. As his title declares, Nichol Smith does not restrict his anthology to *Hamlet* criticism; but he reprints important writings on the play by Samuel Johnson, Charles Lamb, Samuel Taylor Coleridge, and William Hazlitt. Brief excerpts from the earlier critics, British and foreign, form Part I of *Shakespeare, 'Hamlet': A Casebook*, edited by J. D. Jump.

The first detailed critical study of the play was apparently *Some Remarks on the Tragedy of Hamlet*, published anonymously in 1736 and believed to be the work of Thomas Hanmer. Before Hanmer, playgoers and readers seem not to have suspected Hamlet of procrastination. In the seventeenth century they saw him as a bitterly eloquent and princely revenger, and, while in the early and middle decades of the eighteenth century they began to ascribe to him a great delicacy and a more melancholy temperament, both of which David Garrick fully realized in his interpretation of the part, they did not judge him to be lacking in initiative and resolution. Hanmer detected delay, however: 'Had *Hamlet* gone naturally to work, as we could suppose such a Prince to do in parallel Circumstances, there would have been an End of our Play. The Poet therefore was obliged to delay his Hero's Revenge; but then he should have contrived some good Reason for it.'

From the later decades of the eighteenth century, men began to feel sure that Shakespeare could not have failed to contrive 'some good Reason' for Hamlet's delay. They began to look for it. Henry Mackenzie and J. W. von Goethe found it in Hamlet's delicate sensibility. 'Shakespeare meant', writes Goethe, 'to represent the effects of a great action laid upon a soul unfit for the performance of it. . . . A lovely, pure, noble and most moral nature, without the strength of nerve which forms a hero, sinks beneath a burden which it cannot bear and must not cast away.' A. W. von Schlegel and S. T. Coleridge found the reason in an irresolution caused by an excessively reflective or speculative habit of mind. 'Hamlet's character', says Coleridge, 'is the prevalence of the abstracting and generalizing habit over the practical', and a little later he adds, 'I have a smack of Hamlet myself, if I may say so.'

Such comments clearly belong to the period, extending through the nineteenth and into the twentieth century, when character analysis provided the standard critical approach to this as to other plays by Shakespeare. Hartley Coleridge, the poet's son, went as far as to invite his readers to 'put Shakespeare out of the question, and consider Hamlet as a real person, a recently deceased acquaintance.' Critics advanced fresh explanations of Hamlet's delay. One of the more plausible of these was that his conscience restrained him, that he found the wild justice of revenge morally unacceptable. George Bernard Shaw restated this view in terms of his own optimistic evolutionism in the 'Postscript' which he added in 1945 to *Back to Methuselah*. At the opposite extreme, Karl Werder saw Hamlet as an active person hindered in the performance of his duty by difficulties external to himself.

The finest product of the approach to Shakespeare by way of character analysis is undoubtedly A. C. Bradley's *Shakespearean Tragedy* (1904). Bradley rejects all four of the explanations of Hamlet's delay which have been summarized here. In his view, Hamlet has been so deeply shocked by the revelation of his mother's shallowness and sensuality in her hasty remarriage that he has lapsed into 'a boundless weariness and a sick longing for death'. The disclosure of his mother's adultery and of his father's murder overwhelms him while in this state. With the disclosure comes the demand for swift and violent action against his uncle. In his condition of melancholic disgust and apathy he is incapable of this, but he cannot make out why he delays. His various attempts to justify his procrastination are mere rationalizations of an inability to act.

But Bradley does not content himself with analysing the prince. Ophelia, Gertrude, and Claudius also receive his attention; and he detects in *Hamlet*, more than in any other of Shakespeare's tragedies, a 'decided, though always imaginative, intimation of a supreme power concerned in human evil and good'. His discussion of all these matters is remarkable both for its attention to detail and for its balanced view of the work as a whole. Summary inevitably distorts his meaning. Bradley has his limitations; above all, he tends to apply to Shakespeare's characters the kind of analysis that would be more appropriate to those of a nineteenth-century novelist. But his successors, some of whom are highly critical of him, have yet to give us an account of the play as just and as comprehensive as his.

Ernest Jones may be described as a Bradleyite exploiting the new technique of psycho-analysis. As early as 1900, Sigmund Freud had traced Hamlet's irresolution to an Oedipus complex, and Jones, his most eminent British disciple, developed this view in a study of the play that he issued in several versions before publishing it in its finally revised form as *Hamlet and Oedipus* in 1949. He argues that Claudius, by murdering Hamlet's father and entering into an incestuous union with Hamlet's mother, has done something disturbingly similar to what the infant prince must himself have dreamed of doing before the repression of such desires established his Oedipus complex. Now, as he watches his uncle and stepfather, Hamlet's deepest unconscious fantasies threaten to infect his waking mind. There results that paralysing condition of disgust and apathy which Bradley describes so well.

In pointing to these unsuspected hidden depths, Jones writes as a professional psycho-analyst. Students of Shakespeare's play can admit the relevance and the perceptiveness of many of his observations. But in the end they are likely to feel that his Hamlet owes more to Freud's imagination than to Shakespeare's.

Although H. B. Charlton in *Shakespearian Tragedy* emphatically rejects the Freudian interpretation of *Hamlet*, he and Jones start from similar assumptions as dramatic critics. Charlton describes himself as a 'devout Bradleyite'. Seeking to explain Hamlet's delay, he follows Coleridge in ascribing to the prince a 'supreme gift for philosophic thought'. But he gives his own explanation of how this gift inhibits action. It does so by enabling Hamlet to create an ideal world 'and then to mistake it for a true intellectual projection of the real one'. As a result of his error he cannot act properly within the real world; 'or rather, towards those parts of it which the stress of his feeling and the heat of his imagination have made especially liable to intellectual distortion, he cannot oppose the right response. He can kill a Rosencrantz, but not his villainous uncle.' This account rightly stresses Hamlet's exaggerative and generalizing habit of mind, as exemplified by 'Frailty, thy name is woman.' But does it perhaps take 'the stress of his feeling and the heat of his imagination' too much for granted? Are not Jones and Bradley right in thinking that these are precisely what most require explanation?

T. S. Eliot would certainly have said that they are. In his brief essay of 1919 he challenges the collective opinion of mankind formed over a period of three centuries when he pronounces that *Hamlet* is a failure. He objects that, while Hamlet's disgust is occasioned by his mother, it is in excess of the facts as they appear. What is true of him in relation to her is true of Shakespeare in relation to the play as a whole. Like Hamlet, Shakespeare is dominated by an emotion which has no adequate equivalent and which is therefore inexpressible. In all this, the Freudian influence is clear. What notably weakens the essay is Eliot's reliance in it upon the textual fantasies of the Shakespeare-disintegrator, J. M. Robertson. There is a reply to it in Francis Fergusson's *The Idea of a Theater*.

Critics of Bradley sometimes complain that he takes too little account of the facts that Shakespeare intended his plays for stage performance and that they naturally embody a good deal of Elizabethan thought. Without repudiating Bradley, Harley Granville-Barker and John Dover Wilson have sought to repair these omissions.

Granville-Barker had had a distinguished career in the theatre as actor, dramatist, and producer before he started to write his *Prefaces to Shakespeare*, of which the Third Series consists of a single book-length study of *Hamlet*. This is remarkable not for any novel interpretation of the play as a whole but for the constant illumination of detail that proceeds from its author's lively sense of theatrical values. Many of his particular suggestions have been taken up and developed by his successors.

In *What Happens in Hamlet*, the last of his three important publications on the play, Dover Wilson attempts to describe a genuinely Elizabethan *Hamlet*. He argues that the Ghost is an ambiguous figure and that Hamlet has good reason to doubt whether it is his father's spirit or a devil taking that shape to tempt him to murder; that, in ordering him to kill Claudius without compromising

Gertrude, it sets him an extraordinarily difficult task; that Hamlet in
II.ii overhears Polonius's scheme to 'loose' Ophelia to him; and that
Shakespeare intended the audience, but not Claudius, to heed the
dumb-show preceding *The Mousetrap*. The effect of some of these
views, and especially of the insistence upon the ambiguity of the
Ghost, is to focus attention upon the objective difficulties confronting
Hamlet and to suggest that up to a point his inaction is prudent.
Even so, Dover Wilson continues to think sheer procrastination an
important factor, though not as important as Coleridge and his
successors maintained.

So Granville-Barker's determination to see the play in relation to
the theatre and Dover Wilson's determination to see it in relation to
the Elizabethan age stop short of a rejection of Bradley. Other
realists take that further step, however. A. J. A. Waldock in *Hamlet:
A Study in Critical Method* appeals to our experience of the play in
performance in order to challenge the basic assumption of Bradleyite
criticism of it. He maintains that in the theatre Hamlet's procrastination is barely noticeable.

It is not enough to say that Hamlet procrastinates because, as a matter of
fact, and regarding the play somewhat as an historical document, we find
that he did not act for two months or so. If he procrastinates, it is because
he is shown procrastinating. To put it another way, it is not sufficient that
delay should be negatively implicit in the play; it is necessary, for its
dramatic existence, that it should be positively demonstrated. The delay,
in a word, exists just inasmuch as and just to the degree in which it is
conveyed.

Evidently we ought to trouble ourselves less than we do with the old
leading question, 'Why does Hamlet delay?'

At all events, we ought not to put too much effort into answering
it in psychological terms. The more profitable answer is that which
explains the delay as one of the playwright's devices for keeping us
in suspense. L. L. Schücking in *Character Problems in Shakespeare's
Plays* and E. E. Stoll in *Art and Artifice in Shakespeare: A Study in
Dramatic Contrast and Illusion* take this line. Their books tell us much
about the technique but little about the significance and the value of
Hamlet and the other plays they discuss. In a similar fashion, Lily B.
Campbell in *Shakespeare's Tragic Heroes: Slaves of Passion* makes
Shakespeare so much 'of an age'—the Elizabethan—that he can
hardly aspire to be 'for all time'. This is the trouble with the realists:
the plays become more meagre and more provincial things as they
talk about them.

Other critics object that Bradley, in his excessive reliance upon

character analysis, unduly neglects Shakespeare's poetry. They feel
that they can discuss *Hamlet* or any other tragedy to better effect if
they regard it, as G. Wilson Knight puts it in the first chapter of
The Wheel of Fire, 'as a visionary whole, close-knit in personification,
atmospheric suggestion, and direct poetic-symbolism'. Wilson
Knight evidently hopes that his studies of the plays as symbolist
poems will extend rather than contradict the findings of the character
analysts. Others, however, have been less respectful of tradition.

Whereas the stricter realists try to limit Shakespeare too narrowly
to the thoughts current in his day and the modes of expression usual
in the theatre, the symbolist critics feel freer to acknowledge whatever they believe they have found in his work. Certain of them claim
to have discerned some very strange things there. But this is no place
for reviewing the merely eccentric. The best of the symbolist critics
dwell upon the play's poetry in the widest sense, and especially upon
its poetic imagery. Consideration of these leads D. A. Traversi in
An Approach to Shakespeare to a diagnosis of 'Hamlet's malady and its
relation to "the state of Denmark" '. Like Tillyard, he classifies
Hamlet as one of the problem plays. By her writings on Shakespeare's
imagery, Caroline F. E. Spurgeon no doubt helped him, as she has
certainly helped others, to perceive that the distinctive atmosphere
of the work is partly due 'to the number of images of sickness, disease,
or blemish of the body' in it and that 'the idea of an ulcer or tumour,
as descriptive of the unwholesome condition of Denmark morally, is,
on the whole, the dominating one.' In the light of the poetic imagery,
she sees the problem in *Hamlet*

not as the problem of an individual at all, but as something greater and even
more mysterious, as a *condition* for which the individual himself is apparently
not responsible, any more than the sick man is to blame for the cancer which
strikes and devours him, but which, nevertheless, in its course and development impartially and relentlessly annihilates him and others, innocent and
guilty alike. That is the tragedy of Hamlet, as it is, perhaps, the chief
tragic mystery of life.

Wolfgang H. Clemen in *The Development of Shakespeare's Imagery*
shows how language and imagery contribute to define Hamlet himself for us. But Caroline Spurgeon has not been alone in wondering
whether the problem of *Hamlet* is perhaps not the problem of an
individual at all. In a challenging lecture entitled *Hamlet: The
Prince or the Poem?* C. S. Lewis says, 'I believe that we read Hamlet's
speeches with interest chiefly because they describe so well a certain
spiritual region through which most of us have passed and anyone

in his circumstances might be expected to pass, rather than because of our concern to understand how and why this particular man entered it.' In Lewis's eyes, the true hero of the play

is man—haunted man—man with his mind on the frontier of two worlds, man unable either quite to reject or quite to admit the supernatural, man struggling to get something done as man has struggled from the beginning, yet incapable of achievement because of his inability to understand either himself or his fellows or the real quality of the universe which has produced him.

If some twentieth-century critics have questioned the conviction, expressed by Shaftesbury as early as 1710, that the play 'has only ONE *Character* or *principal Part*', others have failed to detect in that character the sweetness and nobility traditionally ascribed to him. Wilson Knight sees him as a sick, cynical, and inhuman prince corrupting a world that is, 'except for the original murder of Hamlet's father . . . one of healthy and robust life, good-nature, humour, romantic strength, and welfare'. In the same essays, included in *The Wheel of Fire*, he discovers in the Claudius whom we are permitted to observe in the play simply 'a good and gentle king, enmeshed by the chain of causality linking him with his crime. And this chain he might, perhaps, have broken except for Hamlet, and all would have been well.' But does not Wilson Knight sweep aside the murder rather too easily? Claudius was no impulsive offender, suddenly acting out of character. He deliberately and treacherously poisoned his mistress's husband, a man who was his brother and his king. His crime discloses the nature of its perpetrator. Can 'all' ever be 'well' while such a man rules?

L. C. Knights rejects Wilson Knight's benevolent view of Claudius but develops his harsh view of Hamlet. He declares that Hamlet's 'attitudes of hatred, revulsion, self-complacence and self-reproach . . . are, in their one-sided insistence, forms of escape from the difficult process of complex adjustment which normal living demands and which Hamlet finds beyond his powers.' This seems excessively censorious. Within the five acts of Shakespeare's play, Hamlet is never lucky enough to face merely the demands of 'normal living'. He confronts an extraordinarily evil situation which is not of his making but which he must set right.

Knights's earlier statement of his opinions occurs in an essay of 1940 which he reprinted in *Explorations*. He does not modify his opinions greatly, though he elaborates them considerably, in *An Approach to 'Hamlet'*. No longer does he charge Hamlet with an inability to face 'normal living'; but he does blame him for 'a sterile concentration on death and evil'.

One other denigrator of Hamlet calls for mention in passing. This is Salvador de Madariaga, who in *On Hamlet* portrays the prince as a ruthless Renaissance egoist.

Those who insist that Hamlet is an unamiable character labour under the same disadvantage as those who maintain that the play is a failure: the testimony of the vast majority of the readers and theatre-goers of more than three centuries contradicts them. Recently critics seem to have become readier once more to acknowledge his sweetness and nobility. Helen Gardner, for example, justifying the historical approach in *The Business of Criticism*, points out that in Elizabethan revenge-plays generally the initiator of the action is the initiator of its resolution, that the villain, in other words, is to some extent the involuntary agent of his own destruction. This being so, the revenging hero does not so much create an opportunity as wait for the one that his victim will unintentionally provide. Hamlet is typical in that he has this waiting role. His guilelessness in it wins our affection, his constancy our approval. Talk of his delay is largely, though not entirely, beside the point.

The constancy which Helen Gardner praises is what Knights blames as 'a sterile concentration on death and evil'. Knights argues his case with sensitivity and subtlety. But it has met with considerable resistance. One of the more genial and persuasive retorts comes from Patrick Cruttwell, who follows Helen Gardner in stressing the prince's constancy and other soldierly virtues. These are not regarded as virtues by those twentieth-century liberal ntellectuals whose thinking is dominated by 'very powerful quasi-pacifist emotions'. Hence Leavis's portrait of Othello, and Traversi's of Henry V. Hence, too, Knights's reference to Hamlet's 'murder' of Rosencrantz and Guildenstern. Cruttwell objects to the term, protesting that Hamlet was engaged in a just war such as might be held to sanction extreme measures. What Hamlet really is, he summarizes at the end of his essay, 'is a conscript in a war. He has done things, as we all do in wars, he would rather not have done; but he believes it to be a just war, and all in all, he has borne himself well.'

Many of the most recent critics, however, are trying to provide not an interpretation of Hamlet's behaviour but an interpretation of the tragedy as a whole. Even D. G. James, who in *The Dream of Learning* ascribes Hamlet's delay to his metaphysical and moral scepticism, feels obliged to recognize 'that we must not see the play as merely an affair of the character of its hero'. Maynard Mack, in 'The World of *Hamlet*', attempts to describe 'the imaginative environment that the play asks us to enter'. He discusses three attributes of this world: 'its mysteriousness, its baffling appearances, its deep consciousness of infection, frailty, and loss'. Following Bradley, he represents Hamlet as a sensitive and idealistic young man, deeply shocked by the events immediately preceding the action of the play. But in the Hamlet who returns from the sea voyage, he discerns a readiness to accept the world as it is. Like Helen Gardner, Mack reminds us that the situation which Hamlet has to face is one that he has done nothing to bring about.

H. D. F. Kitto in *Form and Meaning in Drama* and John Holloway in *The Story of the Night* would presumably be ready to echo this reminder. According to Kitto, Hamlet is inevitably engulfed by the evil that others have set in motion; but he himself becomes the cause of further disaster. The tragedy as a whole shows how evil, once started on its course, so works as to attack and destroy alike the good and the bad; it presents 'the complexive, menacing spread of ruin'. Holloway, too, sees *Hamlet* as a religious drama. In his eyes, the developing spectacle is that of a diseased society deferring to, and placing in distinguished isolation, the revenger who has reluctantly undertaken the role of its purifier, which Providence has forced upon him. Holloway interestingly compares Shakespeare's tragedies with the scapegoat ceremonies that have been performed in many communities.

To these attempts to formulate the total significance of the play may be added Harry Levin's *The Question of 'Hamlet'*, in which he emphasizes its questioning, its doubt, and its irony, and the essay in Jan Kott's *Shakespeare Our Contemporary*, a book which has influenced stage production of the works discussed in it to a quite extraordinary degree. Writing in Poland, a country which has known modern political totalitarianism in a variety of forms, Kott sees *Hamlet* as a political play in which not only the prince but also Laertes, Ophelia, and Fortinbras act parts 'imposed on them from outside'. His purpose is to portray Hamlet for our own times. This is no less the purpose of Helen Gardner and Patrick Cruttwell. But, whereas they try to see him historically, in relation to the Elizabethan age, before suggesting his significance for the twentieth century, Kott proceeds more directly to choose his twentieth-century Hamlet from those which he knows to be realizable on the stage. His best insights as a critic come from his intimacy with the theatre, his worst blunders from his determination at all costs to be modern.

Two other works which happened to appear in the year in which the Shakespeare quatercentenary was celebrated are Terence Hawkes's *Shakespeare and the Reason*, interpreting *Hamlet* and other plays in the light of the medieval and Renaissance distinction between a higher and a lower reason, and Kenneth Muir's useful short introduction designed for undergraduate readers. Since then, Maurice Charney, in *Style in 'Hamlet'*, has rejected over-subtle interpretations in favour of one that sees the play as 'vigorous and active', and Nigel Alexander, in *Poison, Play, and Duel: A Study in 'Hamlet'*, has described the Prince himself as a theatrical device for bringing all human actions into question.

Three collections of essays by various hands call for mention in conclusion. *Shakespeare Survey* for 1956 was devoted mainly to the play. Portraits of thirty-six Hamlets from David Garrick to Sir John Gielgud fill three of its eight full-page plates. In addition to the article by Fredson Bowers already mentioned and other interesting items, the volume includes an excellent descriptive review, 'Studies in *Hamlet*, 1901–1955', in which Clifford Leech outlines and comments judiciously upon the more important contributions both to the textual study and to the critical interpretation of the play. In 1963 the fifth volume of Stratford-upon-Avon Studies was given up to *Hamlet*. The essay by Patrick Cruttwell already discussed is one of several important articles among the ten that it contains. Cruttwell's essay is reprinted in J. D. Jump's *Shakespeare, 'Hamlet': A Casebook* (1968), together with eleven other recent essays, or long extracts from books, by Ernest Jones, Wolfgang H. Clemen, D. G. James, Maynard Mack, H. D. F. Kitto, T. S. Eliot, Harry Levin, Helen Gardner, L. C. Knights, John Holloway, and Jan Kott. Prefacing these are the short extracts from earlier critics that have already been mentioned, and an 'Introduction' from which some borrowings have been made for the present article.

In 'The Decline of Hamlet', his contribution to Stratford-upon-Avon Studies 5, T. J. B. Spencer records with evident regret that some twentieth-century critics have 'tried to convince us that we should abandon the long theatrical tradition of Hamlet as "the Darling of the English Audience"'. In wishing to resist the denigration of Hamlet, Spencer is by no means alone. A number of the most recent critics, without the slightest intention of pushing character analysis as far as does Bradley, or of dwelling excessively upon Hamlet's delay, find the prince a most sympathetic character. He is a likeable young man upon whom an almost intolerable burden has been laid, the action of the tragedy being largely the outcome of his reluctant but dutiful shouldering of it. The world in which he has to act is one in which there is little or no certainty, the society with which he is involved one that is sinking into decay. Such, in outline, is the account of the play that seems to emerge from much that has been said about it in the 1950s and 1960s.

REFERENCES

TEXTS AND TEXTUAL STUDIES

Adams, J. Q. (ed.), *Hamlet* (Cambridge, Mass., 1929).

Bowers, Fredson, 'Hamlet's "Sullied" or "Solid" Flesh: A Bibliographical Case-History', *Shakespeare Survey 9* (1956).

Duthie, G. I., *The 'Bad' Quarto of Hamlet* (Cambridge, 1941).

Farnham, Willard (ed.), *Hamlet* (Pelican Shakespeare, Baltimore, Md., 1957).

Greg, W. W., *The Editorial Problem in Shakespeare* (Oxford, 1942; 2nd edn., 1951).

——, *The Shakespeare First Folio* (Oxford, 1955).

Hubler, E. (ed.), *Hamlet* (Signet Shakespeare, New York, 1963).

Lott, Bernard (ed.), *Hamlet* (New Swan Shakespeare, London, 1968).

Rylands, George (ed.), *Hamlet* (New Clarendon Shakespeare, Oxford, 1947).

Wilson, J. Dover (ed.), *Hamlet* (New Cambridge Shakespeare, Cambridge, 1934).

——, *The Manuscript of Shakespeare's 'Hamlet' and the Problems of its Transmission*, 2 vols. (Cambridge, 1934).

CRITICAL STUDIES AND COMMENTARY

Alexander, Nigel, *Poison, Play, and Duel: A Study in 'Hamlet'* (London, 1971).

Bradley, A. C., *Shakespearean Tragedy* (London, 1904).

Campbell, Lily B., *Shakespeare's Tragic Heroes: Slaves of Passion* (Cambridge, Mass., 1930).

Charlton, H. B., *Shakespearian Tragedy* (Cambridge, 1948).

Charney, Maurice, *Style in 'Hamlet'* (Princeton, N.J., 1969).

Clemen, W. H., *The Development of Shakespeare's Imagery* (London, 1951).

Coleridge, S. T., *Coleridge on Shakespeare*, ed. T. Hawkes (Penguin Shakespeare Library, Harmondsworth, 1969).

Cruttwell, Patrick, 'The Morality of *Hamlet*—"Sweet Prince" or "Arrant Knave"?', *Hamlet* (Stratford-upon-Avon Studies 5, ed. J. R. Brown and B. Harris, London, 1963).

Eliot, T. S., 'Hamlet', in *Selected Essays 1917–1932* (London, 1932).

——, 'Poetry and Drama', in *On Poetry and Poets* (London, 1957).

Fergusson, Francis, *The Idea of a Theater* (Princeton, N.J., 1949).

Gardner, Helen, *The Business of Criticism* (Oxford, 1959).

Granville-Barker, Harley, *Prefaces to Shakespeare: Third Series, Hamlet* (London, 1937).

Hawkes, Terence, *Shakespeare and the Reason* (London, 1964).

Holloway, John, *The Story of the Night* (London, 1961).

James, D. G., *The Dream of Learning* (Oxford, 1951).

Jones, Ernest, *Hamlet and Oedipus* (London, 1949).

Jump, J. D. (ed.), *Shakespeare, 'Hamlet': A Casebook* (London, 1968).

Kitto, H. D. F., *Form and Meaning in Drama* (London, 1956).

Knight, G. Wilson, *The Imperial Theme* (London, 1931).

——, *The Wheel of Fire* (London, 1930).

Knights, L. C., *An Approach to 'Hamlet'* (London, 1960).

——, 'Prince Hamlet', in *Explorations* (London, 1946).

Kott, Jan, *Shakespeare Our Contemporary* (London, 1964).

Leech, Clifford, 'Studies in *Hamlet*, 1901–1955', *Shakespeare Survey 9* (1956).

Levin, Harry, *The Question of 'Hamlet'* (New York, 1959).

Lewis, C. S., *Hamlet: The Prince or the Poem?* (Annual Shakespeare Lecture of the British Academy, London, 1942); repr. in *Shakespeare's Tragedies*, ed. Laurence Lerner (Harmondsworth, 1963).

Mack, Maynard, 'The World of *Hamlet*', *Yale Review*, 41 (1951–2).

de Madariaga, Salvador, *On Hamlet* (London, 1948; 2nd edn., 1964).

Muir, Kenneth, *Shakespeare's 'Hamlet'* (London, 1964).

Schücking, L. L., *Character Problems in Shakespeare's Plays* (London, 1922).

Smith, D. Nichol, *Shakespeare Criticism: A Selection* (World's Classics, London, 1916).

Spencer, T. J. B., 'The Decline of Hamlet', *Hamlet* (Stratford-upon-Avon Studies 5, ed. J. R. Brown and B. Harris, London, 1963).

Spurgeon, Caroline F. E., *Leading Motives in the Imagery of Shakespeare's Tragedies* (Shakespeare Association Lecture, London, 1930).

——, *Shakespeare's Imagery and What It Tells Us* (Cambridge, 1935).

Stoll, Elmer Edgar, *Art and Artifice in Shakespeare: A Study in Dramatic Contrast and Illusion* (Cambridge, 1933).

Tillyard, E. M. W., *Shakespeare's Problem Plays* (London, 1950).

Traversi, D. A., *An Approach to Shakespeare* (London, 1938; revised 1956; 2 vols., revised 1968–9).

Waldock, A. J. A., *Hamlet: A Study in Critical Method* (Cambridge, 1931).

Williamson, C. C. H. (ed.), *Readings on the Character of Hamlet 1661–1947* (London, 1950).

Wilson, J. Dover, *What Happens in 'Hamlet'* (Cambridge, 1935).

11. *Othello*

ROBERT HAPGOOD

TEXTS

Since the hundreds of small differences between the First Quarto and the Folio texts of *Othello* have not yet been satisfactorily explained, the student will find it especially interesting to compare the two versions for himself (Schröer). Modern editions are eclectic, drawing on both texts. Believing that the First Quarto frequently 'vulgarizes' what Shakespeare originally wrote, Alice Walker in the Cambridge edition provides the current text that is closest to the Folio. At the other extreme is Ridley, who in the new Arden edition follows the First Quarto very closely, even to its punctuation. Other editions fall between these extremes. Of these the New Penguin (Muir) and Kittredge (Ribner) may be recommended for the fullness of their glosses; the Signet edition (Kernan) includes some representative commentaries and a translation of Shakespeare's presumed source, a tale from Cinthio's *Hecatommithi* (see also Spencer).

THE MAKING OF *OTHELLO*

Several speculative articles may help the student to imagine Shakespeare at work on his manuscript of *Othello*. Allen is suggestive as to how Shakespeare planned his play. He apparently decided to follow his source very closely in the middle of the action but to invent a beginning that would prepare for it, largely by contrast. Allen argues, in fact, that Shakespeare wrote the second part of the play first, beginning with Act III, showing that its well-known 'double time' results from Shakespeare's use of one time-scheme in the first two acts and another in the last three, which are much faster paced. In a close textual study, Honigmann provides further support for Greg's view that the numerous variants between the Quarto and Folio texts include Shakespeare's first and second thoughts. He thus invites us to see the playwright in the very process of writing and rewriting, substituting and transposing words and phrases as he goes. Looking at the end of this process, Coghill studies the passages that the Folio includes but the Quarto does not. He pictures Shakespeare as putting some finishing touches to his work after he has seen it performed, strengthening its exposition, playing up Brabantio's obsession with Othello's 'foul charms', emphasizing the effect of kneeling, enlarging Emilia's part.

All these studies are conjectural, although knowledgeable and persuasive. Perhaps their surest value is that they encourage the student to regard Shakespeare's text as a working document that a human being composed and changed rather than as a fixed decree, sanctified in print: as a script rather than a scripture.

CRITICISM AND COMMENTARY

The time seems near for some fundamental advances in *Othello* criticism and commentary. Although never generally acclaimed— like *Hamlet* or *King Lear*—as *the* Shakespearian drama, Othello has had a continuously successful life in the theatre and has always been ranked among his finest works. But it has won its place by sheer might not right—as its critics have seen the right.

Not that commentary has been lacking (for extensive notation of its profusion to 1915, see Stoll; thereafter, Heilman). Yet the play still awaits a major commentary that is sympathetic to its distinctive features. Its best appreciations have come from A. C. Bradley and G. Wilson Knight. Bradley remains the best guide to the leading characters and the issues concerning them (how black is the Moor? is he easily jealous? what are Iago's motives?) because he gives a fair-minded survey of the options before developing his own choices. Knight immerses himself in the play's language, showing how the Miltonic 'music' of Othello—'highly-coloured, rich in sound and phrase, stately' yet at times 'sentimental' and 'exaggerated'—is turned to discord by the ugly, cynical intellectuality of Iago. Yet as Helen Gardner brings out in '*Othello:* A Retrospect, 1900–67', the play does not fit the predilections of either critic. Its disturbing finale, with Iago surviving, does not satisfy Bradley's need to feel 'reconciled' to the tragic way of the world. And for Knight, the play is primarily a 'story of intrigue' rather than the 'visionary statement' that he most values.

Like its hero, *Othello* has something alien about it. It has been felt to be more operatic (Shaw) and more novelistic (Bayley) than the Shakespearian norm. Especially, it has resisted consideration as a form of dramatized moral philosophy. When Thomas Rymer finds the play 'very instructive' (presenting 'a warning to all good Wives, that they look well to their Linnen' and a 'lesson to Husbands, that before their Jealousie be Tragical, the proofs may be Mathematical'), his mockery expresses a frustration that many subsequent moralists have shared. To Granville-Barker, indeed, *Othello* seems 'a tragedy without meaning, and that is the ultimate horror of it'. In general the play has appealed less to the reflective reader than to the responding spectator. As Ridley puts it: '*Othello*, to most readers, is not his greatest work, but is his best play, in the narrow sense of "theatre" probably much his best.'

One looks, therefore, to commentaries with a theatrical orientation, but these prove disappointing. At his best, Granville-Barker might well have written the key study. As he moves scene by scene through the play, he contributes numerous insights, such as his fine observation that the contrast between Othello and Iago 'is progressively heightened until a species of conflict is created, not of action, since the story forbids that, but of the very essence of the men'. Yet for the most part he seems uninspired, over-concerned with the surface of the action to the neglect of a fresh and probing treatment of the characters from whom it issues. Stanislavsky's production notes are fragmentary and much given to 'anterior speculation' about the political intrigues of Venice. Stoll occupies a special place in *Othello* commentary, having written more of it than anyone else, and occasioned innumerable replies. Yet the attention thus given to his views far exceeds their value; and for all his talk about 'stage convention', his theories—as Rosenberg has shown—are not really based upon theatrical experience. G. R. Elliott stages a production in his mind and follows it through almost line by line, but the result is a book-length article on the theme of pride rather than the moment-by-moment response to the play's developing sequences that it might have been.

Unfortunately, these commentaries do not reflect the rehearsal phase of theatrical interpretation, where the performer is discovering and selecting from a host of valid possibilities. They are more like accounts of finished productions, and thus do not differ much from orthodox critical articles purporting to have found Shakespeare's 'One Right Meaning'. This is true even of Rosenberg's *The Masks of Othello*. His subtitle is indicative: 'The Search for the Identity of Othello, Iago, and Desdemona by Three Centuries of Actors and Critics'. For him there is for each character only one basic 'identity' that will work in the theatre, and he has discovered it. Instead, therefore, of giving a full and detailed stage history of the play, he spends a third of his book arguing for the rightness of his own formulations of it.

The truth is that Othello, like the other characters, has many identities, and that Shakespeare 'meant' them all. As I have suggested in 'Shakespeare and the Included Spectator', he seems to have imagined not only the world of the play but a whole theatre event, one that includes as well actors and spectators—for whom he has built-in generous latitudes for interpretation and response. This is not to say that there are no wrong interpretations and responses but that there are many right ones. The search, then, is properly for the *best* interpretation, the one that at a given moment best suits the text, the performers, and the audience—or the reader imagining such an event. What follows will suggest how *Othello* commentary to date can aid the student in this search.

Since 1927, when T. S. Eliot described Othello as a self-dramatizer 'cheering himself up' in his last speech, commentators have been preoccupied with the nobility or ignobility of the Moor. Traditionally, Bradley and many others have taken him at his own estimate; Dr. Johnson writes of 'the fiery openness of Othello, magnanimous, artless, and credulous, boundless in his confidence, ardent in his affection, inflexible in his resolution, and obdurate in his revenge' (Wimsatt). After Eliot, a number of critics have challenged the traditional view. With various degrees of stridency they have found in the hero 'a quality of self-deception, revealed, as with Desdemona, in a peculiar romantic fervour' (Nicoll), a 'romantic idealism' (Kirschbaum), a proclivity to 'dramatize as "nobility" his own incapacity to cope with life' (Traversi), an 'obtuse and brutal egotism' (Leavis). Heilman scores 'the unripeness of his sense of his own past, the flair for the picturesque and the histrionic, the stoicism of the flesh unmatched by an endurance of spirit, the capacity for occasional self-deception, the hypersensitivity to challenge, the inexperience in giving, the inclination to be irritable under responsibility and hasty in the absence of superior authority, the need to rely on position'. In rejoinder, a freshly observed reaffirmation of the traditional view has been advocated by Helen Gardner, Bayley, Holloway, and Rosenberg. Among Christian interpreters, a comparable polarity has developed between those who see Othello as damned or as saved (surveyed by West).

In its present adversary form, this dispute has surely gone on long enough. Ranged at one extreme or the other, critics have not been fulfilling one of their chief functions, that of ventilating a full spectrum of interpretative possibilities. In their insistence on a simple hero, they have neglected the possibility of his complexity. Kirschbaum suggests that 'It is the close interweaving of great man, mere man, and base man that makes of Othello the peculiarly powerful and mysterious figure he is.' But he himself shirks close

examination of this interweaving: 'The truly noble aspects of Othello
I have not stressed. They are obvious.' In their concern for consistency, critics have failed to put the two extreme views of the hero
together in one fully worked-out pattern. Holloway, Sewell, and
Prior sketch in their own terms the complete degradation of Othello
from noble man to monster but do not follow the process in
detail.

Hence the student does not have as much critical help as he might
as he seeks the richest possible reading of the text. Such a reading is,
in my view, the prime criterion for the 'best interpretation' of the
play. Another test is that the chosen interpretation suit the interpreter rendering it, whether he is an actor or a reader imagining a
role from the inside. Here individual differences must be respected,
as Olivier's Othello illustrates. In 1961 Rosenberg asked six recent
Othellos whether the hero was prone to self-deception and received
unanimous and emphatic Noes. He concludes: 'Add to these the
voices of Garrick, Foote, Salvini, Booth, Tearle, Stanislavski, and
the interpretations in performance of all the others, and clearly the
weight of acting intuition rejects any interpretation centering on
self-deception or pretended nobility.' In 1964 came Olivier's
epoch-making performance, founded explicitly on his belief that
'the tragic fissure' which destroys the hero is 'self-delusion' (Carlisle).
So much for 'the weight of acting intuition'.

Obviously a third interpretative test must be whether the treatment of one part works with that of others and of the whole. This
is especially true of the relation between Othello and Iago, which
is so intimate as to resemble the interacting aspects of a single
personality (Rogers). An Othello as innocent as Bradley's will
require a corrupter as powerful as his Iago; an Othello as faulty
as Leavis's will scarcely need corruption, and so his Iago is 'merely
ancillary'.

About Iago there has been much wider critical agreement than
about Othello. Interpreters worry Coleridge's phrase concerning
his 'motiveless malignity' (Raysor, Shaffer), arguing about how real
and strong his expressed motivations are (Muir) and how much his
malignity is due to the tradition of the Vice (Spivack), the devil
(Scragg, Bethell), or the Calumniator Credited (Stoll). Taking
Iago's motives as a 'pluralist test-case', Hyman studies him as a stage
villain, Satan, an artist, a latent homosexual, and a Machiavel; but
he leaves it to his reader to interrelate these identities. Interpreters
also differ about the degree of Iago's success, G. R. Elliott treating
him as a bungler, Auden as so masterful that he accomplishes

everything he wishes, including his own destruction. But about Iago's essential nature there is remarkable consensus: his is a spirit of negation—of doubt, hatred, destruction, death.

In contrast, Desdemona has been seen as embodying trust and faith, charity (Heilman), and life (Kernan). Hawkes finds in her a wise and intuitive kind of reason as distinguished from Iago's lower rationality. Such contrasts are frequent: often Othello is regarded as a morality hero, torn between his bad angel and his good. Angelic purity is perhaps better rendered in music—as in Verdi's opera *Otello* (Hartnoll, Kerman)—than on the stage, where it can seem dull. Rosenberg advocates a more human Desdemona. Indeed she has her stern detractors, who find her culpably deceptive (Bonnard) and self-deceiving (Nicoll). As with Othello, Desdemona's interpreters have resisted seeing her as a complex and developing character. Perhaps Heilman takes the most inclusive view of her, suggesting a 'progress from the infatuated girl toward the devoted, enduring wife'.

In seeking the best over-all interpretation of the play, the student faces a problem in synthesis, of putting together the single themes and features that various interpreters have analysed. For the sake o mapping the 'world' of *Othello*, these may be grouped into three patterns.

One pattern is that of *displacement*, signalized when Shakespeare chose his subtitle: 'The Moor of Venice'. His hero is a black man among whites (Jones, Hunter), a soldier in society (Jorgensen, Draper), a primitive among sophisticates; his heroine is a very domestic girl (Knight) who elopes with a very exotic stranger (Van Doren). Commentators differ about the function of Venice: to Heilman and Kernan it represents a sound and supportive society; to Fergusson it seems so sterile that even Desdemona could find nothing in it to command her love and loyalty. But they agree that the outpost on Cyprus is a place in which the characters seem lost. Here the harsh military hierarchy is the nearest thing to a social order, and all the soldiers are sooner or later estranged even from that—as they are passed over, cashiered, or transferred. There is nothing like the sense of great national and cosmic involvement that one customarily finds in Shakespearian tragedy (Hibbard). Thrown on themselves as they are, these displaced persons at the outset also seem remote from one another. As Hazlitt puts it: 'These characters and the images they stamp upon the mind are the farthest asunder possible, the distance between them is immense.' They cluster around the magnetic and expansive Othello. He stands at the centre of a network of bonds (Everett) that soon become bondages, a strange net of relationships that finally enmeshes them all.

One focus of their very intense relationships involves questions of *control*. All the leading characters are strong-willed; none of them knows when to stop. When at the beginning Othello and Desdemona dominate, they feel 'free' and sure of themselves, wonderfully poised and self-controlled. Their self-possession will be lost, utterly (Mack), as their inner and domestic lives are thrown into chaos. As Iago more and more takes control, he more and more defines the atmosphere of the play. It is one of torment and cruelty (Spurgeon), in which impulses toward destruction and self-destruction have been released, in which sexual passion turns perverse to the point of madness, in which the controlled violence of justice becomes a mask for revenge. The consequent sufferings also release overwhelming surges of grief, pity, and—ironically—love. Eventually, the chaos extends so far that Iago himself loses control, and chance and circumstance more and more take charge (Bradley).

These patterns of control are evident to the audience, but Iago is the only character who is much aware of them. The characters are primarily caught up in questions of *fidelity*, of truth to self and others. Here may be grouped the themes on which most commentators rightly dwell: of trust and mistrust, faith and cynicism, integrity and hypocrisy—to the point of prostitution, of honesty in all its senses (Empson, Jorgensen), of deception and self-deception, of seeming and being, of reputation and honour.

Many of these patterns are not of course confined to *Othello*. Yet in their interweavings they help to define a unique 'world', one that moves, furthermore, in characteristic rhythms. In seeking critical help with these rhythms, the student again must piece together fragments of commentary, and not many of these. Bradley suggests a basic pattern: 'In the first half of the play the main conflict is merely incubating; then it bursts into life, and goes storming, without intermission or change of direction to its close.' Fergusson observes how the opening scene 'moves in the agile, sudden rhythms of Iago's spirit', thus contrasting with the subsequent Venetian scenes in which Othello sets the stately pace. Granville-Barker calls attention to the speeding of events and drastic compression of time at Cyprus until Lodovico's arrival; thereafter, he finds 'little or no time-compression' and in the final scene 'none at all'.

As a participant in the whole theatre event, the spectator is himself invited by Shakespeare to enter the world of *Othello* and its rhythms, not only through imagining himself into the world on stage but through his own responses to that imagined world. In many ways the spectator is put in a position analogous to Othello's. He is obliged to determine the trustworthiness of Iago—critics still argue about whether certain statements of Iago are to be credited or not. He is made to feel Iago's all-compelling powers; if Sedgewick is right, Iago masters the audience (along with Brabantio, Roderigo, and Cassio) before he masters Othello. Unless the spectator walks out, he must then suffer helplessly Iago's horrible imaginings, and by Act IV may well feel as compelled as does Othello to find release from these oppressions (Nowottny). Other characters present further analogies. Under the influence of the contrasting verbal styles of Othello and Iago (Clemen, Morozov, Sewell), the spectator may choose to regard the play in an idiom of general glorification, as does Swinburne, or of general vilification, as does Leavis. He may find himself among those critics who judge the characters as self-righteously as does Othello (surveyed in my article) or as compassionately as does Desdemona (H. Wilson). Like Emilia, he may resist the lovers' commitment to tragic absolutes ('The world is a huge thing; 'tis a great price/For a small vice') and yet feel with Burke that this resistance is 'placed' and controlled through her expression of it. The playwright himself seems to enter into the imagined theatre event, as if he were a character in his own play. In the opening scenes, his pace of exposition is as stately as Othello's. In the first Cyprus scene, he seems through his minor characters to share his hero's magniloquence. Throughout, he outdoes Iago in the subtle craft and daring of his plotting. And like all his characters in this play, he drives relentlessly beyond his source to devastating extremes.

The theatre event that Shakespeare imagined thus provides a very generous latitude for interpretation. In making his choices, the interpreter should employ a final criterion: do they centre on what is currently most alive in the play? do they result in an experience that speaks to his condition? Here the student will be very much on his own. Ordinarily, current dramatists are the best guides to what is currently most alive dramatically, but it is not easy to see direct analogies between their work and *Othello*. As it happens, critics who have been particularly concerned with Shakespeare's contemporary relevance, such as L. C. Knights and Jan Kott, have not commented on this play. It is about Iago that the student will find commentators most helpful. If Iago is nothing if not critical, critics, in their detached and sceptical rationality, are by profession all too Iago-like. They know him like a brother, and have readily found in him the attitudes of irresponsible modern science (Auden), positivism (Heilman), and modern war (Goddard). With Othello, they have felt much less at home. His disparagers tend to treat him as if he were a modern 'anti-hero', yet are embarrassed by his heroic achievements. Even his admirers betray a sense of strain, a need to invoke historical attitudes now dead (Holloway, Bayley). Perhaps Paul Robeson is the most helpful. He comments on 'how strikingly contemporary American audiences from coast to coast' found the play: 'in its overtones of a clash of cultures, of the partial acceptance of and consequent effect upon one of a minority group. Against this background the jealousy of the protagonist becomes more credible, the blows to his pride more understandable, the final collapse of his personal, individual world more inevitable.'

I hope that this survey of *Othello* commentary will leave the student with a sense of opportunity. For all their profusion, previous studies of the play have been anything but exhaustive. We still do not have a convincing solution to the puzzle of its First Quarto and Folio texts, a comprehensive stage history, a history of its criticism, a well-balanced survey of its themes and images, a fresh treatment of its characters that takes an inclusive look at their various interpretations, or an aesthetic that accounts for its special powers, especially its contemporary appeal. As I see it, in fact, the most important studies of *Othello* remain to be made.

REFERENCES

TEXTS

Kernan, A. (ed.), *Othello* (Signet Shakespeare, New York, 1963).

Kittredge, G. L. (ed.), revised I. Ribner, *Othello* (Waltham, Mass., 1966).

Muir, Kenneth (ed.), *Othello* (New Penguin Shakespeare, Harmondsworth, 1968).

Ridley, M. R. (ed.), *Othello* (new Arden Shakespeare, London, 1958).

Schröer, M. (ed.), *Othello: Paralleldruck der ersten Quarto und der ersten Folio* (Heidelberg, 1949).

Spencer, T. J. B. (ed.), *Elizabethan Love Stories* (Penguin Shakespeare Library, Harmondsworth, 1968).

Walker, Alice, and Wilson, J. Dover (eds.), *Othello* (New Cambridge Shakespeare, Cambridge, 1957).

THE MAKING OF *OTHELLO*

Allen, Ned B., 'The Two Parts of *Othello*', *Shakespeare Survey 21* (1968).

Coghill, Nevill, *Shakespeare's Professional Skills* (Cambridge, 1964).

Honigmann, E. A. J., *The Stability of Shakespeare's Text* (London, 1965).

CRITICISM AND COMMENTARY

Auden, W. H., *The Dyer's Hand* (New York, 1962).

Bayley, John, *The Characters of Love* (London, 1960).

Bethell, S. L., 'The Diabolic Images in *Othello*', *Shakespeare Survey 5* (1952).

Bonnard, G., 'Are Othello and Desdemona Innocent or Guilty?', *English Studies*, 30 (1949).

Bradley, A. C., *Shakespearean Tragedy* (London, 1904).

Burke, Kenneth, '*Othello*: An Essay to Illustrate a Method', *Hudson Review*, 4 (1951, repr. in *Perspectives by Incongruity*, ed. S. E. Hyman (Bloomington, Ind., 1964)).

Carlisle, Carol Jones, *Shakespeare from the Greenroom* (Chapel Hill, N.C., 1969).

Clemen, W. H., *The Development of Shakespeare's Imagery* (London, 1951).

Draper, John W., *The Othello of Shakespeare's Audience* (New York, 1966).

Eliot, T. S., 'Shakespeare and the Stoicism of Seneca', in *Selected Essays 1917–1932* (London, 1932).

Elliott, George R., *Flaming Minister* (Durham, N.C., 1953).

Empson, William, *The Structure of Complex Words* (London, 1951).

Everett, Barbara, 'Reflections on the Sentimentalist's *Othello*', *Critical Quarterly* 3 (1961).

Fergusson, Francis, *Shakespeare: The Pattern in his Carpet* (New York, 1970).

Gardner, Helen, *The Noble Moor*, British Academy Lecture 1956, repr. in *Shakespeare Criticism 1935–1960*, ed. Anne Ridler (World's Classics, London, 1963).

——, '*Othello*: A Retrospect, 1900–67', *Shakespeare Survey 21* (1968).

Goddard, Harold, *The Meaning of Shakespeare* (Chicago, Ill., 1951).

Granville-Barker, Harley, *Prefaces to Shakespeare*, Fourth Series (London, 1945).

Greg, W. W., *The Shakespeare First Folio* (Oxford, 1955).

Hapgood, Robert, 'The Trials of Othello', in *Pacific Coast Studies in Shakespeare*, ed. W. F. McNeir and T. N. Greenfield (Eugene, Ore., 1966).

——, 'Shakespeare and the Included Spectator', in *Reinterpretations of Elizabethan Drama*, ed. N. Rabkin (English Institute Essays, New York, 1969).

Hartnoll, Phyllis (ed.), *Shakespeare in Music* (London, 1964).

Hawkes, Terence, *Shakespeare and the Reason* (London, 1964).

Hazlitt, William, *Characters of Shakespeare's Plays* (London, 1817; World's Classics, London, 1917).

Heilman, Robert B., *Magic in the Web* (Lexington, Ky., 1956).

Hibbard, G. R., '*Othello* and the Pattern of Shakespearian Tragedy', *Shakespeare Survey 21* (1968).

Holloway, John, *The Story of the Night* (London, 1961).

Hunter, G. K., *Othello and Colour Prejudice*, British Academy Lecture, 1968.

Hyman, Stanley Edgar, *Iago, Some Approaches to the Illusion of his Motivation* (New York, 1970).

Jones, Eldred, *Othello's Countrymen* (London, 1965).

Jorgensen, Paul, *Shakespeare's Military World* (Berkeley, Calif., 1956).
——, *Redeeming Shakespeare's Words* (Berkeley , Calif., 1962).
Kerman, Joseph, *Opera as Drama* (New York, 1956).
Kirschbaum, Leo, 'The Modern Othello', *ELH*, 2 (1944), repr. in *A Casebook on 'Othello'*, ed. L. F. Dean (New York, 1961).
Knight, G. Wilson, *The Wheel of Fire* (London, 1930).
Leavis, F. R., 'Diabolic Intellect and the Noble Hero', *Scrutiny*, 6 (1937), repr. in *The Common Pursuit* (London, 1952).
Mack, Maynard, 'The Jacobean Shakespeare', *Jacobean Theatre* (Stratford-upon-Avon Studies 1, ed. J. R. Brown and B. Harris, London, 1960).
Morozov, Mikhail M., 'The Individualization of Shakespeare's Characters through Imagery', *Shakespeare Survey 2* (1949) .
Muir, Kenneth, 'The Jealousy of Iago', *English Miscellany*, 2 (Rome, 1951).
Nicoll, Allardyce, *Studies in Shakespeare* (London, 1931).
Nowottny, Winifed M. T., 'Justice and Love in *Othello*', *University of Toronto Quarterly*, 21 (1952), repr. in *A Casebook on 'Othello'*, ed. L. F. Dean (New York, 1961).
Olivier, Laurence, 'The Great Sir Laurence', *Life*, 56 (1 May, 1964).
Prior, Moody, 'Character in Relation to Action in *Othello*', *Modern Philology*, 44 (1947).
Raysor, T. M., *Coleridge's Shakespearean Criticism*, 2 vols. (Cambridge, Mass., 1930), repr. Everyman's Library (London, 1960).
Robeson, Paul, 'Some Reflections on *Othello* and the Nature of Our Time', *American Scholar*, 14 (1945).
Rogers, Robert, 'Endopsychic Drama in *Othello*', *Shakespeare Quarterly*, 20 (1969).
Rosenberg, Marvin, *The Masks of Othello* (Berkeley, Calif., 1961).
Rymer, Thomas, *The Critical Works of Thomas Rymer*, ed. C. Zimansky (New Haven, Conn., 1956).
Scragg, Leah, 'Iago—Vice or Devil?', *Shakespeare Survey 21* (1968).
Sedgewick, G. G., *Of Irony, Especially in Drama* (Toronto, 1948).
Sewell, Arthur, *Character and Society in Shakespeare* (Oxford, 1951).
Shaffer, Elinor S., 'Iago's Malignity Motivated: Coleridge's Unpublished "Opus Magnum" ', *Shakespeare Quarterly*, 19 (1968).
Shaw, G. B., 'A Word More about Verdi', *Anglo-Saxon Review* (1901).
Spivack, Bernard, *Shakespeare and the Allegory of Evil* (New York, 1958).
Spurgeon, Caroline, *Shakespeare's Imagery* (Cambridge, 1935).
Stanislavski, Konstantin, *Stanislavsky Produces 'Othello'*, trans. H. Nowak (London, 1948).
Stoll, E. E., *Othello: An Historical and Comparative Study* (Minneapolis, Minn., 1915).
Swinburne, Algernon Charles, *A Study of Shakespeare* (London, 1909).
Traversi, D. A., *Approach to Shakespeare* (London, 1938; 3rd edn., 2 vols., 1968–9).
Van Doren, Mark, *Shakespeare* (New York, 1939).
West, Robert, 'The Christianness of *Othello*', *Shakespeare Quarterly*, 15 (1964).

Wilson, H. S., *On the Design of Shakespearian Tragedy* (Toronto, 1958).

Wimsatt, W. K. (ed.), *Samuel Johnson on Shakespeare* (New York, 1960; repr. as *Dr. Johnson on Shakespeare*, Penguin Shakespeare Library, Harmondsworth, 1969).

12. *King Lear*

KENNETH MUIR

It has been suggested by several critics that *King Lear* has replaced *Hamlet* as the tragedy which finds the most direct response from the modern reader. As L. C. Knights put it, *King Lear* 'is the great central masterpiece, the great exploratory allegory'. This suggestion is certainly borne out by the large number of books and articles on the play which have been published in recent years.

TEXTS

All editions of *King Lear* are based on the two original texts—the First Quarto, published in 1608, and the First Folio, published in 1623—in varying proportions. Until the work of bibliographers and textual critics in the present century, editors chose readings from either text, according to taste. It is now generally agreed that, whatever the basis of the Quarto text, the Folio text of *King Lear* is nearer to what Shakespeare wrote; but, even so, editors are still bound to accept a number of readings from the inferior text and, since there were cuts in the prompt-book from which the Folio text was derived, a number of long passages. The only modern edition that takes the Quarto as its copy-text is the New Temple, edited by M. R. Ridley. As he accepts Folio readings only when the Quarto reading is impossible, his edition is unsatisfactory.

The play appeared, of course, in all editions of Shakespeare's works from 1623 to the present day, but the first separate edition that need be mentioned is H. H. Furness's New Variorum (1880) which gives the readings of all previous editions and a generous summary of previous commentary and criticism. Although much of this material is of little value and although the edition has inevitably been superseded textually and critically, it still contains information not easily obtainable elsewhere.

The most valuable edition from the textual point of view is G. I. Duthie's old-spelling edition. This contains a detailed examination of all the variant readings; but it is so severely textual, without any annotation, that only the scholar will find it useful. Some years later, Duthie collaborated with J. Dover Wilson in the New Cambridge edition. This has a good introduction, succinct notes, a stage history, and a glossary. Fuller annotation is provided in Kenneth Muir's new Arden edition. This, which has been revised several times, also includes a selection of the main sources of the play—Sidney's *Arcadia, King Leir,* Holinshed's *Chronicles,* Spenser's *Faerie Queene, A Mirror for Magistrates.* Russell Fraser's Signet edition contains a shorter selection of sources and some representative criticism; but annotation is restricted to glosses at the foot of the page. Alfred Harbage's Pelican edition has a good and well-printed text, a sensible introduction, and brief glosses. Two other American editions may be mentioned: the Yale, edited by C. F. Tucker Brooke and W. L. Phelps, neat and handy, but with very brief annotations; and that of G. L. Kittredge with a good introduction, a conservative text, and useful notes. G. K. Hunter's New Penguin edition has a freshly considered text and ample annotation.

CRITICISM AND COMMENTARY

So much has been written about *King Lear*—a number of whole books, hundreds of articles, and scores of chapters in books concerned with wider aspects of Shakespeare's work—that in a survey of this kind it will be necessary to make a representative selection. There are useful bibliographies by S. A. Tannenbaum and in *The 'King Lear' Perplex* by H. Bonheim. Others will be found in the books by Heilman and Elton mentioned below and in the New Cambridge edition mentioned above. The criticism written between 1604 (when the play was first performed) and 1904 (when Bradley's *Shakespearean Tragedy* was published) can be considered in roughly chronological order. But during the present century the proliferation has been such that it will be more convenient to consider the criticism under various headings.

The first substantial criticism of the play appeared in Nahum Tate's preface to his adaptation, in which he attempts to justify his alterations by enumerating Shakespeare's supposed faults—the introduction of the Fool, insufficient motive for Cordelia's conduct, insufficient reason for her murder—faults which made the play 'a Heap of Jewels, unstrung and unpolish'd'. So Tate cut out the Fool, made Cordelia enamoured of Edgar and narrowly escape being raped by Edmund, and restored Lear to his throne at the end of the play. This adaptation held the stage throughout the eighteenth century and, although it was condemned by Joseph Addison in *The Spectator,* it was defended by Samuel Johnson in his edition, on the grounds that the death of Cordelia was unbearably painful and a violation of poetic justice. Charles Lamb, who had seen only Tate's adaptation in the theatre, was constrained to argue that Shakespeare's tragedies—and especially *King Lear*—could not be adequately performed. William Hazlitt, in *Characters of Shakespeare's Plays*, quoted Lamb's essay with approval; Kean, influenced by these critics, restored the tragic ending in 1823, but absurdly retained the Edgar-Cordelia love-scenes; and Macready, fifteen years later, reintroduced the Fool.

Meanwhile, the eighteenth-century habit of weighing Shakespeare's beauties against his faults, and the feeling that with all his genius he lacked art—e.g. in Joseph Warton's essays on the play—had given place to the enthusiasm of the Romantics. Schlegel, unlike Warton, realized the function of the Gloucester underplot. Coleridge in his courses of lectures had perceptive comments on several scenes but nothing as striking as his remarks on *Hamlet* and *Othello*. In his *Table Talk* (29 December 1822) he called the play 'the most tremendous effort of Shakespeare as a poet'. Shelley in his 'Defence of Poetry' described the play as 'the most perfect specimen of dramatic poetry existing in the world'. But perhaps the poet who made the most profound remarks about *King Lear* was Keats. In addition to his sonnet, 'On sitting down to read *King Lear* once again', he speaks of the play in his *Letters* and stresses the way in which the disagreeables are evaporated by the intensity of the poetry (21 December 1817). He has also some marginalia in his copy of Hazlitt's *Characters* —stimulated by some of the best criticism in the book—on the relation between the play and Shakespeare's own experience and on the Fool. (These are given in Muir's edition.) D. G. James discusses Keats's views on *King Lear* in an article in *Shakespeare Survey 13*.

The first full analysis of the structure of the play, of the parallelism of the two plots, and of the trio of madness—Lear, Poor Tom, the Fool—in the storm scenes was made by Richard G. Moulton in *Shakespeare as a Dramatic Artist*. A few years earlier, A. C. Swinburne had set the tone for much later criticism by proclaiming in *A Study of Shakespeare* that Gloucester's words, after his blinding—

> As flies to wanton boys are we to the gods:
> They kill us for their sport—

were the keynote of the play. He spoke of Shakespeare's 'tragic fatalism' and declared that 'Requital, redemption, amends, equity, explanation, pity and mercy, are words without a meaning here.' Edward Dowden in what is perhaps the best Victorian book on Shakespeare—*Shakspere: A Critical Study of his Mind and Art*—

stressed the stoical attitude revealed in the play and, in asserting that 'all that is tragically sublime is also grotesque', he anticipated Wilson Knight.

A. C. Bradley's *Shakespearean Tragedy*, the most famous and probably still the best book on the subject, contains two chapters on *King Lear*, which raise all the main questions concerning the play: whether it is a good stage play, whether it is well constructed, whether it can be acted, whether it is pessimistic, to what extent it reflects Shakespeare's personal feelings, whether the opening scene is credible, whether the death of Cordelia is dramatically justifiable, whether Lear is 'redeemed', and what is the function of the animal imagery. Later critics do not always agree with Bradley's answers, but they agree that most of these questions should be asked.

Bradley argued that *King Lear* was Shakespeare's 'greatest achievement, but not his best play'; that it shared the structural weakness of *Timon of Athens* and that the underplot was largely to blame for this; that the first scene was 'strange but not incredible'; that the blinding of Gloucester, acceptable in the study, was too horrible for the stage; that the ending was not inevitable; that the play might be entitled 'The Redemption of King Lear'; and that we should realize that 'our whole attitude in asking or expecting that goodness should be prosperous is wrong.' We have to bear in mind that Bradley never had the chance of seeing an uncut version of the play in the theatre.

Bradley's second chapter is concerned mainly with the characters of the play, and this side of his work has not worn so well. The careful analysis might be useful to actors studying the various roles, but it takes too little note of Elizabethan psychological ideas, of Elizabethan stage conventions, and of the impressionistic, rather than naturalistic, methods of the poetic dramatist. Bradley was criticised by Elmer Edgar Stoll in *Art and Artifice in Shakespeare* and elsewhere for his failure to appreciate the conventions of poetic drama. Lily B. Campbell explained in *Shakespeare's Tragic Heroes: Slaves of Passion* that if *King Lear* were considered in the light of Elizabethan theories, it would be seen as 'a tragedy of wrath in old age'. In the second edition of this book she reprinted two articles in which she criticized Bradley's character analysis, not primarily because it failed to use Elizabethan terminology, 'but because it fails to understand the interrelationships of the things he talks about'. His analysis of character 'was made on a foundation of morality without morals, as well as a psychology untrue to psychological thinking of any period'. Bradley's terminology may sometimes be confused, but neither his morality nor his knowledge of human psychology deserves this intemperate condemnation.

The sources of the play are discussed briefly in most editions. W. Perrett in *The Story of King Lear* made an exhaustive examination of all the versions previous to Shakespeare's; and W. W. Greg made a careful study of Shakespeare's indebtedness to Holinshed's *Chronicles*, Spenser's *Faerie Queene*, *A Mirror for Magistrates*, and the old play of *King Leir*. Neither Perrett nor Greg concerned himself with the underplot: but F. Pyle discussed the use of Sidney's *Arcadia*, arguing that Shakespeare's imagination was fired not so much by the old play as by the tale of the Paphlagonian King and his two sons who were examples of 'true natural goodness' and 'wretched ungratefulness'; and Irving Ribner also wrote on the influence of Sidney's *Arcadia* on the structure of *King Lear*. There are two articles by R. A. Law on Shakespeare's use of Holinshed and *King Leir*. D. M. McKeithan had pointed out earlier that the account of Plangus in *Arcadia* had probably suggested Edmund's deceit of Edgar and Gloucester. K. Muir discussed Shakespeare's use of Samuel Harsnett's *Declaration of Egregious Popishe Impostures*, not merely in the mad scenes, as earlier editors had suggested, but throughout the play; and in his edition he pointed out further echoes of Holinshed, Sidney, and of Shakespeare's *Titus Andronicus*. The influence of Florio's translation of Montaigne's essays, especially on vocabulary, is discussed by G. C. Taylor in *Shakespeare's Debt to Montaigne*; and W. B. Drayton Henderson wrote on the influence of Montaigne's longest essay, the 'Apology for Raymond Sebonde', on Shakespeare's thought. H. B. Charlton compared *King Lear* with earlier versions of the story, in the attempt to throw some light on the dramatist's intentions; and R. W. Chambers made the relevant point that in all previous versions, except the old play, Cordelia commits suicide in prison after being defeated by her nephews—a gloomier ending than Shakespeare's. Edmund Blunden's *Shakespeare's Significances* contains, amongst other interesting points, evidence that Shakespeare echoed two of Horace's poems in the storm scenes. George Gordon in 'A Note on the World of *King Lear*' showed that some of the Fool's questions are to be found in a work of popular philosophy, *The Sapience of Nature*.

The possible influence on the play of the true story of Brian Annesley, who in his dotage was ill treated by his two older daughters and their husbands and succoured by his youngest, Cordelia, is discussed by G. M. Young and, with some scepticism, by Geoffrey Bullough. Bullough's *Narrative and Dramatic Sources of Shakespeare*, vol. 7 (1973) includes the sources of *King Lear*. C. J. Sisson mentions two similar cases concerning Ralph Hansby and Sir William Allen, who both divided their estates among their three married daughters. All Allen's daughters proved unkind; Hansby had one kind daughter, but her name was not Cordelia.

Critics differ as to the skill with which Shakespeare constructed his play from these materials. Allardyce Nicoll saw signs of exhaustion or haste in the play. C. F. Tucker Brooke asserted that 'by the verdict of criticism and theatrical experience alike, *King Lear* is a poor stage play'; and Richard H. Perkinson complained of its 'loose episodic structure'. Bradley listed a large number of defects— most of which would not be noticed in performance, and followed Lamb in supposing that the play was 'two huge for the stage'. Tolstoy took *King Lear* as his main exhibit in his attack on Shakespeare for his triviality, irreligion, immorality, vulgarity, and insincerity; and he tried to prove that *King Leir* was superior to Shakespeare's tragedy. G. Wilson Knight, in his reply to this attack, showed that Tolstoy had made the mistake of treating Shakespeare as a would-be naturalistic writer whose worth depended on his creation of life-like characters. Another effective reply was made by George Orwell in 'Lear, Tolstoy and the Fool'. He argued that Tolstoy's attitude to the play was determined by his dislike of the way Shakespeare had treated the theme of renunciation: the aged Tolstoy was more like Lear than he could ever admit. An article by Y. D. Levin, however, has shown that Tolstoy was not the first Russian writer to complain of the unnaturalness of Shakespeare's plays. Another attack on the play by a foreign writer who, like Tolstoy, appears not to have appreciated the poetry, is to be found in André Gide's *Journals* after he had witnessed Sir Laurence Olivier's performance as Lear. Gide thought that the play was execrable, absurd, contrived, and false. 'Art triumphs. One has only to applaud.' Almost the same complaint of the sacrifice of truth had been made by an English critic, John Middleton Murry, who called *King Lear* an artefact, lacking in spontaneity, and inferior to *Coriolanus*. Although Shakespeare took immense pains in the composition of the play, the result is laboured; and Murry blames the failure on Shakespeare's uncontrollable despair and his 'terrible primitive revulsion against sex'. We should therefore regard the play as 'a tremendous effort towards control'; but it was 'a kind of enforced utterance' at a time when silence would have been more natural and more wholesome. But there is no reason to suppose that Lear's revulsion against sex was Shakespeare's own, since sex nausea was known by the Elizabethans to be a frequent symptom of madness, any more than that a poet writes tragedies when he is 'in the depths' and comedies when he is 'on the heights'.

The only recent critic to share Murry's views is H. A. Mason who suggests in an article in *The Cambridge Quarterly* (reprinted in *Shakespeare's Tragedies of Love*) that most modern critics, including Knights and Traversi, have read qualities into the play which are not really there; that Bradley's complaints were justifiable; that the play is radically incoherent; that Gloucester is a more sympathetic character than Lear; that Edgar indulges in cheap moralizing; and— oddest of all—that the play lacks the intensity of the other great tragedies. On this last point, Mason is diametrically opposed to Keats who told a correspondent to examine *King Lear* as a supreme example of intensity.

Harley Granville-Barker's splendid preface to *King Lear* is the best answer to those critics who think that the play cannot be acted. Not merely does he give admirable advice on how the various parts should be played, he also replies directly to the arguments of Lamb and Bradley by showing how the storm scenes, which were regarded as impossible to perform, should be staged. He allows that it is impossible on a stage which has elaborate scenery and stage devices; but, if played as Shakespeare intended, with Lear personifying the storm, so that the actor impersonates both Lear and the storm, it is supremely effective. Bradley had supposed that the Elizabethan stage, with its more limited resources, was even less able to give an adequate representation of these scenes; but, as Granville-Barker points out, Shakespeare obtains his effects largely by means of the poetry. Sir John Gielgud, in a production for which Granville-Barker was unofficially responsible, was able to validate these arguments; and Gielgud's *Stage Directions* includes the hints made to him by Granville-Barker. (It may be added that Shakespeare did not expect his actor to shout above the noise of the thunder: in the First Folio the stage directions indicate that the thunder occurs between speeches or in natural pauses.)

One of the questions which have provoked most controversy during the present century is whether the play is the expression of pessimism or nihilism, or, as J. C. Maxwell once said, 'a Christian play about a pagan world'. To Bradley's claim that Lear was redeemed, L. L. Schücking retorted that Lear's criticisms of society are the reflection of his mental derangement and that he is not purified by his suffering. But the three moments crucial to Bradley's theory of Lear's development occur either before his madness or after his recovery. To R. W. Chambers, the play presents the world as, in Keats's phrase, a vale of soul-making; and G. L. Bickersteth comes to a similar conclusion. John F. Danby maintains likewise that the play is essentially Christian, with Cordelia as an allegorical, Christ-like figure. Shakespeare, Danby argues, presents the conflict between two conceptions of nature, benignant, rational, and divinely ordered on the one hand, and on the other the assumption that man is governed merely by appetite and self-interest. His view of Cordelia is shared by S. L. Bethell in his *Shakespeare and the Popular Dramatic Tradition* and by Paul N. Siegel in *Shakespearean Tragedy and the Elizabethan Compromise*. D. A. Traversi may also be considered here. His long article, which appeared in *Scrutiny* (1952–3), now appears in a condensed form in the latest edition of *An Approach to Shakespeare*. If it now appears less impressive than it did, this is partly because his views have affinities with those of Danby, Knight, Knights, and Heilman, and partly because they have been absorbed into the critical stream during the last fifteen years. He argues that 'the whole action of the play might be described as a projection of the conflicting issues in the mind of the central protagonist.' He defends Cordelia's initial behaviour, Lear himself being responsible for the breaking up of reciprocal loyalties. He accepts the idea that Lear acquires understanding through suffering, and he stressess the fact that the play is particularly concerned with the nature of justice. The main weakness of Traversi's approach is that he never seems to visualize *King Lear* as a play to be performed.

John Lawlor in his chapter on the play in *The Tragic Sense in Shakespeare* also emphasizes the theme of justice, but he concludes that Shakespeare's 'subject is illusion, and in Lear it is shown as an incurable condition'. A more directly Christian interpretation is that of Terence Hawkes in *Shakespeare and the Reason*. He makes some interesting incidental points, as when he suggests that 'on the level, not of fact, but of function, Cordelia and the Fool can be said to be the same "character". They fulfil identical roles in the play's thematic construction.' Paul A. Jorgensen argued that the King is brought by suffering to an understanding of himself and of mankind. Kenneth Myrick, in 'Christian Pessimism in *King Lear*', says that the play conformed to the orthodox views of Shakespeare's day. D. G. James in *The Dream of Learning* has a valuable comparison between Bacon and Shakespeare, and he suggests that Shakespeare deliberately denied himself any expression of Christian belief but exhibited 'the limits merely of our human experience as they are reached by souls of surpassing excellence and beauty'. Although there is no escape from evil, the good is 'altogether proof against all that is brought against it'. L. C. Knights similarly declared in *Some Shakespearean Themes* that the mind 'is directed towards affirmation *in spite of everything*' since 'the centre of the action is the complete endorsement of a particular quality of being.' H. S. Wilson in his book *On the Design of Shakespearian Tragedy* also declared that the play affirmed 'the value of human love' and was a kind of synthesis of Shakespeare's other tragedies. Virgil K. Whitaker in *The Mirror up to Nature*, while admitting that the word 'salvation' is never mentioned, regards the play as 'profoundly Christian in thought', containing the Christian answer to the problem of suffering.

On the other side of the debate are ranged a large number of modern critics. Barbara Everett attacked all those critics who had tried (as she thought) to turn the tragedy into an allegory or a miracle play. She evoked a number of rather ineffective replies. Nicholas Brooke in his valuable scene-by-scene commentary and in an article argued that the ending is 'without any support from systems of moral or artistic belief at all. It is the most painful thing in our, perhaps in any, literature.' He showed that Edgar's 'morality play is exposed by Lear's experience'. To Sears Jayne the play is harshly pagan; and Helen Gardner in her admirable lecture denied that Lear learns anything from experience. John Holloway argues in *The Story of the Night* that Lear, like Shakespeare's other tragic heroes, is a scapegoat or human sacrifice, and, comparing the play to Job, he stresses the continual sequence of disasters and the meagreness of consolation at the end. Jan Kott in *Shakespeare Our Contemporary* rather absurdly treats *King Lear* as part of the theatre of the absurd, comparing it to Beckett's *End Game*. Edwin Muir, more responsibly than Kott, showed that a poet living in the present age could use his experience of the world to illuminate Shakespeare's play. John D. Rosenberg, while repudiating Kott's account of Lear —'a clown king in a refuse can'—where 'idealisation has been replaced by caricature', complained that 'modern criticism has made the terror and tragedy peripheral to the play.' John Shaw followed up Rosenberg's article with a discussion of the final lines of the play, in which he argued that Albany's penultimate speech, because it resembles the concluding speeches of other tragedies, was deliberately written 'to throw a fresh and shocking emphasis upon the last confused words of the play'. J. K. Walton, writing on Lear's last speech, argues that it is wrong to interpret it to mean that he imagines Cordelia to be alive, as this would alter the direction of the whole movement of the play. J. Stampfer reaches a similar conclusion.

It will be seen from these examples that the critics fall into two opposing parties on this matter. But the fullest and most learned treatment is William R. Elton's *King Lear and the Gods*. After an exhaustive discussion of the evidence, he comes to the conclusion that modern critics are not justified in calling *King Lear* 'a drama of meaningful suffering and redemption, within a just universe ruled by providential higher powers', since Lear is not regenerated or redeemed, since providence 'cannot be shown to be operative', and since 'the devastating fifth act shatters, more violently than an earlier apostasy might have done, the foundations of faith itself.' Elton shows that the characters in the play exhibit four attitudes to providence: Edgar and Cordelia are virtuous pagans; Goneril, Regan, and Edmund are atheists; Gloucester is superstitious; and Lear himself represents the view that God is mysterious and unintelligible to mortal eyes. Elton's strongest arguments are the dechristianizing of the old play; the ironical structure of Shakespeare's play, that is nicely calculated to destroy our faith not merely in poetic justice, but in divine justice; and the dusty answer given to Albany's prayer for Cordelia's safety. All this is true, but it does not inevitably lead to Elton's conclusion. A Christian, after all, need not believe that God intervenes to protect the good, nor suppose that the virtuous triumph in this life; and in the world of the play any question of a future life is properly ruled out. The flagrant injustice of this life cannot be reversed by the operations of divine justice: Shakespeare had to start from the dramatic hypothesis available to a pagan. He shows that the will to power is self-destructive, that the violation of the natural law leads to anarchy, and that the sins of the comparatively good open the door to the worse sins of the evil characters—who are yet not wholly evil—and to the death of the innocent. It may be said that the Christian ethic is vindicated without any support from the Christian hope. As Oscar J. Campbell implies in 'The Salvation of Lear' and as Enid Welsford says: 'The metaphysical comfort of the Scriptures is deliberately omitted, though not therefore necessarily denied.' A chapter in Walter Stein's *Criticism as Dialogue* contains a brilliant reply to Mason, Kott, and Nicholas Brooke.

The imagery of *King Lear* has been the subject of a considerable amount of criticism. Bradley, as we have seen, commented on the significance of the animal imagery and he was making use of an article by J. Kirkman on 'Animal Nature *Versus* Human Nature in *King Lear*' written many years earlier. But Caroline Spurgeon calculated that the dominant iterative image of the play is that of a body racked and tortured. Her article was published in 1930 and incorporated in her big book on *Shakespeare's Imagery*. W. H. Clemen showed in *Shakespeares Bilder*, afterwards revised as *The Development of Shakespeare's Imagery*, how the imagery is fully integrated with the structure of the play, and that the images fall into 'clearly distinguishable patterns'. By the time his revision appeared in 1951, Clemen had had the advantage of reading R. B. Heilman's *This Great Stage*, the most elaborate analysis of the imagery of a single play which has yet been attempted. Heilman showed that Spurgeon's method of concentrating on a single group of images gave an inadequate and one-sided view of the play. He realized, with Clemen, that it was necessary to show 'the interdependence of style, diction, imagery, plot, technique of characterization, and all the other constituent elements of drama'. The various groups of images analysed by Heilman include those relating to sight and blindness, to clothes, to madness in reason and reason in madness, to nature, and to the gods. Blindness has also been treated by J. I. M. Stewart in *Character and Motive in Shakespeare*; clothes by Thelma Greenfield in 'The Clothing Motif in *King Lear*'; nature, as we have seen, by Danby, and by Robert Speaight in *Nature in Shakespearian Tragedy*, and the gods by Elton. Heilman makes use of the repetition of words as well as metaphors and similes. In this respect he was forestalled by F. C. Kolbe's brief study, *Shakespeare's Way*, based on articles written many years before its publication in 1930. Sometimes, it must be admitted, Heilman is lacking in a sense of proportion and he carries his analysis to absurd lengths; and these weaknesses of an important book enabled W. R. Keast in 'Imagery and Meaning in the Interpretation of *King Lear*' to attack its whole method for the circuitous and ponderous way by which it reached platitudinous conclusions. Yet no critic before Heilman had brought out so clearly the basic paradoxes of the play.

One such paradox is to be found in the wisdom of the Fool, so that those who have written of this character have been led into broader questions of interpretation. Enid Welsford shows in a chapter in *The Fool* on 'The Court-Fool in Elizabethan Drama' that Lear's 'tragedy is the investing of the King with motley: it is also the crowning and apotheosis of the Fool.' She, like William Empson in *The Structure of Complex Words*, brings out the importance of an idea which goes back to Erasmus's *Praise of Folly* and beyond. Empson is brilliant, original, and stimulating, but not always convincing. There is a sensible treatment of the subject in Robert H. Goldsmith's *Wise Fools in Shakespeare* and a short article by Carolyn S.

French, entitled 'Shakespeare's "Folly": *King Lear'*. Leslie Hotson discusses the Fool's costume and the first interpreter of the role, Robert Armin, in *Shakespeare's Motley.*

Russell A. Fraser's *Shakespeare's Poetics in Relation to 'King Lear'* may be mentioned here as he deals with Elizabethan ideas on providence, fortune, anarchy, order, and reason as represented in emblem books and as used in the play. Despite its inflated style, the book gives a useful account of the ideas in the minds of Shakespeare's original audience and it should help the modern reader to be on his guard against anachronistic interpretations. Winifred Nowottny has two relevant articles—'Lear's Questions' and 'Some Aspects of the Style of *King Lear'.*

The characters of the play have, of course, been discussed by many critics. Some, influenced by Stoll and Schücking, have stressed the functional role of characters. Leo Kirschbaum, for example, in a chapter called 'Banquo and Edgar: Character or Function', argued against those who attempted to make a consistent character out of Edgar, when he merely serves a dramatic function. Yet Kirschbaum in an article on 'Albany' claims that this character has not been appreciated, and that he develops in the course of the play into a great man. Peter Mortensen's article on 'The Role of Albany' is more cautious. There is a good chapter on Edgar in J. M. Lothian's *King Lear: A Tragic Reading of Life*; and Russell A. Peck argues in 'Edgar's Pilgrimage' that Edgar's search for identity parallels Lear's.

Many critics have concerned themselves with Lear's character. Francis G. Schoff, for example, in 'King Lear: Moral Example or Tragic Protagonist', stresses that Lear was not stupid. The same point is made by G. R. Elliott in *Dramatic Providence in 'Macbeth'* in which he argues that the coronet which is divided between Albany and Cornwall had been intended for Cordelia who, with her husband, would be the real rulers of Britain. But Elliott applies to the play his general theory of Shakespearian tragedy, and he assumes that both Lear and Cordelia are guilty of sinful pride. William Frost, on the other hand, in 'Shakespeare's Rituals and the Opening of *King Lear'*, defends the first scene as allegory, as appropriate to the folkloristic nature of the story, and as producing an effect of nightmarish inevitability. Among other relevant articles may be mentioned Ivor Morris's discussion of 'Cordelia and Lear', T. B. Stroup's 'Cordelia and the Fool', Paul Siegel's 'Adversity and the Miracle of Love in *King Lear'*, Robert P. Adams on 'King Lear's Revenges', and Robert H. West on 'Sex and Pessimism in *King Lear'.*

Early discussions of Lear's madness suffered from the unsatisfactory nature of medical knowledge, though one is sceptical of the diagnosis in H. Somerville's *Madness in Shakespearian Tragedy* and still more of Ella Freeman Sharpe's theory in *Collected Papers on Psycho-Analysis* that the play reflected the loves and hates of Shakespeare's very early childhood. Apart from anything else, the essay contains biographical mistakes. Freud himself, with greater plausibility, remarked that Lear had reached the age when he ought to 'renounce love, choose death, and make friends with the necessity of dying'. More recently Kenneth Muir has discussed the various forms of madness in the play and compared Shakespeare's treatment with that of other Elizabethan dramatists, and Josephine W. Bennett has written of 'The Storm Within: The Madness of Lear'. Harry Levin has a valuable essay, entitled 'The Heights and the Depths', on iv.vi, with some more general comments on the play as a whole.

G. Wilson Knight has two influential chapters on *King Lear* in *The Wheel of Fire*. In one of them he discusses 'the comedy of the grotesque' which Dowden had found in the play, and in the other what he calls 'the *Lear* universe'. He points out the comic aspect of the opening scene, the element of absurdity in Lear's madness, underlined by the Fool, and the ludicrous nature of Gloucester's attempted suicide. He speaks of the 'demonic laughter that echoes in the *Lear* universe'. The basis of the play, in his view, is that 'a tremendous soul is . . . incongruously geared to a puerile intellect.' But Knight does not fall into Kott's error of regarding the play as part of the theatre of the absurd; and, when he played the role, he aimed at sublimity rather than the grotesque. His other chapter touches on several themes that have been elaborated by later critics during the last forty years: the importance of 'nature' (in various senses) in the scheme of the play, the animal imagery, our ambivalent attitude to Edmund, Cordelia as the principle of ideal love, the resemblance of the play to the book of Job, and the play considered as a kind of *purgatorio*. One suggestion in this essay, that Edmund tries to save Cordelia because his heart is kindled by the realization of Goneril and Regan's love for him and by the tragic pathos of their deaths, is more disputable. John Masefield had argued in *Shakespeare* that Edmund is silent for Goneril's sake and that he 'strokes his plumes with a tender thought for the brightness of life that made two princesses die for love of him'.

One of the most satisfying studies of the play is Maynard Mack's *King Lear in Our Time*, not primarily for its perfectly valid argument that Shakespeare's intentions should be respected and that the play should be performed without alterations, but for its insistence on the archetypal nature of the play and, above all, for its final chapter, published originally in the *Yale Review* under the title 'We came crying hither'. He rejects two opposite forms of sentimentality: the view expressed by Oscar J. Campbell and Siegel that Lear is not deceived when he thinks that Cordelia is alive, since she is transported to a better world, and Stampfer's view that the play leads us to believe that 'we inhabit an imbecile universe'. We are rather driven, as Mack says, 'to seek the meaning of our human fate not in what becomes of us, but in what we become'.

Finally, mention should be made of some more general books on Shakespeare which contain chapters, pages, or paragraphs on *King Lear*: Walter Raleigh's *Shakespeare*, Peter Alexander's *Shakespeare's Life and Art*, Theodore Spencer's *Shakespeare and the Nature of Man*, D. A. Stauffer's *Shakespeare's World of Images*, A. Sewell's *Character and Society in Shakespeare*, R. Ornstein's *The Moral Vision of Jacobean Tragedy*, I. Ribner's *Patterns in Shakespearian Tragedy*, G. Kozintsev's *Shakespeare: Time and Conscience*, and Reuben Brower's *Hero and Saint*

REFERENCES

TEXTS

Brooke, C. F. Tucker, and Phelps, W. L. (eds.), *King Lear* (Yale Shakespeare, New Haven, Conn., 1947).
Duthie, G. I. (ed.), *King Lear* (Oxford, 1949).
——, and Wilson, J. Dover, (eds.), *King Lear* (New Cambridge Shakespeare, Cambridge, 1960).
Fraser, Russell (ed.), *King Lear* (Signet Shakespeare, New York, 1963).
Furness, H. H. (ed.), *King Lear* (New Variorum Shakespeare, Philadelphia, Pa., 1880).
Harbage, Alfred (ed.), *King Lear* (Pelican Shakespeare, Baltimore, Md., 1958).
Hunter, G. K., ed., *King Lear* (New Penguin Shakespeare, Harmondsworth, 1972).
Kittredge, G. L. (ed.), *King Lear* (New York, 1940).
Muir, Kenneth (ed.), *King Lear* (new Arden Shakespeare, London, 1952).
Ridley, M. R. (ed.), *King Lear* (New Temple Shakespeare, London, 1935).

CRITICISM AND COMMENTARY

Adams, Robert P., 'King Lear's Revenges', *Modern Language Quarterly*, 21 (1960).
Addison, Joseph, *The Spectator* (16 April 1711).
Alexander, Peter, *Shakespeare's Life and Art* (London, 1939).
Bennett, Josephine W., 'The Storm Within: The Madness of Lear', *Shakespeare Quarterly*, 13 (1963).

Bethell, S. L., *Shakespeare and the Popular Dramatic Tradition* (London, 1944).

Bickersteth, G. L., *The Golden World of 'King Lear'* (London, 1946).

Blunden, Edmund, *Shakespeare's Significances* (London, 1929); repr. in *Shakespeare Criticism, 1919–35*, ed. A. Bradby (World's Classics, London, 1936).

Bonheim, H., *The 'King Lear' Perplex* (San Francisco, Calif., 1960).

Bradley, A. C., *Shakespearean Tragedy* (London, 1904).

Brooke, Nicholas, *Shakespeare: King Lear* (Studies in English Literature No. 15, London, 1963).

——, 'The Ending of *King Lear*', in *Shakespeare 1564–1964*, ed. E. A. Bloom (Providence, R.I., 1964).

Brooke, C. F. Tucker, *Essays on Shakespeare* (New Haven, Conn., 1948).

Brower, Reuben, *Hero and Saint: Shakespeare and the Graeco-Roman Tradition* (New York, 1971).

Bullough, Geoffrey, '*King Lear* and the Annesley Case', in *Festschrift Rudolf Stamm*, ed. E. Kolb and J. Hasler (Berne and Munich, 1969).

——, *Narrative and Dramatic Sources of Shakespeare*, vol. vii (1973).

Campbell, Lily B., *Shakespeare's Tragic Heroes: Slaves of Passion* (Cambridge, 1930; 2nd edn., London, 1961).

Campbell, Oscar J., 'The Salvation of Lear', *ELH*, 15 (1948).

Chambers, R. W., *King Lear* (Glasgow, 1940).

Charlton, H. B., *Shakespearian Tragedy* (Cambridge, 1948).

Clemen, W. H., *The Development of Shakespeare's Imagery* (London, 1951).

Coleridge, S. T., *Coleridge's Shakespearean Criticism*, ed. T. M. Raysor, 2 vols. (Cambridge, Mass., 1930); repr. Everyman's Library (London, 1960).

Danby, J. F., *Shakespeare's Doctrine of Nature* (London, 1949).

——, *Elizabethan and Jacobean Poets* (London, 1964).

Dowden, Edward, *Shakspere: A Critical Study of his Mind and Art* (London, 1875).

Elliott, G. R., *Dramatic Providence in 'Macbeth'* (Princeton, N.J., 2nd edn., 1960).

Elton, W. R., *King Lear and the Gods* (San Marino, Calif., 1966).

Empson, William, *The Structure of Complex Words* (London, 1951).

Everett, Barbara, 'The New King Lear', *Critical Quarterly*, 2 (1960).

Fraser, Russell, *Shakespeare's Poetics in Relation to 'King Lear'* (London, 1962).

French, Carolyn S., 'Shakespeare's "Folly": *King Lear*', *Shakespeare Quarterly*, 10 (1959).

Freud, S., *Collected Papers*, vol. iv (London, 1934).

Frost, William, 'Shakespeare's Rituals and the Opening of *King Lear*', *Hudson Review*, 10 (1958).

Gardner, Helen, *King Lear* (John Coffin Memorial Lecture, London, 1967).

Gide, André, *Journals*, trans. J. O'Brien (New York, 1956).

Goldsmith, Robert H., *Wise Fools in Shakespeare* (East Lansing, Mich., and Liverpool, 1955).

Gordon, George, *Shakespearian Comedy* (London, 1944).

Granville-Barker, Harley, *Prefaces to Shakespeare*, First Series (London, 1927).

Greenfield, Thelma, 'The Clothing Motif in *King Lear*', *Shakespeare Quarterly*, 5 (1954).

Greg, W. W., 'The Date of *King Lear* and Shakespeare's Use of Earlier Versions of the Story', *The Library*, 20 (1940).

Hawkes, Terence, *Shakespeare and the Reason* (London, 1964).

Hazlitt, William, *Characters of Shakespeare's Plays* (London, 1817; World's Classics, London, 1917).

Heilman, R. B., *This Great Stage* (Baton Rouge, La., 1948).

Henderson, W. B. Drayton, 'Montaigne's *Apologie of Raymond Sebond*, and *King Lear*', *Shakespeare Association Bulletin*, 14, 15 (1939–40).

Holloway, John, *The Story of the Night* (London, 1961).

Hotson, L., *Shakespeare's Motley* (London, 1952).

James, D. G., *The Dream of Learning* (Oxford, 1951).

——, 'Keats and *King Lear*', *Shakespeare Survey 13* (1960).

Jayne, Sears, 'Charity in *King Lear*', in *Shakespeare 400*, ed. J. G. McManaway (New York, 1964).

Jorgensen, Paul A., *Lear's Self-Discovery* (Berkeley, Calif., 1967).

Keast, W. R., 'Imagery and Meaning in the Interpretation of *King Lear*', *Modern Philology*, 48 (1950).

Kirkman, J., 'Animal Nature *versus* Human Nature in *King Lear*', *New Shakspere Society Transactions* (1877–9).

Kirschbaum, L., *Character and Characterization in Shakespeare* (Detroit, Mich., 1962).

——, 'Albany', *Shakespeare Survey 13* (1960).

Knight, G. Wilson, *The Wheel of Fire* (London, 1930).

Knights, L. C., *Some Shakespearean Themes* (London, 1959).

Kolbe, F. C., *Shakespeare's Way* (London, 1930).

Kott, Jan, *Shakespeare Our Contemporary* (London, 1964).

Kozintsev, G., *Shakespeare: Time and Conscience* (London, 1967).

Lamb, Charles, 'On the Tragedies of Shakespeare' (1811), repr. in *Shakespeare Criticism: A Selection*, ed. D. Nichol Smith (World's Classics, London, 1916).

Law, R. A., 'Holinshed's Lear Story and Shakespeare's', *Studies in Philology*, 48 (1950).

——, '*King Leir* and King Lear', in *Studies in Honor of T. W. Baldwin*, ed. D. C. Allen (Urbana, Ill., 1958).

Lawlor, John, *The Tragic Sense in Shakespeare* (London, 1960).

Levin, H., 'The Heights and the Depths', in *More Talking of Shakespeare*, ed. J. Garrett (London, 1959).

Levin, Y., 'Tolstoy, Shakespeare, and Russian Writers of the 1860s', *Oxford Slavonic Papers* (1968).

Lothian, J. M., *King Lear: A Tragic Reading of Life* (Toronto, 1949).

Mack, Maynard, *King Lear in Our Time* (Berkeley, Calif., 1965).

McKeithan, D. M., '*King Lear* and Sidney's *Arcadia*', *University of Texas Studies in English*, 14 (1934).

Masefield, John, *Shakespeare* (London, 1911).

Mason, H. A., 'King Lear', The Cambridge Quarterly, 2 (1966-7); repr. in his Shakespeare's Tragedies of Love (London, 1970).

Maxwell, J. C., 'The Technique of Invocation in King Lear', MLR, 45 (1950).

Morris, Ivor, 'Cordelia and Lear', Shakespeare Quarterly, 8 (1957).

Mortensen, Peter, 'The Role of Albany', Shakespeare Quarterly, 16 (1965).

Moulton, R. G., Shakespeare as a Dramatic Artist (Oxford, 1885).

Muir, Edwin, Essays on Literature and Society (London, 1949).

Muir, Kenneth, 'Madness in King Lear', Shakespeare Survey 13 (1960).

——, 'Samuel Harsnett and King Lear', RES, N.S. 2 (1951).

Murry, J. Middleton, Shakespeare (London, 1936).

Myrick, Kenneth, 'Christian Pessimism in King Lear', in Shakespeare 1564-1964, ed. E. A. Bloom (Providence, R.I., 1964).

Nicoll, Allardyce, Studies in Shakespeare (London, 1927).

Nowottny, Winifred, 'Lear's Questions', Shakespeare Survey 10 (1957).

——, 'Some Aspects of the Style of King Lear', Shakespeare Survey 13 (1960).

Ornstein, R., The Moral Vision of Jacobean Tragedy (Madison, Wisc., 1960).

Orwell, George, 'Lear, Tolstoy and the Fool', in Selected Essays (London, 1957).

Peck, Russell A., 'Edgar's Pilgrimage', SEL 7 (1967).

Perkinson, Richard H., 'Shakespeare's Revision of the Lear Story and the Structure of King Lear', Philological Quarterly, 22 (1943).

Perrett, W., The Story of King Lear (Berlin, 1904).

Pyle, F., 'Twelfth Night, King Lear and Arcadia', MLR, 42 (1948).

Raleigh, Walter, Shakespeare (London, 1907).

Ribner, Irving, 'Sidney's Arcadia and the Structure of King Lear', Studia Neophilologica, 24 (1952).

——, Patterns in Shakespearian Tragedy (London, 1960).

Rosenberg, John D., 'King Lear and his Comforters', Essays in Criticism, 16 (1966).

Schlegel, A. W., A Course of Lectures on Dramatic Art and Literature (London, 1846).

Schoff, F. G., 'King Lear: Moral Example or Tragic Protagonist', Shakespeare Quarterly, 13 (1962).

Schücking, L. L., Character Problems in Shakespeare's Plays (London, 1922).

Sewell, A., Character and Society in Shakespeare (Oxford, 1951).

Sharpe, Ella F., Collected Papers in Psycho-Analysis (London, 1950).

Shaw, John, 'King Lear: The Final Lines', Essays in Criticism, 16 (1966).

Shelley, P. B., 'A Defence of Poetry', in Literary and Philosophical Criticism (London, 1909).

Siegel, Paul, 'Adversity and the Miracle of Love in King Lear', Shakespeare Quarterly, 6 (1955).

——, Shakespearean Tragedy and the Elizabethan Compromise (New York, 1957).

Sisson, C. J., Shakespeare's Tragic Justice (Toronto, 1962).

Somerville, H., Madness in Shakespearian Tragedy (London, 1929).

Speaight, Robert, Nature in Shakespearian Tragedy (London, 1955).

Spencer, Theodore, *Shakespeare and the Nature of Man* (Cambridge, Mass., 1942).

Spurgeon, Caroline F. E., *Shakespeare's Imagery* (Cambridge, 1935).

Stampfer, J., 'The Catharsis of *King Lear*', *Shakespeare Survey 13* (1960).

Stauffer, D. A., *Shakespeare's World of Images* (New York, 1949).

Stein, Walter, *Criticism as Dialogue* (Cambridge, 1969).

Stroup, T. B., 'Cordelia and the Fool', *Shakespeare Quarterly*, 12 (1961).

Stewart, J. I. M., *Character and Motive in Shakespeare* (London, 1949).

Stoll, E. E., *Art and Artifice in Shakespeare* (New York, 1933).

Swinburne, A. C., *A Study of Shakespeare* (London, 1880).

Tannenbaum, S. A., *Shakespeare's 'King Lear': A Concise Bibliography* (New York, 1940).

Tate, Nahum, *The History of King Lear* (London, 1681); repr. in *Five Restoration Adaptations of Shakespeare*, ed. Christopher Spencer (Urbana, Ill., 1965).

Taylor, G. C., *Shakespeare's Debt to Montaigne* (Cambridge, Mass., 1925).

Tolstoy, L., *Tolstoy on Art* (Boston, Mass., 1924).

Traversi, D. A., *An Approach to Shakespeare*, 2 vols. (London, 1968–9).

Walton, J. K., 'Lear's Last Speech', *Shakespeare Survey 13* (1960).

Warton, Joseph, '*King Lear*', in *The Adventurer*, 1753–4, repr. in *Shakespeare Criticism: A Selection*, ed. D. Nichol Smith (World's Classics, London, 1916).

Welsford, Enid, *The Fool* (London, 1935).

West, Robert H., 'Sex and Pessimism in *King Lear*', *Shakespeare Quarterly*, 11 (1960).

Whitaker, Virgil K., *The Mirror up to Nature* (San Marino, Calif., 1965).

Wilson, Harold S., *On the Design of Shakespearian Tragedy* (Toronto, 1957).

Young, G. M., *Today and Yesterday* (London, 1948).

13. *Macbeth*

R. A. FOAKES

TEXTS

The new Arden edition by Kenneth Muir offers a very full commentary accompanying the text, substantial extracts from sources in the appendices, and a full introduction notable for its sensible analysis of the work of earlier critics on the play, and its detailed defence of the Porter scene (II.iii). This remains the best edition for the student who wants to work on the play in detail. Dover Wilson's New Cambridge edition has a characteristically eloquent critical appreciation of the play, presenting a very heroic image of Macbeth, and an excellent brief stage-history. Its text suffers from the curious punctuation adopted by the series, and the free revision of stage-directions by the editor. The lengthy notes at the back are less helpful than Muir's, and much of the introduction is devoted to speculation about the text, which the editor thinks is a reworked version of an abridgement by Shakespeare of his original play. If this edition is used, it should be in conjunction with William Empson's convincing defence of the integrity of the text.

Both of these editions are old enough to be caught up in the last flurry of what had been a major debate about the text. Ever since the discovery, usually attributed to George Steevens in 1779, that the full text of the songs indicated by first lines in III.v and IV.i might be found in Thomas Middleton's play, *The Witch*, many commentators have found reasons for disputing Shakespeare's authorship of a variety of scenes, so that, by the early twentieth century, a tradition of regarding parts of the play as suspect came to be taken for granted. Some sense of this may be recovered from the New Variorum edition, notably in its Appendix headed '*The Witch*'. The appendices in this edition are its most useful feature, since they provide a pretty full record of early criticisms, and relevant extracts both from Middleton's play, and from the revision of *Macbeth* staged in 1673–4 by William Davenant. It is possible that Davenant had access to a manuscript of Shakespeare's play, and that it preserved some readings, and a Witches' song, not in the Folio; the evidence is set out in Christopher Spencer's edition of it.

The new Arden edition retains scene-locations, as added by eighteenth-century editors, and it remained for later editors to drop these. The revised Yale edition by Eugene Waith offers brief notes on the same page as the text, with appendices on text, date, and sources. It seems deliberately to pare down extras to a minimum, and concentrates on presenting the text attractively. This has no introduction at all, and though the Bobbs-Merrill edition by R. A. Foakes also deliberately offers no critical introduction, it attempts to provide an ample range of aids to reading the play, including surveys of the background, the history of criticism of the play, and reasonably full notes accompanying the text; also the appendices range more widely than is usual. This edition has a very attractive layout and typeface.

The American Pelican edition by Alfred Harbage has a brief critical introduction which rather overdoes the notion of 'stark simplicity', and it provides minimal annotation accompanying the text. It is less helpful, and less of a pleasure to use, than the English New Penguin edition, although the latter tucks its commentary away at the end. G. K. Hunter's introduction is excellent, not only compressing a great deal of information into a brief space, but providing a critical account of the play that is alert to the dangers of simplification; he is especially concerned to illustrate the process by which Macbeth brings 'his world into conformity with the man he has become'. The Signet edition has an ugly page, with minimal glossing of difficult words below the text, and a brief critical introduction. Its main feature is the inclusion of seventy-five pages of excerpts from various critical accounts of the play. The choice is rather odd, but no doubt it appeals to the student who prefers to avoid using the library; the presentation of the play-text is such that one fears he may avoid reading this too, and merely attend to the commentaries on it.

CRITICISM AND COMMENTARY

Character and Action

'Lady Macbeth is merely detested, and though the courage of Macbeth preserves some esteem, yet every reader rejoices at his fall.' This comment by Dr. Johnson reflects a tendency in the early criticism of *Macbeth* to see the play rather simply in terms of evil or villainy, and to regard the leading figures as 'great criminal characters', in the phrase of Charles Lamb, who associated Macbeth with Iago. The concern of the early critics was principally with character, and in this play it seemed to Dr. Johnson that the conduct of the principal figures was determined by necessity, and that the play had 'no nice discriminations of character'. Nevertheless, an effort began in the eighteenth century to discriminate, notably between Richard III and Macbeth, in order to account for what seemed a richer and more complex character in the later play. The most notable of these comparisons were developed by Thomas Whately, who saw Macbeth as soft and vain in contrast to the hard and proud Richard, and by J. P. Kemble, who, not quite grasping the subtlety of Whately's argument, defended Macbeth as equal in courage to Richard, and as wrought upon by insecurity rather than by fear in his murderous progress.

At the same time, the powerful interpretation of Lady Macbeth by Mrs. Siddons from 1777 onwards helped to create a new esteem for this character, and her deep engagement with the role is apparent from the interesting commentary she wrote on her interpretation. Her sense of a 'frailer frame, and keener feelings' than Macbeth needs to be set against William Hazlitt's account of her performance as full of power and grandeur: 'she was tragedy personified', he wrote. This sense of grandeur in the play, and what Hazlitt called its 'lofty imagination', provided the groundwork for much nineteenth-century criticism, which culminated in two very different readings of the play. In *Shakespeare as a Dramatic Artist* R. G. Moulton stressed the heroic, rugged aspect of Macbeth as 'essentially the practical man, the man of action', finding his antithesis in Lady Macbeth, representing the inner life. By contrast, A. C. Bradley stressed the degree to which Macbeth is possessed by his imagination, which is 'the best of him, something usually deeper and higher than his conscious thoughts; and if he had obeyed it he would have been safe.' For him the greatness of Lady Macbeth lay 'almost wholly in courage and force of will'. Although differing in this way, these critics agreed on the stature of the play ('the most tremendous of the tragedies' according to Bradley), and on an interpretation based on the relationship of Macbeth and Lady Macbeth.

In the twentieth century the pre-eminence of *King Lear* among Shakespeare's tragedies has come to be an article of faith with many critics, so much so that Harold Goddard proclaimed that as *Macbeth* was a lesser play than *King Lear*, it must be earlier in date, although the evidence hardly supports this view. The superiority of *King Lear* is more subtly suggested by William Rosen, who contrasts what he sees as complex questionings at the end of this play with the straightforward optimism of the end of *Macbeth*, though his interpretation depends upon the view that Macbeth 'loses his humanity and descends to the bestial'. The growing influence of the disintegrators, who found reasons for disputing Shakespeare's authorship of many parts of the play (see the section on 'Texts' above), clearly contributed to a diminishing regard for the play. This is most marked in G. B. Harrison's strange account of it as the weakest of the tragedies, revealing Shakespeare as 'slapdash and careless'. It is seen too, perhaps, in a number of studies which appear to simplify the play, as Lily B. Campbell finds it to be 'A Study in Fear', E. E. Stoll discovers an implausible psychological gap between the nature of Macbeth and his deed, Willard Farnham calls it a 'morality play', and Marion Smith, more strictly, 'an inverted morality play'. The discussion of Macbeth by these critics, especially Farnham, is often more subtle and more appreciative than these labels might suggest, but they represent a tendency to depreciate the play which finds its cleverest exponent in R. B. Heilman. In his essay 'The Criminal as Tragic Hero', he argues that too little is demanded of the reader because Shakespeare was too sympathetic with his hero, so that 'we see the world judging Macbeth, but not Macbeth judging himself.' He concludes, 'This is not the best that tragedy can offer.'

No doubt the very intensity of the play, and the prominence in it of Macbeth, have encouraged those critics who have schematized the play in various ways, as a study in evil or ambition or fear, a morality play, or, in H. B. Charlton's words, as an exploration of 'the operations of the human conscience'. Concentration of attention on the character of the hero and on the action seems to tempt the critic to a conclusion like that of Charlton, who says, 'Macbeth destroys human nature in himself. It is all as simple as that.' If, however, the play were so simple, it would presumably not give rise to such contradictory interpretations, for while some, like Charlton, see a 'progressive deterioration' in Macbeth, others, like Dover Wilson and Matthew Proser, have insisted that there is no loss of heroic stature in the play. In *The Heroic Image*, indeed, Proser ingeniously argues that the image of manliness put before Macbeth by his wife (I.vii) emerges in action only in the final scenes, where Macbeth shows true valour in 'facing alone and with dignity, the dreadful end his own acts have determined'. A useful qualification to this line of argument is supplied by E. M. Waith, who shows how partial and limited Lady Macbeth's conception of manliness is, driving Macbeth perhaps rather into 'brutishness' than heroism.

Writing of some of the tendencies I have been discussing, G. K. Hunter remarks, in his judicious survey of commentary on *Macbeth* in the twentieth century, 'most critics, for one reason or another have seemed anxious to de-sentimentalize Macbeth.' The result has been reductive, while the defenders of the 'heroic' Macbeth seem equally to simplify the play. The best criticism, it would appear, ought to find a way of reconciling the opposing views of Macbeth, as both weak and heroic, and of restoring a sense of the play's richness. One way to begin to do this is to focus more on the relationship of Macbeth and Lady Macbeth, as John Russell Brown does in his elementary but useful introduction to the play, which is seen as developing 'through a progressively revealing series of encounters between them'. Another way is represented in J. I. M. Stewart's essay in *Character and Motive in Shakespeare*, in which a specific reply to Stoll on the question of psychological probability turns into a larger recognition of the way Shakespeare deliberately fails to provide 'clear and sufficient motives for action', so bringing home 'not the mere thrill of evil, but its tortuousness and terrifying reach'.

His grasp of a mystery, of something inexplicable in the play, is suggestive, but perhaps more helpful essays in realizing something of the complexity of *Macbeth* are those by John Lawlor and Wilbur Sanders. The first is concerned especially with the way '*Macbeth* demonstrates the failure of illusion, a realized incapacity to sustain the role', and provides a sensitive account of the process by which the hero comes to see himself as a bear tied to a stake. There are two essays on *Macbeth* in the uneven book by Sanders; the second of these is ill informed and disappointing after the excellent long essay called 'An Unknown Fear', in which he tries to unite the 'act of judgement which *sees through* Macbeth' and the 'act of imagination which sees the world *with* him'. He finds here an effect that is paradoxical, and sees the play as poised finally in a 'tremulous equilibrium between affirmation and despair'.

The most sensitive accounts of character and action in *Macbeth* seek to account not just for Macbeth's crime, ambition, or his 'deterioration', but also for what glows through in spite of these, an enormous vitality and attractiveness, those 'sympathetic qualities', noted by John Russell Brown in *Shakespeare's Dramatic Style*, which help to provide the 'sources of Macbeth's life', out of which the crises of the play arise. In a sense, these subtler modern readings of the play may be seen as developments of the brief but incisive comments of S. T. Coleridge, and Lascelles Abercrombie, whose striking formulation of the complex response evoked by Macbeth towards the end of the play dates from 1925: 'For we see not only what he feels, but the personality that feels it; and in the very act of proclaiming that life is ' "a tale told by an idiot, *signifying nothing*", personal life announces its virtue, and superbly *signifies itself*.'

Poetic Imagery and Thematic Interpretations

It has been a commonplace of criticism to remark on the concentrated power of the poetry of *Macbeth*, and Caroline Spurgeon is not alone in finding the play's poetic imagery to be 'more rich and varied, more highly imaginative, more unapproachable by any other writer, than that of any other single play'. She was perhaps the first to apply this awareness in detail to patterns of related images, especially in noticing the images which depict Macbeth as a 'small, ignoble man encumbered and degraded by garments unsuited to him'. Another important essay is that in which Cleanth Brooks analysed the image of the 'naked babe' as a symbol of a future Macbeth cannot control. These show what weight of analysis a single chain of imagery in this play will bear, and indeed W. A. Murray has written an interesting study of the alchemical and religious background to one line, in an effort to explain why Duncan's blood is 'golden': 'His silver skin lac'd with his golden blood.'

Cleanth Brooks overvalued the image of the 'naked babe', and, as O. J. Campbell was quick to point out, pressed strange significances on some passages in the play, but he properly saw its connection with a structure of 'meanings, evaluations, and interpretations'. The study of the language and imagery of the play tends to become a study of themes, ideas, and meanings, and a strong reaction against the emphasis by Bradley and others on character and action led to the proposition by L. C. Knights that 'the only profitable approach to Shakespeare is a consideration of his plays as dramatic poems'; his particular example was *Macbeth*, studied as a 'statement of evil'. This essay is famous for its title, 'How Many Children had Lady Macbeth?', mocking the sort of question asked by Bradley in the appendices to his *Shakespearean Tragedy*. In fact, the later essay on *Macbeth* by Knights in *Some Shakespearean Themes* is a much more incisive analysis of the way that evil is suggested in the play by what is 'unnatural' as opposed to what is 'natural' and by the way time becomes meaningless for Macbeth.

There are other good essays on various aspects of language and imagery. M. M. Mahood emphasizes time and darkness especially in her study of the multiple senses involved in *Shakespeare's Wordplay*, Donald Stauffer is concerned mainly with images of blood, clothes, and the stars in his account of *Macbeth*, while Brents Stirling attempts to show the unifying of poetic mood with dramatic motivation in a study of four 'themes', 'darkness, sleep, raptness, and contradiction'.

In a very good essay on dramatic irony in the play, William Blissett comments especially on air, 'murky' and 'delicate', on sterility and fruitfulness, and on 'the contrast between blood as stain and blood as life'. The extensive commentary on imagery and symbolism in *Macbeth* is well digested in a critical survey by Kenneth Muir, which shows how much this kind of criticism has contributed to the study of the play. At the same time, criticism devoted to poetry and themes has its limitations, as often it neglects dramatic or theatrical aspects, although De Quincey long ago, in his famous little essay on the function of the knocking at the gate in *Macbeth*, pointed the way to a recognition of the importance of symbolism in the action. More frequently attention to themes tends, sometimes rather crudely, to reduce the play to a single idea or statement; so in his first essay on it, in *The Wheel of Fire*, G. Wilson Knight saw it as a 'vision of evil', and Irving Ribner defines it as 'a tragedy about damnation in Christian terms', the whole play supporting a 'thematic statement'. Students, as D. J. Enright notes, are inclined to settle for such simplifying abstractions, and his lively essay on '*Macbeth* and the Henpecked Hero' provides a useful corrective. Wilson Knight's later essay, 'The Milk of Concord', presents a finer reading of the play in terms of the opposition of 'life-themes' and 'death-themes', and his discussion of the interplay between what is natural and what is unnatural has been very influential.

Study of themes and ideas in *Macbeth* somehow has to cope with the question, 'In what sense is this play, in which the hero acknowledges that he has given his soul to the devil,

> mine eternal jewel
> Given to the common Enemy of man

and in which Duncan and Edward are "sainted" or "holy" Kings, a Christian tragedy?' G. R. Elliott provides the simplest and least satisfactory Christian interpretation of *Macbeth* as 'Shakespeare's Tragic Theme of Humanity and Grace'; for him suspense is created by the possibility until the last moment that Macbeth may repent. In *The Time is Free*, Roy Walker takes us line by line through the play, in a reading based on the view that the murder of Duncan is 'profoundly impregnated with the central tragedy of the Christian myth'; the over-all concern with Christian doctrine is far less impressive than the many sharp insights offered incidentally. The same may be said of the essay by J. A. Bryant in *Hippolyta's View*, which imposes a Christian framework on the view that Macbeth's best qualities, bravery and loyalty, pull in opposite directions, and so destroy him.

Harold S. Wilson again hardly needs to 'establish the Christian assumptions that control' this play in order to arrive at his conclusion that we admire Macbeth even while we condemn him. However, those who have tried to preserve a ritualistic or quasi-religious reading while avoiding an explicitly Christian one, have not really found a more persuasive way of interpreting the play. One of the most notable essays of this kind is by John Holloway, who sees the play as 'philosophical' rather than religious, as concerned with a retributive justice operating under 'Fate or Fortune', which makes Macbeth in the end a ritual victim. In *Shakespeare and the Reason*, Terence Hawkes treats the play rather schematically, contrasting the lower world of 'fact' with the 'miraculous' world of 'reality' represented in the 'King's dispersal of evil'. Frederick Turner's treatment is analogous, as he sees Macbeth involved in the world of 'time', and so 'fatally vulnerable to the forces of timelessness' represented by Malcolm.

Like a number of the accounts of *Macbeth* in terms of character and action discussed above, many of the commentaries on imagery or themes tend to schematize the play. In some sense, it is a simple play, and in some sense it is clearly a Christian play; at the same time, critics have sought to reveal its complexities, and to show that it conforms to secular conceptions of tragedy too. Perhaps no one has completely solved the problem of how to allow appropriate weight to what is schematic or what is Christian, while preserving a full sense of the richness and vitality of the drama. Wilson Knight's essay remains impressive because it comes near to achieving this. Certainly it will not do to minimize the Christian stances to the extent of saying 'the authority for morality and the claims of divinity are restricted to the narrower scene of the nature and mind of man', as John Arthos does in *The Art of Shakespeare*, where he stresses the failure of Macbeth to control his imagination by his will.

Background, Sources, and Special Studies

Most of the critical approaches discussed so far touch on the supernatural elements in the play, and the nature of the Weird Sisters. A seminal study of the background of witchcraft and demonology was W. C. Curry's *Shakespeare's Philosophical Patterns*, in which, drawing on scholastic philosophy and theology, he argued that the Weird Sisters 'are in reality demons, opposed to good', and the whole play is 'saturated with the malignant presences of demons'. He also claimed that the play could only be understood 'by reference to defined standards of moral philosophy', but in his long essay he clearly recognizes a greater complexity in *Macbeth* than his scheme for the play suggests; and while most critics now would accept Robert H. West's sensible conclusion that 'The wholeness of the effect requires acceptance of the supernatural as such, but it does not require any one demonological explication', Curry's book has remained influential because of its learning, and its serious investigation into the attributes and powers of witches and demons. Arthur McGee has also shown how the Weird Sisters relate to the Furies, Biblical demons, and fairies of folklore, and cannot be simply identified with any of these.

When writing *Macbeth*, Shakespeare may well have acquired some lore concerning witches, such as their ability to keep spirits in the likeness of toads and cats, from Reginald Scot's *Discovery of Witchcraft*. No doubt he was aware of the King's interest in Witches, James I being author of a tract on *Demonology*. H. N. Paul, making the most of the possible association of the play with the King, and believing it to have been written for performance before him, calls it *The Royal Play of 'Macbeth'*. He thinks the occasion for the first performance was the visit of King Christian IV to London in the summer of 1606, and that the play may be related to other interests of James, who carefully distinguished between a tyrant and a good King in his book of advice to his son, *Basilikon Doron* (published in London in 1603). Paul makes some important contributions to our knowledge of the background to the play, but his passion for finding topical references and his lack of success in applying his findings to a critical account of the play make the book much less useful than it might be.

Several editions of *Macbeth* contain the main source-materials, which are comprehensively presented and discussed in the standard work of reference on this subject, Geoffrey Bullough's *Narrative and Dramatic Sources of Shakespeare*. A judicious survey of the sources, which deals well with the status of the Witches, and with the Scottish background, may also be found in M. C. Bradbrook's essay, in which she attends not only to the sources in chronicles, notably Holinshed, but also points to the connections with *The Rape of Lucrece*. H. N. Paul and others have observed that Macbeth is perhaps the most Senecan of Shakespeare's tragedies, and Inga-Stina Ewbank has found links especially with Seneca's *Medea*. Kenneth Muir's helpful essay in *Shakespeare's Sources* contains a sensible critique of Paul's book, a detailed treatment of the chronicles, and again notes the link with Seneca, particularly the *Agamemnon*. Following a rather different line of investigation, Ruth L. Anderson has traced the background of conventional ideas about ambition and tyranny, and claims that Shakespeare relied on these in creating Richard III and Macbeth. E. M. W. Tillyard also renews the comparison with Richard in a brief essay relating the play to *A Mirror for Magistrates* and the idea of a virtuous king.

Among particular aspects of the play, the porter scene (II.iii) perhaps deserves special notice, if only because of Coleridge's famous objection to it as 'the disgusting passage of the Porter, which I dare pledge myself to demonstrate an interpolation of the actors'. It is easy to dismiss this comment scornfully, but harder to explain just what the function of the porter and the relevance of his speeches is. The study of patterns and themes in the language has brought greatly increased understanding of this episode, and the extensive analysis of it is brought into order in a useful essay by John B. Harcourt. It is important also to grasp the effect of the scene as a theatre-image, which Glynne Wickham seeks to do by relating it to the 'Harrowing of Hell' in medieval cycle plays.

Interpretations of the play, and claims for the importance of source-materials or topical references, need to be set against what can be conveyed in production. Some editions, like the New Cambridge, contain useful but brief stage histories. These can now be supplemented by reference to Bartholomeusz's *Macbeth and the Players*, a detailed account of the treatment of the play on the stage from the beginning in 1606 up to 1964. The author claims that actors and directors have had insights denied to critics, and while this is probably true, it is not easy to demonstrate in relation to the elusive art of the stage. A great actor's interpretation can certainly stimulate a critic, as is shown in Richard David's fine essay, 'The Tragic Curve', based on the performances in the title-role of Paul Rogers and Sir Laurence Olivier.

CONCLUSION

In all this commentary, curiously little attention has been given directly to the structure of the play. If it is in some sense classical, as the Senecan analogies might suggest, then perhaps it ought to be amenable to an Aristotelian analysis. So Francis Fergusson argues, in '*Macbeth* as the Imitation of an Action'—an action seen as a 'desperate race', the key to it being the phrase, 'to outrun the pauser, reason'. In a reply to Fergusson, Julian Markels claimed that the structure of the play is not consonant with the *Poetics*, since *Macbeth* depends so much on what to Aristotle was peripheral, namely, 'the choice of episodes and the visual machinery'. T. B. Tomlinson has also argued that the play is a failure in Aristotelian terms, because it makes the 'subtle introspection' of the chief character primary, and tries, unsuccessfully in his view, to raise this to the status of tragedy. Taking a very different view of the play's structure, R. A. Foakes sees it as falling into three parts, divided by the quasi-choric scenes of the Old Man (ii.iv) and Lennox (iii.vi), marking stages in Macbeth's progress from one murder to 'an endless repetition of that crime, and finally to the recognition that his life has no meaning'.

Perhaps an adequate conception of the play's structure as a tragedy would need to reconcile the classical elements with the Christian, and this task remains to be done. In an analogous way, an adequate interpretation of *Macbeth* needs to accommodate conflicting views of the characters, and to pay sufficient attention to the richness of the poetic texture. Criticism focusing on character and action tends to give too little weight to themes and imagery, while much thematic analysis is inclined to give subtleties of verbal meaning an emphasis that is out of proportion to their impact on an audience. To understand and respond in a balanced way to Christian and classical elements, character and image, action and word, simplicities and complexities in *Macbeth* is no easy task, but at least the possibilities for criticism are by no means exhausted.

REFERENCES

TEXTS

Barnet, Sylvan (ed.), *Macbeth* (Signet Shakespeare, New York, 1963).

Empson, William, 'Dover Wilson on *Macbeth*', *Kenyon Review*, 14 (1952).

Foakes, R. A. (ed.), *Macbeth* (Bobbs-Merrill Shakespeare Series, Indianapolis, Ind., 1968).

Furness, H. H. (ed.), *Macbeth* (New Variorum Shakespeare, Philadelphia, Pa., 1873).

Harbage, Alfred (ed.), *Macbeth* (Pelican Shakespeare, Baltimore, Md., 1956).

Hunter, G. K. (ed.), *Macbeth* (New Penguin Shakespeare, Harmondsworth, 1967).

Muir, Kenneth (ed.), *Macbeth* (new Arden Shakespeare, London, 1951).

Spencer, Christopher (ed.), *Davenant's 'Macbeth' from the Yale Manuscript* (New Haven, Conn., 1961); edition of Davenant's *Macbeth* in his *Five Restoration Adaptations of Shakespeare* (Urbana, Ill., 1965).

Waith, E. M. (ed.), *Macbeth* (Yale Shakespeare, New Haven, Conn., 1954).

Wilson, J. Dover (ed.), *Macbeth* (New Cambridge Shakespeare, Cambridge, 1947).

CRITICISM AND COMMENTARY

Character and Action

Abercrombie, Lascelles, *The Idea of Great Poetry* (London, 1925; repr. with *The Theory of Poetry*, New York, 1968).

Bradley, A. C., *Shakespearean Tragedy* (London, 1904).

Brown, John Russell, *Shakespeare: 'The Tragedy of Macbeth'* (Studies in English Literature No. 14, London, 1963).

——, *Shakespeare's Dramatic Style* (London, 1970).

Campbell, Lily B., *Shakespeare's Tragic Heroes* (Cambridge, 1930).

Campbell, T., *The Life of Mrs. Siddons* (London, 1834; partially repr. in the New Variorum edition of *Macbeth*, ed. H. H. Furness, Philadelphia, Pa., 1873).

Charlton, H. B., *Shakespearian Tragedy* (Cambridge, 1948).

Farnham, Willard, *Shakespeare's Tragic Frontier* (Berkeley, Calif., 1950).

Goddard, Harold C., *The Meaning of Shakespeare* (Chicago, Ill., 1951).

Harrison, G. B., *Shakespeare's Tragedies* (London, 1951).

Hawkes, Terence, *Coleridge on Shakespeare* (Penguin Shakespeare Library, Harmondsworth, 1969; previously published as *Coleridge's Writings on Shakespeare*, New York, 1959).

Hazlitt, William, *Characters of Shakespeare's Plays* (London, 1817; World's Classics, London, 1917).

Heilman, R. B., 'The Criminal as Tragic Hero: Dramatic Methods', *Shakespeare Survey 19* (1966).

Hunter, G. K., '*Macbeth* in the Twentieth Century', *Shakespeare Survey 19* (1966).

Kemble, J. P., *Macbeth and King Richard the Third* (London, 1817).

Lawlor, John, *The Tragic Sense in Shakespeare* (London, 1960).

Moulton, R. G., *Shakespeare as a Dramatic Artist* (Oxford, 1885; revised, Oxford, 1906).

Proser, Matthew N., *The Heroic Image in Five Shakespearean Tragedies* (Princeton, N.J., 1965).

Rosen, William, *Shakespeare and the Craft of Tragedy* (Cambridge, Mass., 1960).

Sanders, Wilbur, *The Dramatist and the Received Idea* (Cambridge, 1968).

Smith, Marion B., *Dualities in Shakespeare* (Toronto, 1966).

Stewart, J. I. M., *Character and Motive in Shakespeare* (London, 1949).

Stoll, E. E., *Art and Artifice in Shakespeare* (New York, 1934).

Waith, E. M., 'Manhood and Valor in Two Shakespearean Tragedies', *ELH*, 17 (1950).

Whately, Thomas, *Remarks on Some of the Characters of Shakespeare* (London, 1785); repr. in *Shakespeare Criticism*, ed. D. Nichol Smith (World's Classics, London, 1916).

Wimsatt, W. K. (ed.), *Samuel Johnson on Shakespeare* (New York, 1960); repr. as *Dr. Johnson on Shakespeare* (Penguin Shakespeare Library, Harmondsworth, 1969).

Poetic Imagery and Thematic Interpretations

Arthos, John, *The Art of Shakespeare* (London, 1964).

Blissett, William, 'The Secret'st Man of Blood. A Study of Dramatic Irony in *Macbeth*', *Shakespeare Quarterly*, 10 (1959).

Brooks, Cleanth, 'The Naked Babe and the Cloak of Manliness', in *The Well-Wrought Urn* (New York, 1947).

Bryant, J. A., *Hippolyta's View: Some Christian Aspects of Shakespeare's Plays* (Lexington, Ky., 1961).

Campbell, O. J., 'Shakespeare and the "New Critics" ', in *Joseph Quincy Adams Memorial Studies*, ed. J. G. McManaway, G. E. Dawson, and E. E. Willoughby (Washington, D.C., 1948).

De Quincey, Thomas, 'On the Knocking at the Gate in *Macbeth*' (*London Magazine*, October 1823); repr. in *Shakespeare Criticism, A Selection*, ed. D. Nichol Smith (World's Classics, London, 1916).

Elliott, G. R., *Dramatic Providence in 'Macbeth'* (Princeton, N.J., 1958).

Enright, D. J., *Shakespeare and the Students* (London, 1970).

Hawkes, Terence, *Shakespeare and the Reason* (London, 1964).

Holloway, John, *The Story of the Night* (London, 1961).

Knight, G. Wilson, *The Imperial Theme* (London, 1931).

——, *The Wheel of Fire* (London, 1930).

Knights, L. C., 'How Many Children had Lady Macbeth?' (Cambridge, 1933, repr. in *Explorations*, London, 1946).

——, *Some Shakespearean Themes* (London, 1959).

Mahood, M. M., *Shakespeare's Wordplay* (London, 1957).

Muir, Kenneth, 'Image and Symbol in '*Macbeth*', *Shakespeare Survey 19* (1966).

Murray, W. A., 'Why was Duncan's Blood Golden?', *Shakespeare Survey 19* (1966).

Ribner, Irving, *Patterns in Shakespearian Tragedy* (London, 1960).

Spurgeon, Caroline F. E., 'Leading Motives in the Imagery of Shakespeare's Tragedies' (Shakespeare Association Lecture, 1930; incorporated into *Shakespeare's Imagery*, Cambridge, 1935).

Stauffer, Donald A., *Shakespeare's World of Images. The Development of his Moral Ideas* (New York, 1949).

Stirling, Brents, *Unity in Shakespearian Tragedy* (New York, 1956).

Turner, Frederick, *Shakespeare and the Nature of Time* (Oxford, 1971).

Walker, Roy, *The Time is Free* (London, 1949).

Wilson, Harold S., *On the Design of Shakespearian Tragedy* (Toronto, 1957).

Background, Sources, and Special Studies

Anderson, Ruth L., 'The Pattern of Behavior Culminating in *Macbeth*', *SEL*, 3 (1963).

Bartholomeusz, Dennis, *Macbeth and the Players* (Cambridge, 1969).

Bradbrook, M. C., 'The Sources of *Macbeth*', *Shakespeare Survey 4* (1951).

Bullough, Geoffrey, *Narrative and Dramatic Sources of Shakespeare*, vol. vii (London, 1973).

Curry, W. C., *Shakespeare's Philosophical Patterns* (Baton Rouge, La., 1937).

David, Richard, 'The Tragic Curve', *Shakespeare Survey 9* (1956).

Ewbank, Inga-Stina, 'The Fiend-like Queen: a Note on *Macbeth* and Seneca's *Medea*', *Shakespeare Survey 19* (1966).

Harcourt, John B., ' "I Pray You, Remember the Porter" ', *Shakespeare Quarterly*, 12 (1961).

James I, King, *Basilikon Doron* (Edinburgh, 1599; London, 1603; reprinted from the 1599 text, Scolar Press, Menston, 1969).

McGee, Arthur R., '*Macbeth* and the Furies', *Shakespeare Survey 19* (1966).

Muir, Kenneth, *Shakespeare's Sources*, vol. i (London, 1957).

Paul, H. N., *The Royal Play of 'Macbeth'* (New York, 1950).

Tillyard, E. M. W., *Shakespeare's History Plays* (London and Toronto, 1944).

West, Robert H., *Shakespeare and the Outer Mystery* (Lexington, Ky., 1968).

Wickham, Glynne, 'Hell-Castle and its Door-Keeper', *Shakespeare Survey 19* (1966).

CONCLUSION

Fergusson, Francis, '*Macbeth* as the Imitation of an Action', *English Institute Essays* (New York, 1952); repr. in *Shakespeare: The Tragedies*, ed. A. Harbage (Englewood Cliffs, N.J., 1964).

Foakes, R. A., '*Macbeth*', in *Stratford Papers on Shakespeare 1962*, ed. B. W. Jackson (Toronto, 1963).

Markels, Julian, 'The Spectacle of Deterioration: *Macbeth* and the "Manner" of Tragic Imitation', *Shakespeare Quarterly*, 12 (1961).

Tomlinson, T. B., 'Action and Soliloquy in *Macbeth*', *Essays in Criticism*, 8 (1958).

14. *Julius Caesar* and *Antony and Cleopatra*

T. J. B. SPENCER

SHAKESPEARE AND PLUTARCH

Probably about seven or eight years separated Shakespeare's writing of *Julius Caesar* and *Antony and Cleopatra*. His dramatic art had developed rapidly in those years; *Hamlet, Othello, King Lear, Macbeth,* and other important and successful plays had intervened.

But there are strong links between *Julius Caesar* and *Antony and Cleopatra,* affecting the criticism of the plays. This is partly because one is a historical sequel to the other (half a dozen of the major characters reappear). But they also both derive from Shakespeare's reading of Plutarch's *Lives of the Noble Grecians and Romans* as translated by Sir Thomas North (first edition 1579, reprinted in 1595 and 1603). The study of Shakespeare's artistry in constructing the plays from historical narratives which he is known to have read often contributes to criticism, and in this case it is uniquely important because of the high quality of North's *Plutarch* and the closeness with which Shakespeare follows it.

The Lives of Julius Caesar, Brutus, and Mark Antony are conveniently available in *Shakespeare's Plutarch,* edited by T. J. B. Spencer, in which the parallel passages from Shakespeare's plays are printed at the foot of the pages. The older editions of selected lives by W. W. Skeat, R. H. Carr, and C. F. Tucker Brooke give references to Shakespeare and helpful introductions in each case. The fifth volume of Geoffrey Bullough's *Narrative and Dramatic Sources of Shakespeare* is devoted to the Roman plays. Besides printing all the relevant texts and re-examining the whole problem of the relationship of Shakespeare to Plutarch, the volume contains useful material outside Plutarch. Kenneth Muir's *Shakespeare's Sources,* volume i, includes a discussion of the Roman plays.

The fullest study of Shakespeare's construction of the plays from Plutarch is still M. W. MacCallum's *Shakespeare's Roman Plays and their Background.* It has outlasted changes of fashion in criticism and remains an indispensable book, even though the later interpreters of the plays have entered regions MacCallum never knew. By modern standards MacCallum's work is somewhat over-laboured and over-explicit. But he was sensible, intelligent, and modest. His purpose was straightforward, and he fulfilled it efficiently. He intended to give a full critical interpretation of three plays, *Julius Caesar, Antony and Cleopatra*, and *Coriolanus*, with the same thoroughness that A. C. Bradley had shown in his study of four plays in *Shakespearean Tragedy*, published a few years before (1904). His method was substantially the same as Bradley's: that is, to study Shakespeare's intentions and achievements in characterization. He analyses and discriminates with a critical subtlety which is not lacking in psychological insight; but his defect is that he rarely takes account of the fact that we are dealing with stage-plays, where 'characterization' means that the author provides a script for the actor to fill out by means of his impersonation. The visual impact of scenes and the means by which emotional situations are built up on the stage are what MacCallum ignores. Nevertheless, these character-studies have a surprising staying-power, while other fashionable modes of writing about the plays pass away. The 'interpretations' we are to give to the dramatic figures of Caesar and Brutus remain subjects of critical debate. They are, moreover, problems for the producer and actor, and not merely for the literary critic; perhaps rather paradoxically, that is one cause of the strength of this kind of Shakespeare criticism.

There are several other studies which deal with the dramatist's use of his raw material in Plutarch: what he took, what he ignored, what he emphasized, what he invented. In *Shakespeare and the Classics* J. A. K. Thomson made the interesting suggestion that Shakespeare may have derived something of the spirit of Greek tragedy from his reading of Plutarch. For the Greek tragic conception, says Thomson, is to be found in the historians as well as in the dramatists.

Nobody can read Plutarch without feeling that he has by nature a strong dramatic sense. But the chief reason why he sees history as drama is that he has been taught to see it so—taught by Homer and Euripides and Thucydides. It is not merely that he is perpetually quoting them; they have formed his mind. He is not pessimistic; he cherishes a gentle philosophy. But he sees the life of Caesar, the life of Antony, as a tragedy—as what the Greeks understood by a tragedy.

And Thomson concludes that 'through the medium of North's Plutarch, Shakespeare divined the true spirit of Greek tragedy'. In an essay on 'Shakespeare and Plutarch' (in *Talking of Shakespeare*) Walter Oakeshott discusses J. A. K. Thomson's idea and has several further interesting observations. This has put Shakespeare's 'classicism' in a new light, making it possible to see that he was closer to an understanding of Greek tragedy than those of his contemporaries who emulated the classics and were more strongly influenced by Seneca's tragedies than he was.

There are several general studies of North's Plutarch which help us to understand Shakespeare's reading. George Wyndham's introduction to the Tudor Translations edition of the complete *Lives* was reprinted in his *Essays in Romantic Literature*. An excellent essay by J. Middleton Murry is to be found in his collection *Countries of the Mind* (Second Series).

GENERAL CRITICISM

An outstanding bibliography of all aspects of the criticism of *Julius Caesar* and *Antony and Cleopatra* is included in J. W. Velz's *Shakespeare and the Classical Tradition. A Critical Guide to Commentary, 1660–1960*. This contains judicious summaries and assessments of the books and articles listed.

A useful account of criticism of the Roman plays in the twentieth century is given by J. C. Maxwell in the tenth volume of *Shakespeare Survey*. This tells the story up to about 1956. Some of the criticism is conveniently selected in *Discussions of Shakespeare's Roman Plays*, edited by Maurice Charney, which also includes the perceptive observations of several of the older critics on *Julius Caesar*, such as Edward Dowden and R. G. Moulton. A brief general survey has been made by T. J. B. Spencer, *William Shakespeare. The Roman Plays*, in the series 'Writers and their Work', with a full bibliography.

Detailed attention has been given to the politics of the plays and to Shakespeare's characterization of politicians in action. H. B. Charlton's pamphlet *Shakespeare: Politics and Politicians* and J. E. Philipps's *The State in Shakespeare's Greek and Roman Plays* are some of the most useful advances on MacCallum's book. In 'Shakespeare and the Elizabethan Romans' (*Shakespeare Survey 10*) T. J. B. Spencer tries to interpret aspects of the plays strictly in terms of the notions of the Roman world which were usual among Shakespeare's contemporaries. An essay by J. Leeds Barroll on 'Shakespeare and Roman History' is a special study of medieval and Renaissance theories of world history which have relevance to interpretations of the position of Julius Caesar and Octavius Caesar in the divine scheme of things.

The new ways of experiencing the plays in more imaginative and symbolic terms are best represented by G. Wilson Knight's *The Imperial Theme*, which has been highly influential. Maurice Charney's *Shakespeare's Roman Plays: The Function of Imagery in the Drama* is a more recent book which tries to combine theatrical and imaginative interpretations without losing sight of historical considerations; his 'imagery' includes what is visually presented on the stage, as well as verbally. L. C. Knights in *Some Shakespearean Themes* and *Further Explorations*, and D. A. Traversi in *The Roman Plays*, have written with their characteristic method of moral probing by means of sensitive response to linguistic and poetic qualities.

JULIUS CAESAR

Texts

Our only early text of *Julius Caesar* is that printed in the First Folio of 1623. The textual problems are comparatively simple. The original text may be read in one of the facsimiles of the Folio (see p. 21). A convenient facsimile of the single play was prepared by J. Dover Wilson and published with a brief introduction and a list of emendations. The New Variorum edition of Furness is now rather old-fashioned. The accumulations of critical comment make a convenient anthology, though the excerpts, summaries, and detached remarks are inevitably imperfect and tend to distort the material. The Variorum should only be used with caution for second-hand quotations from the critics. The most important of recent editions are the New Cambridge by J. Dover Wilson, with an interesting pro-Brutus introduction, and the new Arden of T. S. Dorsch, with an equally valuable (and pro-Caesar) introduction. Paperbacks include the Pelican of S. F. Johnson, the Signet of William and Barbara Rosen, and the New Penguin by Norman Sanders. Kittredge's edition of 1939 has also been reissued as a paperback, revised by Irving Ribner. Maurice Charney's edition for the Bobbs-Merrill Shakespeare Series contains much helpful material.

Criticism

Among the Victorian critics both Edward Dowden and R. G. Moulton wrote well on *Julius Caesar*. The best of early studies was that by the classical scholar W. Warde Fowler on 'The Tragic Element in Shakespeare's *Julius Caesar*'. He sees the play as a double or hybrid tragedy: the fall of Caesar is the tragedy of the turning of Fortune's wheel, but the fall of Brutus is due to his human errors of judgement.

Harley Granville-Barker included *Julius Caesar* in the first series of his *Prefaces to Shakespeare*, and this is one of his best analyses of a play in terms of Elizabethan stage conditions. The scope of the characterization Granville-Barker sees as related to Shakespeare's theatrical artistry. The play is the tragedy of Brutus. But this does not mean that Caesar is unimportant or is belittled; he is a character who must physically disappear after the first third of the play and therefore he should not be felt to be too dominating if the play is not to seem rather empty after his departure. Shakespeare keeps Antony in reserve until after Caesar's death and then reintroduces him in a series of intensely powerful scenes to hold or regain the attention of the audience. Granville-Barker's analysis of Shakespeare's artistry remains an essential contribution to criticism; he taught a method that can be used by others for the discovery of new subtleties of theatrical construction.

The central issues which have for long been the subjects of critical exploration in *Julius Caesar* are 'Who is the hero of the play?' and 'Is Caesar seen favourably or unfavourably?' and 'Is Brutus a noble idealist or a misguided puppet?' The answers have been contradictory.

The various Renaissance attitudes to Julius Caesar are cleverly expounded by Friedrich Gundolf in his *Caesar: Geschichte seines Ruhms*, translated as *The Mantle of Caesar*. This book is a valuable background to our understanding of Shakespeare's attitude. It is not necessary to suppose that, in devising his play for stage-interpretation, Shakespeare was directly acquainted with or influenced by Renaissance historiography. But he could hardly have been unaware that the reassessment and reconsideration of such famous figures as Caesar and Brutus were a common literary activity, not only in poetry and drama (where licence is permissible) but also in straightforward historical writing.

Even in his reading of Plutarch's Life of Caesar, Shakespeare seems to have responded to certain depreciatory hints and developed them. Some versions of the Caesar story in the sixteenth century, including plays, show Caesar as a braggart. But can we regard Shakespeare's Caesar as a typical Renaissance tyrant whose boasting, obstinacy, superstition, vanity, and caprice and malice in the exercise of his despotic power, turn Brutus into a justified and admirable tyrannicide? H. B. Charlton in *Shakespeare, Politics, and Politicians* found the picture of Caesar contemptuous, and he developed his ideas in *Shakespearian Tragedy*, defining the extent to which Shakespeare was affected by Plutarch's notions of history, especially his sense of the role of Fortune in great men's lives. J. Dover Wilson in his introduction to the New Cambridge Shakespeare suggests that 'Written in our day the play might have been called *Caesar and Caesarism*', and he adds: 'the play's theme is the single one, Liberty *versus* Tyranny'. Equally emphatic is Peter Alexander: 'The portrait of Caesar is drawn on lines so startlingly calculated to favour Brutus that we sense some loss of objectivity that blurs the design' (*A Shakespeare Primer*).

To most critics the play is, in spite of its title, Brutus' tragedy. For Dante, Chaucer, and other medieval writers Brutus was guilty of a terrible crime in betraying Caesar, a crime parallel to that of Judas Iscariot. How far did this idea continue in the sixteenth century and into Shakespeare? D. S. Brewer and others have claimed that this attitude tempered the admiration for Brutus felt by the humanists and make it unlikely that Shakespeare would have exalted Brutus in the way Dover Wilson claimed. T. S. Dorsch in his introduction to the new Arden edition gives a hostile view of Brutus, a doctrinaire politician, and of the other conspirators, while emphasizing the greatness of Caesar and Antony. Adrien Bonjour in *The Structure of 'Julius Caesar'* accepts our divided sympathies in the play. It is a double tragedy—both of Caesar and of Brutus. Caesar is no tyrant and has no resemblance to tyrannical characters in other plays. 'Our sympathies are made to oscillate from one hero, and one party, to the other' and in the end they 'are perfectly divided between the victim of the crime and the victim of the punishment'. Sir Mark Hunter's 'Politics and Character in Shakespeare's *Julius Caesar*' claims that there is no single hero. What interests Shakespeare is the interplay of characters in a political situation rather than the analysis of a dominating personality. Ernest Schanzer in 'The Problem of *Julius Caesar*' sees the character of Caesar as being left deliberately ambiguous by Shakespeare, to give a sense of depth, to keep the audience guessing, and so to make the whole dramatic situation more telling. R. A. Foakes in 'An Approach to *Julius Caesar*' sees Caesar and Brutus as less important than they are usually considered to be: the real subject of the play is the conspiracy, its beginnings, its success, and its ultimate defeat. On the whole the most balanced view, fully supported by an analysis of the text, is in John Palmer's *Political Characters of Shakespeare*. This has an essay called 'Marcus Brutus', but it also includes perceptive accounts of Caesar and Antony. The discussion is carried forward in two important more recent papers: Moody E. Prior's 'The Search for a Hero in *Julius Caesar*' and Waldo F. McNeir's *Shakespeare's 'Julius Caesar': A Tragedy Without a Hero*.

There are good discussions of *Julius Caesar* in Mark van Doren's *Shakespeare*, J. I. M. Stewart's *Character and Motive in Shakespeare*, Virgil K. Whitaker's *Shakespeare's Use of Learning*, Ernest Schanzer's *The Problem Plays of Shakespeare*, Northrop Frye's *Fools of Time*, L. C.

Knights's *Further Explorations*, and Norman Rabkin's *Shakespeare and the Common Understanding*.

A number of critical essays and passages from books are conveniently gathered together in *Twentieth Century Interpretations of 'Julius Caesar'*, edited by L. F. Dean, and in *Shakespeare: 'Julius Caesar'* (Casebook Series), edited by Peter Ure.

ANTONY AND CLEOPATRA

Texts

As in the case of *Julius Caesar*, our only early text of *Antony and Cleopatra* is that printed in the First Folio of 1623. A convenient facsimile of this single play was prepared by J. Dover Wilson and published with a brief introduction and a list of emendations. The New Variorum edition of *Antony and Cleopatra* appeared in 1907 and has been reissued as a paperback. It is rather out of date; but it was one of the best of the series and the accumulation of miscellaneous critical opinion and the accounts of other versions of the story make interesting reading. The New Cambridge Shakespeare, edited by J. Dover Wilson, is perhaps a little less comprehensive than the importance of the play demands. The revised Arden Shakespeare, edited by M. R. Ridley, is based upon the original Arden edition by R. H. Case, which is still of value, with many percipient observations in the introduction (partly reprinted by Ridley). There are brief introductions to the Pelican edition by Maynard Mack and to the Signet Classic by Barbara Everett.

Criticism

Although *Antony and Cleopatra* had exercised its fascination from the eighteenth century onwards, the modern criticism of the play may conveniently begin with A. C. Bradley's essay in 1909. He does not treat it as another example of 'Shakespearean tragedy' but as a great play of a different kind. As is usual with Bradley, particularly admirable are his character-studies of Cleopatra, Antony, and Octavius. He is pleasantly free, on the whole, from moral disapprobation; but 'Why is it,' he asks, 'that, although we close the book in a triumph which is more than reconciliation, this is mingled, as we look back on the story, with a sadness so peculiar, almost the sadness of disenchantment?' We do not mourn, he continues, as we mourn for the love of Romeo or Othello. 'And the fact that we mourn so little saddens us.'

L. L. Schücking in *Character Problems in Shakespeare's Plays* made a challenging 'realistic' interpretation of Cleopatra. In the first three acts she is depicted with a pervasive moral condemnation. But in Acts IV and V she is transformed by a kind of penitence that follows Antony's rejection of her (IV. x) and by her experience of his dying. This regenerated Cleopatra can now die 'after the high Roman fashion' with our approval and applause. In an essay on Cleopatra in 1928, which deserves careful consideration, E. E. Stoll vigorously rejected all sentimental or over-subtle interpretations of her character. For the plot of a Shakespeare play is a more important part of the theatrical experience than the characters. If Cleopatra 'changes' in the fifth act of the play, then she changes because that is what the plot requires, and we should not seek for elaborate psychological explanations. Equally interesting and challenging is Lord David Cecil's lecture. He sees *Antony and Cleopatra* more as a historical and political play than as a love-tragedy. 'The love-story is seen always in its relation to the rivalry between Octavius and Antony' and 'a large part of the play is concerned with this only, and not with the love-story at all'. *Antony and Cleopatra* is, after all, a sequel to *Julius Caesar*, and its theme, too, is political success. Dover Wilson's introduction to his New Cambridge edition reacts against all these critics, expressing his warm-hearted response to the magnanimity of Antony and the glory of Cleopatra. 'The play is, in short, its author's Hymn to Man.' But Franklin Dickey in *Not Wisely But Too Well* gives an excellent analysis of the Elizabethan attitudes to love, in relation to this and other love-tragedies of Shakespeare. It is a corrective to our interpreting the play according to modern attitudes to love.

Several critics have pointed out that the language of the play is a necessary guide to our moral reactions. There are some excellent pages in J. Middleton Murry's *The Problem of Style*. Wilson Knight regards *Antony and Cleopatra* as a play of transcendental love, as he finds proved by the imagery and verbal paradoxes of the play. His essays in *The Imperial Theme* (especially 'The Transcendental Humanism of *Antony and Cleopatra*' and 'The Diadem of Love') have been highly influential since their publication in 1931. F. R. Leavis's essay on '*Antony and Cleopatra* and *All for Love*: A Critical Exercise' demonstrates, of course, Shakespeare's superiority to Dryden in poetry and in moral sensibility. S. L. Bethell in *Shakespeare and the Popular Dramatic Tradition* shows that the language of the play gives an effect of grandeur which prevents us from underestimating Antony and Cleopatra, whatever their conduct. Shakespeare thus reduces the pressure of his moralizing source-material. Maurice Charney has an excellent chapter in his book *Shakespeare's Roman*

Plays. The Function of Imagery in the Drama, showing how the style of the play, with its rich vocabulary and hyperbolical phraseology, reflects the half-Oriental culture of Egypt and contrasts with the austere style of most of *Julius Caesar*. D. A. Traversi in *An Approach to Shakespeare* analyses with great subtlety the imagery of the play and deduces important moral suggestions from it. Although there is much emphasis on corruption, yet the transcendent imagery gradually allows tragic greatness to emerge, almost on account of, rather than in spite of, the human imperfections of the two principal characters. David Daiches has a perceptive essay on 'Imagery and Meaning in *Antony and Cleopatra*.'

Many of the earlier critics (MacCallum, Bradley, R. H. Case) wrote adversely about the structure of the play. Harley Granville-Barker's admirable study appeared in the second series of his *Prefaces to Shakespeare* (1930), and he defended and justified the dramatic organization in terms of the representation of action on the Elizabethan stage. 'The layman must remember that he is reading a play, and should be imaginatively translating it into performance as he reads.' Besides interpreting Shakespeare's theatrical intentions, Granville-Barker writes excellently on the characters as they are to be impersonated by actors.

Several complete books have appeared about the play: L. J. Mills's *The Tragedies of Shakespeare's 'Antony and Cleopatra'*; A. P. Riemer's *A Reading of Shakespeare's 'Antony and Cleopatra'*, which, besides a careful and independent study of the play, has a useful chapter on the critics; Philip J. Traci, *The Love Play of 'Antony and Cleopatra'*; Julian Markels's *The Pillar of the World*, which relates the play to other works of Shakespeare, especially to the Histories, *Julius Caesar*, and *King Lear*. A shorter and balanced introduction is Robin Lee's *Shakespeare. 'Antony and Cleopatra'* in the series of 'Studies in English Literature'.

Valuable discussions of *Antony and Cleopatra* are to be found in a number of general books on Shakespeare or on aspects of literary criticism: Theodore Spencer, *Shakespeare and the Nature of Man*; Willard Farnham, *Shakespeare's Tragic Frontier*; J. F. Danby, *Poets On Fortune's Hill*; Brents Stirling, *Unity in Shakespearian Tragedy*; John Holloway, *The Story of the Night*; Ernest Schanzer, *The Problem Plays of Shakespeare*; Virgil K. Whitaker, *The Mirror up to Nature*; Dorothea Krook, *Elements of Tragedy*; T. R. Henn, *The Living Image*.

Some of the more important criticism of the play is gathered together in *Shakespeare: 'Antony and Cleopatra'*, edited by J. R. Brown in the Casebook series.

REFERENCES

SHAKESPEARE AND PLUTARCH

Bradley, A. C., *Shakespearean Tragedy* (London, 1904).

Brooke, C. F. Tucker, *Shakespeare's Plutarch*, 2 vols. (London, 1909).

Bullough, Geoffrey (ed.), *Narrative and Dramatic Sources of Shakespeare*, vol. v (London, 1964).

Carr, R. H. (ed.), *Plutarch's Lives of Coriolanus, Caesar, Brutus, and Antonius in North's Translation* (Oxford, 1906).

MacCallum, M. W., *Shakespeare's Roman Plays and their Background* (London, 1910; new edition with introduction by T. J. B. Spencer, London, 1967).

Muir, Kenneth, *Shakespeare's Sources*, vol. i (London, 1957).

Murry, J. Middleton, 'North's Plutarch', in his *Countries of the Mind*, 2nd Series (London, 1931).

Oakeshott, Walter, 'Shakespeare and Plutarch', in *Talking of Shakespeare*, ed. John Garrett (London, 1954).

Plutarch, *The Lives of the Noble Grecians and Romans* . . . *translated out of Greek into French by James Amyot* . . . *and out of French into English by Thomas North* (London, 1579, etc.); ed. W. H. D. Rouse, Temple Classics, 10 vols. (London, 1898–9); repr. 8 vols. (Shakespeare Head Press, Oxford, 1928); repr. 5 vols. (Nonesuch Press, London, 1929–30).

Skeat, W. W. (ed.), *Shakespeare's Plutarch* (London, 1875).

Spencer, T. J. B. (ed.), *Shakespeare's Plutarch* (Harmondsworth, 1964).

Thomson, J. A. K., *Shakespeare and the Classics* (London, 1952).

Wyndham, George (ed.), *North's Plutarch*, Tudor Translations, 6 vols. (London, 1895–6); introduction repr. in Wyndham's *Essays in Romantic Literature* (London, 1919).

GENERAL CRITICISM

Barroll, J. Leeds, 'Shakespeare and Roman History', *MLR* 53 (1958).

Charlton, H. B., *Shakespeare: Politics and Politicians* (English Association Pamphlet No. 72, 1929).

Charney, Maurice (ed.), *Discussions of Shakespeare's Roman Plays* (Boston, Mass., 1964).

——, *Shakespeare's Roman Plays: The Function of Imagery in the Drama* (Cambridge, Mass., 1961).

Knight, G. Wilson, *The Imperial Theme* (London, 1931; 3rd edn., 1951).

Knights, L. C., *Further Explorations* (London, 1965).

——, *Some Shakespearean Themes* (London, 1959).

Maxwell, J. C., 'Shakespeare's Roman Plays: 1900–1956', *Shakespeare Survey 10* (1957).

Philipps, J. E., *The State in Shakespeare's Greek and Roman Plays* (New York, 1940).

Spencer, T. J. B., 'Shakespeare and the Elizabethan Romans', *Shakespeare Survey 10* (1957).
——, *William Shakespeare. The Roman Plays*, Writers and Their Work (London, 1963; 2nd edn., 1973).
Traversi, D. A., *Shakespeare: The Roman Plays* (London, 1963).
Velz, J. W., *Shakespeare and the Classical Tradition. A Critical Guide to Commentary, 1660–1960* (Minneapolis, Minn., 1968).

'JULIUS CAESAR'

Texts

Charney, Maurice (ed.), *Julius Caesar* (Bobbs-Merrill Shakespeare Series, Indianapolis, Ind., 1969).
Dorsch, T. S. (ed.), *Julius Caesar* (new Arden Shakespeare, London, 1955).
Furness, H. H. (ed.), *Julius Caesar* (New Variorum Shakespeare, Philadelphia, Pa., 1913).
Johnson, S. F. (ed.), *Julius Caesar* (Pelican Shakespeare, Baltimore, Md., 1960).
Kittredge, G. L. (ed.), rev. Irving Ribner, *Julius Caesar* (Waltham, Mass., 1966).
Rosen, William and Barbara (eds.), *Julius Caesar* (Signet Shakespeare, New York, 1963).
Sanders, Norman (ed.), *Julius Caesar* (New Penguin Shakespeare, Harmondsworth, 1967).
Wilson, J. Dover (ed.), *Julius Caesar* (New Cambridge Shakespeare, Cambridge, 1949).
—— (ed.), *Julius Caesar . . . A Facsimile of the First Folio Text* (London, 1928).

Criticism

Alexander, Peter, *A Shakespeare Primer* (London, 1951).
Bonjour, Adrien, *The Structure of 'Julius Caesar'* (Liverpool, 1958).
Brewer, D. S., 'Brutus' Crime: A Footnote to *Julius Caesar*', *RES* 3 (1952).
Charlton, H. B., *Shakespearian Tragedy* (Cambridge, 1948).
Dean, L. F. (ed.), *Twentieth Century Interpretations of 'Julius Caesar'* (Englewood Cliffs, N.J., 1968).
Dowden, Edward, *Shakspere: A Critical Study of His Mind and Art* (London, 1875).
Foakes, R. A., 'An Approach to *Julius Caesar*', *Shakespeare Quarterly*, 5 (1954).
Fowler, W. Warde, 'The Tragic Element in Shakespeare's *Julius Caesar*', *Transactions of the Royal Society of Literature*, 30 (1910); repr. in his *Roman Essays and Interpretations* (London, 1920).
Frye, Northrop, *Fools of Time* (Toronto, 1967).
Granville-Barker, Harley, *Prefaces to Shakespeare*, 1st Series (London, 1927).
Gundolf, Friedrich, *The Mantle of Caesar* (London, 1929).

Hunter, Sir Mark, 'Politics and Character in Shakespeare's *Julius Caesar*', in *Essays by Divers Hands, Transactions of the Royal Society of Literature*, 10 (1931).

Knights, L. C., 'Personality and Politics in *Julius Caesar*', in his *Further Explorations* (London, 1965).

McNeir, Waldo F., *Shakespeare's 'Julius Caesar': A Tragedy Without a Hero* (Mainz, 1971).

Moulton, R. G., *Shakespeare as a Dramatic Artist* (London, 1885; 3rd edn., Oxford, 1901).

Palmer, John, *Political Characters of Shakespeare* (London, 1945).

Prior, Moody E., 'The Search for a Hero in *Julius Caesar*', *Renaissance Drama*, N.S. 2 (1969).

Rabkin, Norman, *Shakespeare and the Common Understanding* (New York, 1967).

Schanzer, Ernest, 'The Problem of *Julius Caesar*', *Shakespeare Quarterly*, 6 (1955).

——, *The Problem Plays of Shakespeare* (London, 1963).

Stewart, J. I. M., *Character and Motive in Shakespeare* (London, 1949).

Ure, Peter (ed.), *Shakespeare: Julius Caesar* (Casebook Series, London, 1969).

Van Doren, Mark, *Shakespeare* (New York, 1939).

Whitaker, Virgil K., *Shakespeare's Use of Learning* (San Marino, Calif., 1953).

'ANTONY AND CLEOPATRA'

Texts

Case, R. H. (ed.), *Antony and Cleopatra* (Arden Shakespeare, London, 1906, revised edn., 1930).

Everett, Barbara (ed.), *Antony and Cleopatra* (Signet Shakespeare, New York, 1964).

Furness, H. H., *Antony and Cleopatra* (New Variorum Shakespeare, Philadelphia, Pa., 1907).

Mack, Maynard (ed.), *Antony and Cleopatra* (Pelican Shakespeare, Baltimore, Md., 1960).

Ridley, M. R. (ed.), *Antony and Cleopatra* (new Arden Shakespeare, London, 1954).

Wilson, J. Dover (ed.), *Antony and Cleopatra* (New Cambridge Shakespeare, Cambridge, 1950).

—— (ed.), *Antony and Cleopatra . . . A Facsimile of the First Folio Text* (London, 1928).

Criticism

Bethell, S. L., *Shakespeare and the Popular Dramatic Tradition* (London, 1944).

Bradley, A. C., 'Shakespeare's *Antony and Cleopatra*', in his *Oxford Lectures on Poetry* (London, 1909).

Brown, J. R. (ed.), *Shakespeare: 'Antony and Cleopatra'* (Casebook Series, London, 1968).

Cecil, Lord David, *'Antony and Cleopatra'*, W. P. Ker Memorial Lecture (Glasgow, 1944), repr. in his *Poets and Storytellers* (London, 1949).

Charney, Maurice, *Shakespeare's Roman Plays. The Function of Imagery in the Drama* (Cambridge, Mass., 1961).

Daiches, David, 'Imagery and Meaning in *Antony and Cleopatra*', *English Studies*, 43 (1962), repr. in his *Modern Literary Essays* (Edinburgh, 1968).

Danby, J. F., *Poets on Fortune's Hill* (London, 1952), repr. as *Elizabethan and Jacobean Poets* (London, 1964).

Dickey, Franklin, *Not Wisely But Too Well* (San Marino, Calif., 1957).

Farnham, Willard, *Shakespeare's Tragic Frontier* (Berkeley, Calif., 1950).

Granville-Barker, Harley, *Prefaces to Shakespeare*, 2nd Series (London, 1930).

Henn, T. R., *The Living Image* (London, 1972).

Holloway, John, *The Story of the Night* (London, 1961).

Knight, G. Wilson, *The Imperial Theme* (London, 1931; 3rd edn., 1951).

Krook, Dorothea, *Elements of Tragedy* (New Haven, Conn., 1969).

Leavis, F. R., *'Antony and Cleopatra* and *All for Love*: A Critical Exercise', *Scrutiny*, 5 (1936–7).

Lee, Robin, *Shakespeare. 'Antony and Cleopatra'* (Studies in English Literature No. 44, London, 1971).

Markels, Julian, *The Pillar of the World* (Columbus, Ohio, 1968).

Mills, L. J., *The Tragedies of Shakespeare's 'Antony and Cleopatra'* (Bloomington, Ind., 1964).

Murry, J. Middleton, *The Problem of Style* (London, 1922).

Riemer, A. P., *A Reading of Shakespeare's 'Antony and Cleopatra'* (Sydney, 1968).

Schanzer, Ernest, *The Problem Plays of Shakespeare* (London, 1963).

Schücking, L. L., *Character Problems in Shakespeare's Plays* (London, 1922).

Spencer, Theodore, *Shakespeare and the Nature of Man* (New York, 1942).

Stirling, Brents, *Unity in Shakespearian Tragedy* (New York, 1956).

Stoll, E. E., 'Cleopatra', *MLR* 23 (1928), repr. in his *Poets and Playwrights* (Minneapolis, Minn., 1930).

Traci, Philip J., *The Love Play of 'Antony and Cleopatra'* (The Hague, 1970).

Traversi, D. A., *An Approach to Shakespeare* (London, 1938; 3rd edn., 2 vols., London, 1968–9).

Whitaker, Virgil K., *The Mirror up to Nature* (San Marino, Calif., 1965).

15. *Coriolanus* and *Timon of Athens*

MAURICE CHARNEY

Coriolanus

TEXTS

Coriolanus first appeared in print in the Folio of 1623, seven years after Shakespeare's death. The printer seems to have used a carefully prepared manuscript, perhaps in the author's own hand. The stage directions are unusually elaborate, and the text is longer than would be normal for an acting version. The chief difficulty is with mislineation, or lines that do not scan properly as blank verse. Most editors rearrange the lines to improve the scansion, but G. B. Harrison argues strongly for following the Folio pattern in most cases. On disputed words and passages that are usually emended, see the discussion in Sisson's *New Readings in Shakespeare*, vol. ii.

For students' purposes, the most useful editions of the play are the New Penguin (edited by G. R. Hibbard) and the Signet (edited by Reuben Brower). The New Penguin has a long and comprehensive introduction, with extensive notes that appear, unfortunately, after the text of the play; the remarks on the dramatic function of each scene are particularly illuminating. Although the Signet edition has many brief notes (chiefly explaining what the words mean), its emphasis is different. Brower's introduction is one of the most original essays on the play, and the volume reprints a generous sampling from North's translation of Plutarch, as well as selections from Bradley, Wyndham Lewis, and Traversi.

The most scholarly modern edition is that by John Dover Wilson in the New Cambridge series. This is the last volume for which Wilson was solely responsible, and the introduction and notes lack some of the fiery inventiveness of his earlier projects. The notes are remarkable for their wide learning and keen insight, especially into problems of lexicography. Furness's New Variorum edition is also very learned, although a good part of its 762 pages culled from critics of the eighteenth and nineteenth centuries now seems merely of antiquarian interest. The notes, however, can be illuminating on particular passages, and they manage to convey a strong sense of the critical tradition. Among other editions, the Pelican by Harry Levin is modest in scope, with a brief and searching introduction. The Laurel has no notes, but it is graced with valuable essays by Francis Fergusson and Sir Tyrone Guthrie. A new Arden edition of *Coriolanus* by J. P. Brockbank has been announced, and it will replace the Arden edition of 1922 by W. J. Craig and R. H. Case, which is still useful but out of date.

CRITICAL STUDIES AND COMMENTARY

When T. S. Eliot in 1919 praised *Coriolanus* for being, 'with *Antony and Cleopatra*, Shakespeare's most assured artistic success', he was paradoxically revaluing the tragedies from Bradley's traditional 'great four': *King Lear, Othello, Macbeth*, and *Hamlet*. It is no longer necessary to defend *Coriolanus* from its imagined detractors. To recent critics it has seemed one of Shakespeare's most original accomplishments, and commentary has been intent on discovering what makes it unique as a tragedy. Fortunately, *Coriolanus* is not still being invidiously compared with earlier tragedies to which it has little resemblance.

In his British Academy lecture of 1912, Bradley was keenly aware that *Coriolanus* stands apart from other tragedies of Shakespeare. 'That peculiar *imaginative* effect or atmosphere is hardly felt', because the play is intensely secular and public and has no natural or supernatural support. As usual, Bradley's descriptive powers are impressive even when we may disagree with his conclusions. The same holds true for O. J. Campbell's argument that *Coriolanus* is a 'tragical satire', full of the spirit of mockery and derision. Although Campbell is too energetic in the pursuit of his thesis, he has an acute sense of what is special in tone and mood. D. J. Enright's essay, '*Coriolanus*: Tragedy or Debate?', is more moderate and subtle than Campbell, but he too is trying to discover why the play cannot be understood within the conventional criteria of tragedy. The range of tone and feeling in the verse 'is unusually narrow for Shakespeare', and the play in general 'has certain qualities of an intellectual debate'. I. R. Browning's answer to Enright, '*Coriolanus*: Boy of Tears', seems to misunderstand the scope of the discussion, because Enright chooses to deal with style and tone, whereas Browning concentrates on a psychological approach to character. Van Doren's emphasis on the 'rhetorical' and 'discussion' aspects of *Coriolanus* offers support for Enright.

In *Shakespeare's Tragic Frontier*, Farnham creates a separate paradoxical world for Shakespeare's final tragedies: *Timon of Athens, Macbeth, Antony and Cleopatra*, and *Coriolanus*. This world of taints and honours waging equally, of deeply flawed yet noble characters, has its most characteristic expression in *Coriolanus*, whose pride produces 'not only everything bad but also everything good by which he comes to be a subject for Shakespearean tragedy'. Even if we disagree with aspects of Farnham's presentation, as Roth does in his long review, we are still indebted to him for trying to discern the place of *Coriolanus* in Shakespeare's development.

One of the most original suggestions about the genre of *Coriolanus* is that of Kenneth Burke, who sees it as a 'grotesque' tragedy resembling a Greek satyr-play. His essay, '*Coriolanus* and the Delights of Faction', is one of the best accounts of the play's tragic structure, derived deductively from Aristotelian principles. Virtues and vices work together to fit Coriolanus for his sacrificial function: his vices make him vulnerable, but his virtues establish his stature as a victim worth the killing. There is a comparable balancing of opposites in Jan Kott's chapter, '*Coriolanus*, or Shakespearian Contradictions' (in *Shakespeare Our Contemporary*), in which political and moral ambiguity lies at the heart of the tragedy. Kott makes it clear why this play appealed so strongly to Brecht and his followers. Northrop Frye deals with *Coriolanus* under the rubric of 'The Tragedies of Nature and Fortune', and Irving Ribner sees the central issue as an old-fashioned tragedy of pride. H. J. Oliver's essay, '*Coriolanus* as Tragic Hero', is a perceptive evaluation of modern thinking on the subject. Samuel Johnson does not deem *Coriolanus* tragic at all—it is 'one of the most amusing of our authour's performances', and Shaw goes so far as to call it 'the greatest of Shakespear's comedies'.

Our interpretation of *Coriolanus* depends, of course, on our own moral values. Critics associated with *Scrutiny* expressed their indignation at the growth of an impersonal, violent, mass society through their comments on Coriolanus, especially in his guise as heroic warrior—heroic values are vigorously reprehended for their harshness and inhumanity. D. A. Traversi is constantly reproaching Coriolanus for being an 'iron, mechanical warrior', a 'human war-machine'. For him, the crucial problem in the play is 'a failure in sensitivity, a failure in living; and it represents a failure on the part of a whole society.' Although L. C. Knights couches his argument (in *Further Explorations*) in terms of 'political wisdom', this too is essentially a moral concept. Tragedy arises from the 'defective humanity' of the central figure, his 'failure to achieve integration', his scorn for 'mutuality' in the state, his lack of 'maturity'. G. Wilson Knight pursues a comparable moral theme in his essay, where War and Love oppose each other as life-denying and life-giving forces.

Roy Battenhouse's long account of the play in *Shakespearean Tragedy* 'reshapes' its meaning according to Christian and humanistic premises.

Whatever one's sympathies for humane values, in the play itself military honour and personal heroism do not merely represent 'a failure in sensitivity, a failure in living'. Brower renders a notable service to students of *Coriolanus* by pursuing his discussion in the heroic, epic mode, and by making cogent comparisons between Shakespeare's protagonist and Homer's Achilles (but a completely Romanized Achilles). Coriolanus 'comes nearest to the essence of Homer's hero in his absoluteness, in his determination to imitate "the graces of the gods", in his will to push the heroic to the limit. . . .' This approach insists on complex moral assumptions, because abstract values are set against a necessary historical background of *virtus* and military honour. Eugene Waith enlightens us on the moral force of the classical tradition by interpreting Coriolanus as a Herculean hero. The whole issue of the degradation of heroic virtue in *Coriolanus* and *Othello* is subtly argued in an important essay by Richard Marienstras.

Knights's questioning of the 'maturity' of Coriolanus raises one of the most often debated (but not necessarily most significant) issues about the play. Is the hero merely a 'boy of tears' (I. R. Browning), a 'huge boy' (Bradley), an 'incorrigible boy' (Granville-Barker), 'one that never became anything but a schoolboy, crazed with notions of privilege and social distinction' (Wyndham Lewis), and can the play properly be called 'a tragedy of youth' (F. H. Rouda)? Psycho-analytic criticism has strongly emphasized Coriolanus's infantile relation to his castrating mother, and Charles Hofling sees the threatened attack on Rome as a sadistic but futile gesture against the mother. Emmett Wilson also interprets the play as the story of a son who is destroyed for his rebellion against his mother. In this schematic representation, both Menenius and Aufidius serve as surrogate fathers for the orphaned hero. To Rufus Putney, the problems of Coriolanus arise from the bleak and loveless atmosphere in which he was raised, so that his overpowering rage against his mother must be displaced on to other objects. David Barron points out that Coriolanus's need to subdue the Roman mob is based on his own personal need to subdue his chaotic, infantile impulses. Other psycho-analytic comment may be found in Holland, *Psychoanalysis and Shakespeare*. Also relevant are D. W. Harding's incisive comments on Volumnia as 'Shakespeare's most blood-chilling study of the destructive consequences of a woman's living out at someone else's expense her fantasy of what manhood should be'.

Although deficient in literary and dramatic understanding, the psycho-analytic critics are at least professional in their methods and assumptions. The older style of character analysis that fills the pages of the New Variorum edition is much more novelistic in intent: small details are assiduously garnered in order to build a vivid, 'rounded' characterization. The elaborate account of the characters in M. W. MacCallum's *Shakespeare's Roman Plays* is the most highly wrought study of this kind. What remains impressive in MacCallum is his careful reasoning and critical insight, which shine through the ponderousness of his approach.

Modern critics have been more interested in character functions than in characterization as an autonomous entity. Dean Frye has investigated the commentary on Coriolanus by other characters, and he reaches conclusions that rehabilitate the protagonist in the eyes of the audience. In a similar line, Una Ellis-Fermor sees the character of Coriolanus revealed by 'secret impressions', especially in his relation to Virgilia. E. A. M. Colman interprets Coriolanus from the perspective of his final speech, which, like Othello's, is exultantly self-assertive. The oddest of all character studies is Charles Mitchell's strident, vituperative attack on Coriolanus, that does not spare to compare him with Milton's Satan. Among many other essays, John Middleton Murry's panegyric of Virgilia, who speaks barely a hundred words, is notable.

On the broad question of politics in *Coriolanus*, Hazlitt's observation that 'Shakespeare himself seems to have had a leaning to the arbitrary side of the question' has not found much support. Modern commentators are more likely to begin with Coleridge's remark about the 'wonderful philosophic impartiality in Shakespeare's politics'. A study of what Shakespeare did with Plutarch supports this notion of a deliberate balancing of the conflict between patricians and plebeians. As Knights insists in 'Shakespeare and Political Wisdom', the politics of the play are not separable from questions of character and morality. John Palmer's pragmatic, commonsensical account of Coriolanus as a 'political character' best illustrates this approach. Coriolanus fares rather poorly in Palmer's scale of values, whereas the Tribunes are seen to be 'Shakespeare's counterfeit presentment of two labour leaders', who work for their party without claiming to be 'working disinterestedly for the nation'. Only Kenneth Muir seconds Palmer 'In Defence of the Tribunes', because they are 'much less unscrupulous than their opponents'. There may be some confusion between 'politic' and 'political', although *Coriolanus* lends itself to amoral speculations about the true source of power in the state. 'Politics' in a more general sense is the theme of Norman Rabkin's '*Coriolanus:* The Tragedy of Politics' and of Rossiter in *Angel with Horns*. Rossiter calls *Coriolanus* Shakespeare's 'only great political play'.

For a more historical approach, Phillips's considerable book on *The State in Shakespeare's Greek and Roman Plays* has a long chapter on the 'Violation of Order and Degree in *Coriolanus*'. Menenius's fable establishes a norm for the political ideology of the play, against which we may measure the excesses of Coriolanus and the Tribunes. David Hale, however, objects to the normative use of the fable of the belly; ultimately, the political analogy cannot be made relevant to the complex issues of the play. Jorgensen's book on *Shakespeare's Military World* has important political implications for understanding the role of Coriolanus; his tragedy arises from his inability to move 'from the casque to the cushion', from military to civic life. There is a useful account of Jacobean politics in the article by Gordon Zeeveld, and Clifford Davidson's essay, 'Coriolanus: A Study in Political Dislocation', is also relevant. The most thorough examination of the contemporary political background is in Clifford Chalmers Huffman's book, '*Coriolanus*' in Context. Huffman, unfortunately, interprets 'context' extremely literally.

The mob as a political force is the subject of Stirling's book, *The Populace in Shakespeare*, and it is quite clear that the Roman mob is conceived in contemporary terms. Stirling notes the topical significance of the enclosure riots in the Midlands in 1607, a point which is developed by E. C. Pettet and Sidney Shanker. As a substantial landowner in Warwickshire, Shakespeare must have been disturbed by the news of this popular insurrection at the very time he was writing *Coriolanus*. There are valuable analogues, especially from Biblical sources, in C. A. Patrides's essay, ' "The Beast with Many Heads": Renaissance Views on the Multitude'.

Our best guide to the classical background of *Coriolanus* is T. J. B. Spencer, who establishes a contemporary context for 'Shakespeare and the Elizabethan Romans.' Spencer's brief treatment of the play in his 'Writers and Their Work' pamphlet also emphasizes Shakespeare's concern 'to get things historically correct, to preserve Roman manners and customs and allusions'. In Spencer's view, 'to write *Coriolanus* was one of the great feats of the historical imagination in Renaissance Europe.' J. Leeds Barroll has a related essay on 'Shakespeare and Roman History'. Brower's introduction to the

Signet edition draws a significant parallel between *Coriolanus* and the heroic, epic tradition, as seen especially in the figure of Achilles. To Brower, Coriolanus is 'the most Roman, the least Christian, of Shakespeare's major heroes'. Kitto explores the topic of *poiesis*, with special reference to classical concepts that lie behind Shakespeare's play, and he notes a striking resemblance between Sophocles' Ajax and Coriolanus. The reader should also consult M. St. Clare Byrne's remarks on 'Classical Coriolanus.'

On the sources, our chief authority is Geoffrey Bullough, *Narrative and Dramatic Sources of Shakespeare*, volume v, which reprints selections from Livy and Florus as well as from Plutarch, and includes historical documents to illustrate the Jacobean context. In his introduction Bullough makes a strong case for Shakespeare's knowledge of Livy. MacCallum's book has a very detailed account of Shakespeare's use of Plutarch, a subject that is also profitably explored by Hermann Heuer, Richard Büttner, and Ernst Honigmann. Kenneth Muir has written extensively about the literary traditions that lie behind *Coriolanus*. If Shakespeare was not actually erudite, he must have read widely and unpredictably in the books and pamphlets of his own time, or at least have been well informed about them. Farnham's book also has a good deal to say about contemporary sources. Plutarch's Life of Coriolanus in North's translation is conveniently available in *Shakespeare's Plutarch* (edited by Spencer), which prints the relevant passages from the play at the bottom of the page.

Our understanding of the poetic quality of *Coriolanus* has been much influenced by G. Wilson Knight, who stresses the imagery of hardness, constriction, and violence: 'We are limited by city walls. And cities are here metallic, our world constricted, bound in by hard walls: and this constriction, this suggestion of hardness, is rooted deep in our theme.' Traversi pursues a similar line of imagery, but with greater sensitivity to the sinuous, muscular movement of the verse. L. C. Knights, in *Further Explorations*, has valuable comments on Shakespeare's poetic achievement in this play. An interesting study by R. F. Hill tries to show how contrarieties in the play are expressed by a pervasively antithetical style. James L. Calderwood has a significant essay on the breakdown of language in *Coriolanus*: 'Wordless Meanings and Meaningless Words'.

Spurgeon's standard work on Shakespeare's imagery has little to point out in *Coriolanus* except the fairly obvious theme of the body and sickness. In *The Development of Shakespeare's Imagery*, Clemen stresses the patrician–plebeian conflict as the source of symbolic contrasts. The most extensive discussion of imagery is in Charney's book on the Roman plays, in which the images are related to their dramatic function. Food, disease, and animals dominate, but the tragedy of Coriolanus is also presented by an imagery of acting and isolation. Maxwell's brief account of the animal imagery is one of the best studies of how a detail of Shakespeare's symbolism can illuminate his poetic method. The animal imagery reveals that '*Coriolanus* is characteristically a play in which the most momentous and vehement statements are made in the most literal form.' In the penetrating article by F. N. Lees, '*Coriolanus*, Aristotle, and Bacon', the animal and god imageries show the hero poised between the alternatives proposed by Aristotle: 'He that is incapable of living in a society is a god or a beast.' Leonard Dean's essay on 'Voice and Deed in *Coriolanus*' adds to our awareness of the acting imagery, while D. J. Gordon's handling of a similar topic, 'Name and Fame', relates Shakespeare to the *topoi* of classical tradition.

Critics pay lip-service to the dramatic power of *Coriolanus*, yet there has been little serious consideration of its dramaturgy, or even of practical problems of staging. Glynne Wickham's comments on the play grow out of his experience in producing it at Bath in 1952, and there is a rewarding sense here of how staging may clarify the text. Sir Tyrone Guthrie's essay in the Laurel edition is also closely related to a theatrical context. Particularly interesting is his emphasis on the role of Aufidius as a worthy antagonist for Coriolanus. The fullest discussion of dramaturgy is in Granville-Barker's *Prefaces*. Unfortunately, *Coriolanus* was the last Preface Granville-Barker wrote, and it shows a certain laboriousness in its points about characters, but its final sections on the dramatic verse and on the use of silence represent the author at his best. He tries to deal with the presented play in its own medium, and this concern gives his work a special freshness and relevance. Charney's book also pays close attention to dramaturgic problems and necessities, especially in the use of a non-verbal, 'presentational' imagery.

The stage history of *Coriolanus* is well summarized in C. B. Young's brief account in the New Cambridge edition. Further details about later versions of the play, often radically rewritten, may be found in Hazelton Spencer's *Shakespeare Improved* and Odell's *Shakespeare— from Betterton to Irving*. Trewin discusses English productions of the twentieth century. There are a few excellent pages on *Coriolanus* from the actors' point of view in Sprague's *Shakespeare and the Actors*. The New Variorum edition has useful material in its appendix on dramatic versions, stage history, and actors' interpretations.

For further discussion of the many books and articles on *Coriolanus* and its background, the reader should consult John W. Velz's bibliography, *Shakespeare and the Classical Tradition*, which goes as far as 1960. There is also valuable commentary on the critical literature in Berman's *A Reader's Guide to Shakespeare's Plays*: in Hibbard's New Penguin edition; in Spencer's 'Writers and Their Work' pamphlet; and in his foreword to the reprint of MacCallum in 1967. Maxwell assesses the main lines of investigation in *Shakespeare Survey 10*, a volume devoted to the Roman plays. There is a collection of essays, edited by Charney, on Shakespeare's Roman plays.

Timon of Athens

TEXTS

There is an air of mystery surrounding the first publication of *Timon* in the Shakespeare Folio of 1623. We know from bibliographical evidence that three pages of *Troilus and Cressida* were already set up and printed when it was suddenly withdrawn, presumably because of difficulties over rights. As a stopgap, *Timon* was inserted in the space left blank between *Romeo and Juliet* and *Julius Caesar*. Whether *Timon* ever would have been published had this contretemps not arisen is an open question, but it seems clear that the manuscript the printer used must have been a rough draft rather than a final version, because it is full of inconsistencies in plot, irregularities in verse, and odd ineptitudes in writing.

It is apparent, for example, from Terence Spencer's fascinating note about money, that Shakespeare either did not know or had forgotten how much a talent was worth, but in the course of writing he found out and then rectified some of his figures. The conclusion from the evidence of the talents seems to be that the play was never 'reasonably completed, polished, or corrected for performance or perusal'. Maxwell has some additional comments on this matter in his edition. The curious history and status of the text of *Timon* are discussed in J. Q. Adams's article, '*Timon of Athens* and the Irregularities in the First Folio'; in Greg's book, *The Shakespeare First Folio*; and in the editions of Maxwell and Oliver. Hinman's brief note in the Pelican edition should also be consulted.

We are fortunate in having excellent scholarly editions of the play: the new Arden by H. J. Oliver and the New Cambridge by J. C. Maxwell. Oliver keeps closely to the Folio text on the principle that 'there are many things in *Timon* about which Shakespeare had presumably not made up his mind at all . . . and I do not myself think it is an editor's business to make Shakespeare's mind up for him.' The notes in this edition are particularly rewarding for their explication of difficult passages, and Oliver's introduction offers a judicious review of the main lines of thinking about the play. Maxwell's introduction and style of editing are more adventurous than Oliver's, so that the two editions complement each other. As in other volumes of the New Cambridge series, there is a special interest in lexicography both in the notes and in the glossary at the end. The New Penguin edition by G. R. Hibbard has full notes and an eclectic and well-balanced introduction.

The notes in the Signet edition by Maurice Charney are much concerned with word-play, and this edition reprints commentary by David Cook, William Richardson, and Roy Walker. Charlton Hinman's Pelican edition has brief notes, but it has the special merit of being edited by one of the leading authorities on the First Folio. Although the Laurel edition has no notes at all, it has a provocative introduction by Francis Fergusson and also an oddly formalistic essay by Kenneth Burke on the function of invective in the play. Sisson, in *New Readings in Shakespeare*, volume II, presents his own editorial views about disputed passages in *Timon*.

CRITICAL STUDIES AND COMMENTARY

Questions about the text of *Timon* impinge closely on interpretation. The older studies of divided or non-Shakespearian authorship are now more or less obsolete, and there is general agreement that the play as we have it is unfinished. But unfinished in what sense? Chambers, in his chapter in *Shakespeare: A Survey*, thinks that parts of *Timon* 'might be rough notes, first drafts of scenes, jotted down in half prose or gnomic couplets, just as they came to the surface in the early stages of composition, to be taken up and worked over again during the process of revision'. The notion that *Timon* is unfinished both in conception and execution has been persuasively developed by Una Ellis-Fermor in her essay, '*Timon of Athens*: An Unfinished Play'. It is 'a play such as a great artist might leave behind him, roughed out, worked over in part and then abandoned; full of inconsistencies in form and presentation, with fragments (some of them considerable) bearing the unmistakable stamp of his workmanship scattered throughout'. This is the heart of the matter, and Miss Ellis-Fermor's later argument about our not really 'knowing' Timon as a character seems to me weak. It is mere frivolity to inquire: 'Why, above all, is he not in love?'

Miss Ellis-Fermor's article, in its wide and enthusiastic acceptance, has had a most pernicious effect on the appreciation of *Timon*. If the play is indeed so chaotic and so fragmentary as it is represented to be, then it is not worth bothering about, and *Timon* has been neglected not only in the classroom, but also in general studies of Shakespeare's tragedies. Even if one admits that it is an unfinished play, the caution Honigmann has proposed is still relevant: 'Stylistic and textual peculiarities have been overstressed while the vital fact that *Timon* appears to be an almost finished play has escaped the attention it deserves.' For all its faults, the poetic interpretation of G. Wilson Knight in *The Wheel of Fire* assumes that the play is a coherent work of art. H. S. Wilson strongly supports Knight: 'as an imaginative conception, as a symbolic poem, *Timon* is splendidly complete in its effect.' It is interesting that in Miss Bradbrook's eloquent inaugural lecture at the University of Cambridge (1966) there is no mention at all of *Timon* as an unfinished play. Perhaps we are now ready to accept the text of *Timon* for what it is without invidiously comparing it to some ideal play in our own minds.

The problem of disappointed expectations also arises in the position usually accorded *Timon* in Shakespeare's development. Older critics tended strongly to think of the play in Coleridge's terms as an 'after vibration' of *King Lear*: 'It is a *Lear* of the satirical drama, a *Lear* of domestic or ordinary life . . . a *Lear*, therefore, without its soul-scorching flashes, its ear-cleaving thunder-claps, its meteoric splendors. . . .' In Bradley's *Shakespearean Tragedy*, *Timon* is confidently placed after *King Lear*, and Bradley devotes Note S and many passing references to exploring their similarities. This pairing is one of the commonplaces of *Timon* criticism, although there is no external evidence at all, or even a specific allusion, by which to date the play. No one would deny similarities of theme and handling between *Timon* and *King Lear*, but, as Honigmann points out, the forms of the two plays are 'so utterly unlike that their collocation can only be misleading'.

Approaching *Timon* with different assumptions, Chambers locates it after *Coriolanus* and before *Pericles*. In this perspective, *Timon* is the last of Shakespeare's tragedies, and it looks ahead to the romances. It is not a failed version of *King Lear*, but something quite different. As Northrop Frye observes, 'It seems to me that this extraordinary play, half morality and half folk tale, the fourth and last of the Plutarchan plays, is the logical transition from *Coriolanus* to the romances, and that it has many features making for an *idiotes* comedy rather than a tragedy.' Clifford Leech develops a similar point of view in *Shakespeare's Tragedies*, where he compares Timon and Leontes. In a wide-ranging essay, 'The Last Tragic Heroes', G. K. Hunter explores the special status of *Timon* (and *Coriolanus*) between *King Lear* and the romances.

If *Timon* cannot be considered a tragedy like *King Lear*, then the question of its genre is once more open to discussion. O. J. Campbell makes a case for 'tragical satire' in the mode of Jonson's *Sejanus* and *Volpone*, but it is difficult to see how satire can be the end rather than the means of the tragedy. Campbell weakens his excellent points about *Timon* by pursuing so narrow a thesis. Farnham's notion of 'paradoxical tragedy' also suffers from the need to prove a thesis about the deeply flawed heroes of Shakespeare's 'tragic frontier'. Unlike Coriolanus, Timon is so thoroughly alienated that there is no norm against which we may understand his tragedy. From the opposite direction, Fergusson's introduction to the Laurel edition makes shrewd observations about the 'high farce' and 'farcical verve' of *Timon*, which displays 'the ironic simplicity of classical comedy'. The 'schematism' of the play is noted by Van Doren, and Charney, in his introduction to the Signet edition, calls the structure a dramatic fable: the 'action separates itself into a series of well-defined episodes related to each other analogically rather than causally.'

In an important article, Collins uses the tradition of the medieval morality play in order to explain the special features of *Timon*. The characters are 'subtilized Virtues and Vices', and their conflict illustrates moral principles. A good deal of squeezing is necessary to fit everything into the allegorical mode, but Collins has a keen sense of what the play is trying to do. To Anne Lancashire, *Timon* is Shakespeare's *Dr. Faustus*, because it so consciously reverses the morality-play expectations of *Everyman*. Traversi also draws on the morality-play aspect of *Timon* to argue the theme of excess. The morality-play context is much invoked by Bradbrook in her wide-ranging lecture, *The Tragic Pageant of 'Timon of Athens'*, but she is also intent on demonstrating that the play is a show, or masque, or pageant, as Jacobean audiences would understand these terms. Bradbrook is strongly conscious of paradox and parody in *Timon*, which she considers not so much a play in the ordinary sense as 'an experimental scenario for an indoor dramatic pageant'—presented, presumably, before the sophisticated audience of the private theatres.

Timon as a character has not fared well at the hands of critics, who have endowed both his philanthropy and his misanthropy with a complexity far beyond the scope of Timon's own limited awareness.

As Samuel Johnson reads the play, 'The catastrophe affords a very powerful warning against that ostentatious liberality, which scatters bounty, but confers no benefits, and buys flattery, but not friendship.' From somewhat later in the eighteenth century, William Richardson offers a perceptive psychological analysis of Timon in *Essays on Shakespeare's Dramatic Characters*. The 'love of distinction' is Timon's ruling passion, and 'through an undue relish for adulation' he comes to solicit distinction, 'not so much for the pleasure it yields him as to remove a disagreeable craving'. Dowden puts a similar emphasis on the dream-like compulsion of Timon in *Shakspere: A Critical Study of His Mind and Art*. On the puzzle about Timon's death, Bernard Paulin argues with trenchant wit that suicide would be most in keeping with his tragic style.

G. Wilson Knight's portrait of Timon, in an essay called 'The Pilgrimage of Hate', is an extravagant idealization. 'Timon himself is the flower of human aspiration. . . . Timon's world is poetry made real, lived rather than imagined. He would break down with conviviality, music, art, the barriers that sever consciousness from consciousness. He would build a paradise of love on earth.' Andor Gomme takes just exception to this sentimentalizing of Timon in defiance of the dramatic context. There is much that is brilliant in Knight's reading of the play as an extended metaphor, but the conclusions seem to be superimposed on the evidence. A study by Jarold W. Ramsey extends Knight's heroic portrait of Timon into a literal imitation of Christ. In an essay that opens the G. W. Wilson Knight festschrift, L. C. Knights quietly demolishes any favourable view of the protagonist. He is particularly interesting on Timon's self-hatred.

Among general discussions of the play, one of the best is by David Cook, who is helpful on the role of Apemantus as 'relentless mentor'. Maxwell has an inventive essay in *Scrutiny* that tries to understand why *Timon* is not more successful, even though it gives promise of being a more profound play than *Coriolanus*. Among older books, F. S. Boas has an excellent chapter on Timon in *Shakspere and His Predecessors*. Of all critics who have written on the play, the most enthusiastic still remains William Hazlitt, who found that *Timon* is 'written with as intense a feeling of his subject as any one play of Shakespeare. It is one of the few in which he seems to be in earnest throughout, never to trifle nor go out of his way. He does not relax in his efforts, nor lose sight of the unity of his design.'

There is general agreement that the world of *Timon* is corrupt and that Athens is a materialistic, money-grubbing city in which virtue is doomed to cynical betrayal. Pettet sees the play narrowly as a 'straightforward tract for the times' on the disruption of feudal morality. Timon in Act 1 is the ideal feudal lord, a dispenser of bounty, but the new forces of commercialism, money, and economic self-interest shatter his traditional beliefs. Karl Marx was particularly drawn to *Timon*, as Kenneth Muir informs us in an important but almost inaccessible article, '*Timon of Athens* and the Cash Nexus.' Everything in Athens has its market value, and the 'sex nausea of *Timon* is an appropriate criticism of a society which is dominated by the acquisitive principle, a society which is bound together by what Marx calls the cash-nexus'. James Emerson Phillips also comments on the social corruption of Athens, chiefly in the light of Renaissance political thinking. Jorgensen adds to this discussion by examining the notion of a 'peace-rotten' society—war is manly and character-building, whereas peace promotes idleness and vice. Alcibiades figures significantly in this argument. Another aspect of the corruption of Athens is the contemporary reputation of Greeks as a 'licentious, luxurious, frivolous, bibulous, venereal, insinuating, perfidious, and unscrupulous' people, as Terence Spencer sums up their national qualities in his essay, ' "Greeks" and "Merrygreeks" '. The subject is also explored by Clifford Leech in *Stratford Papers on Shakespeare, 1963*.

There is no extensive study of the imagery of *Timon*. Spurgeon calls attention to dogs, especially in the sequence of dogs licking sweets to express fawning. 'Timon's Dog' is the subject of a subtle expatiation by Empson in *The Structure of Complex Words* that ranges far beyond its avowed subject. Farnham's chapter on *Timon* puts special emphasis on the beast theme. Knight's essay has many fine perceptions about imagery, but the best brief discussion is in Clemen's book, *The Development of Shakespeare's Imagery*. Hilda Hulme makes some controversial points about the language of *Timon*, especially in defence of a number of Folio readings that are usually emended. '*Timon* and the Conceit of Art' is the topic of a very original study by W. M. Merchant, which he develops further in his book, *Shakespeare and the Artist*.

Timon has been closely related to Shakespeare's life by older critics, who saw in the subject of the play a disturbing expression of Shakespeare's personal troubles. Even so sober and factual a commentator as E. K. Chambers cannot resist the temptations of romantic biography: 'Both *King Lear* and *Timon of Athens* seem to show symptoms of mental disturbance. But mental disturbance may come in waves. It may very likely only be a whimsy of my own that during the attempt at *Timon of Athens* a wave broke, that an illness followed, and that when it passed, the breach between the tragic and the romantic period was complete.' The historical context of this topic is wittily developed in Sisson's British Academy lecture, *The Mythical Sorrows of Shakespeare*. The subject, however, has a medical aspect that equates Shakespeare's physical symptoms with those of Timon, who is not only suffering from megalomania, but also from brain damage brought about by syphilis. This is Somerville's thesis in *Madness in Shakespearian Tragedy*. Andrew H. Woods corroborates the paretic dementia in a learned professional article, and W. I. D. Scott, in *Shakespeare's Melancholics*, treats the same malady under the heading 'Timon: The General Paralytic'. These arguments are satirized in Paulin's account of Timon's death.

The problem of sources is complicated by the fact that, although most critics claim Lucian's dialogue as the main source, there is no contemporary edition of Lucian that Shakespeare can confidently be said to have used. Thomas Heywood first translated Lucian into English in 1637, but Shakespeare could have consulted the Latin version by Erasmus, the French of Filbert Bretin (1582), or the Italian of N. da Lonigo (1536). These matters are discussed at some length in Bullough's introduction to the *Narrative and Dramatic Sources of Shakespeare*, volume VI, but the reader should also consult the provocative and original article by Honigmann, which offers heterodox opinions about many other matters besides sources. Other important contributions are by Clemons and Bonnard. Bond's claim for Boiardo's *Il Timone* is now generally rejected. Farnham has a valuable section in *Shakespeare's Tragic Frontier* on the Renaissance tradition of Timonism.

The relation between *Timon of Athens* and the 'old' *Timon* play, a comedy based closely on Lucian and of apparently academic origin, is still unresolved. There may be a common source now lost, although recent opinion tends to date the 'old' *Timon* after Shakespeare and to see in it echoes of *Timon of Athens*. Muriel Bradbrook has a lively and speculative account of *The Comedy of Timon* as a revelling play of the law students of the Inner Temple, who consciously burlesqued Shakespeare. Bonnard thinks that the comedy may also have borrowed some details from *The Merchant of Venice* and *King Lear*. For other views, see Honigmann's article, Bullough's introduction, and Farnham. The older opinion, which advocated a date for the *Timon* comedy before 1600, is represented by G. C. Moore Smith, 'Notes on Some English University Plays', and J. Q. Adams, 'The Timon Plays'. Goldsmith's paper, 'Did Shakespeare

Use the Old Timon Comedy?', is unsatisfactory in its reasoning.
When Shadwell undertook to rewrite *Timon of Athens* as *The Man-Hater* (1678), he admitted that Shakespeare 'never made more Masterly strokes', yet, he insisted, 'I can truly say I have made it into a Play.' The stage history of *Timon of Athens* is part of literary criticism, because the alterations and omissions of playwrights clearly express their opinion of the original. Some of the earlier history is traced in Hazelton Spencer's *Shakespeare Improved*, and in Odell's *Shakespeare—from Betterton to Irving*. Stanley Williams has a useful article on 'Some Versions of *Timon of Athens* on the Stage'. There are brief accounts by C. B. Young in the New Cambridge edition and by Oliver in the new Arden. For modern productions see Trewin's *Shakespeare on the English Stage 1900–1964*, and an informative presentation in the *Times Educational Supplement* for 30 May 1952. Reviews of specific productions may be found in Kenneth Tynan's *Curtains*; in Roy Walker's 'Unto Caesar' (*Shakespeare Survey 11*); and in H. S. Wilson's book, *On the Design of Shakespearian Tragedy*. Sprague has a brief discussion of the stage business in *Shakespeare and the Actors*.

For a listing and brief description of what has been written on *Timon* up to 1960, see John W. Velz, *Shakespeare and the Classical Tradition*. There is a good evaluation of the critical literature in Ronald Berman's *A Reader's Guide to Shakespeare's Plays*. Francelia Butler devotes a whole book, full of miscellaneous information, to *The Strange Critical Fortunes of Shakespeare's 'Timon of Athens'*, but it is chaotically organized and its judgements are ill considered.

REFERENCES

Coriolanus

TEXTS

Brower, Reuben (ed.), *The Tragedy of Coriolanus* (Signet Shakespeare, New York, 1966); introduction repr. in revised form in *Hero and Saint: Shakespeare and the Graeco-Roman Heroic Tradition* (New York, 1971).

Craig, W. J., and Case, R. H. (eds.), *Coriolanus* (Arden edition, London, 1922).

Fergusson, Francis (ed.), *Coriolanus* (Laurel Shakespeare, New York, 1962).

Furness, H. H., Jr. (ed.), *The Tragedie of Coriolanus* (New Variorum edition, Philadelphia, Pa., 1928).

Harrison, G. B., 'A Note on *Coriolanus*', in *Joseph Quincy Adams Memorial Studies*, ed. James G. McManaway *et al.* (Washington, D.C., 1948).

Hibbard, G. R. (ed.), *Coriolanus* (New Penguin Shakespeare, Harmondsworth, 1967).

Levin, Harry (ed.), *The Tragedy of Coriolanus* (Pelican Shakespeare, Baltimore, Md., 1956).

Sisson, C. J., *New Readings in Shakespeare*, 2 vols. (Cambridge, 1961), vol. ii.

Wilson, John Dover (ed.), *The Tragedy of Coriolanus* (New Cambridge Shakespeare, Cambridge, 1960).

CRITICAL STUDIES AND COMMENTARY

Barroll, J. Leeds, 'Shakespeare and Roman History', *MLR*, 53 (1958).

Barron, David B., '*Coriolanus*: Portrait of the Artist as Infant', *American Imago* 19 (1962).

Battenhouse, Roy W., *Shakespearean Tragedy: Its Art and Its Christian Premises* (Bloomington, Ind., 1969).

Berman, Ronald, *A Reader's Guide to Shakespeare's Plays* (Chicago, Ill., 1965).

Bradley, A. C., '*Coriolanus*', British Academy Lecture 1912, repr. in *Studies in Shakespeare*, ed. Peter Alexander (London, 1964).

——, *Shakespearean Tragedy* (London, 1904).

Browning, I. R., '*Coriolanus*: Boy of Tears', *Essays in Criticism*, 5 (1955).

Bullough, Geoffrey (ed.), *Narrative and Dramatic Sources of Shakespeare*, vol. v (London, 1964).

Burke, Kenneth, '*Coriolanus* and the Delights of Faction', *Hudson Review*, 19 (1966).

Büttner, Richard, 'Zu "Coriolan" und seiner Quelle', *Shakespeare Jahrbuch*, 41 (1905).

Byrne, M. St. Clare, 'Classical Coriolanus', *National Review*, 96 (1931).

Calderwood, James L., '*Coriolanus*: Wordless Meanings and Meaningless Words', *SEL*, 6 (1966).

Campbell, Oscar James, *Shakespeare's Satire* (New York, 1943).

Charney, Maurice (ed.), *Discussions of Shakespeare's Roman Plays* (Boston, Mass., 1964).

——, *Shakespeare's Roman Plays: The Function of Imagery in the Drama* (Cambridge, Mass., 1961).

Clemen, W. H., *The Development of Shakespeare's Imagery* (London, 1951).

Coleridge, Samuel Taylor, *Shakespearean Criticism*, ed. T. M. Raysor, 2 vols. (Cambridge, Mass., 1930; Everyman's Library, London, 1960).

Colman, E. A. M., 'The End of Coriolanus', *ELH*, 34 (1967).

Davidson, Clifford, 'Coriolanus: A Study in Political Dislocation', *Shakespeare Studies*, 4 (1968).

Dean, Leonard F., 'Voice and Deed in *Coriolanus*', *University of Kansas City Review* 21 (1955).

Eliot, T. S., 'Hamlet and His Problems' (1919), in *Selected Essays 1917–1932* (London, 1932).

Ellis-Fermor, Una, 'Coriolanus', in *Shakespeare the Dramatist*, ed. Kenneth Muir (London, 1961).

Enright, D. J., 'Coriolanus: Tragedy or Debate?', in The Apothecary's Shop (London, 1957); repr. in Charney (ed.), Discussions.

Farnham, Willard, Shakespeare's Tragic Frontier (Berkeley, Calif., 1950).

Frye, Dean, 'Commentary in Shakespeare: The Case of Coriolanus', Shakespeare Studies, 1 (1965).

Frye, Northrop, 'The Tragedies of Nature and Fortune', in Stratford Papers on Shakespeare, 1961, ed. B. W. Jackson (Toronto, 1962).

Gordon, D. J., 'Name and Fame: Shakespeare's Coriolanus', in Papers Mainly Shakespearian, ed. G. I. Duthie (Edinburgh, 1964).

Granville-Barker, Harley, Prefaces to Shakespeare, Fifth Series (London, 1947).

Guthrie, Tyrone, In Various Directions: A View of Theatre (London, 1965); essay on Coriolanus repr. from the Laurel Shakespeare.

Hale, David G., 'Coriolanus: The Death of a Political Metaphor', Shakespeare Quarterly, 22 (1971).

——, 'Intestine Sedition: The Fable of the Belly', Comparative Literature Studies, 5 (1968).

Harding, D. W., 'Women's Fantasy of Manhood: A Shakespearian Theme', Shakespeare Quarterly, 20 (1969).

Hazlitt, William, Characters of Shakespeare's Plays (London, 1817; World's Classics, London, 1917).

Heuer, Hermann, 'From Plutarch to Shakespeare: A Study of Coriolanus', Shakespeare Survey 10 (1957).

——, 'Shakespeare und Plutarch: Studien zu Wertwelt und Lebensgefühl im Coriolanus', Anglia 62 (1938).

Hill, R. F., 'Coriolanus: Violentest Contrariety', Essays and Studies, 17 (1964).

Hofling, Charles K., 'An Interpretation of Shakespeare's Coriolanus', American Imago, 14 (1957).

Holland, Norman N., Psychoanalysis and Shakespeare (New York, 1966).

Honigmann, E. A. J., 'Shakespeare's Plutarch', Shakespeare Quarterly, 10 (1959).

Huffman, Clifford Chalmers, 'Coriolanus' in Context (Lewisburg, Pa., 1971).

Johnson, Samuel, Johnson on Shakespeare, ed. Arthur Sherbo (New Haven, Conn., 1968), vol. viii of the Yale Johnson.

Jorgensen, Paul A., Shakespeare's Military World (Berkeley, Calif., 1956).

Kitto, H. D. F., Poiesis: Structure and Thought (Cambridge, 1966).

Knight, G. Wilson, The Imperial Theme (London, 1931).

Knights, L. C., Further Explorations (London, 1965).

——, 'Shakespeare and Political Wisdom: A Note on the Personalism of Julius Caesar and Coriolanus', Sewanee Review, 61 (1953).

——, Some Shakespearean Themes (London, 1959).

Kott, Jan, Shakespeare Our Contemporary (London, 1964).

Lees, F. N., 'Coriolanus, Aristotle, and Bacon', RES, N.S. I (1950).

Lewis, Wyndham, The Lion and the Fox (London, 1927).

MacCallum, M. W., Shakespeare's Roman Plays and Their Background (London, 1910; repr. with a new foreword, 1967).

Marienstras, R., 'La Dégradation des vertus héroïques dans *Othello* et dans *Coriolan*', *Études Anglaises* 17 (1964).

Maxwell, J. C., 'Animal Imagery in *Coriolanus*', *MLR*, 42 (1947).

——, 'Shakespeare's Roman Plays: 1900–1956', *Shakespeare Survey 10* (1957).

Mitchell, Charles, 'Coriolanus: Power as Honor', *Shakespeare Studies*, I (1965).

Muir, Kenneth, 'The Background of *Coriolanus*', *Shakespeare Quarterly*, 10 (1959).

——, 'In Defence of the Tribunes', *Essays in Criticism*, 4 (1954).

——, 'Menenius's Fable', *N & Q* 198 (1953).

——, 'Shakespeare and Politics', in *Shakespeare in a Changing World*, ed. Arnold Kettle (London, 1964).

——, *Shakespeare's Sources*, vol. i (London, 1961).

Murry, J. M., 'A Neglected Heroine of Shakespeare', in *Countries of the Mind* (London, 1922).

Odell, G. C. D., *Shakespeare—from Betterton to Irving*, 2 vols. (New York, 1920).

Oliver, H. J., 'Coriolanus As Tragic Hero', *Shakespeare Quarterly*, 10 (1959).

Palmer, John, *Political Characters of Shakespeare* (London, 1945).

Patrides, C. A., ' "The Beast with Many Heads": Renaissance Views on the Multitude', *Shakespeare Quarterly*, 16 (1965).

Pettet, E. C., '*Coriolanus* and the Midlands Insurrection of 1607', *Shakespeare Survey 3* (1950).

Phillips, James Emerson, Jr., *The State in Shakespeare's Greek and Roman Plays* (New York, 1940).

Putney, Rufus, 'Coriolanus and His Mother,' *Psychoanalytic Quarterly*, 31 (1962).

Rabkin, Norman, '*Coriolanus*: The Tragedy of Politics', *Shakespeare Quarterly*, 17 (1966).

Ribner, Irving, 'The Tragedy of *Coriolanus*', *English Studies*, 34 (1953).

Rossiter, A. P., *Angel with Horns* (London, 1961).

Roth, Robert, 'Another World of Shakespeare', *Modern Philology*, 49 (1951–2) (review of Farnham's *Shakespeare's Tragic Frontier*).

Rouda, F. H., '*Coriolanus*—A Tragedy of Youth', *Shakespeare Quarterly*, 12 (1961).

Shanker, Sidney, 'Some Clues for *Coriolanus*', *Shakespeare Association Bulletin*, 24 (1949).

Shaw, G. Bernard, *Shaw on Shakespeare*, ed. Edwin Wilson (London, 1962; Penguin Shakespeare Library, Harmondsworth, 1969).

Spencer, Hazelton, *Shakespeare Improved* (London, 1927).

Spencer, T. J. B., foreword to reprint of MacCallum, *Shakespeare's Roman Plays* (London, 1967).

——, 'Shakespeare and the Elizabethan Romans', *Shakespeare Survey 10* (1957); repr. in Charney (ed.), *Discussions*.

——, *Shakespeare: The Roman Plays* (Writers and Their Work No. 157, London, 1963).

—— (ed.), *Shakespeare's Plutarch* (Harmondsworth, 1964).

Sprague, Arthur Colby, *Shakespeare and the Actors* (Cambridge, Mass., 1944).

Spurgeon, Caroline F. E., *Shakespeare's Imagery and What It Tells Us* (Cambridge, 1935).

Stirling, Brents, *The Populace in Shakespeare* (New York, 1949).

Traversi, D. A., *An Approach to Shakespeare*, 3rd edn., 2 vols. (London, 1968–9).

——, 'Coriolanus', *Scrutiny*, 6 (1937).

——, *Shakespeare: The Roman Plays* (London, 1963).

Trewin, J. C., *Shakespeare on the English Stage 1900–1964* (London, 1964).

Van Doren, Mark, *Shakespeare* (London, 1939).

Velz, John W., *Shakespeare and the Classical Tradition: A Critical Guide to Commentary, 1660–1960* (Minneapolis, Minn., 1968).

Waith, Eugene M., *The Herculean Hero* (New York, 1962).

Wickham, Glynne, 'Coriolanus: Shakespeare's Tragedy in Rehearsal and Performance', in *Later Shakespeare* (Stratford-upon-Avon Studies 8, ed. J. R. Brown and B. Harris, London, 1966); repr. in *Shakespeare's Dramatic Heritage* (London, 1969).

Wilson, Emmett, Jr., 'Coriolanus: The Anxious Bridegroom', *American Imago* 25 (1968).

Zeeveld, W. Gordon, 'Coriolanus and Jacobean Politics', *MLR*, 57 (1962).

Timon of Athens

TEXTS

Adams, Joseph Quincy, '*Timon of Athens* and the Irregularities in the First Folio', *JEGP* 7 (1908).

Charney, Maurice (ed.), *The Life of Timon of Athens* (Signet Shakespeare, New York, 1965).

Fergusson, Francis (ed.), *Timon of Athens* (Laurel Shakespeare, New York, 1963).

Greg, W. W., *The Shakespeare First Folio* (Oxford, 1955).

Hibbard, G. R. (ed.), *Timon of Athens* (New Penguin Shakespeare, Harmondsworth, 1970).

Hinman, Charlton (ed.), *The Life of Timon of Athens* (Pelican Shakespeare, Baltimore, Md., 1964).

Maxwell, J. C. (ed.), *The Life of Timon of Athens* (New Cambridge Shakespeare, Cambridge, 1957).

Oliver, H. J. (ed.), *Timon of Athens* (new Arden edition, London, 1963).

Sisson, C. J., *New Readings in Shakespeare*, 2 vols. (Cambridge, 1961), vol. ii.

Spencer, T. J. B., 'Shakespeare Learns the Value of Money: The Dramatist at Work on *Timon of Athens*', *Shakespeare Survey 6* (1953).

CRITICAL STUDIES AND COMMENTARY

Adams, Joseph Quincy, 'The Timon Plays', *JEGP*, 9 (1910).

Berman, Ronald, *A Reader's Guide to Shakespeare's Plays* (Chicago, Ill., 1965).

Boas, F. S., *Shakspere and His Predecessors* (London, 1896).

Bond, R. Warwick, 'Lucian and Boiardo in *Timon of Athens*', *MLR*, 26 (1931).

Bonnard, Georges A., 'Note sur les sources de *Timon of Athens*', *Études Anglaises*, 7 (1954).

Bradbrook, M. C., '*The Comedy of Timon*: A Reveling Play of the Inner Temple', *Renaissance Drama*, 9 (1966).

——, *The Tragic Pageant of 'Timon of Athens'* (Cambridge, 1966); repr. in *Shakespeare the Craftsman* (London, 1969).

Bradley, A. C., *Shakespearean Tragedy* (London, 1904).

Bullough, Geoffrey (ed.), *Narrative and Dramatic Sources of Shakespeare*, vol. vi (London, 1966).

Butler, Francelia, *The Strange Critical Fortunes of Shakespeare's 'Timon of Athens'* (Ames, Iowa, 1966).

Campbell, Oscar James, *Shakespeare's Satire* (New York, 1943).

Chambers, E. K., *William Shakespeare: A Study of Facts and Problems*, 2 vols. (Oxford, 1930).

——, *Shakespeare: A Survey* (London, 1925).

Clemen, W. H., *The Development of Shakespeare's Imagery* (London, 1951).

Clemons, W. H., 'The Sources of *Timon of Athens*', *Princeton University Bulletin* 15 (1903–4).

Coleridge, Samuel Taylor, *Shakespearean Criticism*, ed. T. M. Raysor, 2 vols. (Cambridge, Mass., 1930; Everyman's Library, London, 1960).

Collins, A. S., '*Timon of Athens*: A Reconsideration', *RES*, 22 (1946).

Cook, David, '*Timon of Athens*', *Shakespeare Survey 16* (1963); repr. in the Signet edition.

Dowden, Edward, *Shakspere: A Critical Study of His Mind and Art* (London, 1875).

Ellis-Fermor, Una, '*Timon of Athens*: An Unfinished Play', *RES*, 18 (1942); repr. in *Shakespeare the Dramatist*, ed. Kenneth Muir (London, 1961).

Empson, William, *The Structure of Complex Words* (London, 1951).

Farnham, Willard, *Shakespeare's Tragic Frontier* (Berkeley, Calif., 1950).

Frye, Northrop, *A Natural Perspective: The Development of Shakespearean Comedy and Romance* (New York, 1965).

Goldsmith, Robert Hillis, 'Did Shakespeare Use the Old Timon Comedy?', *Shakespeare Quarterly*, 9 (1958).

Gomme, Andor, '*Timon of Athens*', *Essays in Criticism*, 9 (1959).

Hazlitt, William, *Characters of Shakespeare's Plays* (London, 1817; World's Classics, London, 1917).

Honigmann, E. A. J., '*Timon of Athens*', *Shakespeare Quarterly*, 12 (1961).

Hulme, Hilda M., *Explorations in Shakespeare's Language* (London, 1962).

Hunter, G. K., 'The Last Tragic Heroes', in *Later Shakespeare* (Stratford-upon-Avon Studies 8, ed. J. R. Brown and B. Harris, London, 1966).

Johnson, Samuel, *Johnson on Shakespeare*, ed. Arthur Sherbo (New Haven, Conn., 1968), vol. viii of the Yale Johnson.

Jorgensen, Paul A., *Shakespeare's Military World* (Berkeley, Calif., 1956).

Knight, G. Wilson, *The Wheel of Fire* (London, 1930; 2nd edn., 1949).

Knights, L. C., '*Timon of Athens*', in *The Morality of Art: Essays Presented to G. Wilson Knight*, ed. D. W. Jefferson (London, 1969).

Lancashire, Anne, '*Timon of Athens*: Shakespeare's *Dr. Faustus*', *Shakespeare Quarterly*, 21 (1970).

Leech, Clifford, 'Shakespeare's Greeks', in *Stratford Papers on Shakespeare, 1963*, ed. B. W. Jackson (Toronto, 1964).

——, *Shakespeare's Tragedies* (London, 1950).

Maxwell, J. C., '*Timon of Athens*', *Scrutiny*, 15 (1948).

Merchant, W. M., *Shakespeare and the Artist* (London, 1959).

——, '*Timon* and the Conceit of Art', *Shakespeare Quarterly*, 6 (1955).

Muir, Kenneth, '*Timon of Athens* and the Cash Nexus', *Modern Quarterly Miscellany*, 1 (1947).

Odell, G. C. D., *Shakespeare—from Betterton to Irving*, 2 vols. (New York, 1920).

Paulin, Bernard, 'La Mort de Timon d'Athènes', *Études Anglaises*, 17 (1964).

Pettet, E. C., '*Timon of Athens*: The Disruption of Feudal Morality', *RES* 23 (1947).,

Phillips, James Emerson, Jr., *The State in Shakespeare's Greek and Roman Plays* (New York, 1940).

Ramsey, Jarold W., 'Timon's Imitation of Christ', *Shakespeare Studies*, 2 (1966).

Richardson, William, *Essays on Shakespeare's Dramatic Characters*, 2nd edn. (London, 1785; section on *Timon* repr. in the Signet edition).

Scott, W. I. D., *Shakespeare's Melancholics* (London, 1962).

Sisson, C. J., *The Mythical Sorrows of Shakespeare*, British Academy Lecture 1934.

Smith, G. C. Moore, 'Notes on Some English University Plays', *MLR*, 3 (1908).

Somerville, H., *Madness in Shakespearian Tragedy* (London, 1929).

Spencer, Hazelton, *Shakespeare Improved* (London, 1927).

Spencer, T. J. B., ' "Greeks" and "Merrygreeks": A Background to *Timon of Athens* and *Troilus and Cressida*', in *Essays on Shakespeare and Elizabethan Drama in Honor of Hardin Craig*, ed. Richard Hosley (Columbia, Mo., 1962).

Sprague, Arthur Colby, *Shakespeare and the Actors* (Cambridge, Mass., 1944).

Spurgeon, Caroline F. E., *Shakespeare's Imagery and What It Tells Us* (Cambridge, 1935).

'*Timon of Athens*: Some Earlier Appearances', *Times Educational Supplement*, 30 May 1952.

Traversi, D. A., *An Approach to Shakespeare*, 3rd edn., 2 vols. (London, 1968–9), vol. ii.

Trewin, J. C., *Shakespeare on the English Stage 1900–1964* (London, 1964).

Tynan, Kenneth, *Curtains* (London, 1961).

Van Doren, Mark, *Shakespeare* (London, 1939).

Velz, John W., *Shakespeare and the Classical Tradition: A Critical Guide to Commentary, 1660–1960* (Minneapolis, Minn., 1968).

Walker, Roy, 'Unto Caesar: A Review of Recent Productions', *Shakespeare Survey 11* (1958).

Williams, Stanley T., 'Some Versions of *Timon of Athens* on the Stage', *Modern Philology*, 18 (1920).

Wilson, Harold S., *On the Design of Shakespearian Tragedy* (Toronto, 1957).

Woods, Andrew H., 'Syphilis in Shakespeare's Tragedy of Timon of Athens', *American Journal of Psychiatry*, 91 (1934).

16. The English History Plays

A. R. HUMPHREYS

GENERAL

Sources

The sources have been extensively studied: Kingsford ably analysed fifteenth-century chronicles, and there are selections from Holinshed by Boswell-Stone (valuably cross-referenced to other sources), Allardyce and Josephine Nicoll (a handy Everyman's volume), and Richard Hosley (in modernized spelling, annotated, and preserving Holinshed's narrative qualities particularly well). But the indispensable quarry is Bullough's *Narrative and Dramatic Sources*, which describes the authorities Shakespeare found available, the growth of Tudor historiography, and the constructional skill shown in the plays. Hall's chronicle, too, has been repeatedly studied, and the influence upon it, and in general, of Polydore Vergil's *Anglica Historia* has been analysed by Polydore's editor, Denys Hay, and by Campbell, Tillyard (in their studies referred to in the following section), and others. Polydore, an Italian humanist writing under Henry VII's patronage, established the 'Tudor myth' of a kingdom cursed since Richard II's overthrow and redeemed when Lancastrian Henry (VII) married Yorkist Elizabeth. Accepting this pattern, Hall defined Shakespeare's general plan, though how far his influence was direct is uncertain. Borrowings seem detectable in the *Henry VI* plays, but there are no indisputable debts in the *Henry IV–Henry V* trio, and whether Shakespeare studied Hall deeply is doubtful. Daniel's *Civil Wars* was influential, on emotional tone and interpretation: Hall (from Polydore) for theme and scope, Holinshed for material, and Daniel for imaginative spirit—these are the main formative presences. Further debts have been suggested, plausibly or otherwise, to French chronicles, *A Mirror for Magistrates*, Stow's *Annals*, Elyot's *The Governor*, and the church homilies; these latter, Hart convincingly argued, exerted a stronger sway than any treatises on political philosophy in establishing civil obedience as a sacred duty.

General Criticism and Commentary

The attention which, since about 1930, has most illuminated Shakespeare has been that devoted to the histories. Their contribution to

England's self-awareness was recognized a century earlier, and such dramatic individualists as Richard III, Falconbridge, Falstaff, and Henry V have always been found fascinating. But evaluation of the plays as ratifying the Tudor historians' expression of national consciousness is, in general, fairly recent. As Lily Campbell wrote in a seminal study, *Shakespeare's 'Histories'*, 'the Elizabethans expected any work of history to act as a political mirror. The rise of a drama using the materials and subserving the purposes of history was inevitable.' Of this drama, in action, Dover Wilson and T. C. Worsley's *Shakespeare's Histories at Stratford, 1951*, A. C. Sprague's *Shakespeare's Histories: Plays for the Stage*, and J. C. Trewin's *Shakespeare on the English Stage, 1900–1964* are critically interesting and theatrically illuminating accounts. The New Cambridge Shakespeare includes a useful account of each play's stage history.

In particular, England's fifteenth-century wars, foreign and civil, riveted Elizabethan attention, with their dilemmas of union, authority, and succession. Beneath these dilemmas lay the question of God's participation in history. Lily Campbell analyses the conception by which history discloses divine justice and offers rulers a moral-political mirror for their instruction; she bypasses the plays' dramatic qualities yet shows the deep instincts in which they ground themselves, and promotes a revaluation of the *Henry VI–Richard III* sequence, once neglected as immature. 'Behind all the confusion of civil war in Shakespeare's histories', Tillyard observes, 'is the belief that the world is a part of eternal law.' Tudor chronicles, Turner and Williams comment in their introduction to Parts 2 and 3 of *Henry VI*, assume that events, 'while subject to the free will of participants, are nonetheless overseen ultimately by a Providence through which order will eventually be restored to a world rendered chaotic by sin'. Shakespeare wrote dramas, not treatises, yet, developing them through the moral imagination, he offers, as Knights says in *Shakespeare's Politics*, 'a realistic portrayal of the ways of the world and an insistent questioning of the values by which its great men live', 'a continuous exploration and assessment of experience', 'an expression of relationships between particular persons within an organic society'. It was to medieval concepts of the just state that Machiavelli administered the shock so interestingly studied by Mario Praz, and held by Una Ellis-Fermor (in *The Jacobean Drama*) to have precipitated Jacobean pessimism.

The Tudor sense of history is presented in important works by Lily Campbell, Louis Wright, Tillyard, Reese, F. P. Wilson, and Bevington; political, religious, and ethical interests continued and developed medieval traditions. Tillyard (*The Elizabethan World Picture*), Theodore Spencer, Hardin Craig, Joseph, and Danby have studied man in his moral universe; the last of these impressively defines the religious assumptions behind the first tetralogy, assumptions resumed in *Macbeth* and *King Lear*. Those who believe both tetralogies religiously orthodox have clashed with those who play this theme down: Bullough questions Tillyard's contention (in *Shakespeare's History Plays*) that *1 Henry VI* opens with England already under divine punishment, since not cosmic processes but bad practical policies are the play's theme. Ribner, too, doubts the predominance of doctrinal orthodoxy—if a divinely sanctioned establishment contravened England's good, Shakespeare supported England. The revised Arden edition takes the same view about *Henry IV*. The first tetralogy, in particular, plays fascinating variations on the relations of religious and secular history. Throughout, the supreme question is that concerned with the qualities that go to make good rule, and good obedience.

The Shakespearian history play is, then, 'a serious instrument of political education' (Reese). Riggs sees this 'education' as a means less of confirming a providential order than of recalling the heroical ideal, and the examples of great men. Yet Shakespeare offers no predigested answers, though deeply committed to traditional virtues of responsibility, loyalty, wisdom, and harmony. Winny finds as the grounds of the plays man's 'instinctive desire for society and friendship, and for the deeper satisfactions of true allegiance, faithful service, and ordered prerogative'. The 'I-am-myself-alone' individualist is the wicked, and fascinating, outsider.

Political and ethical meanings cannot eclipse the plays' national significance. Much has been heard of them as 'an epic statement of English experience' (Reese), though there are different ways of assessing the epic spirit. The nineteenth century largely neglected the first tetralogy (*Henry VI–Richard III*) in favour of the second (*Richard II–Henry V*), and located the epic statement in *Henry V*. The twentieth, more alive to tragedy, seeks the epic statement as that of a nation tested in trials; Brockbank ('The Frame of Disorder —*Henry VI*') defines it as 'the plight of individuals caught up in a cataclysmic movement of events', with Shakespeare dramatizing the exercise of power not in euphoric enthusiasm but in critical and complex irony. This is equally evident in the 'epic' spirit of both tetralogies.

One answer to the question how the plays find the unity which epic requires is in the evolving theme of king and people; a broader

version of this is the concept of England as hero. Charlton propounded this idea, and it has been cross-fertilized with elements of
the morality-play tradition ever since in 1918 Quiller-Couch saw
Henry IV as the 'Contention between Vice and Virtue for the Soul
of a Prince'. For Tillyard the dramatic hero of *1 Henry VI* is Talbot
but the conceptual hero is England or Respublica, 'after the fashion
of the Morality play', and Reese sees *Henry VI* as a prolonged
morality, with England divided amidst selfish passions.

These interpretations define half-articulated assumptions yet they
risk substituting doctrine for drama, and a counter-movement has
urged that human and dramatic interests are not to be swamped in
doctrine. Dover Wilson insists, in his edition of *Richard III*, that
Shakespeare 'had artistic or dramatic considerations in mind rather
than any concern for the commonwealth or the glorification of the
House of Tudor'. Bullough, Knights, and others assimilate doctrine
to a fully dramatic context, and a stimulating variant of this comes
from Wilson Knight ('Roses at War' in *The Sovereign Flower*) and
Winny; both stress in the first tetralogy 'man's susceptibility to the
impulse of his passionate being [and] the driving energies impelling
growth and change' (Winny). In 'The English History Play'
(*Shakespearian and Other Studies*) F. P. Wilson points out 'how few are
the lay figures, and how sharply the chief characters are placed
before us' even in the conventionally underrated *3 Henry VI*. This is a
valuable reminder of Shakespeare's dramatic humanity even in his
earliest work.

How, then, did Shakespeare conceive of historical drama? His
subject is England's history of the previous century (though with an
extension back to *King John*); his content is largely factual; his
causality is logical (his history has meaning); his structure is unified
by retrospection, foreboding, irony, and Nemesis (and so implies
intelligence, not mindlessness, whether human or providential); and
his historical scene must seem to grow fully out of the nation's being,
creating the sense of time, place, and causative rhythm.

A partial but provocative interpretation is that of Jan Kott. This,
coloured by Continental experience since 1930, focuses on the grim-
ness, the ruthless 'Grand Mechanism', of power. Kott pays scant
attention to the differences between the plays, and Stříbrný's excellent
essay, '*Henry V* and History', criticizes him for treating them all as
exposures of unmitigated *Realpolitik*. Yet by insisting that historical
drama is more than costumed posturing Kott makes the reader
formulate his own sense of it. Kott's sense is tragic, history being
either a desperate struggle for progress or a disastrous cycle of non-

progression, 'a cruel and tragic farce'. Briefly admitting a different
spirit in *Henry IV*, he prefers the 'deeper and more austere' tragedy
of *Richard II* and *Richard III*, and in the histories sees essentially hate,
lust, and violence. His one-sided case registers with great, if repeti-
tious, force.

The two tetralogies offer a magnificent panorama, with the
'Tudor myth' as the general ground. It is unlikely that they are
intentionally 'political', or that each play must be controlled by the
others (so that, for instance, *Henry V*'s heroics need ironic devaluing,
as being deduced from Henry IV's alleged Machiavellism), or
that a total scheme governed Shakespeare from the start (such as
Miss Ellis-Fermor's 'picture of the king', portrayed negatively
through weakness in the first tetralogy, positively through strength
in the second). Still, though unity should not be overstressed, a
century's history has passed through the crucible of one mind and
emerged as the expression of national life and energy.

If in some loose sense there is a 'grand design', where does it
culminate: in *Richard III*, the play about the latest reign, or in
Henry V, the play latest in composition? If in *Richard III*, the tenor of
Shakespearian history may well be thought, as Rossiter, Kott, and
Brockbank have thought it, directed towards tragedy (even though
Richard III is often grimly comic, and though, following the 'Tudor
myth', it establishes Henry VII as England's saviour). If the culmination lies in *Henry V*, the outcome is optimistic (even though the
optimism may be countered with irony and though, probing illness
and remorse, *2 Henry IV* offers its tragic tone). For Rossiter, tragic
and comic complexly interact: rulers' inadequacies contrast all
but tragically with the national destinies under their care, yet in
itself this amounts to ironic comedy. If order-and-degree authori-
tarianism claims reverence for fallible men, there must be critical wit
(from Falstaff, most evidently, yet not from him alone), to deride
'ideal systems which assume that human nature is what it isn't'.
Complexity and irony are themes, too, for Brockbank and Knights,
though the irony is semi-tragic, a Hardyan emotion for men doomed
by remorseless time, their hopes fading with age. And Miss Ellis-
Fermor, exploring the relations between the private and public
personalities of Shakespeare's kings, finds even Henry V tragic, the
ideal public figure 'converted whole' into his function, 'a dead man
walking'. Such a reading, darkening even the most confident of
the histories, seems—however intelligently argued—to contravene the
plain intention, the sense of fulfilled achievement in kingship, which
the emergence of Prince Hal into King Henry betokens. One would

rather see Shakespeare's histories as culminating in a tempered yet assured sense that in unity of king and people each party finds its most rewarding existence.

The marked rehabilitation of *Henry VI* under the growing conviction that all three parts are Shakespeare's has had fruitful results. It has shown how early Shakespeare excelled in construction and comprehension, how brilliantly he set vernacular styles to clash with rhetorical artifice (a theme well developed by Gladys Willcock and by Brooke's essay on *Richard III*), and how strong was his sense of tragic destiny (Kott's insistence on this has been mentioned, and it led R. W. Chambers to rebut the common notion that Shakespeare's first dramatic decade was prevailingly romantic). A superb contribution to this deepened appreciation is *The Wars of the Roses*, by John Barton, aided by Peter Hall, which adapts the first tetralogy as three plays—*Henry VI, Edward IV, Richard III*—with great theatrical effect. As Hall's introduction admits, it 'perpetrates the ultimate literary heresy; Shakespeare cut, rewritten, and rearranged', and the purists protested. But the plays' dynamics of political violences are displayed with stunning power.

The poignancy of tragic history in the first tetralogy goes far beyond what any other dramatist could convey. Yet to extend the same reading to the second would be to distort its rich humanity, which can no more be reduced under the label of tragedy than under that of 'Morality tradition' or political 'Grand Mechanism'. *Henry IV* and *Henry V* bring intense awareness to political issues and the psychology of political men, yet what moves Shakespeare is the fascination of life's vitalities, not of its dooms, an exultance in his fellows' activities and enterprises as, round the statecraft of their governors, they exert their irrepressible energies. In this, ultimately, there is more of the spirit of comedy than of tragedy.

Unfortunately, proper critical appreciation of one of the most decisive interpretations of the histories—the complete *Richard II–Richard III* cycle at Stratford-upon-Avon between 1963 and 1966—is hard to come by. J. R. Brown has provided virtually the only permanent documentation of these productions, but his account needs supplementing by some of the perceptive periodical reviewing of the time. For instance, Brown's reference (in another context) to 'a collection of unsubtle politicians in the history plays of 1964' should be set against T. C. Worsley's comments in the *Financial Times* (18 July 1963) that 'the barons have real weight and distinction. They are nicely differentiated, but . . . nothing is overdone. Their strength and weight are too assured to need over-emphasis.' This theatrical differentiation supports the more observant literary-critical accounts of the barons, but it also extends them: the council table round which the barons regularly assembled was central to Peter Hall's political interpretation, showing, as Worsley added, 'how behind the scenes decisions are cooked up to be ratified later at this table'.

If criticism has insufficiently communicated the rich quality of the histories in performance, it has also not fully expressed the 'perpetually astonishing' range of *Henry IV* (*The Times*, 16 April 1964), which the reviewers saluted. *The Times* stressed this range, from the 'rich comedy' and 'sensual ecstasy' of Hotspur to 'Justice Shallow's ruminations on mortality and the price of cattle . . . written in the disconnectedly self-absorbed idiom which we like to imagine an invention of the twentieth century', and the 'extraordinary poignancy' of Falstaff's dialogues with Doll. Penelope Gilliatt in the *Observer* (10 April 1966) found *Henry IV* 'one of the great marvels of the canon, . . . immensely complex and also very simple': she brought out the crucial appeal of these plays, which the production made unforgettable—'a series of pictures: a crowned father in a narrow black bed envying a political enemy for his son; a red-headed family with split Northumbrian vowels plotting rebellion in the north; a prince mimicking his father's disappointment while he is sitting in a fat man's chair in a tavern; . . . and an archbishop playing deadly politics in a wood, with rooks cawing over his head'.

John Arden, replying to a *New Statesman* review (12 June 1964), threw an interesting light upon critical dispute over *Henry V*: 'The surface meaning of *Henry V* is certainly that "Agincourt was a lovely war", . . . but there are so many corrections of this view in the structure of the play that one is forced to wonder if the author had not . . . written . . . a secret play within the official one.' Considering the ambiguous politics which precede Henry's campaign, Arden found them 'a political situation which we all recognise, [collusion] overlaid with a layer of patriotic rhetoric' so that the audience accepts it. He added, 'I myself constantly write secret plays within my ostensible ones'—an interesting interpretation of elements which criticism often finds contradictory.

What reviews of the 1964 Stratford cycle reveal about the histories is not only their extraordinary richness and range, which critical order-and-degree preoccupations fail fully to reveal, but the notable capacity of *Henry IV* to arouse special enthusiasm, summarized by Kenneth Tynan in reviewing an Old Vic production (quoted by Wood and Clarke): 'I suspected it at Stratford four years ago, and

now I am sure; for me the two parts of *Henry IV* are the twin sum-
mits of Shakespeare's achievement, . . . great public plays in which a
whole nation is under scrutiny and on trial. . . . To conceive the state
of mind in which the Henries were written is to feel dizzied by the air
of Olympus.'

THE EARLIER HISTORIES
(Henry VI; Richard III)

Texts

The three parts of *Henry VI*, edited by A. S. Cairncross in the Arden
Shakespeare, have full discussions of the scholarly problems and
lucid critical commentaries; *Richard III* has so far not appeared in
this series. J. Dover Wilson's New Cambridge edition of *Henry VI*,
though lively in conjecture about authorship and sequence, is less
useful, since much space goes to sharing the texts among supposed
collaborators, and Parts 2 and 3, though separately published, have
a continuous introduction. The New Cambridge *Richard III* discusses
the date and sources carefully, and draws on good traditional criticism for comment on style and dramatic qualities. *1* and *3 Henry VI*
and *Richard III* have valuable accounts of the stage history. The
Signet Classic Shakespeare includes *3 Henry VI*, edited by Milton
Crane, and *Richard III*, edited by Mark Eccles. The introductions
are straightforward and practical, and source material and important critical essays are included in appendices. The New Penguin
Shakespeare includes *Richard III*, edited by E. A. J. Honigmann;
the judicious introduction and full commentary, with textual
apparatus, make it the best edition for general use. The Pelican
Shakespeare has brief but effective introductions to *1 Henry VI*,
by David Bevington, *2* and *3 Henry VI* by R. K. Turner and G. W.
Williams, and *Richard III* by G. B. Evans, though the annotation is
slight. This series is available in the *Complete Pelican Shakespeare*, with
useful introductory essays (for instance, 'The Intellectual and
Political Background' by E. A. Strathmann) and a compact informative introduction to the 'Histories' section by the General Editor,
Alfred Harbage.

Criticism and Commentary

1 HENRY VI: With some important exceptions (like J. Dover Wilson
and F. P. Wilson) most scholars consider Shakespeare as virtually
sole author of *1 Henry VI* and its successors; Cairncross's Arden
introduction charts the currents of opinion well. Dover Wilson,

however, maintains in the New Cambridge edition the older theory of collaboration, believing that while the material for *Henry VI* evolved from one mind—perhaps Greene's—the text emerged jointly from Nashe, Greene, Peele, and Shakespeare. (Whether convincing or not on this, he describes Shakespeare's early-verse style excellently in the introduction to *3 Henry VI*.)

Already in 1903 Courthope had asserted that only Shakespeare could have executed the historical series with 'sufficient grasp of mind to imagine that historic drama as a consistent whole', and Alexander, Bullough, and others have repeated the claim. Alexander vindicates Shakespeare as sole author of the *Henry VI* trilogy, and his positions are accepted in the Arden and Pelican editions, and taken as the bases of critical study by Tillyard and others. Arthos gives a fine account of the human positives offered throughout: he recognizes the irony in conventional rituals of ceremony which clash with the actual realities of violence, yet affirms that this does not devalue human grandeur—'something [remains] of the . . . religious awe of the original ceremoniousness . . . and hope continues to make ordinary men feel like anointed kings.' Even in defeat man is still validated by his energies: 'nothing is being thought of in anything but the largest terms. . . . We are breathing the air of those . . . who bring all their forces to bear as if there were no such thing as fear.'

It has become normal, therefore, to see in the trilogy an ordering mind which, clarifying the mass of chronicle material, achieved an imaginative view of life pulsating with energy (Winny), a 'grand design . . . beneath the broken surface' (Lloyd Evans), and, in each play, a powerful structure. These perceptions, particularly the last, drastically reverse earlier judgements that the plays are a patchwork. In *1 Henry VI* Cairncross discovers 'a new type of drama . . . the drama of England', unprecedented in its organizational skill. (It was indeed unprecedented: there is almost no evidence before 1588 of a historical play on an English subject, whether because of censorship or not, save for one or two academic dramas like *Gorboduc* and *Ricardus Tertius*. Shakespeare, it would seem, actually started the genre.) Tillyard judges the structure of *2 Henry VI* masterly and the apparent formlessness of *3 Henry VI* functional, the right vehicle for the play's meaning. Even Dover Wilson, the disintegrator, thinks *3 Henry VI* structurally impressive, since it 'frames dramatic cosmos out of a chaos of historical events [in] a shapely drama', and the Barton/Hall stage adaptation magnificently vindicated this view.

Henry himself being too amorphous to shape his plays as later kings do (save for John), any shaping agent must be sought elsewhere.

In *Part 1* Talbot is the centre of force, 'a kind of folk-hero' (Lloyd Evans), and it might, Tillyard suggests, be called *The Tragedy of Talbot*. Yet, Cairncross observes, to do so would narrow Shakespeare's scheme, which dramatizes Hall's theme of intestine division—Kitto, seeing Greek analogies with these moral tragedies, instances the Temple-Garden scene (II.iv) as a classic instance of unprincipled faction. For Bullough the form is 'opposition between two forces or principles, one patriotic and constructive, the other destructive and selfish'; for Tillyard its pattern of moral history is the ideal of Order and Degree, whose subversion stands as the trilogy's dreadful warning. And for Richmond, a series of juxtapositions like the medieval device of multiple narrative moves towards 'the contrapuntal complexity of the later history play', one fundamental juxtaposition being that between England's venomous destructive aristocracy and its plebeian enemies—Joan in *Part 1*, Cade in *Part 2* —who, coarse though they are, highlight the nobles' futility by their own fierce energy and shrewd judgement. Shakespeare would hardly have shared in this endorsement of Joan and Cade (qualified though it is), yet to seek meanings thus, rather than yearn for clear narrative which Henry's vacillations cannot provide, is the best way to discover *1 Henry VI*'s form.

Throughout the trilogy further cohesion is offered in the anticipation and foreboding, the ironies of witting or unwitting insight, discussed by Wolfgang Clemen and by Brockbank. To find the play's structure in the dialectic of competing forces, its moral power in the evaluation of these forces and in the problem of God's presence in or absence from history, and its human fascination in the tumultuousness which 'crowds the stage with a mass of events and with animated figures who . . . embody an imaginative view of life' (Winny)—to do this is to value its force and sweep of plot, its demonstrative and thrusting scenes, its collisions of valour and hatred.

2 HENRY VI: Many points about *Part I* relate also to its successors; they too benefit from being presumed authentic. For Tillyard, *Part 2* improves on *Part 1* (the belief in its earlier composition has, since Alexander's study, generally faded); it exchanges a formal, stylized patterning of scenes for greater variety, a wider sense of England, and a stronger sense of personality; its leading personages are 'positive characters . . . at the centre of living', with Shakespeare showing more evidently his skill in animating a mass of material, and the fatalities through which the curse on England moves recall those of the *Oresteia*. Bullough and Cairncross consider it well

ordered, at once faithful to history and intelligently selective from history as, under Queen Margaret's malign power, death extends to her friends and foes alike.

The play moves through a wide field of action with a fine sense of what will interest the audience and, until Humphrey of Gloucester dies, with a moving presentation of his unavailing efforts for England's good. It fills eye, ear, and mind, ranging through the country's life from acrimonious nobles to the common people, these most remarkably presented in the scenes centring on Jack Cade; Shakespeare, as Kott and others remark, shows his humanity in disclosing how war and policy ravage the lives of the poor. Episodic though the source material is, episodic though in many ways it remains in the play, the discord spreading from the centre presents its grotesque tragi-comedy (with tragedy rapidly predominating) as a symphony of dissension. The tribute Turner and Williams pay in their edition is striking, yet justified: 'the mature Shakespeare is noted . . . for unsurpassed skill in dramatic design, for language so pregnant and beautiful that one can only wonder at it, for characters so admirably conceived that they never release their holds upon the imagination, and for as deep an insight into the mystery of things as any writer ever achieved. All these virtues are present, at least in embryonic form, in *2* and *3 Henry VI*.'

3 HENRY VI: Judgements on *Part 3*, that 'study of chaos itself' (Tillyard), vary considerably. It is Shakespeare's approximation to the unorganized chronicle, and though this suits its subject (a chaotic world must look chaotic) Tillyard suspects declining vitality: the occasional 'splendid things' are 'rather islands sticking out in a sea of mediocrity than hills arising from the valleys'—in fact, Shakespeare kindled only over two great war scenes (those of Towton and Wakefield) and over the thrusting ambitions of Margaret, Warwick, and the emergent Richard of Gloucester. Sprague, however, hails its 'greatness', and for Cairncross it is impressively unified by its furies of anger and pride, and its persistent motif of perjury; by its very violences it promotes 'the painful reassertion of the moral and political order against the prevailing anarchy'. Lloyd Evans is still more impressed and comments well on the 'exciting architecture of form'; Shakespeare is 'at the fullest stretch of his imaginative organising talent', constructing his play's necessary chaos around powerful characters and above all around Richard of Gloucester. Bullough, comparing it with its sprawling sources, judges it the *tour de force* of 'an artist in design, whose constructive ability is unequalled

by his contemporaries'. This ability boldly models the main features of Yorkist–Lancastrian strife into a climactic study of 'the larger pattern of England's past in relation to Kingship and Nobility'.

Henry himself has been very variously judged. His weaknesses encourage diabolism, cynicism, and cupidity. As F. P. Wilson puts it in 'The English History Play', 'the saintly yet dangerously ineffective Henry is only dimly aware that but for him and his despairing goodness these cruelties would not be'; Henry's incompetence precipitates his subjects' self-will. Yet he is generally judged with compassion; the vogue of 'moral history', with its respect for religious values, enhances his prestige as the embodiment of these values. His political weakness is undeniable, but the modern trend is to blame the politics for rejecting his goodness, rather than his goodness for mishandling the politics. For Danby, the whole tetralogy turns on the poles of Henry and Richard as symbolic opposites, equally significant; Henry's religious strength balances his political weakness, Richard's diabolism balances his political skill. Dover Wilson considers Henry, by the time he dies, so developed in quality as to deserve far more admiration than the Richard II of a few years later, and 'the only sketch of a saint in the canon'; for Palmer, too, he is 'a saint and a scholar'. None other among Shakespeare's kings, Goddard argues, feels so yearningly for his country's good, or suffers so movingly for her griefs; to Danby he is morally as nearly blameless as a king can be; and to Brockbank ('The Frame of Disorder') 'Shakespeare commands from his audience a full reverence' for his virtues. Milton Crane in his edition sees him as embodying a Christian idealism which defines the savagery of his surroundings, and others trace in *Part 3*, as Dover Wilson had done, the deep humanity which, disciplined by suffering, makes Henry confront his murderer with ironic, measured fatalism and, finally, with grave, religious passion. Though vanquished, Henry emerges to moral authority as 'the regulating principle of traditional society, . . . mercy, pity, love, human kindness, reinforced by God's ordinating fiat' (Danby): in his murder, the appalling secularism of political brutality is blazingly illuminated for what it is.

The trilogy, then, shows much local variety within a powerful common character. Bullough enumerates some shared features— a structure of similar and contrasted scenes, of movements and counter-movements; wave-like risings and fallings of great persons; and the emergence near each play's end of a major character to figure prominently in the next, for onward thrust of movement— Suffolk in *Part 1*, York in *Part 2*, Richard in *Part 3*. Much attention is also paid to patterns of style and plot, which foreshadow the 'tragedy of art' so tremendously achieved in *Richard III*. Rossiter draws a parallel between rhetorical artifices and plot formalities, dramatic structure lying in the 'overall system of paradox' and 'constant inversions of irony', with pendulum-like reversals of expected fortunes in the plot analogous to antithetical turns in the style. Irony of plot and irony of statement are indeed complementary sinews in these plays. To this view, however, Winny offers an interesting amendment, that what should strike us is the contrast between style and plot, rather than the analogy, since the former is showily artificial, the latter nakedly brutal. In this view the irony lies in the discrepancy between the verbal attitudinizing and the hideous conduct lying behind it: both are forms of Senecan sensationalism, intellectual and physical, offering evidence alike that, in Tillyard's words, 'Shakespeare wrote his tetralogy deliberately and academically.' Shakespeare's 'tragedy of art' presents a violently real world, however stylized the presentation.

Indeed, the concluding point must be to the same effect. Much in the plays up to *King John* and *Richard II* is rhetorical tragedy, and R. F. Hill gives a good account in 'Shakespeare's Early Tragic Mode'. But much is not, and shows Shakespeare's line of advance: Gladys Willcock deals well with the interplay of dramatic artifice and realism. Through the first tetralogy reality increasingly breaks through conventional styles. Cade expresses not merely a 'rebel' stereotype but a real social crisis; Joan of Arc's vulgarity shows up the officialism of court rhetoric; and the trilogy shifts hesitantly towards realistic vernacular and naturalistic events—Lloyd Evans distinguishes *Part 2* from *Part 1* by its 'newsreel intensity' after the earlier more ritualistic methods. Richard of Gloucester and, later, Falconbridge in *King John* (both witty outsiders) crack open the official rhetorics with sardonic realism. Flesh and blood speak, not megaphones. Such iconoclasts mark the uninhibited thrust of the world where men know their meanings, rather than the shows of art; they sound a modern (or timeless) note which banishes jaded artifice.

RICHARD III: *Richard III*—'the first English play that has consistently held the stage' (Honigmann, in the New Penguin edition)—needs no such revaluing as has gone to its precursors. Its forcefulness and its hero's compulsiveness, with his 'lifelong unremitting vigilance in relentless simulation' (Rossiter), have never failed to exert their spell, though the spell through the eighteenth and much of the nineteenth centuries was that of Cibber's adaptation (G. B. Shaw admits that he was brought up on it), which ensured for the villain-hero a monopoly of histrionic opportunities; Shaw and Sprague comment interestingly upon it. Shakespeare's version gradually regained the stage in the later nineteenth century, and in the twentieth a contemporary relevance has emerged (as with *Henry VI*) in what once seemed an archaic nightmare. For Kott, understandably, *Richard III* constitutes Shakespeare's testimony on politics; this is the truth, in the actual world.

For others the deduction is different; Richard represents not political truth but a fearful aberration. Shakespeare, Miss Ellis-Fermor remarks, gives short shrift to the type which so engaged Marlowe and Chapman, the lawless individualist (though Marlowe's treatment of ruthless aspiration surely contributed to Shakespeare's fascinated handling of Richard). Reese, for whom Richard exemplifies Machiavellism only by parody, suggests that Shakespeare found him only superficially compulsive, that his play is politically less interesting than *3 Henry VI* because less complex in political analysis, and that he is 'too much of a monster . . . to be taken seriously' (Kott would doubtless demur). In a spirited essay, 'The Unity of *Richard III*', Rossiter discerns in the histories 'a process thoroughly dialectical', in that conflicting political codes are ironically juxtaposed; yet, while *Richard III* abounds in irony, the dialectic merely opposes political virtuosity to political *naïveté* (though with hints, certainly, that under Providence man reaps what he sows).

Relatively unsubtle though it is, however, the play has a perennial fascination; as Lamb remarked, 'we contemplate a bloody and vicious character with delight.' Richard's 'ideal villainy' and 'full intellectual warmth of artistic enthusiasm' (Moulton) are irresistible. Palmer discusses him soundly, and Spivack defines well the consistency of 'his regal ambition, his enormous energy and sovereign force, his bonhomie and craft', as well as the gaily hypocritical malice he derives from the morality Vice—an important point. One falls under Richard's spell, finds little reason to pity his cacophonous foes, and may, as Eccles (in the Signet edition) and others suggest, enact through him, vicariously conscienceless, the archmanipulations one subconsciously aspires to, enjoying the virtuoso's villainies as, less intensely, one enjoys Barabas's in *The Jew of Malta*, or Volpone's, or as, more intensely, one does not enjoy those of Iago or Edmund. Perhaps, Reese suggests, villainy is relished only when turned against those who deserve it.

Yet not much modern criticism devalues the political or ethical significance of *Richard III*. 'Self-mutilation inherent in egotism and isolation' is, for others as well as Knights (in 'Shakespeare's Politics'), a main Shakespearian concern. With the trend toward setting the plays against a religious background, questions are posed about Providence and political morality. Is virtue politically significant? 'Does anything work except "the political"?', as Danby asks in an interesting discussion. *Richard III*, then, is of crucial interest. The machiavel's power marks 'the shift from the absolutes of God and society to the single absolute of the individual' (Danby), and the force of the dislocation is evident. The chroniclers, horrified by fifteenth-century chaos, detected God's hand raised over human sin, and *1 Henry VI*, in Tillyard's view (though not always in others'), sees God's power in the threatening 'stars' and diabolical Joan, 'Assigned . . . to be the English scourge'. In *2 Henry VI* 'the moral order of the universe in its relation to political and judicial acts becomes the central concern' (Richmond). *3 Henry VI* sees the clearest flouting of divine will, in saint-like Henry's murder by Richard. And by the end of *Richard III* the whole tetralogy has shown 'a pageant in which England and man himself work out the expiation of a divinely controlled universal order' (Cairncross). Shakespeare, as Arthos remarks of the *Henry VI* trilogy, does not assert that God controls man's affairs, yet he admits prophecies and premonitions so that 'we are bound to speculate that strange, perhaps spiritual, powers are at work.'

Long ago Moulton interpreted *Richard III* as 'the world of history transformed into an intricate design of which the recurrent pattern is Nemesis', and it is often compared with Greek tragedy, though the supreme power is not Greek Fate but Christianity's God: Richard's eve-of-battle dream is not a secular melodrama of the unnerved criminal but God's subversion of his evil hopes, a prompting of his forfeited humanity, and Lancastrian Henry is virtually a ventriloquist for divine judgement. Brooke's analysis is interesting: it extends into a broader consideration the stylistic point that rhetorical artifices are electrifyingly undercut by pungent bursts of the vernacular. This broader consideration is that Richard, the arch-individualist, sets himself against the massive momentum of history's conventions, set forms, and the generalized, conditioned, type-characters it produces (for all their malevolent energies): he owes much to the Vice, the 'sardonic humorist, by origin a kind of clown, who attracted to himself the attributes of anti-Christ bent on the mocking destruction of accepted values'. But here the Vice-clown becomes tragic, since his individualism, destructive as it is, must

itself be destroyed by the 'orderly predestinate scheme', the irrevoc-
able tendency of history to return to a norm, to annul any Marlovian
'ambition for human self-sufficiency'.

The play, then, seems less strictly either history or personal drama
than demonstrative tragedy, or, indeed, 'not rightly tragedy but
melodrama; the melodrama of genius' (Dover Wilson). Reese offers
the interesting comment that 'In many ways it is Shakespeare's
most mediaeval play in its texture, structure, and attitudes. . . .
Richard III progresses conceptually and dogmatically, not psychologically and pragmatically. . . . It derives from and returns to the
world of myth. . . . The superiority of *Richard III* over *Henry VI* is
obtained at the expense of the history play, rather than by deriving
strength from it.'

Yet Shakespeare is so undoctrinaire that the question how far to
emphasize a 'mythical' or providential interpretation remains open.
Certainly, to read it as a religious morality is to reduce the secular
gusto of Richard himself. Like Dover Wilson, Lloyd Evans considers
that the conclusion, dismissing Richard's memory in the interests
of England's moral convalescence, is an anticlimax; *Richard III*,
he thinks, surpasses its precursors precisely in being less morally
orthodox, and the tremendous impression Richard makes is not to be
annulled by religious sentiments from the insubstantial Henry,
however welcome these were to the Elizabethan mind; Dover
Wilson, too, makes this point firmly at the end of his edition's
Introduction. Theatrical experience will doubtless lean, as it always
has done, to his side and Lloyd Evans's; study of Shakespeare's
ideology will doubtless lean the other way, for while reading the play
it is not difficult to note, with Lily Campbell, the 'unstinted use of
the supernatural', confirming 'the sense of a divine vengeance
exacting a measured retribution for each sin'. Both elements need
holding together—the dramatic exuberance of Richard, and the
deeply felt moral background. Irresistible though Richard's Machiavellism is, it affronts every good instinct of humanity, and, indeed,
gains its effect from doing so. Theatrical zest should go with a sense
of polar good and evil.

Through the tetralogy, then, the sense of Providence is neither so
overriding as morality-tradition enthusiasts make out, nor so temperate as was held before Shakespeare was credited with great intellectual and conceptual power. He created Richard as a human and
dramatic phenomenon, with the keenest creative delight, but his
instincts ran, too, on the deepest values of humanity, and the sense
that 'the world is part of the eternal law' (Tillyard).

THE LATER HISTORIES

(King John; Richard II; Henry IV; Henry V)

Texts

Among the best of the New Variorum edition's exhaustive volumes
are those for *Richard II*, by Matthew W. Black, *1 Henry IV* by
Samuel Hemingway (valuably supplemented by G. Blakemore
Evans in *Shakespeare Quarterly*, 7, 1956), and *2 Henry IV*, by Matthias
A. Shaaber. This edition has disadvantages, however. Shakespeare's
text almost vanishes under the explanatory matter, and, against good
modern practice, *Richard II* and *2 Henry IV* are based on the first
Folio rather than the superior first Quartos. Much more practical
for normal study are the revised Arden editions, with ample introductions, annotation, and source material. The New Cambridge
Shakespeare varies in quality: *King John*, *Richard II*, and *Henry V*
have full, interesting introductions, with good notes and glossary,
and though not all their speculative contentions carry conviction
the editorial enthusiasm is infectious. The *Henry IV* pair are less
satisfactory; the real exploration of them is reserved for a separate
work, *The Fortunes of Falstaff*, and a comparatively scanty introduction is forced to serve for both plays jointly. *Part 2*, so individual a
play, is inadequately examined in the Introduction to *Part 1*, and
has no introduction of its own. The Signet Shakespeare, though less
thorough and critically searching than the revised Arden, has
straightforward introductions and notes by proficient editors, and
includes selections from leading critical essays. The New Penguin
Shakespeare is less of a specialist edition than the Arden but maintains an excellent level of introductory discussion, with critically
annotated lists of recommended reading. The full commentaries and
textual analyses serve both specialist and non-specialist well. The
Pelican Shakespeare has brief but sound introductions to each play,
but the annotation is slight. This series is available in the *Complete
Pelican Shakespeare*, with useful introductory essays. James L. Sanderson's *1 Henry IV* in the Norton's Critical Editions Series has a very
brief introduction but a wide range of selected critical essays, and
extracts from the sources.

Criticism and Commentary

KING JOHN: With *King John* Shakespeare returned from *Richard III*'s
'prestige of art' to a less managed, more realistic type of play, with great
vigour of conflicting positions, and unillusioned analysis of political
behaviour. How the play relates to the anonymous *Troublesome*

Raigne of King John (1591) is unclear; arguments for the priority of *King John* are urged in the Arden and Signet editions, but the New Cambridge seems pretty conclusively to show that only as derivations from *The Troublesome Raigne* are several of *King John*'s details explicable. Reese, also, effectively compares the two plays to illustrate Shakespeare's presumed rehandling. A range of dates from 1590 to 1598 has been offered, arising partly from the mixture of early rhetorical styles with mature ones, there being even touches of the great tragedies' intensity. These matters are still *sub judice*, but the energy of thought and style suggests a date around 1595.

'The play stands higher than it did a generation or two ago', as Sprague notes, though no radical revaluation has taken place: its thrust and mordancy compel respect rather than liking. John is generally thought despicable, his play disjointed in plot and disagreeable in tenor. It has been called hackwork; Reese considers it a relative failure, with verse flogged into energy, its view of history cynical, 'a dark picture [where] issues of right and wrong are debated freely, and every time the wrong prevails'. (This, however, is untrue of the conclusion, where the patriotic Falconbridge ensures succession to the rightful heir.) Yet Spurgeon commends as 'unsurpassed [in] terse pictorial quality' its imagery of bodily movement, and to Tillyard its force of mind and style evinces in Shakespeare a new kind of creative energy.

It has benefited from scrutiny of its structure, from enhanced respect for Shakespeare's political intelligence (evident in its dialectical quality), and from perception that it foreshadows later comic and tragic modes. Goddard credits it with unity, a clear leading idea, and compulsive character interest which points, through John himself, to the psychological ravages of the tragedies. To Bullough it points to a different outcome since, he surmises, by assimilating freely imagined character (Falconbridge) to historical fact Shakespeare broke away from history as rhetorical tragedy bound to his sources, and learnt how to modulate 'from the broadly comic to the epic'. Middleton Murry makes a cognate point in seeing in Falconbridge the bases of both Hotspur's bluff intransigence and Falstaff's ironical wit.

It shares with *Richard II*, though less emotively, a concern for the nature of kingship (does a discreditable king deserve loyalty?) and it also, as Dover Wilson indicates in his edition, presents a second great Tudor concern, the tension between monarchy and Papacy. These themes it presents in dialectic about political values and procedures—'a finely pointed dualism' (Honigmann). Goddard, followed by Calderwood (in 'Commodity and Honor in *King John*') and Matchett (in the Signet edition), postulates a drama of ideas based on the conflict of commodity with truth or honour (including the differentiation of genuine honour from nominal), the play being, in Calderwood's words, 'a dramatic crucible in which Shakespeare explores and tests two antagonistic ethical principles'. Through the juxtaposition of these the play finds its dominating, unifying idea.

The older concept of providential history here dissolves into something near secularism. Professing morality, men act pragmatically. Falconbridge, independent and enterprising, is 'the consciousness of his time' (Danby) and of the Elizabethan thrusting, amoral, 'New Men'; John's political world is as unprincipled as Richard III's, and much less archaic. Yet the play is not presented in entirely secular and modern terms; events may be determined by secular calculations, yet a supernatural shadow falls uncertainly upon them, by prophecy, invocation, or apparent fate. Kitto suggests 'an exact parallel, in technique, effect, and purpose' (though not one Shakespeare intended) between Greek drama's divine retributions and the war which divides France and England after Constance's curses. Tillyard offers a point of some subtlety; admitting weaker divine predominance than in the earlier histories he nevertheless hears a theological undertone: Commodity, cynically invoked, so clearly affronts divine order that by antithesis it provokes religious judgement; it is atheistic materialism, the 'all-changing word' opposing God's ordained Word, and it is held up for clear condemnation.

Modern criticism seeks a viewpoint from which dramatic and moral structures cohere. Bonjour's essay, 'The Road to Swinstead Abbey', has been much echoed: it surveys traditional opinions that the play is inchoate but rejects them by identifying both dramatic and moral centres as the point where John commands the murder of Arthur: Commodity here stands shockingly revealed, and John's kingship turns towards disaster. 'If ever criminal intent was "conscientiously connected" with its due punishment' (Bonjour) it is so here; the residual sense of providential presidence is confirmed. The death of Arthur, in Brockbank's phrase, expresses 'the death of English innocence', and since Arthur inherits the spiritual virtue of Henry VI his death has a religious implication. Hitherto, John has been effective, if unlikeable; henceforth, he courts destruction, England falters, and only Falconbridge rescues her.

Bonjour detects 'the dynamic evolution of two closely connected characters [in a pattern] remarkably balanced', John curving downwards, Falconbridge upwards. Honigmann in the Arden edition offers a variant of this, seeing Shakespeare as organizing his plot by enhancing Arthur's position, a position not particularly significant in the sources, but in the play given a special value as the innocence around which unscrupulousness hovers—'Shakespeare's arrangement of history centres John's problems in Arthur.' A more complex structure is that indicated by Schanzer; there is 'a series of confrontations with moral problems of varying degrees of complexity', from Falconbridge's early choice between legitimacy and advancement to the nobles' late choice between defection from villainous John and patriotism for suffering England. These confrontations, more than any concentration on Commodity or the symbolic Arthur, it is argued, give the play coherence; King John is unified rather by successive dilemmas than by any single theme.

Criticism has dealt much with the natures and relationships of John and Falconbridge. As Tillyard perceives behind cynical Commodity an affronted moral order, so Miss Ellis-Fermor sees, through rulers' selfishness, 'the shadowy suggestion of an opposite quality, . . . Shakespeare's positive ideal of kingship'. Except for Falconbridge, John's reign is unrelievedly distasteful, though Honigmann interestingly argues that, despicable as he is, John is remarkable as the virtuoso politician, destroyed by lack of moral fibre, his energy of intrigue turning to madness. Where, then, seek kingliness? John is 'a King of Commodity governed by short-term views of personal expediency' (Bullough), whereas the opportunist Falconbridge emerges to virtue, if ambiguously so. Is it he who represents kingship? Lloyd Evans doubts the coherence of a character successively cynical, arrogant, subversive, loyal, and valiant, but Calderwood in a good analysis discerns how the ambivalence of Falconbridge's self-consciousness is resolved, turning from specious (opportunist) 'honour' to true honour which saves England and preserves that kingship which, had he maintained his early egocentricity, he could have grasped himself. 'Thus, with what we might call "experienced" Honor dictating the terms to Commodity, King John concludes upon the same theme with which it began' (Calderwood), and Falconbridge, the true upholder of Degree, shows the kingliness which forbids him to be king. Yet this, Danby argues, is secularism à outrance—'a really "blind" feeling for "England right or wrong" '—with reverence for Degree, if not wholly devalued, at least turned specious in a Machiavellian world. Danby's case is a little overstated, but not much. Honour and raison d'état may not be incompatible, as Falconbridge is meant to show, yet their relationship is strained.

King John remains the most discomforting and disconcerting of the histories.

RICHARD II: *Richard II* has been rated rather low in the eighteenth and nineteenth centuries, very high in the twentieth. Sprague gives an interesting account of this change, and John Gielgud shows how modern attention to verse-style has influenced it. Very persuasive in this regard was C. E. Montague's review of Frank Benson's 1899 production: following upon Walter Pater, it established the King as the artist-poet he has been ever since. Notable editions, with good critical commentaries, have furthered the process, particularly those of Matthew W. Black, John Dover Wilson, Peter Ure, and Stanley Wells. Dover Wilson (in his edition) and Tillyard rate this as the most ceremonial of the histories, the culminating vision of 'essential mediaevalism', associated with the presumed influence of Froissart. (Rossiter, on the contrary, rejects a 'sentimental conservative [Shakespeare], looking nostalgically back, like Walter Scott, to the "great age" of chivalry'.) The formality—Dover Wilson wants a ritualistic performance—is the structural reflection, in Tillyard's view, of exceptionally elaborate cosmic references which relate worldly order and degree to heavenly. *Richard II* contrasts strikingly with the realistic histories which follow.

The first tetralogy, Bullough observes, dealt with negatives, with misgovernment and chaos; the second deals with positives, with firm government and order. For many critics *Richard II* presents sacramental kingship dying before mere power; for Brockbank the hieratic conception fades to 'nostalgic emotional consolation', and Richard's death ends the 'ceremonies of authority' which impeded efficient government. *King John* had presented an all-but-secular world; *Richard II* offers fully the emotive potency of Divine Right, only to have events override it. Palmer, Humphreys, and others stress the political case against Richard, countering Richard's personal appeal. 'Which is the more important', Ribner asks, 'the divine sanction of hereditary right, or proven ability to rule?' The Elizabethan answer is hardly in doubt; rulers must rule well.

The sources have been much discussed, especially in Dover Wilson's, Ure's, and Black's editions, and Black's article. Reyher argued for indebtedness to Froissart and other French chroniclers: Wilson and Black concur, but Ure is sceptical, and Wilson's theory of a non-extant earlier play which combined several sources ready for Shakespeare's use has been little supported: Bullough discusses the matter with his usual fine discrimination. Influences from

Daniel and, in conception, from Marlowe's *Edward II* are generally admitted. *Woodstock* is discussed by Wilson, Rossiter (in *Angel with Horns*), and Bullough: Ure is uncertain which play influenced which.

The psychological interest lies in Richard and Bolingbroke, and their relationships. Bolingbroke's enigmatic nature may be that of the calculating conspirator, or, as in Holinshed, that of the virtual victim of events, or, as seems evident, that of the man who, without contriving, seizes chances as they arise. He contrasts, markedly, with the voluble Richard, 'the interested spectator of his own ruin, dressing it with illuminating phrases and exquisite images' (E. K. Chambers). 'This dramatic use of the silent figure', Bradbrook comments, 'implies a grasp of full theatrical perspective', and for Ure his silence in the deposition scene has 'a positive quality', though his motives are too uncertain to warrant a Machiavellian interpretation. Humphreys, recognizing—as others do—Machiavellian elements (Henry's reign includes the Gaultree treachery in *2 Henry IV*), sees these as so involved with tragic unease throughout the *Henry IV*s that Machiavellism is an inadequate formula. Bolingbroke has what England needs: Shakespeare, tacitly endorsing him, tones down the militarism of his insurrection and ascribes Richard's deposition to his own histrionic, self-humiliating nature.

The stage history reveals relative neglect until the late nineteenth century, caused by dislike of Richard himself and the lack of overt action. Then, with *fin-de-siècle* romanticism, Pater, Yeats, and others idolized the aesthete-King. The balance has now steadied, and whereas the play was 'too often read as the tragedy of a private man' (Palmer), and England's welfare ignored, the contrasting theme is generally acknowledged. Richard's magnetism is poignant indeed; the Yeatsian view persists in Goddard's (that 'anyone with a distaste for a combination of worldliness and intelligence' will prefer Richard to Henry) and perhaps in Hill's, that openness of nature (Richard's) is preferable to inscrutability: the New Penguin editor, too, leans towards Richard (in Richard's later mode—'a voice with tears in it' —rather than his earlier). Such reactions arise, rightly, from sympathetic stage productions, and from sensitiveness to poetry. Yet Reese with equal justice deprecates 'the moody but gifted dreamer', Traversi recognizes Richard's negligence of his office and his shrewdness vitiated by self-deception, Rossiter censures his dilettantism, and Humphreys, observing that Richard is responsible alike for his misrule and his fall, argues that Bolingbroke's receptive expediency crossed with remorse impels his career more truly towards tragedy than does Richard's self-centred pathos. Palmer insists on the play's political seriousness; he cuts through Richard's magnetism with the sharp judgement that compared with Henry VI he is no saint or scholar, compared with Brutus he is no man of principle, compared with Hamlet he is no grown man exploring his own nature and life's realities but 'a wilful child "pretending" '. Palmer ends with the startling suggestion that, unlike as they are, Richard of Bordeaux and Richard of Gloucester are akin, mono-maniacs of egoism at odds with the world and its needs.

The old suspicion that *Richard II* is undramatic was confirmed, even as its poetic supremacy was affirmed, when Pater praised its lyrical qualities as 'a single melody [with] a simple continuity', as of a song or ballad. Dover Wilson and Tillyard, as already mentioned, stress its ritual and ceremony, its difference from *Henry IV* lying in its pattern and symbolism instead of the dynamic structure and expressive vernacular which mark the 'post-mediaeval world'. Inter-pretation, however, now admits its dramatic variousness. Events may, as the New Penguin editor remarks, 'seem to occur of them-selves or by a remote, divine will rather than as the result of human volition, [yet] movement can be of the mind as well as of the body'; the play is 'immensely complex and unusually self-conscious'; Richard, poeticizing his suffering, is as dramatic as characters more overtly active. This 'deliberate experiment in sophisticated lyricism' (Traversi) offers variety, not monotony. M. C. Bradbrook distin-guishes the multiple points of view in what is not a one-man, one-style play; Clemen indicates the interplaying facets of Richard's nature, and of contrasting political positions. Rossiter points out that much of the play contrasts sharply with ritualism, and Traversi observes that 'this effort to diversify artificial forms, to make the elaboration of contrasted styles answer to the tensions which consti-tute the true tragic theme, is possibly the most original feature of the play.'

Its qualities of style have attracted much attention. Reacting against Pater, Rossiter finds them 'heavily over-written Elizabethan High-Renaissance'. This is the theme of many comments, such as those of Madeleine Doran and Clemen on the imagery—that it is, in general, decorative and explicit rather than organic and implicit. The imagery and motifs are finely analysed by Altick who (partly anticipated by Mark Van Doren on imagery of speech and utter-ance, and partly supplemented by Dean) enriches one's sense of imaginative reference. That the artifices are dramatically expressive, despite their relative superficiality, is recognized by Clemen, Traversi (since they provide 'psychological correspondence' to Richard's

mercurial nature), and Hill ('the rhetorical projection of psychological intensity').

Finally, the political positions have been clarified. Elements of
divinity have always invested kingship but in feudal times this
association was ambiguous. Alfred Hart's *Shakespeare and the Homilies*
finds it gaining authority only with Tudor centralism and through
the homilies themselves. In *Richard II* the issues are balanced:
'*Richard II* is a favourite play with historians; it develops the political
issue in all its complexity and leaves judgement upon it to the
spectators' (New Cambridge edition). The poetical display of one
mercurial personality broadens into a many-faceted humanization
of a great political dilemma: Richard, though unrivalled in dramatic
magnetism, is only the centre of competing forces. Tillyard, Campbell, Humphreys, and others explain the contrasting positions, which
are well summarized in Matthew Black's essay on the sources; this
praises 'that even-handed justice and breadth of vision which could
take the [sources'] conflicting views' and reconcile them in so subtle
a portrait as that of Richard himself. 'I have never found that
quality of imagination in any other writer to the degree to which it is
manifest here'—so Black sums up, and so others agree.

1 AND 2 HENRY IV: *Henry IV* marks 'an astonishing development in
the direction of inclusiveness, . . . realised only because Shakespeare's
genius for construction matched his receptivity' (Barber). This inclusiveness Tillyard instances as evidence of epic qualities and
varied styles unmatched earlier and hardly rivalled later. In the
theatre this richness of effect has been particularly striking, as the
reviews already cited make apparent (see pp. 245–6).

The sources for this comprehensiveness are well given by Boswell-
Stone and Bullough. Ward (see *Henry IV: Sources*) examines the
anonymous *Famous Victories of Henry V*, and Elson's study of *Woodstock* ('The Non-Shakespearean *Richard II* and Shakespeare's
Henry IV, Part I)', suggests an influence thence, in comic subplots
organically related to the theme of the disturbed kingdom. Important studies by Dover Wilson and Oliver (for both, see *Henry IV:
Sources*) analyse the Wild-Prince legends, and the Arden introductions
to both parts survey a broad sweep of certain or probable material.

The morality-play tradition struck Quiller-Couch when he saw
the plays as 'a Contention . . . for the Soul of a Prince'. Studies by
Law, Spargo, and Shirley reinforced the argument, which threatened
to become one-sided; others, however, have provided a counter-
poise by pointing out that the moralities' spiritual conflict is missing

and the Prince's soul is never endangered. The Arden *1 Henry IV* relates the morality substratum to other elements but declines any implication that would reduce Falstaff's rich variety to the limitations of the morality Vice.

Its wealth of national feeling is *Henry IV*'s outstanding feature as history, expressed by Tillyard as a turn from the sacramental to the secular world, with the widest perspectives of metropolitan and provincial detail, the epic unfolding of England's life. For Lloyd Evans, as for others, these two plays are the most consistently exciting of all, with their 'gradually widening and deepening conception . . . of what constitutes a nation'.

Their political sense is deep, though not easy to define. A tendency to read them as near-tragic analyses of human frailties within the politico-social world prompts some caveats; as Jenkins remarks, it suggests 'a dislike of Shakespeare's political ideals [combined] with a search for ironies alien to his art'. Judgement of the political motives can be austere; Danby's is the most mordantly striking, with 'symbols of Power and Appetite [as] the keys to the plays' meaning: . . . the two symbols of Commodity [in an England] neither ideally ordered nor happy'. Richmond even detects in Henry's reign 'the evil genius of the new England' and in *Part 2* 'the most shocking illustration of the disintegration of healthy standards'. Less extravagant is Traversi's view that *Part 2* changes in spirit from the comic to the severely moral, in the mood of *Measure for Measure*. The best-considered of such judgements is that of L. C. Knights, in *Some Shakespearean Themes*; his criticism of *Part 2* balances well between the rigours of morality and the sympathy of understanding, the 'outgoing sympathy—even, at times, liking—for what is so firmly judged in the Falstaff comedy'. Over-earnest criticism has reacted against such euphoric views as Dover Wilson's, that '*Henry IV* is Shakespeare's vision of the "happy breed of men" that was his England', but it has in turn provoked a counter-reaction since, however responsible the plays are in their rendering of human nature, they are certainly not intended as monitors of private or public life. For Bradbrook they are 'about human relationships and heroic acts, not about politics', moral history being here subordinate to the appreciative celebration of human life; for Madeleine Doran, too, the whole tetralogy, whatever it implies about England's fate, centres not on moral judgement of political societies but on the natures of men. This indeed would seem the true Shakespearian intention.

The austerer interpretation takes *Henry IV* as leaning towards tragedy. This is tenable of *Part 2*, and Traversi and Knights stress its 'sombre realism'. Such readings, acceptable in the study, are less so on the stage, where the engrossing action, and the nation's rescue from dangers, brighten the scene. The life of Eastcheap and Gloucestershire may be—as for Danby it is—that of 'bawdy house and thieves' kitchen', of corrupt authority and victimized peasantry. But stage experience—as already instanced—offers Eastcheap (however coarse) and Gloucestershire (however absurd) as guaranteeing an irrepressible, irresistible, popular life.

Two aspects of structure have been much canvassed: one relates the history to the comedy, the other relates *Part 2* to *Part 1*. Charlton, in his essay on Falstaff, paralleled the King and the knight, since both endeavour to exploit the realms they command (for Winny, too, both are 'thieves'): the history and comedy stand equally on moral unscrupulousness. The earlier idea that the two are unconnected has vanished. The connection, however, is viewed in various lights. In 'Notes on Comedy' Knights holds that both plots 'express the vision which is projected into the form of the play', with (as in Charlton) Falstaffian duplicity 'in solution . . . throughout'. But in the most captivating study of the plays, *The Fortunes of Falstaff*, and more briefly in his edition of *Part 1*, Dover Wilson offers a less limiting mode of unification, virtually organizing the plays round Hal as relationships with others (Henry, Hotspur, Falstaff) develop his education as ruler. Tillyard continues the theme, of Hal poised among moral choices, as the structural bond, and Brooks and Heilman likewise conclude that 'for the reader for whom [*1 Henry IV*] does achieve a significant unity it may well seem that here Shakespeare has given us one of the wisest and fullest commentaries on human actions possible to the comic mode.' The *comic* mode, one notes; for the stricter moralist the play hints at tragedy; for the broader, it is (as surely it should be) comedy.

2 Henry IV, often undervalued, has benefited from the search for coherence even when coherence is not prima facie evident; studies by Traversi, Leech, and Knights (in *Some Shakespearean Themes*) have demonstrated how richly the play orchestrates its material, and the Arden introduction owes much to their insights in interconnecting history and comedy.

Whether the two parts are separate entities or an inseparable pair, a ten-act double drama, has been argued for two centuries. G. K. Hunter, surveying other Elizabethan two-part plays, decides that their unity is as likely to consist in a parallel disposition of incidents as in any narrative continuity, and that this is what happens in

Henry IV. The main ten-act proponents are Dover Wilson (who suggests that Shakespeare expanded an original single play and retained in its double form the characteristic curve of five-act construction, with Shrewsbury its keystone) and Tillyard (who treats both parts as one play testing Hal first for Chivalry and second for Justice). These views have been countered by Law, Shaaber, Cain, and others, and *Part 2* has even been called a hastily written encore. This is not tenable. Had *Part 1* failed, *Part 2* might have been left unwritten, but that Shakespeare should arouse expectation of Hal's accession and Falstaff's downfall without any real intention of so climaxing his story is inconceivable. Jenkins argues persuasively that Shakespeare expected to encompass Henry's reign within one play, and wrote three acts before finding his material too ample, where-upon he substituted a Shrewsbury climax (with Hal redeemed) instead of a King's deathbed climax and, when a continuation was justified, provided a second, parallel, princely redemption. The Arden *2 Henry IV* admits the appeal of this theory but thinks that from *Part 1*'s inception, or at least its earliest phase, its scope and development would demand a remoter denouement than one play could offer, and that a long post-Shrewsbury period is required for the moral pattern. Bullough surveys the conflicting opinions and concludes, as seems likely, that from the start Shakespeare thought in terms of two closely linked stages of Henry's troubles and Hal's reform.

The plays' stylistic vitality is widely recognized. For Tillyard, as already mentioned, it expresses the variety of England's life. Clemen finds a striking integration of imagery and thought, particularly in *Part 2*, and Madeleine Doran analyses the increasingly rapid, elliptical mode of utterance. A study by Dorius ('Prudence and Excess in *Richard II* and the Histories') displays the patterns of imagery which help to define the idea of good government throughout the tetralogy. Halliday briefly but alertly demonstrates how expressive the sound and rhythm are, and Traversi defines the 'exuberance firmly founded on common realism' in Falstaff's delivery (*Shakespeare from 'Richard II' to 'Henry V'*). The Arden introductions are particularly concerned to bring out the energetic and graphic spirit of the dramatic styles. A valuable study of idiomatic vitality is that in Brian Vickers's *The Artistry of Shakespeare's Prose*.

The main characters have always seized the attention. Most of them are historical persons, and the power with which this historical actuality is imaginatively incarnated is enthralling. The King is variously judged as 'one of the most subtly drawn . . . hypocrites in literature' (Goddard), a virtual tragic hero, a Machiavellian submerged in expediency, 'a good ruler, . . . confessing [his] crooked ways' (Tillyard), an able king care-worn and guilt-oppressed, and a leader becoming—in his shrewd aloofness—less than fully human under the imperatives of rule. Interpretations of the plays correspond closely to those of Henry himself. If he comes to power involuntarily, a man of worth, by firmness repelling anarchy, by remorse afflicted to death, he is seen as burdened to restore his realm, and his realm as maintained by his sacrifice—not Richmond's land of 'universal decay' but Tillyard's 'stable society', imbued with Elizabethan vitality. This encouraging national vision leads Tillyard to view Henry as a good man and king, and Hal as the humane sharer in popular life, 'a man of large powers, Olympian loftiness, and high sophistication'. If, on the contrary, kingship is read as Bolingbrokian 'policy', emergent in *Richard II*, dominant in *Henry IV*, and unscrupulously victorious in *Henry V*, the progression will run, as it does for Richmond, from the 'few sinister effects' of *Part 1* to the 'overtly diseased society' of *Part 2* and the 'black threads in the weave' of *Henry V*. But such readings deny the exultant life with which the plays pulsate.

Estimates of Hotspur range from Halliday's 'only major character in the English histories whom it is possible . . . to admire' to Tillyard's 'engaging barbarian'. His vitality is captivating, though his reckless 'honour' is hubristic and outmoded, his impetuousness anarchic, and his moral indignation ill based: Tillyard sees in him the Aristotelian excess of his qualities. Yet he is unique in the histories in having his married life shown comically and delightfully, within the limits of space; the wit and teasing between him and Lady Percy in *Part 1*, and Lady Percy's heart-rending commemoration in *Part 2*, should annul censure. Rossiter, in 'Ambivalence: the Dialectic of the Histories', comments well that in her war-widowhood Lady Percy touches a spring of sympathy which renders moralistic condemnations of her husband inept. As for Hotspur's appearance with his allies in the central scene of *Part 1*, J. R. Brown offers a striking comment: 'At Stratford-upon-Avon in 1951, at least two reviewers agreed that the short episode presenting Glendower, and Mortimer and Hotspur with their wives, was the most moving scene in the whole play . . .; and almost every other reviewer paid special attention to this scene. Now in critical accounts of *Henry IV*, the so-called Welsh scene often goes entirely unnoticed'— which shows how easily critics can take Shakespeare's humanizing genius for granted while they seek for moral or technical structure.

Hotspur's faults may be warnings against extravagance; they are also, like his virtues, dramatically splendid.

Hal, the focus of dramatic expectancy, has received more attention than Henry, though much less than Falstaff. For Bradley a chip off the Bolingbrokian block (with qualities both admirable and questionable); for Danby a (temperate) machiavel, counting strategy as virtue; for Goddard a reincarnation of paternal hypocrisies; for Traversi a purposeful intelligence seeking political advantage; he nevertheless finds admirers. Dover Wilson in *The Fortunes of Falstaff* calls him the prince in whom Shakespeare 'crowns *noblesse oblige*' and celebrates selfless devotion to duty; Tillyard sees in him the spirit of *sprezzatura*, the felicitous achievement of success. 'Opinion, led by Tillyard and Dover Wilson, has not only replaced Hal on his pinnacle but given him a more solid basis in Elizabethan ideals of courtesy and political morality' (Jenkins). Such an estimate is as widely held as the alternative, and may be expressed as Maynard Mack does in his Signet edition, that Hal, tested by different codes, emerges to maturity having 'met the claims of Hotspur's world, of Falstaff's, and of Henry's, without narrowing himself to any one', and combines 'valor, courtliness, hard sense, and humor, in an ideal image of the potentialities of the English character' wherein Shakespeare incorporates his optimism about England's true nature.

'Unimitated, unimitable Falstaff' (in Johnson's phrase) has inspired criticism as ample as himself. His evolution is explained by Baeske, Dover Wilson, and Oliver (their accounts are listed among the plays' sources, pp. 280–1), and in the Arden edition. Morgann's famous essay of 1777 still gives pleasure; if it depends on assumptions outside the plays, or only tenuously inside them (as with the 'secret impressions' of Falstaff's 'courage'), nevertheless its intelligence is as fresh as its enthusiasm is infectious. Bradley too, in a classic defence, claims that Falstaff is not a coward, and that he unlocks the shackles of ordinary life through 'the bliss of freedom gained in humour': 'we share his glory.' Bradley's appreciation has been repeatedly endorsed; Priestley's essay glows warmly and vivaciously; Sen Gupta is eloquent on Falstaff's 'amoral philosophy of joy, . . . a philosophy of instincts . . . anterior to moral evaluation'. 'In the most satisfying interpretations of Falstaff', Jenkins observes ('Shakespeare's History Plays: 1900–1951'), 'something of Bradley survives; though incorporating many traditional figures he is yet an original creation expressing with the utmost exuberance a universal principle of human nature in which we may properly delight'—even though his witty anarchism must ultimately be restrained. Auden's essay makes, with a new verve (sometimes engaging, sometimes tiresome), the familiar point that 'sober reflection in the study may tell us that Falstaff is not, after all, a very admirable person, but Falstaff on the stage gives us no time for sober reflection.' His account is oddly sentimental; for instance, Falstaff 'loves Hal with an absolute devotion . . . [as] the son he has never had', and even while pressing his Gloucestershire victims he addresses them as individuals, and shows 'the justice of charity which treats each person, not as a cipher, but as a unique person'. Sober judgement rejects this extravagance; yet criticism so rose-coloured is testimony to the spell of Falstaff seen in action, not analysed upon the page. A rewarding study in the Bradleyan tradition, and throwing light on stage practice, is Sprague's 'Gadshill Revisited'. Vickers analyses Falstaff's nature and prose style well, and Kaiser sets him enlighteningly in a context of Renaissance wisdom and folly.

But Falstaff has not had things all his own way. Realists and moralists maintain, opprobriously, that he is the stage coward-braggart, with glutton and parasite thrown in. Danby sees 'predatory Falstaff about to sweep on the body politic', and for Richmond the corruption of Henry IV's England 'crystallizes in . . . Falstaff'. Falstaff was due for desentimentalizing, but not so drastically. Generally, criticism balances between his liberating and his dangerous traits, between enjoying his exuberance and endorsing his dismissal, and consequently has more truly judged Hal. This balance owes much to Dover Wilson's brilliant discussion in *The Fortunes of Falstaff*; this develops a splendid sense of the plays' course and tone, and of the wealth of English life, neither tragically nor censoriously judged, as the action celebrates it.

Studies of non-naturalistic Elizabethan stage practice have helped, along with recognition that the great figures of popular comedy cannot fit into the straitjacket of consistency. Falstaff is not a naturalistic character, to be made consistently explicable, but a complex of shifting facets, dramatically 'ambiguous'. Tillyard writes well of his function in releasing enjoyable rebelliousness yet compelling recognition of social order, and needing no more coherence than the incomparable aplomb with which he supports his multiple functions. Waldock's essay and the Arden introductions argue against unifying his paradoxes in simplified formulas. Empson's important essay contends that he fascinates by the very fact that irreconcilable qualities must be entertained simultaneously, and to Lloyd Evans his popularity results not from 'recognised actuality' but from 'the audacious principles and practice by which the deprived, the expedient, and the eternally optimistic' must live. Not a 'real' character, then, Falstaff is liberating yet unruly, comic in manifold variability. In this kaleidoscope Barber makes out the popular festival's Lord of Misrule, and Stewart, followed by Philip Williams, associates Falstaff's rejection with residual myths of Golden-Bough-type parricide or sacrificial victim slain for the land's renewal—an idea which would surely have surprised the dramatist who dismissed Falstaff with as much fairness as possible to all concerned.

Attitudes towards the dismissal correlate with those towards Falstaff himself. Shakespeare over-reached himself, Bradley thought, since Falstaff is so engaging that his humiliation, though deserved, is too painful a betrayal of friendship. Dover Wilson's defence is important; it is that Hal's intimacy with Falstaff is generally exaggerated (throughout he hints at the expected break), that Falstaff is increasingly disreputable and his gleeful hope of anarchy needs public rebuke, that the Fleet prison was the not-dishonourable lodgement of Elizabeth's noblemen, and that the 'fracted' heart of *Henry V*, so distressing to critics, is an afterthought occasioned by stage circumstances. Hal's soliloquy, 'I know you all', is no callous ambush but an impersonal, choric foretelling of Wild-Prince redemption; the rejection is no heartlessly sprung duplicity but follows many open hints. Bradley himself notes how the rejection is prepared through *Part 2*, in Hal's increasing gravity, Falstaff's increasing coarseness, and the minimal contact between them. Tillyard, strong for Hal, argues that his attitude throughout is so critical that only Falstaff's complacency could ignore it; for Reese, too, the divergence is such that 'in the end there will be no betrayal.' Bullough supports the Johnsonian line that, all allowance being made for Falstaff's magnetism, his affection for Hal was 'always based on self-interest . . . and the expectation of plenty'. Lloyd Evans defends the rejection as just and inevitable, foreseen early in *Part 1*, looming through *Part 2*, and finally forced upon a Hal who is the more humane partner, Falstaff's concern being only to make the world serve himself. Hazlitt's famous contention that the rejection is unforgivable and Falstaff 'the better man of the two' seems critically outmoded. The current valuation interrelates serious and comic plots, each criticizing and being criticized by the other, with Falstaff alerting us to the human comedy which rulers must forgo, and also to the integrities he himself flouts.

Part 2's darker tone is not a regrettable decline from high comedy. It reflects the tragic unease of Daniel's *Civil Wars* and movingly marks the retribution doomed to Henry, Falstaff, and the rebels. It has been much discussed, by Bradley and others. For Knights, *Part 2* is perhaps the first masterpiece of 'the great Shakespeare', sombre in its honesty yet not pessimistic. Traversi also praises the 'sombre realism' which yet achieves a superb inclusiveness. And Leech finely analyses the clouded themes with which Henry's reign concludes. Tillyard and Dover Wilson, however, are less ready to envisage tragedy; Tillyard's sense that England, however faulty, is given in its irrepressible humanity, and Dover Wilson's interpretation in terms of moral wisdom, have influenced the Arden edition's analysis, which recognizes the dark motifs yet sees the total effect as one neither of comedy nor tragedy but as an amalgam in which Shakespeare's interpretation of human nature achieves a richness of feeling nowhere excelled even by himself.

HENRY V: As usual, Bullough illuminates the critical problems finely by the light of Shakespeare's sources. Lily Campbell and Walter (Arden edition) set the play among sixteenth-century historical, political, and military assumptions; together with Dover Wilson (New Cambridge edition) and Bullough, they indicate how Shakespeare enhanced Henry's distinction by importantly modifying the material.

Whatever the reservations of critical scrutiny, in the theatre *Henry V* is 'in a perfectly satisfactory sense—stagey' (Bradbrook): Henry's grandiose or histrionic qualities, Stoll observes, belong to the Elizabethan conception of royalty in action, especially stage action. And in performance his play's masterfulness averts the scepticism which reading may provoke.

Is it an 'epic'? Nineteenth-century critics (with exceptions, like Hazlitt) took it—to quote one of them—as 'a song with trumpets', unambiguous about national triumph, and such indeed seems its intention. Victorian enthusiasm for warrior-valour almost warranted the extreme reaction against Henry expressed by Yeats and echoed by Shaw and others. Yet the reaction was excessive, and much modern criticism (not all) holds that *Henry V* is a valid celebration of national courage, unironic and unambiguous though not simpleminded. Its evidence is curiously difficult to assess, and can be read in contradictory ways: John Arden's interesting comments on its ambiguities have already been mentioned (see p. 245). As against the Shakespeare of national heroics some critics seek a Shakespeare shrewdly unillusioned about political duplicities; Gerald Gould, in the anti-war mood of 1919, judged *Henry V* a savage satire on imperialism, and Henry the perfect hypocrite. More recently Goddard has portrayed a Shakespeare gratifying his playgoers' 'windy chauvinism' yet morally bound to disclose, through strong irony, the sophistries underlying virtuous political pretensions. Palmer, more subtly, suggests that Henry plays the ideal king superbly while in fact being the acute opportunist, and that Shakespeare is not satirical about this, but recognizes that realities in politics must differ from appearances.

The play's enjoyable vigour satisfies the unsceptical but not, for instance, Granville-Barker: for him the play, however professionally skilful, must have shown Shakespeare how inadequate is the mere man of action. (Shaw held that Shakespeare must have thought *Henry V* a mistake and failure. Charlton, like Yeats, considered Henry 'the magnificent commonplace', popular only by sheer efficacy.) Shakespeare, Granville-Barker argues, needed to pass from external actions to the tragedies' internal ones: Henry neither provides real temperamental interest nor finds anything truly interesting to do—his play lacks the 'spiritually significant idea' great drama needs. Yet to others this is not so; this significance is defined by E. K. Chambers as the heightened self-consciousness of Elizabeth's England, and by Dover Wilson in his edition as the heroical ideal Sidney praises in his *Apology for Poetry*, which 'inflameth the mind with a desire to be worthy': so the informing idea is the honour men earn through courage. Yet Dover Wilson sees more than mere heroic tableaux: under the stress of war Henry moves from the Marlovian king-warrior to much deeper humanity, showing 'the real man behind the traditional heroic mask', and his play's spirit changes from jingoism to gravity. And Richmond, while detecting 'black threads' in a play 'less simply epic than has usually been assumed', also takes it as developing from epic brashness and political finesse to a deep code of humanity and responsibility. The significant idea, to the Arden editor, is a complex of Elizabethan values—unity, honourable stock, national duty—and in the conception of the Christian king as Erasmus and others defined him. One of the better definitions is Traversi's—'the establishment . . . of an order based on consecrated authority', which nevertheless involves the ruler in near-tragic tensions between his human nature and the superhumanity of his office, so that the play's idea is 'maturity [gained] through consciously accepted mortification': Henry achieves virtue by accepting the constraints of his vocation. The New Penguin Introduction suggests that, above darker tones hinting at 'tentatives towards an altogether deeper realisation of its subject', there grows a confidence climaxed in Henry's Agincourt speech with its 'neighbourliness, and humour, and hope, and proper pride', with the King, matured by trial, by no means a figure of tragedy. If there are satirical elements, Battenhouse contends, they are of a warm, Chaucerian temper; Henry accepts his duties boldly, and the play's standpoint is that of 'heroic comedy'. In a notable essay Stříbrný argues that national fellowship can coexist with unideal politics without becoming less valid. And Lloyd Evans, rejecting the questionable-kingdom-under-questionable-king view, takes the play to harmonize the national and cosmic schemes of things, mirroring 'an order which . . . encompasses the kingdom of heaven and of earth'.

Henry has been many things to many men. The fairest interpretations conclude that Shakespeare has unironically maintained the popular hero, externally rather than inwardly characterized (yet earnestly realized before Agincourt), while recognizing the moral limitations which condition him. The current estimate, not uncritical yet taking him (as Stoll, Dover Wilson, Bullough, and Sprague do) within the relatively unsophisticated context of the Elizabethan public stage, accepts him in the fairly straight terms the play offers; he is the embodiment of his valiant nation, humanized by imperfections, yet not rendered false by them. Playgoers, for whom the play is meant, can judge shrewdly; they can, Quinn suggests, see flaws in a ruler yet relish his rule—'Such an audience might recognise Henry as ruthless, calculating, sanctimonious, even hypocritical, and still find him wholly admirable as king and military leader.' They might, certainly. Yet even so this sequence of epithets is too damaging: it would explain why Henry appeals to the jingo, but not why he differs so profoundly from Richard III.

The style, finally, has been variously viewed. It is that of public address, and objectors find it unimaginative, bombastic, and alternating between the rhetorical and the perfunctory. On the other hand Halliday hails its clarity, majesty, and dynamism, Hill contrasts the shallow rhetoric frequent in *Richard II* with the passion of Henry's Ceremony speech, and for Sewell 'a particular address, a royal address, is transformed into poetry.' Vickers praises the prose as running 'across all levels of society and across all the dramatic resources open to Shakespeare', and Stříbrný resumes for *Henry V* the claim Tillyard makes for *Henry IV*, that 'the great variety of style, climbing from the depths of London taverns up the flights of court poetry, is in full accord with the basic idea-content of the play.' *Henry V* may offer neither lyrical enchantments nor expressive intensity, yet its writing moves with a confident and melodious energy, as public rather than private utterance, and the national temperament sounds in it with an appropriate zest.

REFERENCES

GENERAL

Sources

Boswell-Stone, W. G. (ed.), *Shakespere's Holinshed. The Chronicle and the Historical Plays Compared* (London, 1896).

Bullough, G. (ed.), *Narrative and Dramatic Sources of Shakespeare*, vol. iii, *Earlier English History Plays*; vol. iv, *Later English History Plays* (London, 1960, 1962).

Daniel, Samuel, *The Firste Fowre Bookes of the Civile Warrs between the two Houses of Lancaster and Yorke* (London, 1595).

Elyot, Thomas, *The Boke named The Governour* (London, 1531); ed. S. E. Lehmberg (Everyman's Library, London, 1962).

Griffiths, John (ed.), *The Two Books of Homilies appointed to be read in Churches* (Oxford, 1859).

Hall, Edward, *The Union of the Two Noble and Illustre Famelies of Lancastre and Yorke* (London, 1548); ed. Henry Ellis (London, 1809, and Scolar Press, Menston, 1970).

Hart, Alfred, *Shakespeare and the Homilies* (Melbourne, 1934).

Holinshed, Raphael, *Chronicles of England, Scotland, and Ireland* (London, 1577, revised 1587); ed. Henry Ellis (London, 1807–8).

Hosley, Richard (ed.), *Shakespeare's Holinshed: an Edition of Holinshed's Chronicles (1587)* (New York, 1968).

Kingsford, C. L., *English Historical Literature in the Fifteenth Century* (Oxford, 1913).

Myrroure for Magistrates, A (London, 1559); ed. Lily B. Campbell (Cambridge, 1938).

Nicoll, Allardyce and Josephine (eds.), *Holinshed's Chronicle, as used in Shakespeare's Plays* (Everyman's Library, London, 1927).

Stow, John, *The Annales of England* (London, 1592).

Vergil, Polydore, *The Anglica Historia of Polydore Vergil, A.D. 1486–1537*, ed. Denys Hay (Camden Society, 3rd Ser. 74, London, 1950).

General Criticism and Commentary

Armstrong, W. A. (ed.), *Shakespeare's Histories: an Anthology of Modern Criticism* (Penguin Shakespeare Library, Harmondsworth, 1972): includes, sometimes abridged or excerpted, items listed in this section for Reese, Ribner, Sen Gupta, and Sprague; under *Henry VI* for Brockbank; under *Richard III* for Rossiter; under *King John (Texts)* for Matchett; under *Richard II* for Ure (*Texts*), and Gielgud; and under *Henry IV* for Humphreys (*Texts*) and Jenkins.

Bevington, D. M., *Tudor Drama and Politics: a Critical Approach to Topical Meaning* (Cambridge, Mass., 1968).

——, 'Shakespeare the Elizabethan Dramatist', in *A New Companion to Shakespeare Studies*, ed. K. Muir and S. Schoenbaum (London, 1971).

Bradbrook, M. C., *Shakespeare and Elizabethan Poetry* (London, 1951).

Brockbank, J. P., 'Shakespeare: his Histories, English and Roman', in *English Drama to 1710*, ed. Christopher Ricks, vol. iii of *A History of Literature in the English Language* (London, 1971).

Brown, J. R., *Shakespeare's Plays in Performance* (London, 1966; Penguin Shakespeare Library, Harmondsworth, 1969).

Campbell, Lily B., *Shakespeare's 'Histories': Mirrors of Elizabethan Policy* (San Marino, Calif., 1947).

Chambers, R. W., 'The Elizabethan and the Jacobean Shakespeare', in his *Man's Unconquerable Mind*, expanded from *The Jacobean Shakespeare and 'Measure for Measure'*, British Academy Lecture 1937 (London, 1939).

Charlton, H. B., *Shakespeare, Politics and Politicians*, English Association Pamphlet 72 (Oxford, 1929), repr. in Hunter (see p. 281).

Clemen, W. H., *The Development of Shakespeare's Imagery* (London, 1951).

Craig, Hardin, *The Enchanted Glass: the Elizabethan Mind in Literature* (New York, 1936).

Danby, J. F., *Shakespeare's Doctrine of Nature* (London, 1949).

Dean, L. F. (ed.), *Shakespeare: Modern Essays in Criticism* (New York, 1957).

Doran, Madeleine, *Endeavors of Art: A Study of Form in Elizabethan Drama* (Madison, Wis., 1954).

Dorius, R. J. (ed.), *Discussions of Shakespeare's Histories: from Richard II to Henry V* (Boston, Mass., 1964): includes, sometimes abridged or excerpted, items listed in this section for Rossiter and Sewell; under *Richard II* for Yeats; under *Henry IV* for Bradley, Jenkins, Leech, Morgann, and Stewart; and under *Henry V* for Stoll.

Duthie, G. I., *Shakespeare* (London, 1951).

Ellis-Fermor, Una, *The Frontiers of Drama* (London, 1945).

——, *The Jacobean Drama* (London, 1936).

Goddard, H. C., *The Meaning of Shakespeare* (Chicago, Ill., 1951).

Halliday, F. E., *The Poetry of Shakespeare's Plays* (London, 1954).

Hill, R. F., 'Shakespeare's Early Tragic Mode', *Shakespeare Quarterly*, 9 (1958).

Humphreys, A. R., *Shakespeare's Histories and the 'Emotion of Multitude'*, British Academy Lecture 1968 (London, 1970).

——, 'Shakespeare and the Tudor Perception of History', in *Stratford Papers on Shakespeare, 1964*, ed. B. W. Jackson (Toronto, 1965), repr. in *Shakespeare Celebrated*, ed. L. B. Wright (Ithaca, N.Y., 1966).

Jenkins, Harold, 'Shakespeare's History Plays: 1900–1951', in *Shakespeare Survey 6* (1953).

Joseph, B. L., *Shakespeare's Eden: The Commonwealth of England 1558–1629* (London, 1971).

Knight, G. Wilson, 'This Sceptred Isle: A Study of Shakespeare's Kings', in his *The Sovereign Flower* (London, 1958).

Knights, L. C., *Shakespeare's Politics: with some Reflections on the Nature of Tradition*, British Academy Lecture 1957 (London, 1958), repr. in his *Further Explorations* (London, 1965) and Quinn (see p. 283).

——, *Poetry, Politics, and the English Tradition* (London, 1954), repr. in his *Further Explorations* (London, 1965).

——, 'The Public World', in his *Some Shakespearean Themes* (London, 1959).

Kott, Jan, *Shakespeare our Contemporary* (London, 1964).

Lloyd Evans, G., *Shakespeare I* and *Shakespeare II* (Oliver and Boyd's 'Writers and Critics', Edinburgh, 1969).

Murry, J. Middleton, *Shakespeare* (London, 1936).

Palmer, John, *Political Characters of Shakespeare* (London, 1945).

Praz, Mario, *Machiavelli and the Elizabethans*, British Academy Italian Lecture 1928 (London, [1929]).

Reese, M. M., *The Cease of Majesty: a Study of Shakespeare's History Plays* (London, 1961).

Reyher, Paul, *Essai sur les idées dans l'œuvre de Shakespeare* (Paris, 1947).

Ribner, Irving, *The English History Play in the Age of Shakespeare* (Princeton, N.J., 1957).

——, *Patterns in Shakespearian Tragedy* (London, 1960).

Richmond, H. M., *Shakespeare's Political Plays* (New York, 1967).

Riggs, David, *Shakespeare's Heroical Histories; 'Henry VI' and its Literary Tradition* (Cambridge, Mass., 1971).

Rossiter, A. P., 'Ambivalence: the Dialectic of the Histories', in his *Angel with Horns* (London, 1961).

Sen Gupta, S. C., *Shakespeare's Historical Plays* (London, 1964).

Sewell, Arthur, *Character and Society in Shakespeare* (London, 1951).

Spencer, Theodore, *Shakespeare and the Nature of Man* (New York, 1942).

Sprague, A. C., *Shakespeare's Histories: Plays for the Stage* (The Society for Theatre Research, London, 1964).

Spurgeon, Caroline F. E., *Shakespeare's Imagery and What it Tells Us* (London, 1935).

Stoll, E. E., *Shakespeare Studies* (New York, 1927).

Tillyard, E. M. W., *The Elizabethan World Picture* (London, 1943).

——, *Shakespeare's History Plays* (London, 1944): extract, 'The First Tetralogy', in *Shakespeare Criticism, 1935–60*, ed. Anne Ridler (World's Classics, London, 1963), and 'Henry IV and the Tudor Epic' in Hunter (see p. 281).

Traversi, D. A., *An Approach to Shakespeare* (London, 1938; 2nd edn., London, 1956; 3rd edn., 2 vols., London, 1968–9).

——, *Shakespeare: from 'Richard II' to 'Henry V'* (London, 1957).

Trewin, J. C., *Shakespeare on the English Stage, 1900–1964* (London, 1964).

Van Doren, Mark, *Shakespeare* (New York, 1939).

Waith, E. M. (ed.), *Shakespeare: the Histories: a Collection of Critical Essays* (Prentice-Hall's Twentieth-Century Views, Englewood Cliffs, N.J., 1965): includes, sometimes abridged or excerpted, items listed under *General Criticism and Commentary* for Campbell, Reese, and Tillyard; under *Henry VI* for Brockbank; under *Richard III* for Rossiter; under *King John* for Calderwood; and under *Henry IV* for Wilson.

Willcock, Gladys D., *Language and Poetry in Shakespeare's Early Plays*, British Academy Lecture 1954 (London, 1955).

Wilson, F. P., *Marlowe and the Early Shakespeare* (Oxford, 1953).

——, 'The English History Play', in his *Shakespearian and Other Studies*, ed. Helen Gardner (Oxford, 1969).

Wilson, J. Dover, and Worsley, T. C., *Shakespeare's Histories at Stratford 1951* (London, 1952).

Winny, James, *The Player King: a Theme of Shakespeare's Histories* (London, 1968).

Wood, Roger, and Clarke, Mary, *Shakespeare at the Old Vic: 1954–5* (London, 1956).

Wright, L. B., *Middle-Class Culture in Elizabethan England* (Chapel Hill, N.C., 1935).

THE EARLIER HISTORIES

Texts

Bevington, David (ed.), *Henry VI, Part One* (Pelican Shakespeare, Baltimore, Md., 1966).

Cairncross, A. S. (ed.), *Henry VI, Part One* (new Arden Shakespeare, London, 1962).

Ryan, L. V. (ed.), *Henry VI, Part One* (Signet Shakespeare, New York, 1967).

Wilson, J. Dover (ed.), *Henry VI, Part One* (New Cambridge Shakespeare, Cambridge, 1952).

Cairncross, A. S. (ed.), *Henry VI, Part Two* (new Arden Shakespeare, London, 1957)

Freeman, A. (ed.), *Henry VI, Part Two* (Signet Shakespeare, New York, 1967).

Turner, R. K., Jr., and Williams, G. W. (eds.), *Henry VI, Part Two* (Pelican Shakespeare, Baltimore, Md., 1967).

Wilson, J. Dover (ed.), *Henry VI, Part Two* (New Cambridge Shakespeare, Cambridge, 1952).

Cairncross, A. S. (ed.), *Henry VI, Part Three* (new Arden Shakespeare, London, 1964).

Crane, Milton (ed.), *Henry VI, Part Three* (Signet Shakespeare, New York, 1968).

Turner, R. K., Jr., and Williams, G. W. (eds.), *Henry VI, Part Three* (Pelican Shakespeare, Baltimore, Md., 1967).

Wilson, J. Dover (ed.), *Henry VI, Part Three* (New Cambridge Shakespeare, Cambridge, 1952).

Eccles, Mark (ed.), *Richard III* (Signet Shakespeare, New York, 1964).

Evans, G. Blakemore (ed.), *Richard III* (Pelican Shakespeare, Baltimore, Md., 1959).

Honigmann, E. A. J. (ed.), *Richard III* (New Penguin Shakespeare, Harmondsworth, 1968).

Wilson, J. Dover (ed.), *Richard III* (New Cambridge Shakespeare, Cambridge, 1954).

Criticism and Commentary

Henry VI

See entries for Boswell-Stone, Bullough, Hosley, and Nicoll under *General: Sources* (p. 273).

Criticism

Alexander, Peter, *Shakespeare's 'Henry VI' and 'Richard III'* (Cambridge, 1929).

Arthos, John, *Shakespeare: the Early Writings* (London, 1972).

Barton, John, in collaboration with Peter Hall, *The Wars of the Roses* (London, 1970).

Brockbank, J. P., 'The Frame of Disorder—*Henry VI*', in *Early Shakespeare* (Stratford-upon-Avon Studies 3, ed. J. R. Brown and B. Harris, London, 1961), repr. in Armstrong (see p. 273) and Waith (see p. 275), and in the Signet *Henry VI, Part 3*, ed. Milton Crane (New York, 1968).

Clemen, W. H., 'Anticipation and Foreboding in Shakespeare's Early Histories', in *Shakespeare Survey 6* (1953).

——, 'Past and Future in Shakespeare's Drama', British Academy Lecture 1966 (London, 1967), repr. in his *Shakespeare's Dramatic Art* (London, 1972).

Courthope, W. J., 'On the Authenticity of Some of the Early Plays Assigned to Shakespeare', appendix to his *A History of English Poetry*, vol. iv (London, 1903).

Kitto, H. D. F., 'A Classical Scholar Looks at Shakespeare', in *More Talking of Shakespeare*, ed. John Garrett (London, 1959).

Also see entries under *General Criticism and Commentary* (pp. 273–6), particularly for Bradbrook, Chambers, Danby, Doran, Goddard, Halliday, Hill, Kott, Lloyd Evans, Reese, Ribner, Richmond, Riggs, Sewell, Sprague, Tillyard, Willcock, F. P. Wilson, Winny.

Richard III

Sources

See entries for Boswell-Stone, Bullough, Hosley, and Nicoll under *General: Sources* (p. 273).

Criticism

Alexander, Peter, see under *Henry VI*.

Arthos, John, see under *Henry VI*.

Barton, John, see under *Henry VI*.

Brooke, Nicholas, *Shakespeare's Early Tragedies* (London, 1968).

Clemen, W. H., see under *Henry VI*.

Moulton, R. G., '*Richard III*: how Shakespeare weaves Nemesis into History', and 'A Picture of Ideal Villainy in *Richard III*', in his *Shakespeare as a Dramatic Artist* (London, 1885).

Palmer, John, 'Richard of Gloucester', in his *Political Characters of Shakespeare* (London, 1945).

Rossiter, A. P., 'The Unity of *Richard III*', in his *Angel with Horns* (London, 1961), repr. in Armstrong (see p. 273) and Waith (see p. 275).

Shaw, G. B., '*Richard III*', in *Shaw on Shakespeare*, ed. Edwin Wilson (New York, 1961; Penguin Shakespeare Library, Harmondsworth, 1969).

Spivack, Bernard, *Shakespeare and the Allegory of Evil* (New York, 1958).

Also see entries under *General Criticism and Commentary* (pp. 273–6), particularly for Bradbrook, Chambers, Danby, Doran, Goddard, Halliday, Hill, Kott, Lloyd Evans, Ribner, Richmond, Sewell, Sprague, Tillyard, Willcock, Wilson.

THE LATER HISTORIES

For sources and general criticism and commentary, see pp. 273–6.

Texts

Honigmann, E. A. J. (ed.), *King John* (new Arden Shakespeare, London, 1954).

Matchett, William H. (ed.), *King John* (Signet Shakespeare, York, 1966).

Ribner, Irving (ed.), *King John* (Pelican Shakespeare, Baltimore, Md., 1962).

Wilson, J. Dover (ed.), *King John* (New Cambridge Shakespeare, Cambridge, 1936).

Black, Matthew W. (ed.), *Richard II* (New Variorum Shakespeare, Philadelphia, Pa., 1955).

——, *Richard II* (Pelican Shakespeare, Baltimore, Md., 1957).

Muir, Kenneth (ed.), *Richard II* (Signet Shakespeare, New York, 1963).

Ure, Peter (ed.), *Richard II* (new Arden Shakespeare, London, 1956).

Wells, Stanley (ed.), *Richard II* (New Penguin Shakespeare, Harmondsworth, 1969).

Wilson, J. Dover (ed.), *Richard II* (New Cambridge Shakespeare, Cambridge, 1939).

Davison, P. H. (ed.), *Henry IV, Part One* (New Penguin Shakespeare, Harmondsworth, 1968).

Hemingway, S. B. (ed.), *Henry IV, Part One* (New Variorum Shakespeare, Philadelphia, Pa., 1936); with supplementary material by G. Blakemore Evans in *Shakespeare Quarterly* 7 (1956).

Humphreys, A. R. (ed.), *Henry IV, Part One* (new Arden Shakespeare, London, 1960).

Mack, Maynard (ed.), *Henry IV, Part One* (Signet Shakespeare, New York, 1965).

Sanderson, James L. (ed.), *Henry IV, Part One* (Norton Critical Editions, New York, 1962); includes, sometimes abridged or excerpted, items listed under *General Criticism and Commentary* for Tillyard and Traversi;

and under *Henry IV* for Bradley, Brooks and Heilman, Doran, Knights, Shaaber, Sprague, Stewart, and Wilson.

Shaaber, Matthias A. (ed.), *Henry IV, Part One* (Pelican Shakespeare, Baltimore, Md., 1957).

Wilson, J. Dover (ed.), *Henry IV, Part One* (New Cambridge Shakespeare, Cambridge, 1946).

Chester, Allan G. (ed.), *Henry IV, Part Two* (Pelican Shakespeare, Baltimore, Md., 1957).

Holland, Norman L. (ed.), *Henry IV, Part Two* (Signet Shakespeare, New York, 1965).

Humphreys, A. R. (ed.), *Henry IV, Part Two* (new Arden Shakespeare, London, 1966).

Shaaber, Matthias A. (ed.), *Henry IV, Part Two* (New Variorum Shakespeare, Philadelphia, Pa., 1940).

Wilson, J. Dover (ed.), *Henry IV, Part Two* (New Cambridge Shakespeare, Cambridge, 1946).

Brown, J. R. (ed.), *Henry V* (Signet Shakespeare, New York, 1965).

Harbage, Alfred (ed.), *Henry V* (Pelican Shakespeare, Baltimore, Md., 1967).

Humphreys, A. R. (ed.), *Henry V* (New Penguin Shakespeare, Harmondsworth, 1968).

Walter, J. H. (ed.), *Henry V* (new Arden Shakespeare, London, 1954).

Wilson, J. Dover (ed.), *Henry V* (New Cambridge Shakespeare, Cambridge, 1947).

Criticism and Commentary

King John

Sources
See entries for Boswell-Stone, Bullough, Hosley, and Nicoll under *General: Sources* (p. 273).

Criticism
Bonjour, Adrien, 'The Road to Swinstead Abbey: a Study of the Sense and Structure of *King John*', *ELH*, 18 (1951).

Calderwood, J. L., 'Commodity and Honor in *King John*', *University of Toronto Quarterly*, 29 (1960), repr. in Waith (see p. 275).

Kitto, H. D. F., see under *Henry VI*.

Schanzer, Ernest, *The Problem Plays of Shakespeare* (London, 1963).

Also see entries under *General Criticism and Commentary* (pp. 273–6), particularly for Brockbank, Campbell, Danby, Ellis-Fermor, Goddard, Lloyd Evans, Reese, Richmond, Sprague, Tillyard, Willcock.

Richard II

Sources
See entries for Boswell-Stone, Bullough, Hosley, and Nicoll under *General: Sources* (p. 273), and editions by Black, Ure, and Wilson. Also:

Black, Matthew W., 'The Sources of *Richard II*', in *Joseph Quincy Adams Memorial Studies*, ed. J. G. McManaway, G. E. Dawson, and E. E. Willoughby (Washington, D.C., 1948).

Criticism

Altick, R. D., 'Symphonic Imagery in *Richard II*', *PMLA*, 62 (1947), repr. in the Signet edition.

Chambers, E. K., *Shakespeare: a Survey* (London, 1925).

Dean, L. F., '*Richard II*: the State and the Image of the Theater', *PMLA*, 67 (1952), repr. in Dean (see p. 274).

Doran, Madeleine, 'Imagery in *Richard II* and *Henry IV*', *MLR*, 37 (1942), repr. in Sanderson (see p. 278).

Gielgud, John, *Stage Directions* (London, 1963), repr. in Armstrong (see p. 273).

Hill, R. F., 'Dramatic Techniques and Interpretation in *Richard II*', in *Early Shakespeare* (Stratford-upon-Avon Studies 3, ed. J. R. Brown and B. Harris, London, 1961).

Humphreys, A. R., 'Shakespeare's Political Justice in *Richard II* and *Henry IV*', in *Stratford Papers on Shakespeare 1964*, ed. B. W. Jackson (Toronto, 1965).

——, *Shakespeare: 'Richard II'* (Arnold's Studies in English Literature, 31, London, 1967).

Montague, C. E., *Manchester Guardian* review of Frank Benson's *Richard II*, repr. in *Specimens of English Dramatic Criticism, xvii–xx Centuries*, ed. A. C. Ward (World's Classics, London, 1945).

Palmer, John, 'Richard of Bordeaux', in his *Political Characters of Shakespeare* (London, 1945).

Pater, Walter, 'Shakespeare's English Kings', in his *Appreciations* (London, 1889), repr. in the Signet edition.

Ribner, Irving, 'The Political Problem in Shakespeare's Lancastrian Tetralogy', *Studies in Philology*, 49 (1952).

Rossiter, A. P., '*Richard II*', in *Angel with Horns* (London, 1961).

Traversi, D. A., '*Richard II*', in *Stratford Papers on Shakespeare 1964*, ed. B. W. Jackson (Toronto, 1965).

Wilson, J. Dover, 'The Political Background of Shakespeare's *Richard II* and *Henry IV*', *Shakespeare Jahrbuch*, 75 (1939).

Yeats, W. B., 'At Stratford-upon-Avon', in his *Ideas of Good and Evil* (London, 1903), abridged in Dorius (see p. 281).

Also see entries under *General Criticism and Commentary* (pp. 273–6), particularly for Bradbrook, Brockbank, Campbell, Clemen, Goddard, Reese, Reyher, Richmond, Rossiter, Sprague, Tillyard, Traversi, Van Doren.

Henry IV

Sources

See entries for Boswell-Stone, Bullough, Hosley, and Nicoll under *General: Sources* (p. 273). Also:

Baeske, Wilhelm, *Oldcastle-Falstaff in der englischen Literatur bis zur Shakespeare*, *Palaestra*, 50 (Berlin, 1905).

Elson, John, 'The Non-Shakespearean *Richard II* and Shakespeare's *Henry IV*, Part 1', *Studies in Philology*, 32 (1935).

Oliver, L. M., 'Sir John Oldcastle, Legend or Literature?', *The Library*, 5th Ser. 1 (1947).

Ward, B. M., '*The Famous Victories of Henry V*', *RES*, 4 (1928).

Wilson, J. Dover, 'The Origins and Development of Shakespeare's *Henry IV*', *The Library*, 4th Ser. 26 (1945).

Criticism

Auden, W. H., 'The Fallen City', *Encounter*, 13 (1959), repr. as 'The Prince's Dog' in his *The Dyer's Hand* (London, 1963), and in Hunter (below).

Barber, C. L., *Shakespeare's Festive Comedy* (Princeton, N.J., 1959), section on *Henry IV* repr. in Dean (see p. 274), Dorius (below), Hunter (below), and Young (see p. 282).

Bradley, A. C., 'The Rejection of Falstaff', in his *Oxford Lectures on Poetry* (London, 1909), repr. in Sanderson (see p. 278), Dorius (below), Hunter (below), and Young (see p. 282).

Brooks, Cleanth, and Heilman, R. B., *Understanding Drama* (New York, 1946), repr. in Sanderson (see p. 278).

Cain, H. E., 'Further Light on the Relation of 1 and 2 *Henry IV*', *Shakespeare Quarterly*, 3 (1952).

Charlton, H. B., 'Falstaff', *Bulletin of the John Rylands Library* (Manchester, 1935), repr. in his *Shakespearian Comedy* (London, 1938).

Doran, Madeleine, 'Imagery in *Richard II* and *Henry IV*', *MLR*, 37 (1942), repr. in Sanderson (see p. 278).

Dorius, R. J., 'A Little More than a Little', *Shakespeare Quarterly* 11 (1960).

——, (ed.), *Twentieth Century Interpretations of Henry IV Part One* (Englewood Cliffs, N.J., 1970): includes, sometimes abridged or excerpted, items listed under *Texts (Henry IV)* for Humphreys, and in this section for Barber, Bradley, Empson, and Jenkins.

Empson, William, 'Falstaff and Mr. Dover Wilson', *Kenyon Review*, 15 (1953), repr. in Hunter (below).

Hunter, G. K., '*Henry IV* and the Elizabethan Two-Part Play', *RES*, N.S. 5 (1954).

——, (ed.), *Shakespeare: King Henry IV Parts 1 and 2* (Macmillan Casebooks, London, 1970); includes, sometimes abridged or excerpted, items listed under *General Criticism and Commentary* for Charlton and Tillyard; and in this section for Auden, Barber, Bradley, Empson, Jenkins, Knights, Morgann, Stewart, and Wilson.

Jenkins, Harold, *The Structural Problem in Shakespeare's 'Henry the Fourth'* (London, 1956), repr. in Armstrong (see p. 273), Dorius (above), Hunter (above), and Young (see p. 282).

Kaiser, Walter, *Praisers of Folly: Erasmus, Rabelais, Shakespeare* (London, 1964).

Knights, L. C., 'Notes on Comedy', in *Determinations*, ed. F. R. Leavis (London, 1934), repr. in *The Importance of 'Scrutiny'*, ed. Eric Bentley (New York, 1948), and in Sanderson (see p. 278).

——, 'Time's Subjects: The Sonnets and *King Henry IV*, Part 2', in his *Some Shakespearean Themes* (London, 1959), repr. in Hunter (above) and Young (below).

Law, R. A., 'Structural Unity in the two parts of *Henry the Fourth*', *Studies in Philology*, 24 (1927).

Leech, Clifford, 'The Unity of 2 *Henry IV*' in *Shakespeare Survey 6* (1953), repr. in *Shakespeare Criticism 1935–60*, ed. Anne Ridler (World's Classics, London, 1963), and in Dorius (see p. 281) and Young (below).

Morgann, Maurice, *Essay on the Dramatic Character of Sir John Falstaff* (London, 1777), in *Shakespearian Criticism*, ed. D. A. Fineman (Oxford, 1972); also in *Eighteenth Century Essays on Shakespeare*, ed. D. Nichol Smith (Oxford, 1903), *Shakespeare Criticism*, ed. D. Nichol Smith (World's Classics, London, 1916), Dorius (see p. 281), and Hunter (above).

Priestley, J. B., *The English Comic Writers* (London, 1925).

Quiller-Couch, Arthur, *Shakespeare's Workmanship* (London, 1918).

Sen Gupta, S. C., *Shakespearean Comedy* (Calcutta, 1950).

Shaaber, M. A., 'The Unity of *Henry IV*', in *J. Q. Adams Memorial Studies*, ed. J. G. McManaway, G. E. Dawson, and E. E. Willoughby (Washington, D.C., 1948), repr. in Sanderson (see p. 278).

Shirley, J. W., 'Falstaff an Elizabethan Glutton', *Philological Quarterly*, 17 (1938).

Spargo, J. W., 'An Interpretation of Falstaff' (Washington University Studies, Humanistic Series, 9.2, St. Louis, Mo., 1922).

Sprague, A. C., 'Gadshill Revisited', *Shakespeare Quarterly*, 4 (1953), repr. in Sanderson (see p. 278).

Stewart, J. I. M., 'The Birth and Death of Falstaff', in his *Character and Motive in Shakespeare* (London, 1949), abridged in Dorius (see p. 281), Sanderson (see p. 278), and Hunter (above).

Stoll, E. E., *Poets and Playwrights* (Minneapolis, Minn., 1930).

Vickers, Brian, *The Artistry of Shakespeare's Prose* (London, 1968).

Waldock, A. J. A., 'The Men in Buckram', *RES*, 23 (1947).

Williams, Philip, 'The Birth and Death of Falstaff Reconsidered', *Shakespeare Quarterly*, 8 (1957).

Wilson, J. Dover, 'The Political Background of Shakespeare's *Richard II* and *Henry IV*', *Shakespeare Jahrbuch*, 75 (1939).

——, *The Fortunes of Falstaff* (Cambridge, 1953), abridged in *Shakespeare Criticism 1935–60*, ed. Anne Ridler (World's Classics, London, 1963), Waith (see p. 275), Sanderson (see p. 278), Hunter (above), and Young (below).

Winny, James, *The Player King* (London, 1968).

Young, David P. (ed.), *Twentieth Century Interpretations of Henry IV, Part Two* (Englewood Cliffs, N.J., 1968): includes, sometimes abridged or excerpted, items listed under *General Criticism and Commentary* for Rossiter, Tillyard, and Traversi; and under this section for Barber, Bradley, Jenkins, Knights, Leech, and Wilson.

Also see entries under *General Criticism and Commentary* (pp. 273–6), particularly for Bradbrook, Brown, Campbell, Charlton, Clemen, Danby, Doran, Dorius, Ellis-Fermor, Goddard, Halliday, Jenkins, Lloyd Evans, Palmer, Reese, Richmond, Rossiter, Sen Gupta, Sprague, Stoll, Tillyard, Traversi.

Henry V

Sources

See entries for Boswell-Stone, Bullough, Hosley, and Nicoll under *General: Sources* (p. 273). Also Ward under *Henry IV: Sources* (see pp. 280–1).

Criticism

Battenhouse, R. W., '*Henry V* as Heroic Comedy', in *Essays on Shakespeare and Elizabethan Drama in Honor of Hardin Craig*, ed. R. Hosley (Columbia, Mo., 1963).

Chambers, E. K., *Shakespeare: a Survey* (London, 1925).

Gould, Gerald, 'A New Reading of *Henry V*', *English Review*, 29 (1919), repr. as 'Irony and Satire in *Henry V*' in Quinn (below).

Granville-Barker, Harley, *From 'Henry V' to 'Hamlet'*, British Academy Lecture 1925 (London [1926]), revised in *Studies in Shakespeare*, ed. P. Alexander (London, 1964), and abridged in Quinn (below).

Hazlitt, William, *Characters of Shakespeare's Plays* (London, 1817; World's Classics, London, 1917).

Hill, R. F., see under *Richard II*.

Quinn, Michael (ed.), *Shakespeare: 'Henry V'* (Macmillan Casebooks, London, 1969): includes, sometimes abridged or excerpted, items listed under *General Criticism and Commentary* for Ellis-Fermor, Knights, Sprague, and Van Doren; and under this section for Gould, Granville-Barker, Stoll, and Stříbrný.

Shaw, G. B., *Shaw on Shakespeare*, ed. Edwin Wilson (New York, 1961; Penguin Shakespeare Library, Harmondsworth, 1969).

Stoll, E. E., '*Henry V*' in *Poets and Playwrights* (Minneapolis, Minn., 1930), slightly abridged in Dorius (see p. 281) and Quinn (above).

Stříbrný, Zdeněk, '*Henry V* and History', in *Shakespeare in a Changing World*, ed. A. Kettle (London, 1964), repr. in Quinn (above).

Vickers, Brian, *The Artistry of Shakespeare's Prose* (London, 1968).

Also see entries under *General Criticism and Commentary* (pp. 273–6), particularly for Bradbrook, Campbell, Charlton, Goddard, Halliday, Lloyd Evans, Palmer, Reese, Richmond, Sewell, Sprague, Tillyard, Traversi.

17. *Henry VIII, The Two Noble Kinsmen,* and the Apocryphal Plays

G. R. PROUDFOOT

Henry VIII

TEXTS AND AUTHORSHIP

Henry VIII was first printed in the First Folio of 1623, where it appears in chronological sequence of subject as the last of the histories, in a good text with unusually full and elaborate stage directions. Its date is established by the fact that the Globe playhouse was destroyed on 29 June 1613 by a fire which started when wadding from a cannon (required by the stage direction at 1.iv.49) ignited the thatched roof during a performance of it. One eye-witness, Sir Henry Wotton, called the play a new one and described it, under the title *All is True*, as containing 'some principal pieces of the reign of Henry VIII'. It seems likely that it was written with performance at the Blackfriars playhouse also in mind, as that playhouse occupied the very room in which the trial of Queen Katharine (II.iv) took place in 1527. Though never one of Shakespeare's most read plays, it has had a consistent history of success in the theatre. Criticism has been bedevilled by controversy about the authorship.

R. A. Foakes, in his new Arden edition, gives the fullest commentary and the most comprehensive critical account of the play, laying stress on its unity of design and deducing from this a unity of conception which he finds hard to reconcile with the orthodox theory of absolute division of authorship between Shakespeare and John Fletcher. J. C. Maxwell and A. R. Humphreys, in their New Cambridge and New Penguin editions, accept the theory of divided authorship and accord the play only a qualified artistic success. F. D. Hoeniger, in the Complete Pelican Shakespeare, recommends 'scholarly caution' in the matter of authorship and sees the play as truly Shakespeare's final work, both in its experimental use in a historical play of 'some of the themes and devices and even the symbolism of the Romances' and in its completion of the pattern of English history 'begun in the early histories by extending the view to the birth of Queen Elizabeth, in a sense even to 1613'.

The history of the controversy about the authorship of *Henry VIII* cannot be considered without some critical judgements being involved. Doubts about the integrity of *Henry VIII* were expressed in the later eighteenth century, and since 1850 many critics and scholars have argued that, in spite of its inclusion in the First Folio, the play is not wholly by Shakespeare but a product of his collaboration with John Fletcher. This view appears to have originated with Tennyson, but it was first aired in public in 1850 by James Spedding in a long article entitled 'Who Wrote Shakespeare's *Henry VIII*?', in which dissatisfaction with the play's attitude to its subject, and especially with its morally equivocal handling of the King and its evasion of the Reformation, goes hand in hand with stylistic and metrical arguments tending to shift the onus for its alleged failure on to John Fletcher. In the same year Emerson developed the view that two styles were distinguishable in the play, of which only one was Shakespeare's, and suggested that his role in it was only that of a reviser. Both arguments used metre as a feature distinguishing the styles. There followed a period in which metrical statistics of varying accuracy and significance were presented, generally in support of a slightly modified version of Spedding's scene-by-scene division of the play between Shakespeare and Fletcher. The reassertion of Shakespeare's sole authorship by Swinburne in *A Study of Shakespeare* was the first powerful challenge to Spedding's hypothesis. His objection was simply that many speeches assigned to Fletcher, such as Buckingham's farewell (II.i.55–136), had 'a comparative severity and elevation which will be missed when we turn back . . . to the text of Fletcher', but he also regarded the play as one of Shakespeare's earliest works.

The two opinions of the play are still current. The theory of collaborative authorship has been reinforced by closer stylistic and linguistic analysis, notably by Marco Mincoff in '*Henry VIII* and Fletcher' and by A. C. Partridge in *The Problem of 'Henry VIII' Reopened*. Mincoff's stylistic analysis is not statistical and takes full account of the observed effects of collaboration on Fletcher's style in the plays he wrote with Francis Beaumont. He finds in *Henry VIII* both the characteristic sentence structure and imagery of Fletcher and his typical humour, while agreeing with Swinburne that Fletcher here achieved an untypical success, a success which Mincoff attributes to the influence of 'another mind behind Fletcher's'.

Partridge's aim is to support the findings of the metrical tests, which have come in for deserved criticism, with evidence for two patterns of linguistic usage in the play. Among the distinguishing features he specifies are uses of the auxiliary verb *do*, the use or avoidance of the third person singular present tense ending in *-th*, and individual habits of contracting personal pronouns in colloquial contexts.

After Swinburne, the next influential advocate of Shakespeare's sole authorship was Peter Alexander in 'Conjectural History, or Shakespeare's *Henry VIII*', an essay which drew attention to the play's participation in the 'compassionate outlook' of Shakespeare's latest period and argued that the stylistic variation observed by the disintegrators could be seen as the deliberate device of Shakespeare for his own artistic ends and that variation as extreme was to be found in many of his plays. These positions were elaborated at great length by G. Wilson Knight, whose estimate of the play as 'the only fitting culmination of Shakespeare's work' remains a minority view, despite the fertility of his essay, '*Henry VIII* and the Poetry of Conversion', in ideas about the play's themes and leading characters. The consistency of the play's use of its historical source materials has been seen as arguing for unity of authorship by, among others, Geoffrey Bullough in his introduction to a reprint of the sources.

Necessarily, all the evidence for Fletcher's hand in *Henry VIII* is internal, so that the question which is to be asked must remain 'Did Fletcher write any of the play and, if so, how much?'

CRITICISM AND COMMENTARY

The fortunes of *Henry VIII* have been happier in the theatre than in the study or class-room. The dispute about the authorship has been in part responsible for critical neglect of the play, as well as itself stemming from doubts about the play's achievement. Dissatisfaction with *Henry VIII* has been variously explained as resulting from its episodic structure, from its lack of a strong central character, from its ambiguous attitude to its historical material, even from its failure to tackle those aspects of the reign of Henry VIII which its critics regarded as the most significant. Attempts to relate it to Shakespeare's earlier histories are hampered by the gap of thirteen years of dramatic experience which separate it from *Henry V*, while its relation to the last comedies is equally complicated by its historical subject and its offer of 'truth'. Though England and kingship and penitence and rebirth may be among its themes, it is neither simply a political play nor a romance.

The play has never lacked admirers. Dr. Johnson laid his finger on two sources of its appeal in his comment that it 'still keeps possession of the stage, by the splendour of its pageantry. . . . Yet pomp is not the only merit of this play. The meek sorrows and virtuous distress of Catherine have furnished some scenes which may be justly numbered among the greatest efforts of tragedy.' Its pomp has motivated revivals on the occasion of several coronations from 1727 to 1953, while its leading roles, especially Katherine, Wolsey, and Henry himself, have attracted the leading Shakespearian players of every period, from Thomas Betterton (who is said to have learned the part from John Lowin, the original Henry) and Sarah Siddons to John Gielgud and Peggy Ashcroft. In the nineteenth century, the play was lavishly presented with huge processions and meticulously historical settings and costumes: such productions as Charles Kean's and Henry Irving's, in 1855 and 1892 respectively, are described by G. C. D. Odell, who also reveals the cost in textual cuts (often including the whole of Act v) of such scenically lavish presentations. The twentieth century has seen notable revivals and the restoration of the full text. Tyrone Guthrie's 1953 production at Stratford did much to revive critical curiosity about the play, although even so admiring a reviewer as Muriel St. Clare Byrne suggests that some of the producer's virtuosity was obtrusive. Trevor Nunn's Stratford production in 1969 was a straightforward account of the play, distinguished by the forceful though deeply puzzled King of Donald Sinden and a Katherine of exemplary quiet dignity from Peggy Ashcroft. The religious bearing of the action (tentatively traced by Gervinus in 1863), in which the English Reformation, though never directly treated, is implied by the falling fortunes of Wolsey and Queen Katherine and by the rise of Anne Bullen and Cranmer, was clearly projected and did much (despite the eccentric and fussy playing of Cranmer as a near-simpleton) to answer the familiar charge that Act v is irrelevant and uninteresting. The subtle interrelation between the stage history of *Henry VIII* and the course of criticism of it is only one of many aspects of the play discussed by A. C. Sprague in the final chapter of his *Shakespeare's Histories: Plays for the Stage*.

Sprague's praise of the play reaches a happy balance between the uncritical adulation and the impatient dismissal which it more often provokes. Character criticism has fallen into some disrepute, but the peaceful action and unheroic mode of *Henry VIII*, together with the insistence of the prologue on its 'truth', set it apart from the earlier histories and may justify a critical emphasis on individual psychology. Such an emphasis, at least, does little to blur the perceptive reading of the play in Gervinus's *Commentaries* and remains one organizing principle of the more loosely thematic discussion by G. Wilson Knight in *The Crown of Life*.

Aspects of *Henry VIII* which have received critical attention in the present century include its imagery of 'the human body seen in endlessly varied action', which Caroline Spurgeon described in her lecture on 'Shakespeare's Iterative Imagery' for the British Academy, and its treatment by painters, which W. Moelwyn Merchant handles in *Shakespeare and the Artist* with particular reference to Blake's five versions of Queen Katherine's vision and to Henry Harlow's painting of 'The Kemble Family' in the scene of her trial (II.iv).

Most modern critics have been drawn towards the interrelated questions of the play's historical and political ideas, its structural and thematic unity, and its relation to the rest of Shakespeare's latest plays.

The central position of the King affords a clear link with the earlier histories, but in no other play is the disparity between the King's private actions and his public significance so marked. R. A. Foakes, in the fresh and substantial introduction to his new Arden edition, proposes that Henry's central position resembles that of Prospero, both rulers being 'central in as much as they are permanent, influencing others, and uniting a complex plot'. His emphasis on Henry's 'growth in spiritual stature during the play' stems from a consideration of the King's emergence from Wolsey's domination into full self-awareness and beneficent exercise of his royal power, as this is reflected in Henry's role in the four trials, of Buckingham, Queen Katherine, Wolsey, and Cranmer, which are the major crises of the action. He here develops Frank Kermode's view of the play as 'a new "Mirror for Magistrates" ', a morality in which Henry presides over three tragic falls before intervening in the role of Mercy to save Cranmer. Foakes regards Shakespeare's choice of an historical subject as an intelligible step in his gradual renunciation of supernatural intervention in the plays from *Cymbeline* to *The Tempest*: 'Perhaps after abjuring magic as a means to his end, the dramatist turned to real life again, to fact in the form of history.' Developing this point in a later book, Foakes relates it to Shakespeare's emphasis on the 'truth' of his action, which comprises 'human activities within a framework of government or rule'. Simple judgement is forbidden by 'the variety of perspectives' on men and their motives, and 'the generosity of providence' in the birth of Elizabeth shines the brighter among the 'fumbling inadequacies of men and their laws in a given historical situation'. Compassing at once the historical particularity of the action and its constant suggestion of spiritual significance, this view of the play serves to differentiate it from the earlier histories, whose concern with political dogma and dynastic struggles it does not share, and provides an answer both to the complaint of Irving Ribner that *Henry VIII* 'does not give us a coherent and meaningful philosophy of history' and to E. M. W. Tillyard's disappointment at its lack of dramatic 'event'.

A similar view of Henry's development is presented by H. M. Richmond in 'Shakespeare's *Henry VIII*: Romance Redeemed by History'. He associates Henry's lesson in 'the need for temperance in the administration of all justice' not only with Prospero but with the Duke in *Measure for Measure*.

Not all critics are so happy to see *Henry VIII* as a sequel to *The Tempest*. Madeleine Doran, reviewing Foakes's edition, wisely urged some caution in relating it too closely to the last romances. To his claim that 'a contrast between private suffering and public good, or private sorrow and public joy' serves to unify the play, she replied with a reminder of the play's uneven quality—'One difficulty is that the private sorrow is so much more moving than the public joy.' Of the earlier histories, that to which *Henry VIII* has most often been related is *King John*. Cumberland Clark, in *A Study of Shakespeare's 'Henry VIII'*, anticipated Tillyard's description of the two plays by calling *King John* the prologue and *Henry VIII* the 'epilogue to the historical dramas', having in common a concern with 'the victory of Protestantism'.

The Two Noble Kinsmen, and the Apocryphal Plays

TEXTS, AUTHORSHIP, AND CRITICISM

The canon of Shakespeare's dramatic work was established in 1623 by John Heminges and Henry Condell in their epistle 'To the great Variety of Readers' prefaced to the First Folio, where they add to their claim to offer good texts of such plays as had previously been published the promise that their book also includes 'all the rest, absolute in their numbers, as he conceived them'. Despite this specific claim, substantial reasons have been found for attributing to Shakespeare at least a share in a few plays excluded from the Folio and for challenging the integrity of a few of the plays in it.

The possibility of Shakespeare's hand in plays outside the Folio wins some support from the discovery that problems encountered in the course of printing nearly led to the exclusion of *Troilus and Cressida* and that only its near exclusion left room for the printing of *Timon of Athens*. Although in either eventuality, the great variety of readers might have been notified, it seems unlikely that the desire for inclusiveness was pursued so assiduously as to leave no room for doubt. Even before 1623, plays had been published as Shakespeare's which Heminges and Condell omitted. *The London Prodigal*, 'By William Shakespeare', was published in 1605 and *A Yorkshire Tragedy*, '*Written by* W. Shakspeare', in 1608. They were followed, in 1609, by *Pericles, Prince of Tyre*, 'By William Shakespeare'. During these years, the reluctance of the King's Men to release Shakespeare's plays for publication gave printers added incentive to misattribute plays to him, and this is probably what happened with the first two, although *Pericles* presents a different problem and is generally held to be substantially Shakespeare's work.

When a second issue of the Third Folio of 1663 was published in the following year, these three plays were added as a supplement together with four more, alleged on even flimsier grounds to be Shakespeare's because of claims made on the title-pages of earlier quarto editions of each. One, *The First Part of Sir John Oldcastle*, was written in 1599 by Antony Munday, Michael Drayton, Robert Wilson, and Richard Hathway as a retort to Shakespeare's Falstaff plays, but was fraudulently attributed to Shakespeare in the second edition, falsely dated '1600', though printed in 1619 as part of Thomas Pavier's surreptitious attempt at publishing a collected edition of 'Shakespeare'. The others were only attributed by initials to 'W.S.', as sole author of *The Life and Death of Thomas Lord Cromwell* (1602) and *The Puritan, or the Widow of Watling Street* (1607, perhaps the work of Thomas Middleton), but merely as overseer and corrector of *The Lamentable Tragedy of Locrine* (1595). None of the three plays affords internal evidence for the identification of 'W.S.' with William Shakespeare.

Other plays have seemed to have stronger claims to be considered as containing Shakespeare's work although not attributed to him in his lifetime. *The Tragedy of Master Arden of Feversham* (1592) and *The Reign of King Edward III* (1596) were both written about 1591–2, when Shakespeare was beginning to make a name as a playwright. Neither was attributed to him, except haphazardly in booksellers' catalogues, until Edward Capell edited *Edward III* in 1760 with a tentative suggestion of his authorship and Edward Jacob did likewise for *Arden of Feversham* in 1770. As both cases depend exclusively on the internal evidence of style and linguistic usage, and as both plays date from a time before Shakespeare's style had fully diverged from that of his immediate forerunners, conviction has not been reached about either attribution, although the evidence for *Edward*

III is immeasurably stronger and more various than that for *Arden of Feversham*. The documentary mode and 'naked' style of *Arden of Feversham* contrast with Shakespeare's early addiction to classical allusion and elaborate rhetoric, whereas *Edward III* is linked by vocabulary, imagery, structure, and thematic concerns not only with Shakespeare's early histories and sonnets but with other plays of much later date. Kenneth Muir gives a clear account of the main arguments for Shakespeare's participation in the play together with an account of its use of its historical material in his *Shakespeare as Collaborator*.

Shakespeare's hand as collaborator or reviser has also been suggested in other plays, for instance, in the additions first printed in the reprints of Kyd's *The Spanish Tragedy* in 1602 and of *Mucedorus* in 1610. Fuller and more convincing arguments have surrounded *The Book of Sir Thomas More*, a play which survives in a single manuscript that has undergone extensive revision and which was first edited by Dyce in 1844. Dates proposed for the composition of this play have ranged from about 1591 to about 1601, with some weight in favour of an early date. Two additions to the manuscript, one a three-page scene in its author's hand, the other a scribal copy of a single speech, have come to be regarded as very likely the work of Shakespeare as the result of long controversy since the publication in 1871 of Richard Simpson's broader claim that much of the manuscript was in Shakespeare's hand. Two landmarks in the history of this question were W. W. Greg's edition of 1911, which not only provided the best text to date but laid the basis for identification of the hands in the manuscript, and the collection of essays edited by A. W. Pollard in 1923 as *Shakespeare's Hand in the Play of 'Sir Thomas More'*, in which the contributions of Sir Edward Maunde Thompson on the handwriting of the longer addition and of Shakespeare's signatures and R. W. Chambers on the political ideas of the additions and Shakespeare's English and Roman histories remain among the strongest links in the chain of evidence connecting Shakespeare with the play. The case for the shorter addition was greatly reinforced by J. M. Nosworthy's analysis of the speech in relation to passages within the Shakespeare canon.

The remaining important attributions to Shakespeare are of plays belonging to the latest years of his career and are thus associated with the doubts which have been frequently expressed, especially since 1850, about his sole authorship of *Henry VIII*. In each case, it is claimed that Shakespeare collaborated with his younger colleague John Fletcher, who was soon to succeed him as principal playwright for the King's Men. *The Two Noble Kinsmen*, a tragi-comedy written in 1613 and based on Chaucer's *Knight's Tale*, was printed in 1634 as a play 'Presented at the Blackfriars by the King's Majesty's servants, with great applause' and with an attribution to Fletcher and Shakespeare. The printers used a good manuscript bearing traces of performance by the King's Men about 1625–6. Most attentive readers have found in the play clear indications of two styles, not always in distinct scenes, which can reasonably be identified as those of Fletcher and of Shakespeare in his latest period. In the case of *The Two Noble Kinsmen*, where internal evidence similar to that in *Henry VIII* has been offered in attempts to assign the authorship of particular passages to one or other of the authors named on the title-page, the question which is still most frequently asked, is 'Did Shakespeare write any of it?'

Controversy about the authorship of *The Two Noble Kinsmen* has run parallel with that about *Henry VIII* (cf. pp. 284–6), although it began sooner, and particularly engaged the attention of writers in the early nineteenth century, among them Charles Lamb, whose description of the two styles in the play remains classic. Systematic division of the play got under way with W. Spalding's *Letter on Shakespeare's Authorship of the Drama Entitled 'The Two Noble Kinsmen'* (1833), and followed a course similar to that of *Henry VIII*. The case for Shakespeare's participation was greatly strengthened by H. Littledale's collection of parallels of thought and expression between the parts of it assigned to him, chiefly in the first and last acts, and plays in the Shakespeare canon. From the 1840s, when Charles Knight included it in his *Pictorial Shakespeare*, the play has gradually moved from its initial position among the plays of Beaumont and Fletcher, which it joined in the Second Folio of 1679, towards a place on the fringes of Shakespeare's works. Although Shakespeare's hand in the play has often been denied, divided authorship has rarely been so and P. Bertram stands alone in contending that the play is the unaided work of Shakespeare. This position is the central weakness of a study which does much to illuminate the history of the play and is particularly cogent in its criticism of the lack of rigour in many of the tests used by nineteenth-century investigators of the authorship, and it can only be sustained by ignoring much of the best evidence for dual authorship, such as A. Hart's analysis of the vocabulary. Recent contributions to the controversy (and to the disputes about the integrity of other plays such as *Titus Andronicus*, *1 Henry VI*, and *Henry VIII*) are summarized by D. Erdman and E. Fogel in *Evidence for Authorship*, while S. Schoenbaum gives a cautionary account of the whole history of disputed authorship in *Internal Evidence and Elizabethan Dramatic Authorship*.

A play called *Cardenno* or *Cardenna* was acted at court by the King's Men in the winter of 1612–13 and on 8 June 1613. 'The History of Cardennio, by Mr. Fletcher. & Shakespeare' was registered by Humphrey Moseley in the Stationers' Register on 9 September 1653. This lost play would seem to have used the episode of Cardenio and Lucinda from Cervantes's *Don Quixote*, which was translated into English by Thomas Shelton and published in 1612. Over a century later, Lewis Theobald claimed to have rescued a lost play by Shakespeare, which he had performed, in a text adapted by himself, in 1727 at Drury Lane. It was published in 1728 as *Double Falsehood, or the Distress'd Lovers*. Though the characters' names have been altered, it is based on Shelton's 1612 version of the Cardenio episode in *Don Quixote*. Theobald's silence, after 1728, about his claim that the play was Shakespeare's lent weight to the general view that it was a forgery, but it has been possible for modern scholars to reopen the question and to argue that a Jacobean play lay behind Theobald's avowedly thorough adaptation. The scanty internal evidence for two styles in the original was presented by E. H. C. Oliphant, who held that that original was a collaborative play by Fletcher and Shakespeare; a stronger train of external links is traced back from Theobald to the early seventeenth century by J. Freehafer, who at least indicates that Theobald's story of obtaining several manuscripts of the play need not be dismissed out of hand as incredible.

Apart from the additions to Kyd's *Spanish Tragedy* and *Double Falsehood*, which was edited in 1920 by Walter Graham, these plays are in *The Shakespeare Apocrypha*, edited by C. F. Tucker Brooke, who provides fairly reliable texts, except of *Sir Thomas More*, but sparse annotation and a brief introduction which is largely devoted to late nineteenth-century opinion on the authorship of the plays and which is seriously out of date in many matters of fact. The large-scale edition of *The Two Noble Kinsmen* by Harold Littledale remains an indispensable source for commentary on the play and gives a full account of early critical comment on it. Useful students' editions include those of *Sir Thomas More* by Harold Jenkins, *Arden of Feversham* and *A Yorkshire Tragedy* by K. M. Sturgess, *Edward III* by W. A. Armstrong, and *The Two Noble Kinsmen* by Clifford Leech and by G. R. Proudfoot. A balanced and fully documented account of the ascription to Shakespeare of plays excluded from the First Folio constitutes Chapter X of E. K. Chambers's *William Shakespeare: A Study of Facts and Problems*. This may be supplemented with studies of

Locrine, *Thomas Lord Cromwell*, *The London Prodigal*, *The Puritan*, and *A Yorkshire Tragedy* by Baldwin Maxwell, in which sources, historical context, and authorship are thoroughly explored.

Much of what has been written about the apocryphal plays has concentrated on the question of their authorship, but critical commentary, sometimes extended, will be found in many of the editions just cited and especially in the books by K. Muir and B. Maxwell.

Various critics have tried to define and account for the divided nature of *The Two Noble Kinsmen*, notably Theodore Spencer in a bravura piece in which he presents the play as emanating from the imagination of an ageing and exhausted Shakespeare, and, in more moderate terms, Philip Edwards, who discerns a thematic pattern in the opening and closing acts which collaboration has blurred and left incomplete but which both serves to bring the play into relation to *The Winter's Tale* and also suggests that it represents a new departure in Shakespeare's art and in his view of love as radical and as disturbing as that of *Troilus and Cressida* after *Twelfth Night*. G. R. Proudfoot traces the effect on the play of its two authors' very different responses to Chaucer's *Knight's Tale*. Una Ellis-Fermor finds that the style of the scenes usually attributed to Shakespeare is 'not strictly dramatic' and concludes that he cannot have written them. Discussions of the imagery of the play by M. Mincoff, E. A. Armstrong, and P. Bertram are equally involved with the issue of authorship.

Of the many general studies of the drama of the period which pay attention to other apocryphal plays, mention can be made of Irving Ribner's *The English History Play in the Age of Shakespeare* for its systematic reference to the historical plays in the group and to Wolfgang Clemen's *English Tragedy before Shakespeare* for its account of the rhetoric of *Locrine*.

REFERENCES

Henry VIII

TEXTS AND AUTHORSHIP

Alexander, Peter, 'Conjectural History, or Shakespeare's *Henry VIII*', *Essays and Studies* 16 (1931).

Bullough, G. (ed.), *Narrative and Dramatic Sources of Shakespeare*, vol. iv (London, 1962).

Emerson, R. W., *Representative Men. Seven Lectures* (London, 1850).

Foakes, R. A. (ed.), *Henry VIII* (new Arden Shakespeare, London, 1957).

Hoeniger, F. D. (ed.), *Henry VIII* (Pelican Shakespeare, Baltimore, Md., 1966).

Humphreys, A. R. (ed.), *Henry VIII* (New Penguin Shakespeare, Harmondsworth, 1971).

Knight, G. Wilson, 'Henry VIII and the Poetry of Conversion', in *The Crown of Life* (London, 1947; 2nd edn., London, 1948).

——, *Shakespearian Production* (London, 1964).

Maxwell, J. C. (ed.), *Henry VIII* (New Cambridge Shakespeare, Cambridge, 1962).

Mincoff, M., 'Henry VIII and Fletcher', *Shakespeare Quarterly*, 12 (1961).

Partridge, A. C., *The Problem of 'Henry VIII' Reopened* (Cambridge, 1949; repr. in his *Orthography in Shakespeare and Elizabethan Drama*, London, 1964).

Spedding, J., 'Who Wrote Shakespere's *Henry VIII*?', *Gentleman's Magazine* 178 (Aug.–Oct. 1850).

Swinburne, A. C., *A Study of Shakespeare* (London, 1880).

CRITICISM AND COMMENTARY

Byrne, Muriel St. Clare, 'A Stratford Production: *Henry VIII*', *Shakespeare Survey 3* (1950).

Clark, C., *A Study of Shakespeare's 'Henry VIII'* (London, [1931]).

Doran, Madeleine, review of *Henry VIII*, ed. R. A. Foakes (London, 1957), in *JEGP* 59 (1960).

Foakes, R. A. (ed.), *Henry VIII* (new Arden Shakespeare, London, 1957).

——, *Shakespeare: the Dark Comedies to the Last Plays* (London, 1971).

Gervinus, G. G., *Shakespeare Commentaries*, translated by F. E. Bennett, 2 vols. (London, 1863).

Kermode, F., 'What is Shakespeare's *Henry VIII* About?', *Durham University Journal*, N.S. 9 (1948); repr. in *Shakespeare's Histories*, ed. W. A. Armstrong (Penguin Shakespeare Library, Harmondsworth, 1972).

Knight, G. Wilson, 'Henry VIII and the Poetry of Conversion', in *The Crown of Life* (London, 1947; 2nd edn., London, 1948).

Merchant, W. Moelwyn, *Shakespeare and the Artist* (London, 1959).

Odell, G. C. D., *Shakespeare—from Betterton to Irving* (New York, 1920).

Ribner, Irving, *The English History Play in the Age of Shakespeare* (Princeton, N.J., 1957; 2nd edn., London, 1965).

Richmond, H. M., 'Shakespeare's *Henry VIII*: Romance Redeemed by History', *Shakespeare Studies* 4 (1968).

Sprague, A. C., *Shakespeare's Histories: Plays for the Stage* (London, 1964).

Spurgeon, Caroline F. E., 'Shakespeare's Iterative Imagery', British Academy Shakespeare Lecture 1931, repr. in *Studies in Shakespeare*, ed. Peter Alexander (London, 1964).

Tillyard, E. M. W., *Shakespeare's History Plays* (London, 1944).

——, 'Why did Shakespeare write "*Henry VIII*"?', *Critical Quarterly*, 3 (1961).

Wimsatt, W. K. (ed.), *Samuel Johnson on Shakespeare* (New York, 1960; repr. as *Dr. Johnson on Shakespeare*, Harmondsworth, 1969).

The Two Noble Kinsmen, and the Apocryphal Plays

TEXTS, AUTHORSHIP, AND CRITICISM

Armstrong, E. A., *Shakespeare's Imagination* (London, 1946; 2nd edn., Lincoln, Nebr., 1963).

Armstrong, W. A. (ed.), *Edward III*, in *Elizabethan History Plays* (World's Classics, London, 1965).

Bertram, P., *Shakespeare and 'The Two Noble Kinsmen'* (New Brunswick, N.J., 1965).

Brooke, C. F. Tucker (ed.), *The Shakespeare Apocrypha* (Oxford, 1908; 2nd impression, Oxford, 1917).

Capell, E. (ed.), *King Edward III*, in *Prolusions, or Select Pieces of Ancient Poetry* (London, 1760).

Chambers, E. K., *William Shakespeare: A Study of Facts and Problems*, 2 vols. (Oxford, 1930).

Chambers, R. W., 'The Expression of Ideas—Particularly Political Ideas—in the Three Pages, and in Shakespeare', in *Shakespeare's Hand in the Play of 'Sir Thomas More'*, ed. A. W. Pollard (Cambridge, 1923).

Clemen, Wolfgang, *English Tragedy before Shakespeare*, translated by T. S. Dorsch (London, 1961).

Dyce, A. (ed.), *Sir Thomas More* (Shakespeare Society, London, 1844).

Edwards, P., 'On the Design of *The Two Noble Kinsmen*', *A Review of English Literature*, 5 (1964); repr. in *The Two Noble Kinsmen*, ed. Clifford Leech (Signet Shakespeare, New York, 1966).

Ellis-Fermor, Una, '*The Two Noble Kinsmen*', in *Shakespeare the Dramatist*, ed. Kenneth Muir (London, 1961).

Erdman, D. V., and Fogel, E. G. (eds.), *Evidence for Authorship* (Ithaca, New York, 1966).

Freehafer, J., '*Cardenio*, by Shakespeare and Fletcher', *PMLA*, 84 (1969).

Graham, W. (ed.), *Double Falsehood* (Cleveland, Ohio, 1920).

Greg, W. W. (ed.), *The Book of Sir Thomas More* (Malone Society Reprints, Oxford, 1911; repr. with *Supplement* by H. Jenkins, Oxford, 1961).

Hart, A., 'Shakespeare and the Vocabulary of *The Two Noble Kinsmen*', *RES*, 10 (1934); repr. in his *Shakespeare and the Homilies* (Melbourne, 1934).

Jacob, E. (ed.), *Arden of Feversham* (Faversham, 1770).

Jenkins, H. (ed.), *Sir Thomas More*, in Sisson, C. J. (ed.), *William Shakespeare: The Complete Works* (London, 1953).

Knight, C., *The Pictorial Shakespeare* (8 vols., London, 1838–43).

Kyd, T., *The Spanish Tragedy*, ed. Philip Edwards (Revels Plays, London, 1959).

Lamb, Charles, *Specimens of English Dramatic Poets* (London, 1808).

Leech, Clifford (ed.), *The Two Noble Kinsmen* (Signet Shakespeare, New York, 1966).

Littledale, H. (ed.), *The Two Noble Kinsmen* (New Shakspere Society, London, 1874–85).

Maxwell, B., *Studies in the Shakespeare Apocrypha* (New York, 1956).

——, 'Conjectures on *The London Prodigal*', in *Studies in Honor of T. W. Baldwin*, ed. D. C. Allen (Urbana, Ill., 1958).

Mincoff, M., 'The Authorship of *The Two Noble Kinsmen*', *English Studies*, 33 (1952).

Muir, Kenneth, *Shakespeare as Collaborator* (London, 1960).

Nosworthy, J. M., 'Shakespeare and *Sir Thomas More*', *RES*, N.S. 6 (1955).

Oliphant, E. H. C., *The Plays of Beaumont and Fletcher* (New Haven, Conn., 1927).

Pollard, A. W. (ed.), *Shakespeare's Hand in the Play of 'Sir Thomas More'* (Cambridge, 1923).

Proudfoot, G.R. (ed.), *The Two Noble Kinsmen* (Regents Renaissance Drama Series, Lincoln, Nebr. and London, 1970).

——, 'Shakespeare and the New Dramatists of the King's Men, 1606–1613', in *Later Shakespeare*, ed. B. Harris and J. R. Brown (Stratford-upon-Avon Studies 8, London, 1966).

Ribner, Irving, *The English History Play in the Age of Shakespeare* (Princeton, N.J., 1957; 2nd edn., London, 1965).

Schoenbaum, S., *Internal Evidence and Elizabethan Dramatic Authorship* (Evanston, Ill., 1966).

Simpson, R., 'Are there any extant MSS. in Shakespeare's Handwriting?', *N & Q* 4th Ser. 8 (1871).

Spalding, W., *A Letter on Shakespeare's Authorship of the Drama Entitled 'The Two Noble Kinsmen'* (Edinburgh, 1833; repr. in *Transactions of the New Shakspere Society*, London, 1876).

Spencer, Theodore, '*The Two Noble Kinsmen*', *Modern Philology*, 36 (1939); reprinted in *The Two Noble Kinsmen*, ed. Clifford Leech (Signet Shakespeare, New York, 1966).

Sturgess, K. M. (ed.), *Arden of Faversham* and *A Yorkshire Tragedy*, in *Three Elizabethan Domestic Tragedies* (Harmondsworth, 1969).

Thompson, Sir E. M., 'The Handwriting of the Three Pages Attributed to Shakespeare Compared with his Signatures', in *Shakespeare's Hand in the Play of 'Sir Thomas More'*, ed. A. W. Pollard (Cambridge, 1923).

NOTES ON THE CONTRIBUTORS

Maurice Charney is Professor of English at Rutgers University. His books include *Shakespeare's Roman Plays*, *Style in 'Hamlet'*, and *How to Read Shakespeare*.

Philip Edwards is a Professor of Literature at the University of Essex; before this he was Professor of English Literature at Trinity College, Dublin. His studies of sixteenth- and seventeenth-century literature include books on Ralegh and Shakespeare, and editions of Kyd and Massinger.

R. A. Foakes is Professor of English in the University of Kent at Canterbury. He has edited plays for the new Arden and New Penguin Shakespeare series, and his writings include a critical study, *Shakespeare, the Dark Comedies to the Last Plays*.

Robert Hapgood is Professor of English and Chairman of the Department at the University of New Hampshire. His publications include the English Institute prize essay, 1968, 'Shakespeare and the Included Spectator', and numerous other articles and theatre reviews.

G. R. Hibbard is Professor of English in the University of Waterloo, Ontario. He is the author of *Thomas Nashe: a Critical Introduction*, and has edited several volumes in the New Penguin Shakespeare.

A. R. Humphreys is Professor of English at the University of Leicester. He has edited and written about several of Shakespeare's history plays, and has also published studies of eighteenth-century English literature, and of Melville.

Michael Jamieson is a Lecturer in English at the University of Sussex. He has edited *Three Comedies* by Ben Jonson and published a short study of *As You Like It* as well as articles on the Elizabethan boy actor and on modern stages for Shakespeare.

John Jump is John Edward Taylor Professor of English Literature in the University of Manchester. He has written on Arnold, Byron, and Tennyson, and has edited several plays by contemporaries of Shakespeare.

Kenneth Muir, King Alfred Professor of English Literature in the University of Liverpool and editor of *Shakespeare Survey*, has edited four of Shakespeare's plays. His books on Shakespeare include *Shakespeare's Sources*, *Shakespeare's Tragic Sequence*, and *Shakespeare the Professional*.

J. M. Nosworthy, Reader in English in the University of Wales, is the editor of *Cymbeline* (new Arden Shakespeare) and *Measure for Measure* (New Penguin Shakespeare), and the author of *Shakespeare's Occasional Plays*.

G. R. Proudfoot is a Lecturer in English at King's College, London. He has edited *The Two Noble Kinsmen* and is general editor of the Malone Society, for which he has edited *A Knack to Know a Knave* and *Johan Johan the Husband*.

Gāmini Salgādo is a Reader in English at the University of Sussex. He has edited *Three Jacobean Tragedies, Three Restoration Comedies, Conycatchers and Bawdybaskets,* and a Casebook on *Sons and Lovers.*

D. J. Palmer is a Senior Lecturer in English Literature at the University of Hull. He is the author of *The Rise of English Studies,* a General Editor of Stratford-upon-Avon Studies, and the editor of two Macmillan Casebooks, on *The Tempest* and *Twelfth Night,* and of *Tennyson* (Writers and their Background).

Norman Sanders is Professor of English at the University of Tennessee. He has edited *Richard II, A Midsummer Night's Dream, The Two Gentlemen of Verona,* and *Julius Caesar* for various Shakespeare series, and Robert Greene's *James the Fourth* for the Revels Plays.

T. J. B. Spencer is Professor of English and Director of the Shakespeare Institute, University of Birmingham. He is General Editor of the New Penguin Shakespeare, for which he has edited *Romeo and Juliet,* and of the Penguin Shakespeare Library, for which he has edited *Shakespeare's Plutarch* and *Elizabethan Love Stories.* He is the author of *Shakespeare: The Roman Plays,* and other studies of Shakespeare.

John Wilders has taught at Princeton and Bristol Universities and is now a Fellow of Worcester College, Oxford, and a University Lecturer in English. He has edited Samuel Butler's *Hudibras* and a Casebook on *The Merchant of Venice.* For nearly ten years he was Director of the Royal Shakespeare Theatre Summer School.

THE EDITOR

Stanley Wells, Reader in English Literature and Fellow of the Shakespeare Institute, University of Birmingham, is the author of *Literature and Drama: with special reference to Shakespeare and his Contemporaries* and of *Shakespeare: A Reading Guide.* He is Associate Editor of the New Penguin Shakespeare, for which he has edited *The Comedy of Errors, A Midsummer Night's Dream,* and *Richard II.* He succeeded John Wilders as Director of the Royal Shakespeare Theatre Summer School.